THE SUN AND HER STARS

THE SUN *and* HER STARS

SALKA VIERTEL *and* HITLER'S EXILES *in the Golden Age of Hollywood*

DONNA RIFKIND

Other Press New York

Production editor: Yvonne E. Cárdenas
Text designer: Julie Fry
This book was set in Whitman with Alternate Gothic.

Endpapers: The garden of the house on Mabery Road, 1940s.
(Wienbibliothek im Rathaus)

1 3 5 7 9 10 8 6 4 2

 Printed in the United States of America
on acid-free paper. For information write to Other Press LLC,
267 Fifth Avenue, 6th Floor, New York, NY 10016.
Or visit our Web site: www.otherpress.com

Library of Congress Cataloging-in-Publication Data
Names: Rifkind, Donna, 1961– author.
Title: The sun and her stars : Salka Viertel and Hitler's exiles
in the golden age of Hollywood / Donna Rifkind.
Other titles: Salka Viertel and Hitler's exiles in the golden age of Hollywood
Description: New York : Other Press, 2020. |
Includes bibliographical references and index.
Identifiers: LCCN 2019942339 | ISBN 9781590517215 (hardcover) |
ISBN 9781590517222 (ebook)
Subjects: LCSH: Viertel, Salka. | Screenwriters—United States—Biography. |
Hollywood (Los Angeles, Calif.)—History. | Los Angeles (Calif.)—History.
Los Angeles (Calif.)—Biography. | Hollywood (Los Angeles, Calif.)—
Social life and customs. | Los Angeles (Calif.)—Social life and customs.
Classification: LCC PN2287.V47 R54 2019 | DDC 812/.52 [B]—dc23
LC record available at https://lccn.loc.gov/2019942339

To my husband and sons, and in memory of
my parents, sister, and brother

Mankind is divisible into two great classes:
hosts and guests.

—MAX BEERBOHM, 1918

There are no minor characters.

—JANE GARDAM, 2014

CONTENTS

INTRODUCTION

THE LOOK, THE SOUND, AND THE SPEECH of Hollywood's Golden Age did not originate in Hollywood. Much of it came from Europe, through the work of successive waves of immigrants during the first half of the twentieth century. The last several of those waves brought a group of traumatized artists who were lucky enough to escape Hitler's death trains and extermination camps. All were antifascists; a few were Communists; most were Jews. These were Hitler's gift to America—prodigious individuals who enriched the film culture and the intellectual life of our nation, and whose influence continues to resonate. Plenty of writers have explored the ways these refugees, exiles, and émigrés managed to escape from Europe. Fewer have told about the Americans who had the courage to take them in. Of those heroic citizens, at the top of the list for her uncompromising conviction and generosity, was a too-often-forgotten screenwriter in Santa Monica named Salka Viertel. This is her story.

Salka Viertel was a recently naturalized American when Hitler's war began, having arrived from Berlin on a visitor visa in Hollywood with her husband during one of the earlier waves of emigrating filmmakers, in 1928. She became a proud and grateful U.S. citizen in February of 1939, only months before the official outbreak of war in Europe on September 1 of that year. It was her very Europeanness that had alerted her early on to the growing conflagration across the Atlantic, well before Hitler took power in 1933. She had been raised in a well-heeled Jewish family in a garrison town in Galicia called Sambor, on the fringes of the Austro-Hungarian Empire, where she'd been born in 1889. And she came of age as an actress on the stages of many European cities, most notably Weimar-era Berlin. Long before the advent of National Socialism made anti-Semitism official state policy in Germany, Salka Viertel was quite familiar with its lethal intentions. Thus after 1933 she was extra sympathetic to the attempts of the panicked human beings who began to launch themselves desperately, in any way they could, toward the possibility of safety in America. An estimated ten thousand refugees from Germany and Austria settled in greater Los Angeles between 1933 and 1941, a significant part of "the most complete migration of artists and intellectuals in European history" up to that time, according to California historian Kevin Starr. Members of Salka Viertel's own family were among those refugees, as were hundreds of her friends and many more strangers. In Santa Monica, she made it her mission to provide a refuge for them in her own home and to absorb them into her social and professional network, all to help them survive in a wholly unfamiliar new world.

America's own deeply rooted anti-Semitism, the eruptions

of homegrown fascism that emerged in the 1930s with rallies sponsored by the Silver Shirts and the German American Bund, and widespread anti-immigrant sentiments stoked by such fearmongers as Father Coughlin were factors in the Roosevelt administration's reluctance to alter strict immigration policies that had been further tightened during the Great Depression. While Roosevelt was not unsympathetic to the plight of Europe's Jews, during the early years of his administration his chief concerns were domestic, focused on boosting employment and fostering an economic recovery. His administration chose to maintain the stringent quotas for refugees that had been established in 1924, reluctant to stir up an already robust homegrown xenophobia. Later, after 1941, he concentrated almost exclusively on winning the war. And so it became clear that rescue for the Jews, as Hitler set out methodically to kill them all, was not likely to originate with U.S. government agencies. It would be individual efforts such as Salka Viertel's, synchronized with organizations like Hollywood's European Film Fund and Varian Fry's Emergency Rescue Committee, that saved the lives of hundreds of refugees during the earlier stages of National Socialism's twelve-year domination, and which then mobilized to help those refugees adapt to life in America.

As I began to read the histories of the two intersecting arenas where Salka Viertel rang up her accomplishments during the 1930s and 1940s—the film studios of Hollywood's Golden Age and the gathering places of the antifascist emigration—I found myself asking again and again: where are all the women? I read dozens of thoughtful, entertaining, even groundbreaking works about Hollywood in which women who were not wives, secretaries, or movie stars scarcely make an appearance. Yet women worked in every department of the studios. They were screenwriters, editors, researchers, readers, publicists, costumers, hair and makeup artists. Often below the line and unglorified, women were nonetheless vital to the success of these vast, complex organizations, and some of them wielded genuine influence if not actual power. Where are their stories?

In the documentation about the antifascist intellectuals who fled from Hitler's Germany, I found a similar absence. Jean-Michel Palmier's monumental *Weimar in Exile: The Antifascist Emigration in Europe and America* gives the unintentional but unmistakable impression that fully half of the population he writes about—the women—had little or no involvement in this epic human exodus. You would not think, reading Palmier's book and others, that women witnessed their homes and property and livelihoods stolen away from them, and scrambled to uproot themselves, and waited endlessly in airless bureaucratic offices for documents and visas, and suffered the penury and humiliation of exile, along with the men. You would not discover that it was Nelly Mann who more or less carried her seventy-year-old husband Heinrich Mann over the Pyrenees in the stifling heat of an early October day in 1940 as they tried to evade capture and certain arrest. Or that it was Erika Mann, Heinrich's niece and Thomas Mann's eldest daughter, who risked her life by sneaking into Nazi-dominated Munich in the summer of 1933 to rescue her father's manuscript of *Joseph and His Brothers* from the Mann family home, which was then under constant Gestapo surveillance. Or that it was Marta Feuchtwanger who planned and implemented the escape of her novelist husband Lion Feuchtwanger from the concentration camp at Les Milles in southern France at the end of the summer of 1940. Or that it was two women, Liesl Frank and Charlotte Dieterle, who carried out most of the paperwork-heavy, unglamorous, but effective rescue work of the European Film Fund (EFF) in Hollywood. All of these women were like-minded friends and colleagues of Salka Viertel, whose work inspired and was inspired by their commitment and their bravery.

It is more often in the imaginative literature about Hollywood and the 1930s exiles, rather than in the histories, that women play prominent roles and emerge as fully fleshed characters: Anna Trautwein in Lion Feuchtwanger's novel *Paris Gazette*, for example; or Erich Maria Remarque's heroines in *Shadows in Paradise* and *The Night in Lisbon*; and Salka herself, who appears in fictional form in Joseph Kanon's *Stardust*, Elizabeth Frank's *Cheat and Charmer*, Gavin Lambert's *Inside Daisy Clover*, Christopher Hampton's *Tales from Hollywood*, Irwin Shaw's short story "Instrument of Salvation," and, fleetingly, in the film *The Way We Were*. Yet these glimpses can't compensate for the absence of real women in the copious nonfiction, where at best they are underrepresented and at worst virtually erased.

Fortunately, but glacially, the landscape is changing. Martin Sauter's *Liesl Frank, Charlotte Dieterle, and the European Film Fund* not only provides the first comprehensive study of the EFF but also properly credits Frank and Dieterle as the chief administrators of the fund—credit that has previously been granted to its more high-profile male directors, Paul Kohner and Ernst Lubitsch. In his book, Sauter aims specifically to remedy the exclusion of women in the histories of Hollywood and the antifascist emigration. He underscores British professor S. Jay Kleinberg's creditable assertion that women are "systematically omitted from the accounts of the past. This has distorted the way we view the past; indeed it warps history by making it seem as though only men have participated in the events worthy of preservation." Other scholars are also working to redress the oversight. Cari Beauchamp's *Without Lying Down: Frances Marion and the Power of Women in Hollywood*; Erin Hill's *Never Done: A History of Women's Work in Media Production*; Evelyn Juers's *House of Exile: The Lives and Times of Heinrich Mann and Nelly Kroeger-Mann*; and Emily D. Bilski and Emily Braun's essay about Salka Viertel, "The Salon in Exile," from *Jewish Women and Their Salons: The Power of Conversation* have all begun to fill in the blanks. Significant, too, is the robust state of exile-studies scholarship in Europe. Katharina Prager's German-language biography of Salka Viertel, *"Ich bin nicht gone Hollywood!,"* is especially noteworthy, as is her examination of Viennese modernism, *Berthold Viertel: Eine Biografie der Wiener Moderne*. But in America there is much more work to be done.

SALKA VIERTEL has the double distinction, during her lifetime and after, of being both maligned and dismissed. When they have bothered to mention her at all, writers about the era have described her variously as a gossipmonger, a money-grubber, a vengeful lesbian, an incompetent fraud, and a horrible witch. (That last, from a letter Kurt Weill wrote to his wife Lotte Lenya, may be the most excusable, for distraught refugees were brittle, often depressed, and prone to lashing out at friends and benefactors.) Such vituperation may seem extreme toward a woman who titled her memoir *The Kindness of Strangers* and who is remembered, if at all, for inviting people to parties on Sunday afternoons. But Salka had a strong, confident personality and wielded a degree of influence, for a time, in a Hollywood embittered by chronic discord, frustration, jealousy, and misogyny both casual and institutional. Never prone to self-pity or cowering, she learned early that survival in Hollywood required a thick skin, and toughened herself up accordingly.

Worse than the insults, in my mind, is the neglect. While biographical information may be scarce about, say, Charlotte Dieterle, or such women as Miriam Davenport and Mildred Adams, who worked with Varian Fry at the Emergency Rescue Committee, this excuse does not apply to Salka Viertel, who in 1969 published one of the earliest and, it turns out, the most comprehensive personal record of Hollywood's affiliation with Europe before and during the time of Hitler's rise. *The Kindness of Strangers* has thus been eagerly plumbed again and again by scholars and researchers for its anecdotes about such luminaries as Greta Garbo, Arnold Schoenberg, and Albert Einstein, all the while studiously ignoring the woman who participated in and then chronicled those very anecdotes.

In addition to her memoir, Salka Viertel left behind a trove of letters and diaries, much of which has found a home at the extraordinary center for exile literature called the Deutsches Literaturarchiv (DLAM), in the town of Marbach in southern Germany. Salka's letters to and from her husband Berthold Viertel are of world-class literary quality in several languages. The eloquence of the German letters was clarified for me by two marvelously sensitive translators, Pamela Selwyn, who worked with me at the DLAM, and Friedel Schmoranzer in Los Angeles. When I first arrived at the DLAM and introduced myself to the archivists, one of them said to me, "We're so glad you are here for Salka. Almost everyone comes for Berthold." The balance has shifted since my visit, with research on Salka Viertel accelerating among European scholars, but for me, as an American, the archivist's sentiment still resonates.

Nor did Salka's famous friends, including Thomas Mann and Bertolt Brecht, feel much compunction to mention Salka in their memoirs or diaries beyond an occasional reference to the excellent coffee and cake she served them. Charlie Chaplin pays her a brief compliment in his autobiography, and producer Gottfried Reinhardt states correctly in his that "the history of Hollywood, which is not yet written, is incomplete without an appreciation of Salka Viertel's distinct talent for human relationships." Of the writers whom Salka counted among the closest in her wide interlocking social circles, only Christopher Isherwood provides a generous portrait of her in his diaries, noting her charisma, her energy, her emotionality, her humor, her gift for friendship, and glimpses of both her family life and her working life as a screenwriter—all with his usual novelistic flair for detail.

Salka Viertel has been more or less forgotten in America because too few people believed that what she accomplished was important. To survive and flourish in the hostile environment of the Hollywood studio system; to use her influence at the studios to petition for sponsors, affidavits, and jobs for refugees; to turn her home into the endpoint of a transatlantic routing network for those refugees, providing welcome, food, shelter, camaraderie, and introductions to potential employers;

to speak out against intolerance, censorship, political inquisitions, and the curtailing of human rights in the name of national security—all seeds of fascism in the United States that threatened to sprout as poisonously as they had in Germany: in the end, none of this has been deemed thus far to be worthy of our attention. It was just one woman's response to the events of her day—events that, clear as they may seem in hindsight, were as bewildering in their time as those in our time are to us.

I'm writing this book in mid-2017, while an even larger human migration is taking place around the world, forced by civil war, ethnic cleansing, poverty, and climate change. Once again, the fate of refugees has become a prolonged incendiary debate in our country. And once again, as in every generation, anti-Semitism has found a new energy. I've been writing about the rise of the National Socialists in 1930s Germany while neo-Nazis are rallying murderously in America's cities, chanting "Jews will not replace us"; while synagogues and Jewish cemeteries in America are vandalized and desecrated; and while authoritarian pronouncements demonizing immigrants and inviting racism, layered insouciantly with lies and misinformation, are issuing almost daily from the commander in chief on Twitter, just as they did from the radio in Hitler's time.

The questions Salka asked herself about one's responsibility in the face of bigotry and exclusion are the same questions we're asking today. The treatment of refugees was not at that time a political issue and it is not now, though it has become politicized in both eras. It is a moral issue, a human issue. It asks us, as Salka asked herself: What is our duty toward the displaced of the world? Who can remain neutral, who unfeeling?

What do those who have homes owe those whose homes have been destroyed? Who will open the door to the stranger?

What kept the luckiest of the 1930s refugees going, as Elie Wiesel wrote about Adam in the book of Genesis, is that God gave them a secret: not about how to begin, but how to begin again. Yet it was impossible to begin again without the help of people like Salka Viertel, who welcomed them into a community after their own had been eradicated.

It was a personal financial crisis that had brought Salka Viertel to California in 1928, and it was another that forced her to leave, in the early 1960s, to begin a self-imposed exile in the Swiss Alps. Both predicaments had come about through a larger political context, but they were not, in the end, a political story. They were, and are, a human story. A woman, finding good fortune in a foreign land, comforted and fed and housed the survivors of an overseas genocide. In her old age, when her fortune was gone, only a few family members and friends remained to feed and comfort her, and to remember her after her death. As witnesses to this story, we might ask again: what does it say about our values that we have chosen to dismiss so large and estimable a life as Salka Viertel's?

1

THE WISHING SEASON

HAUS ELIANA, DOGGILOCHSTRASSE,
KLOSTERS, SWITZERLAND
JANUARY 1963

IT IS A HOLIDAY TOWN. After the first snows of the year, the hotels and chalets begin to swell with the ski crowds, with Christmastime bringing revelers up from Zurich by the trainload. Among them are so many movie stars that the little Alpine village has come to be called Hollywood on the Rocks. At the train station they arrive in a merry commotion, snugly wrapped up in their youth and glamour and money, none of which have belonged to Salka Viertel for a long time. In her second-floor apartment above the butcher's shop, she worries now over every franc and depends on her son Peter, who lives nearby, for monthly handouts. Her furniture is falling apart. Her clothes have gone threadbare. The last time she was in Davos she ordered the cheapest new dresses she could find and still gasped at the expense.

Poverty in youth is something to be vigorously outrun; at life's end, it is a prison. She can't make plans, can't travel to see her other two sons who live in Los Angeles and Massachusetts.

They are nearly as financially strapped as she is, and her worries about them seep into the corners of her day and keep her thrashing in her bed at night. There are grandchildren in the States who barely know her; even a tiny step-great-grandson now.

And the granddaughter she helped to raise has been claimed by Peter, who is her father after all, and was shuttled away at age ten to a British boarding school, closed off from Salka now except for a few holidays. Christine, her darling, her Puck and her Ariel: the last great love of her life. For some years Salka fed and bathed her, and sang her lullabies, and kissed away her sorrows, too many sorrows for any little girl. She has to be careful to spare Christine most of what she knows, and to keep the good memories alive. Their mutual mourning is a large part of what links her with Christine and she can hardly stand the distance from her now. Her longing for the child is a genuine physical ache.

Yet for all of Salka's troubles she is an optimist out of long habit, and at seventy-three she doesn't always feel so hopeless. If it's true that her body, that reliable engine, is not as indomitable as it was—her back bothers her, she worries about her heart—her spirit still feels strong. She enjoys the young admirers who come to pay her visits and bask in her counsel. And for herself, there is still so much she wants to do. Work, as always, sustains her. She keeps a daily diary and is trying, with difficulty, to finish her memoirs, although sometimes she thinks she has lived too long and seen too much to get out on top of her life, to see it whole. With luck she will convince a decent American publisher to buy the memoirs and grant her a bit of financial freedom, but she shudders to think she might be forced to sell her life too cheaply. Already the few who have read her drafts—all men—have blanched at every hint of womanly mess, of love affairs and menstruation and childbirth. They insisted that she take it all out.

When she's not struggling with her memoirs she dreams up scenarios for pictures. Every day, sparks of ideas come to her as they always did: a vignette from Chekhov or Turgenev, or a story about refugee servants in America. She tries not to care that too few people these days are interested in hearing them. It seems another life, all those years ago in Metro's heyday, when she was one of Thalberg's favored Scheherazades.

Salka Viertel in Klosters, Switzerland, early 1960s.

Christmas and New Year's have come and gone, the end of "the wishing times," once her favorite time of year. As a child in Galicia, on the eastern fringe of the Austro-Hungarian Empire, she couldn't wait for Christmas, which her family celebrated twice, on December 24 and then two weeks later for the Ukrainian servants. She has loved it even more as an adult, with the candid delight of all the Hollywood Jews. In her living room in Santa Monica, to the distress of her American-born neighbors, her angel-topped tree was always alight with real candles. Today, in her sitting room darkened by the unadorned spruces of the Selfranga hills outside the window, on the outskirts of the movable Yuletide feast that sets up for the winters in Klosters, cast aside among the endless snows and the freezing black rush of the Landquart River and the clanking cowbells and the pretty young skiers and the vacationing film stars, she misses California and she is not in a holiday mood.

Of course, when she was in California she longed as fiercely for Europe. Forever uprooted. She thinks of this time as her exile in the Alps, the last stop in a series of exhausting rebeginnings. If there is a defining truth in all she has lived over this long century, it's the speed with which she has seen houses and homelands snatched away, their inhabitants forced out into different kinds of wilderness, obliged to rebuild what they could with whatever opportunities they managed to seize. What an effort she has made to keep creating the spirit of all her homes, over and over again, for herself and for others. Her childhood house—her dear rambling Wychylowka—gone. The rye and wheat fields; the orchards and the little forest. Galicia itself—many times destroyed. The apartments of her vagabond theater days in Vienna, Munich, Dresden, Berlin—vanished. Her house in California by the shore: how she misses it but there was no choice, she could not make the payments. A house filled with the dispossessed, all of them drawn to her compassion and her European cooking. The current of energy that flowed through her Sunday afternoon gatherings as she strode to the kitchen to check on the food: Arpège and cigar smoke, a tumult of piano chords, the confidential lilt of German, and, through the open terrace doors, the ionized breath of the sea.

Now, in her solitude, even on her good days she thinks the attempt to invent yet another haven from these Swiss rooms will defeat her. Anyway, so many of those she cared for are gone. Too many to count. Too hard to think about.

How extraordinary to think that so many of her loved ones, hounded out of Europe in the 1930s, returned there almost immediately after the war, harried this time by the House Un-American Activities Committee. She had taken them all in, the wild-eyed and desperate, when they had found themselves so improbably in Los Angeles, and then, as soon as they could, they had gone back. Brecht and Helli Weigel, disappearing with no regrets behind the curtain of East Berlin. Thomas and Katia Mann, leaving the house they'd built in Pacific Palisades for a staunch manor in the hills above Zurich. Katia is still there, eight years after Thomas's death, as sharp and imposing as ever. And Salka's own husband Berthold, dead now a decade, who had settled with a sigh of cosmopolitan relief back into Vienna and the Burgtheater when the war was over. She's acutely aware that, were it not for the quirk of timing that brought her and Berthold to Hollywood in 1928 before the deluge, they would have been among Hitler's victims. Aware also that after the war was over she would no longer be in demand at Metro or Warners. She wasn't exactly on the blacklist, but by then it didn't matter. The Committee had already succeeded in wrecking her livelihood.

Now she too has abandoned America, with infinite regret. How strange to find herself in this sanitized version of Europe, going about its gay daily business as though the war had never happened. Impossible today for a *galitzianer* Jewess to look up at these mountains, just a few miles from the Austrian border, and fail to feel amazed at being alive in this time and place, and more or less intact. Impossible not to wonder about the former peasants turned waiters in the luxury hotels of this recently chic town as they serve platters of *tête de moine* and *Bündner-fleisch* to the rosy-cheeked tourists. The young woman who does some typing for her, hired part time as a gift from Peter, likes to regale her with tales of her dead father's Nazi past.

So much is dreamlike about her life these days. At midnight at Irwin Shaw's New Year's Eve party, he had been the first to kiss her. Then she had found herself approached to be kissed by every man in the room, most of them perspiring unpleasantly. The scene had a troubling dream's truthfulness: it's not vanity but only fact to say that all her life and even now, with her nimbus of white hair, she has been accustomed to fielding the frank expectations of men. Plenty of young men always, though it was the old men she tended to remember, for the urgency and pathos in their plans of conquest.

At last in the New Year's parade of sweaty kissers she had arrived to face her long-ago love, Gottfried. With Silvia—his official Mrs. Reinhardt—off somewhere out of earshot, he had held her against him and kissed her deeply as he had in the old days, and whispered, "*Weisst du noch?*" Of course she remembers, but his kiss itself was like a dream of their dead passion. She remembers many of the New Year's Eves they spent together when he made her so unhappy with his drinking, and then the next day he would play his little seducing games to win her back. She feels not the slightest sentiment for him now. For some reason she thinks of the time a handful of years ago when he arrived at her Westwood apartment to take her to a party and noticed a torn seam in his pants. He had taken them off so she could make the repair for him, and while he sat there in his shorts she had been surprised to find how distasteful she found the sight of his bare legs. She'd tried not to look at him as he waited silently in the airlessness of the late afternoon, and she had marveled to herself at the idea of her once-crazy obsession with that same body.

All her life, it occurs to her, she has loved extravagantly, heedlessly. It may have been her greatest achievement, but it has cost her, maybe too much. One day last summer in Klosters she was walking along the road when her son Peter happened to drive up behind her and gave her a ride. Of late he had been behaving coldly toward her and she impulsively asked him why he does not like her. "I like you," he replied, "but I am not as demonstrative as you." Demonstrative? It's only that she loves him. She has always loved him. She has demonstrated it all her life.

She knows Peter loves her too, even if he is always running away. Of her three sons, he most resembles her. Their faces are similar and they have the same walk, headlong but with a slight hesitation in the step of the right leg. Peter has her social ease, her gift for friendship, her avid way of engaging with the world. But too much has happened between them over the years and their bond has gotten very complicated and often tense. Sometimes he is proud to be her son, proud of her connections to international celebrities and the old-guard movie folk. At other times he is ashamed: of her refusal to be a normal American mother, her insistence on clinging to her European ways.

Between Berthold and Peter it was different. Difficult also, but perhaps in some ways less complicated. Peter never mentions his father these days. Yet one need not pay the sky-high fees of a Hollywood psychoanalyst to tease out the relationship between this Viennese father and his Dresden-born middle son, a boy who always and only wanted to be an American. At a young age, during Berthold's long absences from Santa Monica, Peter had hung on to their neighbor Oliver Garrett, whose sporty New England urbanity Peter loved and admired. And later, Peter had thought to be amusing when he dedicated his first novel, *The Canyon*—published, to her surprise, when he was just nineteen—to "the foreign family up the street." She and Berthold had not been amused. They had felt the sting of accusation at that time and ever since.

Some years later Peter sent a copy of *The Canyon* to Ernest Hemingway after they had become friends. Peter made no secret of caring more for Ernest's flattery than for the praise he'd received from Berthold. And so developed Peter's dogged and largely successful pursuit of substitute fathers. There was Hemingway, certainly, and also her own old ally John Huston: big, brawling, globe-trotting men who possessed Berthold's brilliance and his fiery temper and his love of excess but who were also solidly, and, most crucially for Peter, *American*. Hemingway the hero of literature and war, and Peter his worshipper; it's hardly even a stretch that the world calls him Papa. Peter who still talks like the Marine lieutenant he was, a character Hemingway might have invented, ordering Greta into the car when she comes to visit during the summers as if she were the lowliest of GIs and not the Divine Garbo, and Greta rather loving every minute of it.

In the meantime, now that Hemingway has been erased from their lives with his final violent act of self-dispatch, Peter has found himself another *Ersatzpapa*, Orson Welles, who recently departed from Klosters after spending the winter holidays. Orson is only a few years older than Peter but he fills the bill in every other way. Just as it was with Hemingway, the friendship was sealed by their devotion to the infernal sport of bullfighting and by the writing advice Orson has offered Peter over the years. More recently they worked together on a doomed film, and last August Peter wrote an admiring profile of Orson for *Life* magazine that to Peter's chagrin was scrapped as well. Early this winter Orson announced he was coming to Klosters to give his little daughter a white Christmas. His wife arrived as well, a very beautiful Italian, quite a few years younger than he. There are whispers of an estrangement. No doubt there are people who find this information compelling, but many years ago Salka learned the value of inoculating herself against Hollywood rumors. It could be true or not. Either way it's of little use to her.

Orson when he arrived was catastrophically fat, his bulk draped in acres of soft dark clothing, a cape, a slouchy hat on his giant head, a cigar cradled in his hand. As he picked his way across the snow-banked path toward Peter's house, pausing for a moment near the two frozen ponds by the barn, he looked like a miniature black mountain among mountains, dwarfed only by the tall pines and the white-frosted peaks rising up behind him. Later, seated next to Salka for Christmas dinner, he was loud and to her mind not terribly interesting.

In his grossness he reminded her a little of Heinrich George, the Weimar actor turned Nazi collaborator who had spent his last days in a Soviet concentration camp. Then again, nearly everyone these days reminds her a little of someone she knew long ago. She supposes Orson is more intelligent than George, with a better education. He has recently finished making a film of Kafka's *The Trial*, produced by a blithe Russian whose contributions had gone uncredited on one of Greta's earliest pictures in Germany. Orson said he would have preferred to make *The Castle* instead, but the Russian had no money and was keen on *The Trial* because he thought that it was in the public domain. Not true, as it turned out, but by then they were stuck with *The Trial* and somehow the Russian scraped the money together and Orson was grateful to him for taking a chance when no one else was interested. In that way Orson is very much like Salka's husband Berthold had been, drawn to seat-of-the-pants producers because he had already alienated the powerful ones, the Zanucks and the Selznicks who avoided his calls even as they praised him to the skies as a great genius of the cinema.

Orson told Salka that he had shot much of *The Trial* in the deserted old Gare d'Orsay in Paris, because it was enormous and cheap and available. Fortuitously it was also a place that came to speak to him of Kafka, of unstamped visas and the haunted hopelessness of refugees. She's not sure what refugees have to do with Kafka and she was only half listening as Orson rambled on, distracted by Peter who seemed bored and impatient with his guests. At last she acquiesced to Welles and found herself telling him about her long-ago days in Prague, about her friendships with Kafka and Max Brod. He was interested and in the end quite nice and she was carried away by her memories, though she is perturbed to think she might have gone on too long . . .

MOST OF WHAT SALKA REMEMBERS ABOUT PRAGUE is hunger. It was the spring of 1918. She was twenty-nine years old and a newlywed, and the last good meal she had eaten recently was the wedding dinner her mother had brought to Vienna from her childhood house: home-cured ham, roast turkey, bread, butter, and a small cake. She and Berthold had each recently and triumphantly managed to secure theatrical contracts. He would direct for three years at the Royal Saxonian Theater in Dresden while she joined the actors of the Kammerspiele in Munich. But for the moment Berthold had taken a position as a theater critic for the *Prager Tagblatt*, an appointment he had eagerly accepted upon his release from the army after three miserable years of active duty on the Eastern Front.

Berthold Viertel in uniform, c. 1915–16.

The war was taking its fateful turn and the unimaginable was beginning to seem possible for the Hapsburg monarchy. The Czechs were adamant in their refusal to sell the bounty of their farms to the German-speaking locals, and so the abiding topic for her and Berthold and everyone they knew in Prague was where to find enough to eat. On a few lucky occasions, Salka found that by speaking Polish she could briefly catch a shopkeeper's attention.

It was not the first time she would know hunger in her life and it would not be the last. In Prague, a city to which she has never returned, her deprivation had visual as well as visceral dimensions, as if it were a giddy Technicolor hallucination. The month of June had brought a profusion of cherries to the markets. Though they could never appease her cravings for a solid dinner, those baskets of cherries in the street stands delighted her anyway, their extravagant bursts of scarlet splashed against the sober stone palaces and the greenery of the Castle District.

They had rented a furnished room in the house where Berthold's pregnant sister Helene and her husband, a tenor with the Staatsoper, were living. What breakfast there was Salka cooked on an alcohol burner, while they took their other meager meals with Willi and Helene. Sometimes Max Brod and Franz Kafka came for supper, bringing with them a Viennese journalist named Anton Kuh, a satirist with a monocle and a stinging wit. Kuh reminded Salka of Berthold's great friend Karl Kraus, but without Kraus's clarity. Once when she cooked a dinner for the three men that consisted chiefly of spinach, Kuh made antic political jokes about it that she was at a loss to understand. Kafka, on the other hand, was very quiet. Salka was too shy to talk much to him though she saw him quite often, mostly at Brod's house. Kafka was tall and handsome and so brown and robust-looking that Salka had trouble believing he suffered from tuberculosis.

Her greatest pleasure in Prague had been the opera. At that time the choir director was Anton Webern, who was a friend and colleague of her brother Edward, both of them protégés of Arnold Schoenberg. During the many evenings she and Berthold spent with Webern and his wife, discussing the war and the revolution in Russia, their most urgent conversations were about food—how to get it and where. Webern had little children, and she saw him once looking longingly into the window of a store that boasted a few sausages and a single can of sardines. He spoke no Czech and the prices were beyond him, so he only stared.

It sounds grim, this honeymoon time she spent in Prague, and yet she and Berthold had had so much there: wonderful music and theater, an abundance of stimulating friends, their youth and their ambition and their early love. But the world was at war, and they were always hungry. The surplus of culture thriving alongside threats to basic human survival was a double-edged path that she would continue to navigate in different places through most of her life, in which it seemed she was forever cobbling together one meal after another for people whose hunger—for food, but also for consolation—could never be satisfied. These days she is almost never hungry. Sometimes she wonders why she is feeling so dizzy and weak, and then she scolds herself and has a bit of meat and a cup of coffee and she feels a little better. Unless she is invited to the Shaws' or to Peter's, she gets little pleasure from eating, as if food that is not shared, not offered to someone needier than she, has lost its satisfaction. Even so, she tells herself, she really ought to stop eating her suppers while standing over the sink. It is too depressing.

AGAIN SHE WISHES she had not gone on so long to Orson about her memories of Prague. His Kafka would never be hers and she should not have attempted to offer him an alternative. Orson's version is a grand, masculine, spectacular Kafka, loud and vast enough to fill the Gare d'Orsay. A Kafka reeking of paranoia, forever asking in a shout why he is being punished. And a Kafka, moreover, who has been forced to serve as an oracle for all the evils that have befallen Europe after his death. Her own Kafka is more private and more elliptical, fixed firmly in his place and time, a gentle, watchful man who wakes from troubled dreams, who is affable company in coffeehouses and drawing rooms, who silently fears his father. *Ein Hungerkünstler* whose very existence invites misinterpretation. She supposes that she and Orson have each taken possession of a Kafka composed mainly of themselves. But enough of this. She should keep these thoughts for her memoirs. They are all that belong to her these days.

In the 1940s she had had a few run-ins with Orson at the studio, always about projects for Greta. At one point he'd been after Salka to write a picture about the poet Gabriele D'Annunzio's affair with the actress Eleonora Duse, a farce, if one could believe it, to star Greta and Charlie Chaplin. Orson was mistaken to think that such a serious story could be played for laughs, even after *Ninotchka*, and they had all told him so. This took place after Charlie's *Monsieur Verdoux* unpleasantness and it was interesting to see Orson still wrangling to direct Chaplin, who of course declined again for all kinds of reasons.

Ah, Charlie, darling faithful friend of her California years, ever since the early 1930s. She has known only two geniuses in her life, Brecht and Schoenberg, but if Charlie has not the same kind of genius he is still a great artist, one of the greatest, as Greta was. He has been very generous to her over the years, even helping to save her Santa Monica house from foreclosure. She last saw him this past autumn when she had stopped in Vevey on her way back to Klosters from a trip to San Sebastián, which Peter had been eager to show her and which she had found enchanting.

Even Charlie thinks that his manor house in the village of Corsier just above Vevey is pretentious. But he and Oona and their brood have settled in so happily there, on their thirty-seven acres with the enormous lawn that frames the mountains and the lake. There are orchards and a pool and of course a tennis court: Charlie is never so serious as when he risks losing a point, and has always so hated to lose. His five daughters are beautiful in their white cotton dresses and their pigtails, and the new baby, Christopher, is a darling. Everywhere Charlie walks or drives, the Swiss give a cheerful shout of "Bonjour, Charlot!" which he enjoys, and in restaurants or during meals at home he is never above indulging a guest or his children with his old dance of the dinner rolls from *The Gold Rush*, with forks stuck in the rolls so that they look like feet.

Oona is unchanged, sweet and intelligent. But their life of luxury is a cocoon from which they hope never to emerge. They eat wild strawberries and cream on the terrace, which he savors ostentatiously, and once in a while, he confesses, when he and Oona are alone they take out the caviar and champagne and they revel in the private indulgence.

Salka understands, of course, that everything with Charlie including his art stems from the almost unbelievable misery of his childhood, the poverty and the hunger—more dire hunger than she has ever known—and the fear and the loneliness. He has asked her to read his memoirs which he is writing with a copy of Fowler's *The King's English* and a dictionary always at hand, declaring that he is entirely self-taught, hoping to impress the reader with his vocabulary. The first parts are the best, especially when he writes about his early years of movie making. But his philosophy is a rather hilarious mixture of socialism, undigested Marxism, and the worst parvenu capitalism, and his dictionary-plucked word choices are pompous and often wrong. She felt compelled to tell him that his overblown language makes it hard for the reader to understand him, that he should try to write simply and clearly, and she thinks he resents her for her honesty. Not too long ago he had read bits from her own memoirs and told her he was fascinated. But she doubts he believes her criticisms of his efforts. He is proud and does not want to hear them.

She and Charlie are exactly the same age and both are hard at work revisiting their respective pasts. Their childhoods are like photographic negatives: hers was straight out of Turgenev in a big country house full of servants and music, while his was the purest Dickens, industrial and desperate. She had the advantages of the early tutoring of governesses and a boarding school in Lemberg; his education came from the terrors of the Lambeth workhouse and the London streets, his lessons only about survival and escape. Neither of them has ever really recovered from their early years, she from the security she took for granted, nor he from the humiliations he swore to avenge.

And now that they are old, each of them stashed away in their Swiss exiles, how the negatives have been switched: he under his glass bell of comfort and she without more than a handful of coins in her pocket. When she visited him she did not have enough money to tip his servants and she had had to ask Oona to lend her forty francs to get home. They were always so kind to her, yet in the end she was eager to leave. Late in the evenings she had been tired, and yearned silently to go to bed while Charlie talked on and on.

She is flattered that he mentioned her briefly in his manuscript, writing about her "interesting supper parties" in Santa Monica and comparing her to the great eighteenth-century hostess Madame de Staël. Perhaps she should be less modest about her reputation as a salonnière, though she never thought of herself in such lofty terms, only as a friend looking after other friends. But if she is remembered at all, it may be for her parties—along with the unshakable murmurs of gossip that she and Greta were lovers. Nobody will recall that she was once a good actress, or after that a screenwriter. Already too many people doubt that she even wrote those pictures at Metro. They believe that her name on the titles was just a hollow payment for playing gatekeeper between Greta and the studio. Well, let the naysayers believe what they wish. She doesn't care.

All the same, it is a bit painful to compare her life with Charlie's, to note how substantial his achievements are, how indelibly the Little Tramp will remain engraved on the public consciousness. He built a studio with his own hands, composed the music for his own films, he can point to *City Lights* and *Modern Times* and all the rest as the tangible artifacts of his immortality.

And she? She leaves no monuments. She has only her life as her magnum opus, and what will anyone remember of it? The taste of her chocolate cake. The cadence of her voice. Her shadowy image in an upstairs bedroom with a view of the Pacific, as she lofts a billowing sheet over a mattress. Little things, quick to fade away.

She would like to be remembered for her courage. For the way she rose to meet the twentieth century, maneuvered through its dangers across the wide screen of the world. "And meet the time as it seeks us," as Shakespeare said in *Cymbeline*, the epigraph her doomed friend Stefan Zweig chose for his own haunted memoir. Unlike Zweig, she has never been trapped in the world of yesterday, yearning after its lost charms, paralyzed by the thought of the future. She has stepped forward with an open heart. For all the horrors life has shown her, she still believes in its goodness, and its infinite possibilities.

2

CARRIED ACROSS

BERLIN, NEW YORK, AND LOS ANGELES
MARCH 1928

SALKA AND BERTHOLD VIERTEL had decided they would go to America. Their last weeks in Berlin were filled with parties, like a celluloid montage of farewell tableaux. The party Salka remembered most vividly was a reception for the French singer Yvette Guilbert. It was hosted by Salka's friend Francesco von Mendelssohn at his family's majestic Grunewald villa, in the white music salon among the celebrated collection of Corots. In attendance were ambassadors, socialites, and film stars, all in evening dress. Guilbert performed her chansons while the audience regarded her still-blazing red hair and her long figure, made famous by Toulouse-Lautrec in his drawings, and her now-ruined face and her fluttering hands. Afterward, during supper and dancing, Salka and Berthold were pleased to sit with the Belgian director Jacques Feyder, who had signed a contract from MGM and was also on his way to Hollywood with his actress wife and their three sons, who were around the same age as Salka's boys.

Midnight arrived and there appeared in the drawing room a sudden mirage, orchestrated by the slyly outrageous Francesco: a flight of bicycle racers, another collection of his beautiful young men, muscled and tattooed under their dirty striped T-shirts. They had just arrived from one of Berlin's great spectacles, the six-day round-the-clock racing competition at the Sportpalast. The ambassadors and their wives discreetly evaporated as the party took on its louche new dimensions and the young changelings busied themselves about their pleasures, like something, Salka later recalled, out of Max Reinhardt's *A Midsummer Night's Dream*.

It was her last impression of Berlin. She would not return until forty years later, after both she and the city had withstood events beyond anyone's imagination. Half a decade after Salka left for America, the feverish pageantry of her Berlin would fall, of course, into barbarous hands. The Mendelssohn palace would be seized and its Corots distributed among thieves. Francesco and his sister Eleonora von Mendelssohn—a talented Nefertiti-eyed actress, named for her godmother, Eleonora Duse—would be forced to flee to New York, their world in exile shrunken to the exigencies of melancholy and drug addiction. And what of Francesco's white Lancia convertible, with its ermine seat covers, and his red leather suit, and the yellow dressing gown he often wore to parties: in whose possession did those land? And what about his beautiful young Berlin men, who can say what happened to them? *Beware, oh wanderer, the road is walking too*: Rainer Maria Rilke, whom Salka had met in Munich in 1918 while she was playing Paulina in *The Winter's Tale*, knew a few things himself about the ruthlessness of change, and wrote that sentiment in his diaries.

SALKA AND BERTHOLD were joining an early wave of artists who had been lured to Los Angeles to work in the film industry. Although it was some years before many thousands of their fellows throughout Europe would begin to be expelled—and worse—by the looming National Socialist catastrophe, by 1928 the signs were already more than evident in the war-torn old cities they were leaving behind. From Salka's apartment window in Düsseldorf, where she had gone to perform and teach at the Schauspielhaus in the mid-1920s, she had often watched young men in steel helmets pushing people off the sidewalks while singing the *Horst Wessel Lied*.

Yet in 1928 it was not politics but economics that was propelling Salka and Berthold to Hollywood. Their finances were in total disarray, and the money Berthold had been promised by the Fox Film Corporation, a weekly salary of $600 to write and direct, plus a travel allowance of $1,200, was far more than he could hope to earn in Germany's vertiginously uncertain economy.

The Viertels had been married for ten years and they were not young. Salka was thirty-nine and Berthold was forty-three. But they had not yet become their full selves. In time, the New World would tell them definitively who they were. As she prepared for the journey, Salka wanted to go to Hollywood but she was also reluctant to go. She had created contingencies to soothe herself: they were leaving their three little sons with a nanny in Berlin until they felt more confident that their "great adventure" would pay off. Their youngest child, Tommy, was two years old. They were anxious parents, and with reason. As a toddler their middle son Peter had nearly died of pneumonia, while a few years later their eldest, Hans, had contracted scarlet fever.

Just after she booked passage, Salka suffered the full force of her misgivings. "Suddenly the thought of the six thousand miles separating me from my sons made me panicky," she wrote decades later in her memoir. "If it had not been for Berthold and our determination to start a new life together, I would have stayed in Berlin."

Their plan was to return to Europe in one year, or three, or five—as quickly as they could manage to rebuild their finances. If Hollywood was good to them, maybe they would stay longer. Either way, they were making a forceful break. As they told themselves and each other again and again, it was to be a new life.

Leaving Berlin required Salka to pass up another offer for a good acting job there. And who knew how many more there might be for her, coming up on the wrong end of forty? She had been a working actress for twenty years and had dreamed of a life in the theater since she was five, when she had built a stage in the corner of her bedroom and created performances that lasted for days, using paper cutouts from her mother's fashion magazines while she spoke all the parts. She had fought hard to enter the profession and to succeed within it, battling against a general presumption that actresses were only slightly less vulgar than prostitutes. Never a star and not a classical beauty, she was nonetheless as employable in Europe as an actress of her age and station could hope to be. She was tall enough to be authoritative, with broad shoulders, a full bosom, and lovely legs. Her auburn hair was fine, with a tendency toward frizz. She drew audiences in with a blue-eyed gaze that was natural but not naive.

Two views of Salomea Sara Steuermann as a young actress.

Each new acting job was hard-won, each position tenuous. Even her name was protean. While her legal name was Salomea Sara Steuermann and her childhood nickname was Salka, sometimes she appeared in playbills as Mea Steuermann, sometimes as Mia, sometimes as Salka; for some productions she was Steuermann-Viertel, for others Viertel-Steuermann. Her identity was as variable as the roles she played in the many cities to which she routinely traveled to play them.

Berthold was acutely aware of the sacrifice Salka was now ready to make in giving up her stage career in Europe. "It saddens me deeply that you should not immediately pursue your livelihood as an actress. And I do not at all think that a trouble-free paradise awaits in Hollywood—that exists nowhere," he had written to her with the voice of a man living in a supremely destabilizing time and place. "But fate calls us and we must follow." Yet if she were no longer to be an actress, what else could she possibly be?

Salka was also abandoning the double edge of economic upheaval and cultural innovation that gashed the air of the Weimar Republic, that caused her and everyone she knew in Berlin to veer many times daily between alarm and elation. The gray streets were filled with the unemployed, with real and fake cripples from the Great War, with shiny-booted prostitutes and skinny rent boys on every corner. *Garçonnes* wearing trousers and sporting monocles pushed their way past corseted and rouged young men as jazz tangos spilled from the open doors of the Königin-Bar and the Eldorado. Lurid images of sex murders splashed across the pages of tabloids and on painters' canvases. Foreign opportunists had plenty of money and spent it shamelessly, while many natives of the city went hungry. Throughout a series of disastrously failed governments, the German mark had until recently been plummeting from one stomach-dropping depth to another. What little food available in the city was hoarded and furiously bartered. "*Hunger* is what I remember from those years," Salka told the journalist Otto Friedrich when he interviewed her in the 1970s. "I was always hungry and cold. And sometimes slightly drunk, because that was one thing you could always get if you had any money at all."

Yet in this jumpy milieu and out of nothing, it seemed, art was happening everywhere, and Berlin's many theaters rarely lacked for audiences. During the inflationary crisis of the early 1920s, Salka and Berthold had launched a repertory company of their own called *Die Truppe*, a longtime dream come true. They hoped to offer performances that reflected the hurly-burly of contemporary Berlin. But for practical reasons their first offering, *The Merchant of Venice*, did not provide a commentary on the increasingly pernicious anti-Semitism that *Die Truppe*'s Jewish directors encountered. Instead they designed the production to showcase the company's star, Fritz Kortner, along with jarring geometric sets by a pair of Bauhaus artists. Their next two shows—Eugene O'Neill's half-Expressionist, half-realist *Emperor Jones*, followed by Knut Hamsun's *Driven by the Devil*, starring Salka—spoke more to the moment, tackling current questions about race and class. Next came *Vincent*, a farce by Robert Musil about the fluidity of sexuality and the power of money. The last was a failure, proving far too intellectual even for Berlin's sophisticated audiences.

Remembering the wildly lurching economy of the Weimar Republic, Salka later wrote: "I was amazed that there were still people who would buy tickets, but they did; and tottering but determined, *Die Truppe* continued its frail existence." The company's production of *Side by Side*, Georg Kaiser's New Objectivity play about the hyperinflation, with sets designed by George Grosz, played to sold-out houses every night in November of 1923. Yet each morning the Viertels awoke to learn from the newspapers that they were as broke as ever. "It was a cold and wet winter and the dollar now stood at between two and three billion marks," Salka wrote.

> We got paid every day; at noon we would appear at the cashiers, our billions and trillions stuffed into large paper bags or suitcases, and those of us who lived in boarding houses would rush home to deliver cash to our distraught landladies, who hastened to the stores and bought food before the Stock Exchange closed and another deluge of marks swept away the value of the old ones.

Die Truppe struggled to stay afloat. But its death knell came in March 1924 with Berthold's staging of a pair of one-act plays by his friend Karl Kraus, to honor the twenty-fifth anniversary of Kraus's satirical journal *Die Fackel* (The Torch). The premiere was packed with the very same theater critics upon whom Kraus had lavished his harshest invective, and while many in the audience cheered at the company's courage, the occasion was more of a wake than a celebration. In the days that followed, the critics retaliated. One of the troupe's key sponsors, a currency speculator seeking cultural cachet, suspended his financial support. The Viertels declared bankruptcy, sending them into considerable personal debt.

Salka and Berthold went back to chasing piecemeal theater work in whichever city they could find it, dwelling fleetingly in boardinghouses or dreadfully furnished apartments in Munich, Dresden, Leipzig, Hamburg, Berlin, Vienna, Düsseldorf. They were nomads of a rarefied intellectual sort, hauling their children and their belongings from city to city, throwing themselves into play after play. Salka was Strindberg's Laura at the Volksbühne in Leipzig. She was Medea in Hamburg, catching the night train to Dresden after her Sunday performances to spend twenty-four hours with her sons and with Berthold, who was directing at the Dresden Schauspielhaus. Then she rushed back to Hamburg on Tuesdays in time to take up Medea again and to murder her make-believe children offstage. The train, the curtain, the train, the children and Berthold, the train, the stage. She was Schiller's Mary Stuart in Düsseldorf. She was Friedrich Hebbel's Judith in Berlin.

They were citified bohemians with many addresses but no home. When Salka and Berthold were together, there were late nights at their table at the Romanisches Café in Berlin, where on any evening they might sit with Bertolt Brecht, say, and the actor Alexander Granach, and the young Communist Otto Katz, and with scores of other friends who would pop up again at different times in their lives in different cities. They knew just about everyone worth knowing. Through Salka's brother Edward Steuermann, a notable pianist, they had met all the important composers: Schoenberg, Webern, Hanns Eisler. They befriended Berlin's wild young things, many of them from culturally patrician families and all brimming with plans to *épater le bourgeois*: Pamela Wedekind, Anna Mahler, Klaus and Erika Mann, Eleonora and Francesco von Mendelssohn. While Salka and Berthold were in Vienna, there were long nights in coffeehouses with Karl Kraus and his circle when Salka was nine months pregnant with Tommy and dying to go to bed. She did not go to bed. She stayed at the table to answer the lacerating wits, glazed and half-delirious, hoping the waiters would turn out the lights.

Steeped as they were in the theater, she and Berthold were interested in the possibilities of cinema, and willing to gamble on its future as a serious art form. Berthold had written a scenario for *Nora*, based on Ibsen's *Doll's House*, for Universum-Film AG in 1923, and soon thereafter he wrote and directed *The Wig*, which became an Expressionist classic, for Westi Film. He directed a picture called *Adventures of a Ten-Mark Note* for Fox Company Europe in 1926, in which the musically prodigious Francesco von Mendelssohn played the role of "Ein Klavierspieler."

Around the time of the success of the landmark film *Sunrise* in 1927, its director F. W. Murnau asked Berthold to be the writer for his pictures. At that time the Westphalia-born Murnau was already working in Hollywood, where he'd been coveted by the studios as yet another must-have European genius like Lubitsch and Stiller, and signed to an enormous salary by William Fox.

Salka had known Murnau—colossally tall, ginger-haired, fiercely reserved—since her earliest days in Max Reinhardt's theaters. They had acted together in *Penthesilea*, when he was a Greek soldier and she a saucy Amazon. She had once thought Murnau unbearably stuffy, but in time, with warmth and humor, she found she was able to soften his Prussian inflexibility. Hollywood loosened up Murnau as well, although his relationship with the equally headstrong Berthold remained fraught from the beginning. In November of 1927, just after staging *Peer Gynt* for Reinhardt's theaters in Berlin, Berthold completed the scenario for *4 Devils*, the second of Murnau's three Hollywood films. (This circus picture, starring a young Janet Gaynor, became one of the great "ghost films" of the silent era, all copies of which were lost.) Now, in 1928, Murnau was impatient to get Berthold to the Fox studios in California to begin writing his next film, to be called *Our Daily Bread*.

Salka thought most of the early movies she saw to be vulgar. She considered one a masterpiece—Eisenstein's *Potemkin*—and a few others remarkable: Robert Wiene's *The Cabinet of Dr. Caligari*, Paul Wegener's *Golem*, Ernst Lubitsch's *Anne Boleyn*, the first pictures of Fritz Lang and the great Swedish director Mauritz Stiller. Salka would always remember the collective gasp in the movie house during Stiller's *The Saga of Gösta Berling* when the luminous eyes of a very young Greta Garbo took over the screen. But she, like nearly everyone she knew, reserved her highest admiration for the faraway legend of Chaplin's Little Tramp.

In Berlin in the early summer of 1925, Salka had written a film treatment of her own, an adaptation of a novel by the nineteenth-century French writer Jules-Amédée Barbey d'Aurevilly. It would be some years before she would begin to imagine herself as a writer. Yet she was inspired by the hectic artistic activity flourishing around her, and she conceived a scenario with the encouragement of Hjalmar Lerski, the brilliant cameraman for Berthold's picture *The Wig*. Pluckily she forged ahead, scrawling her work longhand on big sheets of paper in a single exhilarating session. She sold the treatment to the Hungarian producer Gabriel Pascal, whose film company then promptly went bankrupt. While Salka's picture was never produced, she managed to collect her payment of five thousand rentenmark, the currency issued by the Weimar government in a vain attempt to control hyperinflation.

BERTHOLD WAS A SERIOUS POET, essayist, and novelist as well as a director and screenwriter. Deeply intellectual and prone to philosophizing, he recognized the radical power of the medium of film—the first new form of storytelling to come along in five hundred years—and noted its vulnerability to manipulation. It was, as he saw it, "an immense political tool of the future." With the ubiquity of screens in our era, it's difficult to imagine how grand and strange those first films seemed to audiences, how shocking the notion of pictures that moved. Pictures that offered the grandest exotic vistas, and pictures so intimate that a kiss filled an auditorium, its viewers rapt and furtive in the secrecy of the dark. Pictures that could reach into every corner of the planet in a way the theater never could—not even

Max Reinhardt's 360-degree extravaganzas and his tireless world tours could approach cinema's range. Just as the Great War had been the first industrialized war, the movies were an industrialized art form, deployed to seize vast audiences and to change the way they would see the world. Berthold was more correct about film being a political instrument than even he could imagine. It happened sooner than he expected: in America mostly for profit, in Germany for control and subjugation.

Convinced by the achievements of Stiller and Chaplin, the Viertels were gambling on novelty. They would leave the stage, their ancient beloved, into which they had infused modern ideas and techniques. They would take up the screen, investing the new technology with all the classic old stories. As they prepared to cross the Atlantic for the first time, Berthold was intent on using this moment to remake himself as well. A lover of excess—too many cigarettes; too many rich desserts; an extravagant temper; a chronic sexual thrall to actresses who momentarily caught his eye—he now fervently hoped, for his and Salka's sakes, to rein himself in. The previous year, on their tenth anniversary, he had written to Salka: "I often wish you had a worthier man, a stronger, better-looking, smarter, richer, and better husband. But I beg you from the bottom of my soul to keep me the way I am with all of my failings." He now swore to smoke only twenty cigarettes a day (he would count them) and to curb his frequent raging. "Ever since I have known you there is no greater fear for me than that I might lose you," he had written. "I've never said that to another human heart and probably never will be able to again."

If Salka was feeling similar urges toward transformation, she did not mention it. She, too, was prone to rages and fits of serious melancholy. She, too, had had love affairs, some retaliatory and fleeting, one or two more meaningful. She'd begun and ended a serious romance with a friend of Berthold's, a Viennese art historian named Ludwig Münz. She'd had an intense emotional relationship with Luise Dumont, her adviser at the Düsseldorf Schauspielhaus.

There is a story about Salka from her theater days. Its details are lost now, but here's the fragment that remains. During some night on an unremembered stage, Salka was performing alongside a well-known actor with whom she was having an affair. The scene demanded that her head be positioned very close to that of the actor, who took the opportunity to whisper to her so that only she could hear. "When?" he said. She responded with a suggestion, sotto voce. Then the actor whispered, "Where?" and she replied again, meeting the challenge headlong. Throughout her life Salka was defiant about "asserting my rights to love and to live," as she wrote decades later, regardless of collateral damage.

Despite their mutual betrayals and disappointments, Salka and Berthold were not ready to give up on their marriage. They had spent a holiday week in Venice in the summer of 1927, a second honeymoon in which they pledged to attempt repairs. Unlike Berthold, Salka now made no declarations toward self-improvement. Most likely, putting an ocean between herself and her children, her parents, and her siblings was change enough for her. Their landlady and Francesco von Mendelssohn took them to the train station in Berlin. As she always did at moments of farewell, Salka broke down and cried.

The Viertels got off the train in Hamburg and sailed from Cuxhaven on the *Albert Ballin* on February 22, 1928. Berthold mentioned that in the "mountainous heights" of first class the passage seemed like a stay at a spa, with rich meals and games and casual flirtation. Salka remembered that among the fifteen hundred or so passengers there was a stowaway, discovered in the hold once they had started westward. There was also a dead American soldier from the Great War who had been disinterred from his grave in France and sent off to be buried on home soil. She noted the addition of six thousand canaries, all being ferried to America to be sold as pets. The birds were as cosseted as the first-class passengers. When one of them fell ill, the purser brought it to his cabin to oversee its convalescence.

A dense fog cheated Salka of the melodrama of the approaching New York skyline. Even so, her arrival was momentous, as she had crossed an irreversible border. Though she did not know it yet, she had been translated. From the death of her old self she was emerging into an American life, whatever that might mean. The feeling of this moment of unmooring would return throughout her life. It would feed her compassion for the thousands of her *Landsleute* who would make this same voyage, in far greater states of panic and disorientation, in the decades to follow.

They were emigrants first of all and only after that were they the people they really were.

— LION FEUCHTWANGER

WHEN THE *ALBERT BALLIN* DOCKED, three reporters and a German-speaking publicity man from Fox met the Viertels in the ship's salon. As the reporters began to interview Berthold, out of nowhere a bleached-haired young German woman showed up, braying about how seasick she'd been during the crossing. In split seconds the reporters' cameras veered away from Berthold and clicked away at the girl as she dangled her legs off the arm of a sofa. She had a contract with Universal, but Salka had never heard of her, and she never would again.

They left the boat, and Salka tried hard to grasp the immensity of New York. The city seemed alien and disturbingly beautiful. Its jagged geometries reminded her of the visions of the painter Lyonel Feininger, while its symphonic stink recalled the teeming ghetto in Przemyśl, a Galician city not far from her hometown. Immediately upon arriving at their Central Park South hotel, she and Berthold ran into an exhausted-looking Max Reinhardt, surrounded by his Berlin entourage. The theater impresario—whose portrait had been on the cover of *Time* magazine the previous year, and who was named "the Barnum of world theater" by the *New York Herald Tribune*—told them he was departing that day for the Coast after completing another successful program of Schiller and Shakespeare on Broadway. Salka had not spoken to Reinhardt personally since the day of her first audition for him when she was twenty-two, though she'd had major roles on his stages for over a decade. With great cordiality Reinhardt said he hoped to see the Viertels in Hollywood. And then, just as affably, one of his associates predicted Salka's unavoidable failure as an actress there and her swift return to Berlin.

The performances the Viertels saw during their three weeks in New York left them cold, except for several wonderful Negro musicals and a dazzling all-black production of *Porgy*, directed by Rouben Mamoulian. Otherwise they found Broadway thoroughly unexciting, while the Theater Guild people they met through an introduction from the journalist Dorothy Thompson were baffling. These Americans considered Max Reinhardt a mere entrepreneur, admired the most conventional aspects of German theater, and had never heard of Brecht or Wedekind.

Salka had been studying a primer called *A Thousand Words of English*. Her command of the language was improving but still limited; the strange vowels and the *th* sound would continue to bewilder her. New York seemed just as alienating as the harsh sounds of its speech. She would revisit the city many times and in her later years would briefly live on the Upper West Side, but she always found Manhattan loud, dirty, and dispiriting.

Murnau's anxious telephone calls from Hollywood propelled them at last onto the westward train, a marvel of modern luxury and speed. Over the four-day journey, the shifting landscapes kept Salka staring out the window, transfixed by the strange beauty of the purple rock formations in New Mexico and Arizona, the spiky Joshua trees and the impressionistic mounds of sagebrush. In Berlin, cactuses were popular houseplants and familiar subjects in the still-life paintings of the New Objectivity. There they'd been symbols of otherness, of captivity and claustrophobia. But here, set among the panoramas flickering outside the train window, they were for Salka a revelation of breadth, of prodigality, of endless star-bright desert nights. She was as astonished as a schoolgirl by everything she saw.

On the fifth day she woke up to the overpowering smell of orange blossoms. Outside the window were groves and groves of citrus trees. They had reached California.

THE SKIES WERE GRAY and the air was chilly when the sleek, efficient *Chief* pulled into the Pasadena train station on a late-winter day in 1928. The Viertels rode to the Roosevelt Hotel in a chauffeur-driven car with yet another publicity man from the Fox studio and Berthold's new secretary, a tall, heavy-set actor named Herman Bing. Their route to Hollywood took them along Sunset Boulevard in order to skip the crush of cars downtown. Along the way Salka noted the fantastic eclecticism of the houses and shops they passed on the way: roofs shaped like mushrooms, a restaurant shaped like a hat. She must have missed—because surely she would have remarked on them—the many rooms-for-rent signs on boardinghouses that warned NO ACTORS, NO JEWS, NO KIDS OR PETS, a list that perfectly described Salka and her household.

"I expected California to be all sunshine and flowers," Salka wrote. But the sun she had been warned repeatedly to avoid was nowhere in evidence in a sullen March sky. Outside the limousine window, Los Angeles was a fast-paced Autopia. Its main industries were oil, agriculture, and motion pictures, but for the people who lived there, it was a city built largely to support houses and cars. The sight of so many automobiles had surprised other recent emigrants, many of whom had perhaps read too many Karl May novels and were expecting some sort of Wild West settlement. The director Ernst Lubitsch had this to say about his arrival from Berlin in 1922:

> I went to Hollywood with the feeling of making a voyage of discovery in a dark continent. I imagined Hollywood as a semi-wild nest surrounded by a big fence of wilderness. And when I got off

> the train in Los Angeles, I saw the traffic of a modern metropolis: skyscrapers towered in the air, thousands and thousands of cars whizzed around on the paved roads, a gigantic traffic jam made the city alive . . .

Salka herself had had little idea what to expect. She had not even known where Hollywood was. On a visit home to Wychylowka the previous summer, her father had been obliged to find a map so he could show her. She now realized that Hollywood was actually a neighborhood within a larger city which was coming into focus. She and Berthold would need a car, and driving lessons. They would need a house. Their days in Europe had been lived in apartments and on trains, in orderly vertical metropolises where people went about their business on foot or public transport. Their new life would be lived in this elliptical, self-driven place. It might as well be a new planet for the complex vocabulary they would have to learn in order to maneuver within it.

For the moment, though, their lives as urban nomads played on at the Roosevelt Hotel, a Spanish Colonial Revival fantasy which had opened the previous year, financed by the likes of Mary Pickford, Douglas Fairbanks, and Louis B. Mayer as a fancy way station for visiting film folk. In their too-warm suite they found ingratiating gifts from the studio. A big bouquet of red roses for Salka. A case of Prohibition whiskey for Berthold, stashed, with cheeky cliché, in the bathtub.

After all of Murnau's fretful telephoning, it turned out that he was busy shooting tests and would not need Berthold that day. This was an inauspicious beginning. Berthold interpreted the hurry-up-and-wait as a sign of Murnau's insufferable arrogance, and was furious.

Instead the Viertels had lunch with a German journalist of their acquaintance, and then, before they even got a glimpse of the studios, Salka begged to see the ocean. They headed toward the beach town of Santa Monica, named by eighteenth-century Spanish missionaries after the patron saint of difficult marriages and disappointing children because some local freshwater springs had reminded the good Franciscans of Saint Monica's tears. At the end of Pico Boulevard, a long highway heading west, Salka got her first glimpse of the Pacific. She described it on that gray day as iridescent, as if it were a vast sheet of mother-of-pearl.

They stopped the car in front of a large hotel shaded by sycamores and cypresses, then crossed the street to find themselves on the rim of a cliff. To their right were the bay and the canyon, dotted with trees and only a few houses. To the left was the pier. They drove up to its entrance and Salka was instantly smitten: with the yellow hippodrome and the merry-go-round inside it, with its hand-carved painted horses and old-fashioned music; with the ice cream stands and the fish markets and the bait stalls; with the day fishermen casting from atop the pier, and the swaying boats below; and with the Filipina bedecked in sequins who was telling fortunes out of a shack.

Salka had been raised near a river that flowed out of the Carpathian Mountains and emptied, after a long haphazard course, into the Black Sea. The river was called the Dniester and the section of it that flowed near her childhood home was unpredictable, with sudden deep and roiling chasms. Her memory of its wildness answered a secret call that she sometimes heard. It rose up in protest against Berthold's unassailable Viennese urbanity and her own self-discipline on the stage and at home. Looking out beyond the pier at the expanse of this foreign sea, she recognized that same wildness and it called to her again.

Amid the gaudy melodies of the carousel's orchestrion and the fresh brine of the air, here along the pier was a sense of openness and possibility. Here, for the moment, was a counterpoint to all those days and nights in the crowded cafés of Vienna and Berlin, with their hours upon hours of talk. Talk of art and politics and the path toward the future, talk that was weighty and nervous and much of it brilliant, all those ideas, all those convictions, and all of this talk on top of the daily difficulties of theater rehearsals and scrounging for food and soothing sick children and endless cooking and arranging and tidying. On the Pacific shoreline Salka recognized how much of her old existence had been exhausting her, while here the world seemed to be taking a silvery breath. She pleaded with Berthold to let them find a house in Santa Monica.

But the implacable world was not standing still, even among the eternal holiday-makers on this peaceful American shore. In fact, dramatic change and conflict had been routine here long before the Spanish missionaries had forcibly relieved the indigenous people of their beachfront land. Those people, the Tongva, had thrived on it for more than seven thousand years, and clashed regularly and violently with other hunter-gatherers, including the Chumash, their neighbors to the north. More recently, in 1828, rights to the land had been vigorously disputed among several Mexican families who had been granted grazing rights. After the city of Santa Monica was officially incorporated in 1886, development had marched insistently forward with the building of hotels, private clubs, bathhouses, and pleasure arenas, its progress punctuated now and then by large fires with dubious origins, destruction followed by eager and bigger reconstruction.

By 1928, Hollywood's elite had entrenched itself on the beach, with actors Pickford and Fairbanks and the Talmadge sisters venturing from their inland neighborhoods in Hollywood and Beverly Hills to stake out second and third homes on choice stretches of sand below the California Incline that extended north toward the canyon. Then, as now, the houses were built backward. The balconies and fenestrations of their revival-style architecture faced the water, while blankly forbidding gates and garages fronted the street. In 1926, MGM studio chief Louis B. Mayer commanded his art director at Metro to conjure up a house for him at 625 Pacific Coast Highway as quickly as possible. In six weeks, with three construction shifts working around the clock, a sturdy twenty-room Spanish Colonial with a red-tile roof and an onyx-and-marble bathroom materialized like a film set, at a cost to Mayer of $28,000 (about $412,500 in 2019 dollars). Many more Hollywood folk followed into this neighborhood. It came to be known as the Gold Coast and the American Riviera.

Hollywood was coming to the shore for prestige, not for its health. For the leisure-seeking crowds, the sea air of Santa Monica in 1928 was thought to be anything but wholesome. When Berthold casually mentioned at Fox that Salka was keen to live there, he met with scandalized protests. No, no, the studio people said, the Viertels would become rheumatic, the dampness would bring on recurring bronchitis and gout. Gold

Coast mansions—most famously the house built for the film star Norma Shearer and her husband, the chronically unwell MGM executive Irving Thalberg—were climate-controlled, double-windowed, and soundproofed to block the toxic air and the perilous surf.

About all this Salka was skeptical. But she gave in when Herman Bing noted that living in Santa Monica would add an extra half hour to Berthold's daily commute. Defeated by visions of the mad rush her husband would have to endure, she rented the least expensive house she could find in Hollywood, a pleasant mock-Tudor on North Fairfax Avenue, near the foothills of Laurel Canyon.

THERE WAS A WELCOME PARTY for the Viertels that echoed the farewell parties in Berlin. A cabaret singer presided over this gathering, as Yvette Guilbert had appeared in Francesco's salon, though this one had not sung professionally for years. She was a chic Frankfurt-born blonde named Gussy Holl, a former film star and *diseuse*, and she was married to the German actor Emil Jannings. The Janningses hosted the party at the house they were renting from Joseph Schenck, the American film pioneer who was at that time the chairman of the board of United Artists.

Schenck's place was luxurious, if not as august as the Mendelssohn villa. Sitting on a fashionable stretch of Hollywood Boulevard, its three-acre grounds included a tennis court and a swimming pool that was routinely emptied in order to water the citrus orchard. The interiors shone with onyx and tile, oak and mahogany. Salka noted that the enormous living room boasted a wondrous variety of lamps, a common feature, as she would discover, among the swanky parlors of film folk.

Ernst Lubitsch and the actor Conrad Veidt were among the guests—both, Salka noted, with "uninteresting pretty wives." Despite Lubitsch's renown in America, she found him unchanged since the early 1920s in Berlin, when she had watched him pull off practical jokes during rehearsals on Max Reinhardt's stages. Further blending her new life with the old, on this Hollywood evening Max Reinhardt himself made an appearance, declaring himself besotted with California, while their host Emil Jannings, who had taken no time to familiarize himself with his surroundings, professed to hate it. At the party too was a director named Ludwig Berger, a big success in Germany but a troubling loss for the Paramount executives who had brought him over and now could not find a use for him. Salka vowed to remember Berger's predicament as "a warning to European directors"—no doubt thinking of her own husband, to whose fortunes she was yoked.

On this evening there was anxious speculation about the looming adoption of sound technology in film, with its potential to ruin the Hollywood careers of foreign actors with heavy accents. The Viertels had seen *The Jazz Singer* in New York and Berthold had been wondering what the advent of talking pictures might mean for his contract at Fox. Salka thought *The Jazz Singer* was hopelessly banal. Comparing it with silents like King Vidor's *The Crowd* or Murnau's *Sunrise* was for her "sheer blasphemy." Yet it was hard to ignore the long lines of patrons outside the Warner Bros. theaters who were waiting to hear Al Jolson warbling "Blue Skies" and speaking sentimentally to his mother. And it was easy to imagine that the talkies might offer greater opportunities for a writer and director such as Berthold—even if Murnau, the wizard of silent cinema, looked upon all notions about sound in films with loathing.

Reassurances for the actors' concerns were scarce on this California evening with the hint of a chill in its early spring air. Salka was glad to see the evening's mood lighten with the entrance of two ebullient young friends from her Berlin days, Klaus and Erika Mann, newly arrived in Hollywood as part of a pleasure trip they were taking around the world. Into the Janningses' sedate living room the Mann siblings injected the irreverence of Berlin's night life, a welcome jolt of enthusiasm among the roomful of glum expatriates.

Years after that night, the gossip columnist Louella Parsons would name the Janningses' house "the Jinx Mansion," because of the calamities that befell so many of its residents over the decades. There had been the freak death by runaway boulder of grocery magnate George Albert Ralphs back in 1914; the dramatic suicide of Jack Cudahy, heir to a meatpacking fortune, in 1921; and the recently crumbling marriage of the house's current owners, Joseph Schenck and Norma Talmadge.

The arrival of talking pictures played its own role in the shifting fortunes of the Jinx Mansion's current resident, Emil Jannings. Within the year, his thick German accent deemed incomprehensible to American audiences, Jannings would be dismissed from his contract with Paramount. It was a terrible blow for the actor, whose egotism was as outsized as his screen presence. His career in Hollywood was finished. He returned to Germany, where he costarred with Marlene Dietrich in UFA's *The Blue Angel* in 1930 and tyrannized that production with rococo displays of his vanity.

Marlene Dietrich left Berlin for America on the night of *The Blue Angel*'s premiere, in April 1930, as the Weimar Republic was collapsing. She did not return to her hometown until after the war was over. During those fifteen years she became first a proud American citizen and then a tireless participant in the U.S. armed forces, traveling from one dangerous war zone to another to entertain the troops. Jannings in the meantime remained in Germany and starred in films promoting the glory of Nazism from 1934 onward. In 1936, two years before the Mendelssohn villa was expropriated by the National Socialists, Jannings was made a *Staatsschauspieler*, or "artist of the state," by Hitler's propaganda minister, Joseph Goebbels.

"Fate calls, and we must follow," Berthold had written to Salka about their decision to come to America. But as they and their compatriots flowed forward and back across the Atlantic, they were not quite as passive as he suggested. Fate called, but they also made their choices, while they could. The boundary between the new world and the old was porous only for a few years longer. After the gates closed, there would be no more choice.

AS SOON AS THE VIERTELS MOVED into the Fairfax Avenue house, they threw themselves into learning to navigate their strange surroundings. Berthold's secretary Herman Bing gave them English lessons and taught Salka to drive their new Buick. She took to motoring with panache if not exactly with finesse, set off in high spirits, and never looked back. Bing next tried to teach Berthold, who stalled the car on his first attempt behind the wheel, then smashed a bumper and tore off two fenders. Berthold instantly abandoned all hope of driving and they hired a chauffeur to take him to and from the studio.

Tenuously, the roots of their new life unfurled and began to cling. They felt no less foreign, but as the days and weeks went by their English improved and their familiarity with the landscape grew. The spring weather, at first so aloof, now turned munificent, the evening air thick with the smell of jasmine and eucalyptus and ringing with the trills of mockingbirds, the noontimes benignly sunny and warm. Salka sat in the garden in a summer dress and read *Boston* by Upton Sinclair. Berthold made a good first impression at Fox, offering advice everywhere, doctoring other people's films, jumping whenever Murnau called. Berthold was thought to be eccentric, but they were paying him for that, for his foreign intellect and originality.

After a month or so the Viertels determined that they would stay for a while in Hollywood. Salka made arrangements for her sons—aged eight, seven, and two—to make the journey across the Atlantic with Nena, their *Kindermädchen*. During a blistering heat wave at the end of May, Salka traveled across the country on the *Chief*, by herself this time, to meet the *Albert Ballin* in New York. Then she accompanied Hans, Peter, Tommy, and Nena back to Los Angeles on the four-day ride that had so entranced her the previous March. While she was gone, Berthold wrote her a sweet, grateful letter in which he told her that he loved the "Hollywood Salka" even more than every other Salka he had known. She was the one who drove his life, he said wryly, alluding to his hopelessness behind the wheel. She was the globetrotter of his world (*Weltenbummler* is the charming word he used: "world window-shopper"), and she was, he believed without a doubt, the American driver of their luck.

Peter and Hans Viertel, Berlin, 1926.

After their long voyage across the ocean and then the continent, the three Viertel boys were very glad to reach California. They fell in love immediately with De Witt Fuller, the new chauffeur, and the housekeeper, Emma. Their German nanny was distinctly less enchanted with the servants, harboring an ingrown distrust of "*die Schwarzen,*" whose like she had probably never encountered in Europe. Emil Jannings, too, had warned he would never have a meal in Salka's house while her Negro servants were there. But Salka appealed to Nena's Christian morals and coaxed her into a grudging politeness.

Salka and the boys spent the next several months taking English lessons with a tutor and making trips to the Santa Monica pier to ride the merry-go-round. She was glad to be able to send fifty dollars here or five dollars there to her parents, as money back home at Wychylowka was tight. Her seventy-eight-year-old father was no longer practicing law, and when the weather was cold her parents could not always rely on the vacationers they took in as boarders to supplement their income, nor on the fruit from their orchards that they sold to pay their bank loans. Letters to Salka from her mother showed much curiosity about life in California. "Are there snakes on the beach?" she asked. "What about mosquitoes? How is it that such splendid fruit grows in the desert? Are the film stars interesting upon closer acquaintance?"

Berthold and Salka began to be invited to Fox studio parties. There Salka paid special attention to the wives, whom she tended to respect more than the husbands. She found Berthold's producer, Sol Wurtzel, intolerably coarse. But she had warm feelings for Wurtzel's wife Marion, who invited her to lunch and on shopping excursions. One afternoon, Salka watched as Mrs. Wurtzel spent three hundred dollars on fripperies in an expensive boutique. She explained to Salka that, as a poverty-stricken Jewish girl in her small Polish hometown, she had had to share a single pair of shoes with her sister. So it was of no small consequence to her now to be able to buy things she didn't need.

Some of the other wives passed their days playing golf. The director Jacques Feyder and his actress wife Françoise Rosay, whom Salka had seen at the Mendelssohn gala in Berlin, were also recent arrivals in Hollywood, and Françoise gamely suggested to Salka that they give golf a try. They abandoned the idea almost at once. Casting about for a role in this environment, Salka was firm about at least one thing: "We were professional women," she decided, "and to survive in Hollywood we had to work."

For the moment, though, work was Berthold's province alone. Murnau had been struggling from the beginning with his third Fox picture, and things were not getting better. There were problems with casting. There were disagreements about the story. *Our Daily Bread* was to be, as Murnau had explained to the studio chief William Fox in a letter at the end of 1927, "a tale about wheat, about the sacredness of bread, about the estrangement of the modern city dwellers and their ignorance about Nature's sources of sustenance." Under pressure, Berthold's versions of the script became more and more spare, cutting out the expensive visual effects that had reflected Murnau's original vision. Berthold wrote three drafts in all, with further contributions by a screenwriter named Marion Orth, who had also worked on Murnau's last picture, *4 Devils*. Filming was delayed for months while various crises mounted, including Murnau's hospitalization for appendicitis in early July.

At the end of August, the production was ready to travel to the town of Pendleton in northeastern Oregon, where Murnau planned to shoot essential scenes including the picture's climactic wheat harvest. Aboard the train, Berthold wrote to Salka that he had never before seen such hot weather, not even in Serbia during the summertime miseries of his army duty. In the days after his arrival in Oregon, Berthold sat in the hotel making script revisions while Murnau, on location forty-five minutes away, communed with the field of standing wheat which the studio had bought and would sell, thriftily, once the harvest was in and the picture was done. Berthold had little to do during this time except write, swim in the hotel pool, and continue his English lessons with Herman Bing, his only companion. "In this way," he wrote to Salka, "the illusion of my existence as a prisoner is perfect." He drifted through the town, bought Native American figurines and toy boats for the boys, asked Salka if she would like him to buy her a shawl.

In the meantime Salka enrolled her two older boys in elementary school, doing her best to allay their worries that their limited English might put them with younger children. Thanks to their tutor and the help of Emma and De Witt, after only three months in America the boys had made good progress. Salka was proud to report that Hans had landed properly in third grade while Peter, in the second, declared his satisfaction with the school and with his teacher. "She speaks very slowly," he told his mother, "and I understand every word she says."

Salka did not mind being the driver of their family life. She was accustomed to its requirements and she threw herself briskly into the work. It was not in her nature to complain. But lately she had been feeling unwell, suffering from back pain that had emerged from an operation she'd had several years ago, which now triggered an attack of melancholy.

It was in this low state, in early September, when she was tidying Berthold's perennially messy study and happened to read a sentence in one of his open notebooks that overwhelmed her with rage. It was a dramatic and also an unequivocally literary moment: an emotional conflagration sparked by ink on a page, like something out of the life of Sofia Tolstoy, who read the Count's diaries, which were displayed on a table at Yasnaya Polyana for the entire household to see. Berthold had written: *Marriage is sex without desire*. The bald statement revived many buried grievances in Salka while inflicting a new one, even as, in the bitter exchange of letters and phone calls from Oregon over the next two weeks, Berthold tried to deny that he'd written such a thing.

I'd gone to America to start my life over with you, he wrote to her after her first recriminations; *but in difficult times I believe that you want to make me feel: too late, my dear!* And he, further: *I never thought that you could harden so against me in a foreign land, where we represent home to each other.* Salka responded: *Only one thing has changed between us. You were the one person I felt I could talk to, but now has come something that I can't manage, and I can manage a lot. It eats and tears at me. It's a pity about youth: that it leaves you, but you cannot grow older while it happens.* (Salka had turned forty the previous June.) *You have it better: you can write. I have only my life and my love to create, while you are able to create with writing.* In answer to his wounded sense of betrayal that they were not able to be a refuge for each other in a strange land, she had this to say: *I'm not one iota more in a foreign country here than I was in Dresden, Berlin, or Düsseldorf. If you ever had any idea how dismal and lonely I felt when I was walking around on the Rhine Bridge—but you never asked me about it. The only kind of home that I had was the stage. It may have been a pseudo-life and meant little, but now in order to live I have become homeless. It's over and there is no point in talking about it. But just to soothe you, California is not a bit more alien to me than Germany.*

It was as desolate a time as she had ever known. When they spoke of home, they both used the German word *Heimat*, with its centuries of contradictory volatile meanings, a word as likely to evoke exile and loss as belonging and fulfillment—and a word, moreover, which was soon to be grotesquely exploited in the blood-and-soil propaganda of the National Socialists. For the moment, Salka's insistence that she and Berthold could never represent home to each other in the New World, and that he had never done so for her in any previous city, was the true instant of her arrival. She had loved and admired him since the first night they met, in a café in Vienna in 1916, when he had fixed his dark eyes on her and calmly announced that he was going to marry her, even though at the time he was married to somebody else. She loved and admired him still, and their fortunes were chained together. But she had been lonely in Europe and she was lonely now. For some time a link had been broken between them, a much more damaging impairment than the dull tarnish of his stupid little infidelities. Her grievance was not, she had told him, a question of geography. It was a question of self, of one's place in the world.

The only kind of home that I had was the stage. And now, for Berthold's sake, in this newfangled city of sets and costumes but virtually no live theater, she was exiled from her calling. What could home mean for her now? Her childhood Eden, her Wychylowka, the place now in serious disrepair since the looting and burning it had sustained during the Great War, her parents straining to make ends meet, would never again be her refuge. The grand houses she had seen—their interiors gleaming with the patina of the Mendelssohn villa or glaring with the nouveau lamps in the Janningses' rented mansion—none was steadfast, all were vulnerable. They were only as alive as the inhabitants who infused them with their character.

Character, finally, was everything in the meaning of home. What kindnesses or cruelties breathe through the walls and floorboards? For whom do the doors unlock with welcome, and against whom do they close? Salka had been blown across the ocean to venture toward this hard lesson: home was not a privilege conferred on her by others, but an obligation that she would have to perform over and over again, alone.

3

A GREAT HOUSE FULL OF ROOMS

LOS ANGELES
1929–1932

IN MAY 1929, the Viertels' marriage was holding a truce. On the outside they were flourishing. They put all their energy toward the building and maintenance of their small domestic empire in the rented house on Fairfax Avenue. Their sunny mood matched the Los Angeles spring weather, which after a winter of heavy rain had produced carpets of green around the homes of Hollywood and a fanatical abundance of roses.

Berthold was directing his first feature at Fox, a picture called *The One Woman Idea* that turned out to be the studio's last silent film. It was a busy romance set in some notion of Persia, chock-full of minarets and veiled dancing girls and starring the suave screen idol Rod La Rocque. Berthold's direction was inventive and sure-footed. The shoot went so well that Fox picked up his option and doubled his salary.

It was during these florid hopeful months that Salka got Berthold's permission to look for a house near the ocean, as long as they rented it only for the summer. On a balmy afternoon, the air rinsed to clarity after an early rain shower, she drove straight to Santa Monica.

She remembered that there was a real estate office near Inspiration Point, where Ocean Avenue meets Palisades Park. An agent agreed to show her several houses, the first of which was just below, on a sloping street called Mabery Road at the entrance to Santa Monica Canyon. From the end of Mabery the beach was only a short walk away, down some steps and through a little tunnel under the Coast Highway.

The house on Mabery Road, Santa Monica, 1930s.

The breeze at the doorway of the house smelled of honeysuckle and the pink Belle of Portugal roses that hung in an overgrown tangle on the fence. A magnolia tree with huge waxy flowers spread its branches over the arched front door, flanked by two pines. Built in 1926 in the popular "English style," painted white with a pitched green roof and green timber framing, the house was currently in receivership and owned by a local bank. It could be theirs for $900 for the three summer months—about $13,000 in 2019 dollars.

Inside, the rooms were spacious and comfortable, perfect for a busy family. On the ground floor was a large living room with a fireplace and a glass door leading out to the back porch and garden. There was a sizable kitchen with a separate breakfast area, and a dining room. Upstairs were four bedrooms with a view of a faraway slice of the sea. A garage and servants' quarters stood in the back next to the garden, which was planted with hibiscus and a fig and an apricot tree. Salka noticed a single lilac bush struggling to survive in front of a rusting incinerator. The estate agent told her that the lilac had never bloomed. One day, she would see that it did.

Salka took Berthold to see the house and he liked it. In June, after the school term was over, the Viertels moved—just for the summer months—from Fairfax Avenue to Mabery Road.

And you are to love those who are strangers,
for you yourselves were strangers in Egypt.
—DEUTERONOMY 10:17–19

THERE WERE LILAC BUSHES under the front windows of Salka's childhood home, Wychylowka, whose name came from a Polish word that means "leaning out." The estate was situated just outside a town called Sambor. There was an orchard with hundreds of fruit trees, and a thriving kitchen garden.

Just across the road from the house was a wood, which the Steuermann family called the little forest, with the chain of the Carpathians hazy in the distance. In the little forest Salka often hid from her tutor and governess and wandered among the arthritic old trees for hours, dreaming of her magnificent future as a leading lady on the world's stages. A short walk from the house was the Dniester River, on whose banks Salka invented long impromptu melodramas with her younger brother and sister in the supporting roles, and beyond that were the potato and wheat fields.

On their river outings the Steuermann children were sometimes accompanied by their nurse, whom they called Niania, a small Ukrainian woman who wore peasant skirts and an elaborate headdress that was common among the married women of her village. Illiterate but immensely clever, Niania was in charge of running the entire household, including the kitchen. Thus Salka remembered Niania in constant barefoot motion, "moving swiftly like a figure in a puppet show; rushing from the stables to the poultry yard, from the vegetable garden to the meadow, and over the fields." It was to Niania that Salka appealed for consolation during her parents' frequent and sometimes violent quarrels, and it was through Niania that Salka cultivated a love for animals, for outdoor country life, and for garden-inspired recipes. From Niania she also inherited a variety of deep-seated superstitions, including a dread of Friday the thirteenth, that she would spend a lifetime trying to shed.

There was a roadside inn on the outskirts of the little forest. Here the peasants stopped for vodka on their way home from the market. The inn was owned by a tall, white-bearded Orthodox Jew named Lamet. Salka's parents were also Jewish but they had little interest in any kind of religion including their own, and they did not speak Lamet's language. Sometimes Salka would sneak over to peer curiously through the windows of the inn as old Lamet and his tiny bewigged wife and his many children and grandchildren gathered to light the Sabbath candles.

As a girl, Salka's mother, Auguste Amster, had hoped to become an opera singer. After Auguste's father suffered a string of economic misfortunes, she settled instead for marriage to Salka's father, Josef Steuermann, a prosperous lawyer in the garrison town of Sambor, forty miles southwest of Lemberg. (In time, Josef Steuermann would become Sambor's first and only Jewish mayor.) Auguste's people had been Russian Jewish landowners and their large country houses had been filled with guests who stayed for a week or a month or sometimes a year or more. Music wafted through these estates; the family spent many of their leisure hours around the piano. The two kitchens in Salka's great-grandmother's house—one strictly kosher for the observant guests and one run by an imperious French chef—steamed and clanged and sent out meals around the clock.

Auguste Steuermann ran Wychylowka as her mother and grandmother had presided over their households, and much as Salka in Santa Monica would run her own. Wychylowka was, by any standard, an open house. Its rambling rooms were crowded with people throughout Salka's girlhood. There were dances and garden parties in the warmer months and skating and sleigh rides in the winter. Sundays were reserved for salonlike gatherings, often featuring musical performances. As the years passed and Josef Steuermann's law practice began to dwindle, many of the houseguests became paying boarders, though all were treated with the same hospitality. By the time Salka was establishing herself in Hollywood in 1929, her parents had turned Wychylowka into something of a proto-Airbnb in order to pay its substantial bank loans and bills. Auguste wrote to Salka in May 1929: "A woman from Lemberg wants to come with three children and a servant for four to six weeks, she seems to be a nice, modest woman and will not disturb us too much." By December of that year, as the reverberations from the American stock-market crash resounded around the world, the Steuermanns were unable to find boarders for Wychylowka. Auguste asked Salka to send them three hundred dollars to pay the coal bill.

For as long as Salka could remember, Auguste had been a tireless organizer of Sambor's soup kitchens and food drives. In 1914, with the outbreak of World War I, Auguste had worked with other town women to provide a buffet service at the railway station, seeing to it that all soldiers, not just officers, would be fed. Outside the garden fence at Wychylowka was an ammunition dump where Russian prisoners of war were loaded and unloaded onto nearby freight cars. At night these men, starving and suffering from typhoid, would crawl under the fence to receive a bowl of cabbage and potato soup that Niania had cooked for them.

Every beggar in the town came to Wychylowka and none was refused: the Christians on Thursdays and the Jews on Fridays, with the Gypsies coming and going on any day they pleased. Instructed by Auguste, Niania handed out copper coins or food. Those lines of destitute people made a searing impression on the very young Salka. "They were a nightmarish procession of misery," she recalled, "crippled, whining old men and women, young paralytics and drooling imbeciles, some so severely maimed and afflicted that they crawled on all fours like animals. Their knees were padded with dirty rags, many were blind. Most pitiful were the children they dragged along, whom they cursed and beat with sticks."

The idea of home as the center of intense moral, civic, and cultural engagement was Salka's most enduring inheritance from her mother. For both Auguste and Salka, notions of morality existed outside the rituals of the synagogue, yet were no less passionately observed. (In her letters and diaries Salka mentioned often that she believed in God and had spiritual impulses, but she did not specify what kind of God she had in mind.) In 1957, at the age of sixty-eight, Salka wrote in her diary: "I have no ties to any traditional Jewishness—my parents did not have them—and the 'antireligiousness' of my family when I speak of it to strangers is interpreted (I feel it so often) as a denial of Jewishness. As if Jews did not have any other heritage but religion! The Apostate—the Revolutionary—the Prophet—they had to leave the 'Covenant' when they wanted to talk to the world."

Although their rejection of ceremonial Judaism was total, both mother and daughter nevertheless had a gene for hospitality, a blueprint for compassionate behavior that had been handed down through centuries of Jewish life ever since Abraham, as the legend goes, kept all four corners of his tent open to welcome strangers. For the Jews, whose origin story is that of a people cast out of their homeland and forced to wander, the act of opening one's home to the displaced and the hungry has always been the expression of an essential Judaic principle, known in Hebrew as *hachnasat orchim*, the taking in of guests. It's a code motivated at least in part by survival, one that says: I am glad to take you in and offer you comfort, with the hope that one day, should it be necessary, you might do the same for me. Salka was almost certainly unaware of this principle, having been raised to embrace Enlightenment German and not Hebraic culture, to recite Schiller's verses rather than psalms. Yet she and her mother and their female forebears embodied it nonetheless.

Ever since Auguste had been forced to give up her dream of singing professionally in the capitals of Europe, resigning herself to life in a small town on the fringes of the empire, she determined that if she could not step out into the world, she would do what she could to bring the world to Wychylowka. She operated socially in the tradition of such famous eighteenth- and nineteenth-century Jewish salonnières as Rahel Levin and Ada Leverson. These were women who defied their double exclusion from society, as women and as Jews, by collecting influential figures—politicians, artists, writers, composers—within the confines of their own homes, the only arenas in which they exercised any power.

Wychylowka's houseguests may have been somewhat unsophisticated in comparison with Levin's and Leverson's statesmen. But Auguste did the best she could to wield some cultural influence, inviting, among others, a professor from the university in Lemberg and an eccentric but educated Englishwoman whom she had met at a spa in Kissingen. Attended also by a steady parade of cavalry soldiers from the garrison, Auguste's Sunday afternoons featured the Steuermanns clustered around Salka's brother Edward at the piano as the family sang arias and chorales by Mozart, Wagner, and Strauss, and lieder by Schumann and Brahms.

Salka took careful note of her mother's role as Wychylowka's salonnière. As soon as she had established herself in Santa Monica, Salka began to translate Auguste's instincts for friendship and hospitality into a foreign vocabulary. And as a global cataclysm gathered its forces, Salka turned her own Sunday afternoons at home into a place of welcome on a much larger, higher-stakes scale.

FOR THE MOMENT, Berthold and Salka's chief concerns were more immediate and more pecuniary. When the summer of 1929 ended, they extended the lease on the Mabery Road house for another year and renewed their government-issued visitors' permits, too ambivalent at that moment to take the next step to apply for immigration visas. Their family and friends were pressuring them to come back, and in those early Hollywood days, Salka confessed, she "was counting the days till [her] return to Europe." But Berthold was still doing well at Fox and the Viertel sons were thriving, spending much of their free time at the beach and becoming strong swimmers. In no time they had changed from pasty little *Jungen* in short pants and overcoats to bronzed California boys who answered their parents' German questions in vernacular English and raced off through the little highway tunnel to go bodysurfing in the ocean.

Salka did what she could to add some style to the house, covering its hideous black-velvet furniture with slipcovers, renting a piano, and finding shelves for all their books that had been sent from Berlin.

When the stock market crashed at the end of October 1929, Hollywood was slow to feel the shock. But the Viertels themselves were immediately affected. Berthold had invested their savings in Fox Theater Corporation shares, whose value had been climbing vertiginously until the crash. Now they were wiped out. Although he and Salka had managed to pay off the debts from their theater company and they still had a bit of savings for a return trip to Germany, they delayed any plans for leaving. The Viertels were accustomed to setbacks. They renegotiated their rent for the house to a lower figure of $150 per month and resolutely began again.

Berthold's next directing job for Fox was an "all-talker" called *Seven Faces*, a showcase for the Yiddish theater actor Paul Muni, whose real name was Muni Weisenfreund and who had been born in Lemberg, not far from Salka's hometown. In *Seven Faces*, Muni played the caretaker in a wax museum whose figures come to life during a dream sequence. The film carries cinematic echoes back to 1924, to the silent German Expressionist horror picture *Das Wachsfigurenkabinett*, and looks forward toward our era, to the *Night at the Museum* franchise of 2006 and onward. In addition to playing the caretaker, Muni also played most of the waxwork figures, which included Franz Schubert, Don Juan, and Napoleon. For the small part of the waxwork Catherine the Great, the production supervisor recommended Salka, who'd been continuingly unhappy about the interruption of her acting career. Jumping at the chance, Salka worked hard to learn her lines in English, while her accent managed to sound Slavic enough to seem authentic.

For an actress who until quite recently had been accustomed to striding across stage after stage in leading roles, the experience was a shock. “My face, my neck, my whole upper body had to be modeled in wax,” Salka recalled. “A company specializing in death masks did the work, during which I was allowed to breathe only through a thin straw, plastered over with plaster. I felt as if I were a model for my own tomb.”

Salka’s participation in the shoot lasted for only four days. The rest of her scenes were filmed using only her wax figure. It made for a funny story—she relished that, and didn’t mind laughing at herself—but only in the way that extreme humiliation is funny. To be encased in her own stiff shroud, unable to move and barely to breathe, and then to be erased from the proceedings with only the waxen shell of her outline in use: this was what a forty-year-old actress at the time could expect from a casting opportunity. Salka’s name was obscured as well: in reviews for the film she was listed in the credits variously as “Salka Stenermann” and “Salka Stensrmann.” Of the experience, she wrote with characteristic wryness that “acting in fragments is like drinking from an eyedropper when you are parched.”

Salka would appear as an actress in three more pictures between 1929 and 1931, all of them German-language versions of American films, shot quickly on the same sets as the American versions, sometimes at night while the English-language productions were shooting during the day. (Before the innovations of dubbing and subtitles in the mid-1930s, this was how Hollywood studios exported talking films to their still very lucrative foreign markets.) Two of the pictures were Warner Bros. productions: *Die heilige Flamme*, or *The Sacred Flame*, based on a Somerset Maugham play, for which Salka was paid the handsome sum of five hundred dollars per week; and *Die*

Maske fällt, or *The Way of All Men*, directed by William Dieterle, a good friend of the Viertels' from Germany.

The best-known of Salka's three pictures, released in December of 1930, was a German-language remake of MGM's *Anna Christie*, marketed as the first film in which "Garbo Talks!" It was Greta Garbo's personal favorite of all her pictures. Salka played Marthy Owens, the waterfront prostitute who'd been portrayed to great effect in the film's English-speaking version by the great American actress Marie Dressler. Salka was nowhere near as enamored of the film as Garbo was. She hated her makeup and her costumes and felt uncomfortable when her scenes began shooting. But she used some of her time on set to help the director, her friend Jacques Feyder, with the German dialogue. "I got excellent reviews and fan mail from Germany," Salka wrote about her role in *Anna Christie* in the German edition of her memoirs, "but nothing could change my conviction that [as an actress] I belonged to the stage and not the movies."

Salka never acted again after these small roles, in films or on the stage. It was an acute sort of exile for her, a death of self that she mourned for the rest of her life. "It made me miserable that I, who had started to act at the age of seventeen, had to be idle in my best years," she wrote. Yet her flair for drama lived on, unofficially, during her crowded Sunday parties on Mabery Road. The novelist Christopher Isherwood later offered a description of Salka during those afternoons:

> She greeted newcomers warmly and got them involved in conversation with earlier arrivals, then she disappeared into the kitchen to see how things were going. I remember her most vividly at this

moment of greeting: she was strikingly aristocratic and unaffected. Her posture, the line of her spine and neck, was still beautiful; you could believe that she had been a great actress.

When she first arrived in Hollywood, Salka had written to Berthold during one of their worst quarrels that "the only kind of home that I had was the stage." Because she recognized, as feminist scholars have noted, "that home and estrangement were not geographically determined," she was especially well suited to create an alternative home for others. Now and for the rest of her life, although Salka never stopped wishing it were otherwise, the most effective stage she would have would be her home.

ONE CHILLY EVENING, Ernst Lubitsch and his wife gave a party at their six-columned Southern Colonial Revival estate on Beverly Drive. (Some film scholars believe it took place in the spring or around Christmas of 1929, while others claim it was in 1930 or 1931.) It was a formal gathering of about forty people. The servants balanced trays of bootleg booze as they sidestepped around the incoming guests. In the well-appointed living room the men huddled to talk about work, dressed in black tie, their voices booming. Their host was at the center, stocky and dapper, his dark hair meticulously parted, an eternal cigar between his teeth, his demeanor both amused and discerning.

In the opposite corner the ladies were clustered, laughing delicately, showing off their evening gowns. A lone man had joined their circle: Jacques Feyder, the Belgian director. He gestured a welcome to a woman friend of his, smartly dressed in a tailored cocktail dress, who'd arrived to join the group. It was Salka Viertel, Lubitsch's colleague from their years as actors in Reinhardt's theaters, whom Feyder had met at the Mendelssohn villa in Berlin.

Salka and her husband Berthold had decided to attend the party out of nostalgia. The occasion, Salka noted later in her memoir, was to honor a visiting German movie star whose husband, a producer, was someone Berthold had known in Berlin. Feyder ushered Salka over to a sofa on which the movie star was holding court. She was engulfed in a dress with voluminously flouncy skirts. The dress took up most of the sofa except for another woman, who sat squashed into the only remaining space. The squashed woman wore a severe black suit instead of an evening gown. Salka had never met her before, but recognized immediately that she was Greta Garbo.

As there was no room for her on the couch, Salka suggested that Garbo join her outside on the veranda. When they got there they saw that the night was cold enough for the few outside guests to see their own breath. Feyder rejoined the two women with a bottle of champagne and the talk grew animated. Salka spoke about *The Saga of Gösta Berling*, the only one of Garbo's films that she had seen, and about her own work in the theater. Salka found Garbo intelligent, totally unaffected, and droll, joking about her poor German and her English, both of which were actually quite good. Eventually Berthold joined them and the four of them kept talking until late in the evening.

Salka wrote later that there was always something startling about the loveliness of Garbo's face, as if, on every viewing, one was seeing it for the first time. Garbo was then in her middle twenties and approaching the height of her fame. She was fixated on her need for privacy and rightly so: fans and reporters hounded her relentlessly.

On Mabery Road the next day, the Viertel family was just finishing lunch when the doorbell rang. When Salka went to the front door she saw the famous face again, peering through the open window of the entrance. She noted that Garbo looked even more beautiful in the sunny light of noontime. She was makeup-free except for mascara on her naturally long eyelashes. She looked a bit sunburned and was wearing a well-cut shirtwaist and slacks.

The actress was in a merry mood. She was living nearby at the moment, she said, and was hoping to continue their conversation from the previous night. In fact Garbo stayed all afternoon. She chatted with the three Viertel boys and patted their waggy-tailed dog, Buddy. She and Salka strolled on the beach in the golden air, up past the Santa Monica pier with its merry-go-round. Later they sat talking in Salka's bedroom as the light grew deeper and more shadowy. In the evening Berthold and Salka walked with Garbo back to her rooms at the Hotel Miramar, where they said warm goodbyes and made their way back home. Berthold said to Salka that he found Garbo absolutely charming, polite, and attentive. He noted her oversensitivity but also her resilience. Salka answered that Garbo's fame must prevent her from living an authentic life. Berthold agreed, saying it was a high price to pay.

In her memoir, Salka devoted less than a page and a half to her first encounters with Garbo, reporting them without fanfare and concluding rather vaguely: "She came very often early in the morning when the beach was deserted, and we took long walks together." But that first meeting in Ernst Lubitsch's living room was an electrifying moment for both women. It sparked the longest and most important relationship either of them would ever have in Hollywood. Instinctively they must have known that each had what the other needed. As a major film star at the peak of her earning potential, Garbo had power, while Salka had stability, patience, ironclad loyalty, and a gift for advocacy. Along with advice and total discretion, Salka offered Garbo a refuge on Mabery Road, where the actress could be herself, relaxed and without airs. Garbo moved into eleven different houses during her years in California, but each of these was a fortress, not a place of comfort. They could never be home, as Mabery Road came to represent for her. And Garbo offered Salka as much if not more in return. Salka wrote to a friend in the mid-1960s that Garbo "is a kind of deus ex machina responsible for the strange turn my life took, and kept me in America."

Salka's loyalty to Garbo was possibly the reason for her declining to mention in her memoir the name of the German film star whom Lubitsch was honoring at his party the night she and Garbo met. Cinema devotees have guessed for years that this was Marlene Dietrich, who was being welcomed by Hollywood's film community from the time of her arrival there on March 31, 1930. (The American premiere of Dietrich's *The Blue Angel* took place in December of that year.) If it's true that Lubitsch gave the party in honor of Dietrich, Salka would have had good reasons for neglecting to mention Dietrich in this portion of her memoir. (She does mention a "Mary Dietrich" once in an earlier section, when she tells of acting with her in Max Reinhardt's 1911 Berlin production of Heinrich Kleist's *Penthesilea*, in which the two young women played Amazons and showed off their legs. But this actress was not Marlene Dietrich, who would have been too young to perform with Salka at that time.) Salka was first and always loyal to Garbo, who was locked into a decades-long, studio-fostered rivalry with Dietrich. Thus Salka would have felt compelled to erase Dietrich's name from the scene in her memoir when she first meets Garbo by simply calling her, as she does, "a visiting German film star." In any case, Salka and Dietrich knew each other well, and Dietrich frequently showed up at Salka's Sunday afternoons in Santa Monica. The two women shared a passionate dedication to antifascism and a mutual if wary respect. Salka's son Peter later observed that "my mother thought [Dietrich] something of a *poseuse*, playing Mother Earth off the screen."

BERTHOLD HAD TOLD SALKA admiringly that she was the "driver" of their family life. As she searched for ways to channel the energy she had reserved for acting into other kinds of work, she discovered that she was just as good at helping to drive the professional affairs of her friends. As Salka's footing in America grew surer, she improvised a volunteer job for herself as a social ambassador between the newcomers who were flocking to Hollywood and the Americans and Europeans who were already established there. Much of this took place at her increasingly popular parties on Mabery Road. There Salka welcomed the playwrights, novelists, and journalists who'd been summoned from New York to the West Coast, having found themselves suddenly in demand as dialogue writers when the silents gave way to talking pictures. She made introductions on their behalf to director friends like William Dieterle and to actors like Charles Boyer. She also made a place at the table for Berthold's new assistant, a twenty-three-year-old aspiring filmmaker from Vienna named Fred Zinnemann, who had arrived in the States on the day of the stock-market crash in October 1929.

Salka performed her role as a connector of people with genuine warmth and panache. In making introductions she was witty when she spoke and careful when she listened. On Sunday afternoons at her house, alliances formed and circles expanded around her as she commanded the room—something she had not had an opportunity to do since her last days on theater stages.

Her pro bono human resources work extended well beyond the Sunday parties. In 1930 and 1931, she became a de facto manager for two of early cinema's most notable figures: F. W. Murnau, the Expressionist master who had been responsible for bringing Berthold to Hollywood; and the visiting Soviet director Sergei Eisenstein. Both were men of enormous artistic sensitivity who found themselves at odds with a studio system that had gone to great expense to lure them to Hollywood and then did not know how to work with them.

By mid-1930, Murnau's directing contract with Fox was reaching an unhappy end, while Eisenstein—whose landmark *Potemkin* was the only silent picture that Salka considered a masterpiece—had accepted a six-month contract with Paramount. Each man, for different reasons, confided his immense frustrations to the Viertels. Murnau's last Fox picture, the Oregon wheat-field epic which Berthold wrote, had been retitled *City Girl* and butchered by the studio, which had added extra footage and a clumsy dialogue track to stay current with the transition into talkies. Eisenstein's scenarios for Paramount—one about the 1849 California gold rush and another about a house made entirely of glass—were both moldering away in Paramount's files, never to be made. Nor did anything come of Eisenstein's final attempt at a film for Paramount, an adaptation of Theodore Dreiser's novel *An American Tragedy*.

In separate ventures, Murnau and Eisenstein each decided to make an independent picture far away from the confines of the Hollywood studios. Salka and Berthold offered their support as Murnau scraped financing together and headed to the South Seas to film a feature called *Tabu* with the well-known documentarian Robert Flaherty. The Viertels were equally sympathetic when Eisenstein set off to make a historical travelogue—"a colorful film symphony," as Eisenstein described it—in Mexico. Eisenstein financed his long-hoped-for venture with the help of the muckraking socialist writer Upton Sinclair, whose novel *Boston* Salka had admired, along with some well-heeled Pasadena women who were sympathetic to Sinclair's politics.

By acting as an adviser and advocate for both Murnau and Eisenstein throughout their voyages, Salka served a kind of apprenticeship that would prove critical for the work she would do for hundreds of artists in the years that followed. She saw Murnau off from the harbor at San Pedro with a gift of two pounds of Malossol caviar, an act that moved the stoic Prussian to tears. And then, via letters and telegrams, she proceeded to offer advice during every phase of the South Seas film shoot.

Hans, Peter, Berthold, Thomas, and Salka Viertel on F. W. Murnau's yacht, 1928.

Things went badly for Murnau in Tahiti. His collaboration with Flaherty fell apart and the production ran out of money. Yet Murnau still managed to return with completed footage for *Tabu*. The symphonic music for the score would cost another $50,000. Never able to refrain from helping a project they believed in, Salka and Berthold loaned the director all their newly restored savings to help pay an advance to the film's composer.

At last Murnau managed to complete *Tabu*, which he successfully sold to Paramount. But fate intervened again, this time shockingly. Only a week before the film's New York premiere, on March 11, 1931, Murnau died from injuries he sustained in an automobile crash near Santa Barbara. Hours before the crash, he had stopped at Salka's house to pick up sandwiches for his motoring trip up the coast. He was forty-two years old.

It fell to Salka to inform Murnau's mother in Germany of his death. Salka and Berthold were among only eleven people, including Garbo, who gathered at a Los Angeles funeral home for a last farewell before Murnau's body was shipped back to his homeland. Hints of a scandal had most likely kept away other studio folk, who feared their careers might suffer if they were spotted at the memorial. Gossip was spreading that before the crash Murnau had been "servicing" his teenaged male Filipino chauffeur while the boy was driving. The boy allegedly lost control of the car, which then rolled down an embankment.

Thus without fanfare but with plenty of whispered disparagement, Hollywood lost an international giant of the silent cinema. Bestriding the backlots of the Fox Film Corporation, Murnau had enriched the technologically advanced but idea-poor American film industry of his era with an indelible stylistic legacy. Among those who watched and learned from Murnau at Fox were the American directors John Ford and Frank Borzage, whose own films became infused with Murnau's pioneering brand of cinematic poetry. Murnau's first American picture, *Sunrise*, is endlessly and justly cited as a major cinematic landmark. Its enormous sets were used again and again by Ford and other filmmakers, while Murnau's pictorial language pulses throughout American film history, engraved on the work of Alfred Hitchcock and Werner Herzog and continuing more recently in the work of Terrence Malick and Barry Jenkins.

From Tahiti, Murnau had written to his mother: "I am never at home anywhere—I feel this more and more the older I get—not in any country or in any house or with anybody." If Murnau could be said to have found any kind of rapport in Hollywood it would have been among his longtime friends Salka and Berthold Viertel, who understood his genius, with its distinctively European sources, and who did what they could to help him translate it so that baffled studio chiefs might be able to understand. Instinctively, Salka went out of her way to provide literal sustenance for Murnau (that caviar, those road-trip sandwiches) while pragmatically she was flexing her capacity to protect a specialized group of artists, among whom she counted Berthold and herself. Artists who act outside conventional expectations and are often, as Murnau said, never truly at home in any country.

With Sergei Eisenstein and *Que Viva Mexico!*, Salka was an even more hands-on advocate than she had been with Murnau. Eisenstein asked Salka to be a witness when the financing agreement for his Mexico film was signed with the writer Upton Sinclair, Sinclair's wealthy wife, and their group of Pasadena investors on November 24, 1930. Salka had plenty of misgivings. Few of the Pasadena women knew who Eisenstein was, and Salka said she was certain that "they would have been horrified had they ever seen one of his films."

In December 1930, Salka drove Eisenstein and two of his filmmaking colleagues to Union Station as they departed for Mexico. Sinclair and his wife, along with a few reporters, were on hand to witness the director's disappointed farewell to Hollywood, whose culture Eisenstein had declared so garish that it was as if "decadence and blight wrote a last chapter to history." Once he reached Mexico, Eisenstein's film shoot tried to move forward despite delays from bad weather and illness. But the Pasadena group's original investment of $25,000 quickly evaporated. Eisenstein asked Salka to persuade his sponsors to add more financing, which she did. He also appointed Salka to be his representative in Hollywood to view the rushes, which had to be sent to Los Angeles because there were no facilities in Mexico for developing the film. It became Salka's job to explain each of Eisenstein's camera angles to the Pasadena women, in an attempt to justify what they saw as his needless extravagance.

In January 1932, Eisenstein wrote to Salka in a desperate mood. He had four-fifths of a completed film, with footage that Salka noted was some of the most extraordinary ever to be caught on camera. "The Christian-pagan rites and processions, the peons and Indians, the desert and the forests were breathtakingly beautiful," Salka wrote. (Much of it, "still shown and admired in film museums all over the world," Salka noted in the 1960s, is available on YouTube.) But Sinclair and his investors had run out of patience. They accused Eisenstein of continuing idleness and waste, and insisted on halting the financing altogether. Eisenstein begged Salka to intervene with Sinclair and his wife, who controlled the purse strings. "Use your Medea flame," Eisenstein urged Salka in an exchange of letters, "and convince him (but especially *her*) to let us finish our film."

Salka was not successful this time. She did manage to make a persuasive case to David O. Selznick, at that time the young and promising production head of RKO. Through the

Hollywood connections she was cultivating, Salka had already gained enough of a reputation to be taken seriously by a studio chief. After she vouched for the picture, Selznick told her he was interested in seeing the footage. But once again Sinclair and his wife were implacable. According to the contract, the uncompleted film belonged to the Pasadena group, they insisted, and could not be sold to or financed by anyone else. As a grieving Eisenstein wrote to Salka, it was fated to remain a "mutilated stump with the heart ripped out."

Eisenstein never recovered from the public failure and humiliation he suffered during his Mexican venture, or more generally from his experience in Hollywood, whose executives treated him at best with bemusement and at worst with indifference. His point of view was, to say the least, utterly foreign to them. As his friend Léon Moussinac remarked, Eisenstein was "a man of universal genius for whom the costume of the time was too small." Yet he was also firmly fixed in his time and place. Many of this polymath director's cinematic ideas, including his groundbreaking theory of montage, were born in the context of his participation in the Soviet revolution and as a citizen of the burgeoning USSR. Eisenstein disapproved of professional actors, preferring to use regular citizens in his pictures. He spurned the very notion of a film industry driven by profits.

During his months at Paramount, Eisenstein became the victim of a malicious anti-Semitic and anti-Communist smear campaign, mounted by a right-wing agitator named Major Frank Pease. In a twenty-four-page pamphlet titled *Eisenstein: Messenger of Hell*, Pease ranted that the director was part of a "Jewish-Bolshevik conspiracy to turn the American cinema into a Communist cesspool." (Eisenstein's father's family were "Christianized Jews" from Germany and Latvia; his mother was not Jewish.) The harassment was similar to the vigorous round of hate speech that greeted Charlie Chaplin during his visit to Berlin around the same time, when the National Socialists denounced Chaplin as a "Jewish Communist millionaire" and a "Jewish film clown." (Chaplin was not Jewish.) As the hounding of Eisenstein escalated, Paramount executives Jesse Lasky and B. P. Schulberg—who were Jewish themselves, and reluctant to call any more attention to the fact—decided the Russian director was more trouble than he was worth. They terminated his contract.

Eisenstein was forced to return to the USSR. Upon his farewell he gave Salka some photographs of himself with her on the beach in Santa Monica. He would later say that these were the only films he had managed to make in America. Though he continued to make pictures, Hollywood had diminished him. Back in Moscow, his idiosyncratic views of art and film clashed with the increasingly totalitarian strictures of Stalin's regime, and his health failed early. He was found dead of a heart attack on the floor of his flat, alone, in February 1948 at age fifty.

Sergei Eisenstein and Salka Viertel on the beach in Santa Monica, early 1930s.

"I am very sad because I am not going to see you anymore and I have the feeling that all I have to ask you this time is to send me a family photo of all of you," Eisenstein had written to Salka in another letter shortly after he had left Hollywood. "You have helped me in the most difficult years of my life and this shall never be forgotten." Hailing Salka's theatrical talents as she attempted to intercede for him ("use your Medea flame"), he also appreciated her flair for creating and sustaining a home and a growing community of friends, and was comforted by her welcome.

With compassion and esprit, Salka made Eisenstein's and Murnau's lives a little better in difficult circumstances. These men were cruelly derided for being homosexual, Jewish, and Communist in an America where such hatreds were routine. The hatred would crescendo to near-hysterical panic in decades to come. Being labeled as any of those was equivalent to being called a criminal and could easily cost a job or an entire reputation. To Salka's constitutionally open mind, this was ridiculous. For her there were no outsiders. Or, just as true, everyone in Hollywood was an outsider. The very industry was created in America by its "others"—that is, by Jews and immigrants. To simplify a human being for the purpose of malice and exclusion was to insult every belief Salka upheld. Defying the nativist vitriol heaped on her artist friends in Los Angeles, she did everything she could to support them.

Across the Atlantic, at just that time, a disaffected Austrian demagogue-to-be was exploiting the social and economic emergency in Germany to build a political platform that gathered strength through the demonization of Jews, Communists, and homosexuals. On November 18, 1930, Salka's sister Rose wrote from Dresden to report that "I can feel Hitler's influence already everywhere." The American press had been carefully tracking Adolf Hitler's political activities since the early 1920s. By 1930, the *New York Times* was still dismissing him as a buffoon. Yet National Socialism was already making substantial gains. In March 1929 the Nazi candidates in the parliamentary elections won barely 1 percent of the vote, yet by July 1930 they captured 18.3 percent, and doubled it two years later.

The ways in which people chose to treat those who were different among them would soon turn out to define the boundary between civilization and barbarism. The gestures of acceptance that Salka extended to Murnau and Eisenstein, in a time of institutional bigotry on both sides of the Atlantic that is not difficult to imagine today, was anything but minor. It was quietly but transgressively courageous.

BY 1931, Berthold Viertel was feeling as frustrated as Murnau had been at Fox. He lost faith that his studio colleagues would ever appreciate his ideas or see him as anything other than a baffling eccentric. "I became aware that we were constantly explaining ourselves to our American friends," Salka wrote of this time, "trying to convey our identity and what really possessed us, who we were." Berthold was reduced to hiding in the men's room at the studio to read Kierkegaard and Kant, despairing of making his ambitions understood in the "primitive vocabulary" of his superiors. When his contract expired, Berthold signed immediately with Paramount, where he was relieved to witness the evident intelligence of his new boss, head of production B. P. Schulberg. Over the years the

Schulberg family would become entwined with Salka's in ways both beneficial and fraught. For now, Salka enjoyed meeting Schulberg's energetic and progressive wife, Ad, and their gifted teenaged children, Budd and Sonya.

Berthold directed four pictures for Schulberg at Paramount, several of which sent him to New York for filming from August 1931 until February 1932. While he was away, his family did its best to keep him current. His youngest son Tommy, now five years old, wrote to him in stalwart block letters: "WE HAVE A NEW DOG NAMED DUKE. HE IS AN ENGLISH 'UPSETTER,' BECAUSE HE KILLED THE NEIGHBOR'S RABBITS."

Tommy, Hans, and Peter continued to spend all their free time at the beach or roaming among the neighborhood creeksides with the local Mexican children, whose families had once owned all the land in the canyon. The Viertel boys were besotted with the liberty of their American lives, in which every day brought a chance to swim and ride their bikes and go fishing in mud ponds, and to stage Western scenes from their favorite Karl May and Fenimore Cooper tales. Their romantic boyhood inventions echoed Salka's long-ago theatrics on the banks of the Dniester River with her siblings.

While Berthold was in New York, the Mabery Road establishment grew more and more thoroughly into Salka's house. She cleaned and organized, scheduled and shopped. In the garden she planted begonias, deadheaded roses, watered the fruit trees and the lilac, which had started to bloom. She sprinkled lavender in the linen closet and pine oil in the bath. She cooked goulash and stuffed cabbage, and an earthy Galician version of vichyssoise. ("You want a prevailing leek and potato taste," she said years later as she prepared it for her step-granddaughter.)

She baked *Kugelhopf* and a flourless chocolate cake so addictive that it became an obsession for nearly everyone who tasted it. Along with Salka's cooking, every bit of house business on Mabery Road—the supervision of homework and tutoring for the boys, the preparations for the Sunday parties—was stamped with her *Lebenskunst*, her art of living. Her domestic style hybridized an adherence to European decorum with casual Californian improvisation. She required her children to bow when greeting visitors, yet gave her dogs the run of the house, granting them the same privileges as family members.

A further improvisation unfurled while Berthold was away in New York. The Viertels had become friendly with a neighboring family on Mabery Road: the successful screenwriter Oliver H. P. Garrett, his wife Louise (both in their early thirties), and their son Peter. In Berthold's absence, Salka and Oliver began an affair that lasted two years. It was an open liaison, most of the time endured if not endorsed by both Louise Garrett and Berthold. The families continued to mingle socially, with Oliver and Louise joining in at Salka's Sunday afternoons. Oliver played football and baseball with the Viertel boys, who adored him, and took them to see the professional teams play. During the Halloween evenings of those years, Salka stood at her front door passing out candy while her sons went trick-or-treating with young Peter Garrett and the Mexican boys from the neighborhood. Christmas Day gift exchanges always included the Garretts as well.

In her account of her relationship with Oliver, Salka stated that she was always the less invested of the pair, insisting that "My life with Berthold was always predominant." She made it clear that she would not leave her marriage, especially at the end of the affair, when Oliver's marriage fell apart and Louise asked for a divorce. Nonetheless Oliver was a consequential figure in Salka's life. Full of brio and an impressive Yankee sophistication, he motored around the canyon in a late-model convertible, his baldness obscured by a jaunty beret. Oliver came from a distinguished Massachusetts family and had enlisted in the Great War in 1917, after which he worked as a newspaper reporter in New York and then signed a lucrative long-term contract to write for Paramount in Hollywood. All the important New York journalists who'd been lured to the Coast to write for the pictures—among them Ben Hecht and Dudley Nichols—gathered on Oliver's Mabery Road front porch to drink and swap war stories.

Salka recognized that her foreignness was what attracted Oliver to her. He saw her, she wrote, as "part of that ancient, baffling continent of which he had caught a distorted glimpse during the war, and for which, like so many young Americans, he had brought home an unappeased longing." If for Oliver she represented Old World sensuality and savoir-faire, for Salka he provided a valuable entrée to the complexities of America and Hollywood. He educated her in his left-leaning belief in democracy and his knowledge born of experience as a screenwriter in the trenches of the picture business. It was through Oliver's introduction that Salka got the chance to appeal to David Selznick on Sergei Eisenstein's behalf. And as a founding member of the Screen Writers Guild, Oliver did much to influence Salka's interest in Hollywood's early labor negotiations.

More personally, she appreciated Oliver's chivalrous conduct toward her, noting that other "devoted husbands" felt free to make unwanted passes at her. Clearly there was much Oliver and Salka were able to do for each other beyond the boundaries of sex—although control over her sex life was always, for Salka, an indispensable prerogative. She insisted on her right to sleep with Oliver regardless of the tensions it caused in the daily lives of both families. Through this sexual relationship Salka was expressing a variety of feelings not only toward Oliver but to Berthold as well. Husband and wife spoke volumes to each other through their infidelities, which were demonstrations of fear and hurt and anger as much as they were love affairs. "I don't feel guilty about . . . Oliver," Salka mused nearly thirty years later in her diary.

> I felt sorry, heartbroken about hurting Berthold. But also I was terribly impatient and angered with myself and with him, because I was convinced that a lot of his suffering was due to hurt vanity. I remember the words he said to me when I was jealous and miserable, when he was in love with [X] or [Y]. He said that he expects me to be generous and maternal in my emotions. I did not expect him to be paternal towards me but when I was asserting my rights to love and to live I was not his wife anymore. I was his sister and friend . . . I could not combine the two things: lover and mother. Never. As a lover I was not a "mother." To nobody. I *loved*. Basta. I never diluted passion—with motherliness—My tenderness was sexual—

AS HER ACTING PROSPECTS SPUTTERED, Salka's professional idleness continued to nag at her. "Why don't you write?" asked a sympathetic Garbo, and Berthold agreed, saying, "You would bear Hollywood much better if you worked." Salka was not new to writing, after all: she had written and sold that film treatment to Gabriel Pascal in 1925, back in Berlin. Garbo's suggestion began to percolate. In July and August of 1930, while waiting for her takes during the filming of the German version of *Anna Christie*, Salka had read a recently published biography of Queen Christina of Sweden. She began to think about adapting it as a picture for Garbo.

Salka's interest in the subject was auspicious. Garbo was negotiating a new contract with Metro that would pay the actress a staggering salary of $250,000 per picture for a two-picture deal. Even better, it offered her the unprecedented power to choose her own director and costars. She would have plenty of influence over the choice of film properties as well. Garbo was tired of being cast as vamps and prostitutes and eager for the chance to portray her homeland's idiosyncratic seventeenth-century queen, whose "masculine education and complicated sexuality made her an almost contemporary character," as Salka put it. Garbo made it clear that her next picture for Metro would be about the life, rule, and eventual abdication of Queen Christina of Sweden. Though other writers, including Garbo's friend Mercedes de Acosta, were keen to develop the project, Garbo designated Salka as its screenwriter.

Salka began to construct a film treatment, in German, of the early part of Queen Christina's life. Berthold felt her work was promising and urged Salka to have it translated into English so she could present it to Metro. Ad Schulberg recommended a friend, Margaret "Peg" Le Vino, who spoke German and could help with the translation. Peg had no prior film experience, though her husband, Albert Shelby Le Vino, was a

Paramount screenwriter. Peg was likable and smart: she and Ad Schulberg had recently founded the Progressive School in Hollywood, modeled on pedagogical ideas of the English philosopher Bertrand Russell. At first Peg dismissed the *Christina* project, declaring that historical films had no chance in Hollywood. But as soon as Ad mentioned that the treatment was a vehicle for Garbo, Peg became mightily interested, and Salka had herself a collaborator.

In February 1932, just as Berthold was returning from his film shoot in New York, Salka received news that her father had died suddenly at home in Wychylowka. She had hoped to be able to visit her parents during the upcoming summer, with Berthold's promise that he would stay with the children. Now it was too late. She would never see her proud, honorable Papa again. In her grief she took note of the obituaries in the Polish press, which applauded Josef Steuermann as a lawyer and a patriot, and later commented that it was the last time in Piłsudski's Poland that Jews and Gentiles would mourn together. (In 1918, after World War I dissolved the Austro-Hungarian Empire, Salka's homeland of Galicia had become part of Poland.)

The death of Josef Steuermann caused Salka to feel deeply unmoored. Nothing seemed secure, particularly her economic future. Berthold's Paramount contract had not been renewed and his prospects for studio work were vague. The previous year Salka had begged Berthold to give up the film business, to pursue his own poetry and fiction writing. Even with the physical distance between husband and wife and despite her affair with Oliver, Berthold was still the fulcrum of Salka's life. He and their boys were the only truths that remained unwavering in a bewildering world. She was willing to go back with him to Berlin if he insisted. She even began to imagine that her treatment for Garbo's *Christina* might be sold and filmed on the Continent. But she was reluctant to uproot her happy Californian sons and she was worried about Europe's instability. At this point in 1931, she wrote, "the world was just as insecure as in 1919." "The Nazis . . . [were] gaining power in Germany, and anti-Semitism and racism were spreading." She did her best to retain her newly hatched American optimism:

> The Depression was at its worst. Hitler's hideous, demented voice carried across the Atlantic, but I believed in the future. Often on the road I gave a ride to hitchhikers from the East Coast or the Middle West, who had come to California because it was less cold and hungry than back home. Our housekeeper, Jessie, kept a big pot of soup on the stove for them, when they came to the door. It reminded me of Niania feeding the Russian prisoners of war. But I . . . was sure that the misery would not last.

In March 1932, as if to underscore Salka's ambivalence about returning to Europe, the family's visitor visas expired. To remain in America, the Viertels would need to apply for admission into an immigration quota. According to a law passed in 1924, the U.S. Immigration and Nationality Act restricted the total number of immigrants who were legally permitted to enter the United States to a fixed 153,774 people per year. Of those, more than 50 percent were to be from Great Britain and Ireland. In September 1930, as the Great Depression took hold, alarming unemployment levels led to further immigration restrictions. The Hoover administration denied entry to those who were "likely to become a public charge"—that is, people who would be unable to support themselves without assistance. To comply with the "LPC clause," immigrants were required to provide elaborate documentation about their identity, financial resources, and health histories. This paperwork, which included an affidavit from local police confirming their good character and many copies of their birth certificates, often proved so daunting that many were too discouraged to apply.

After their visitor visas became invalid, the Viertels spent hundreds of dollars for legal help in assembling their documentation so they could take the steps that would allow them to remain in America. Because of their varying birthplaces, the process was more difficult: Berthold and Tommy were applying for an Austrian quota number, Hans and Peter for a German, and Salka for a Polish. The law then required the Viertels to leave the country and wait to receive their quota numbers while outside the territorial boundaries of the United States. They did not know how long this would take, but they hoped to be gone for only a couple of days. If their numbers were approved, they could then reenter as legal immigrants who had declared an intention to become permanent citizens.

And so, in March 1932, the Viertels loaded up their boat-like secondhand Cadillac and steered south across the border, headed for the Mexican seaport town of Ensenada. Once they left the States, the changed landscape reminded them of Europe in different ways. The narrow, rutted roads and the colorfully dressed peasants in the fields reminded Salka happily of Poland. For her thirteen-year-old son Peter, the border officials in Tijuana brought back fearful memories of the trips he had taken across Europe when he was small, when strident soldiers at "arbitrary frontiers" questioned them in languages he could not understand. The crowds of begging children reminded him of the joyless streets of Berlin.

When they reached Ensenada, the Viertels booked in at a fancy hotel with a casino, echoingly vacant now because of the Depression, while waiting for their quota numbers to arrive. There they spent a strange, fretful week, their mood at odds with the holiday atmosphere of the sun-drunk city by the sea. "We were the only guests in the hotel," wrote Salka. "Before our windows a long sickle of soft, silvery sand hugged the bluest, most serene ocean." But after three days the gloom of the ghost hotel, its ballrooms silent and its baccarat tables covered in sheets, brought on a sense of mordant claustrophobia. "I heard my mother ask what my father would do if the government refused to grant us our entry permits," Peter wrote later, in a fictionalized account of the episode in his novel *Bicycle on the Beach*. "I was only thirteen and a half years old, and yet I felt frightened at the thought of losing America forever."

After six days, their quota numbers arrived and the Viertels were allowed to cross the border again and to resume their American lives. Their signed declarations of intent from the Department of Labor read, in part: "it is my intention in good faith to become a citizen of the United States of America and to reside permanently therein"; they had up to seven years in which to petition for naturalization. As soon as they were back on Mabery Road, Peter wrote: "I went immediately down to the beach, and when I found the cool water of the sea again, with the gentle surf breaking on the shore, I felt as if I had escaped some awful fate, and that I was safe again in the land of the free."

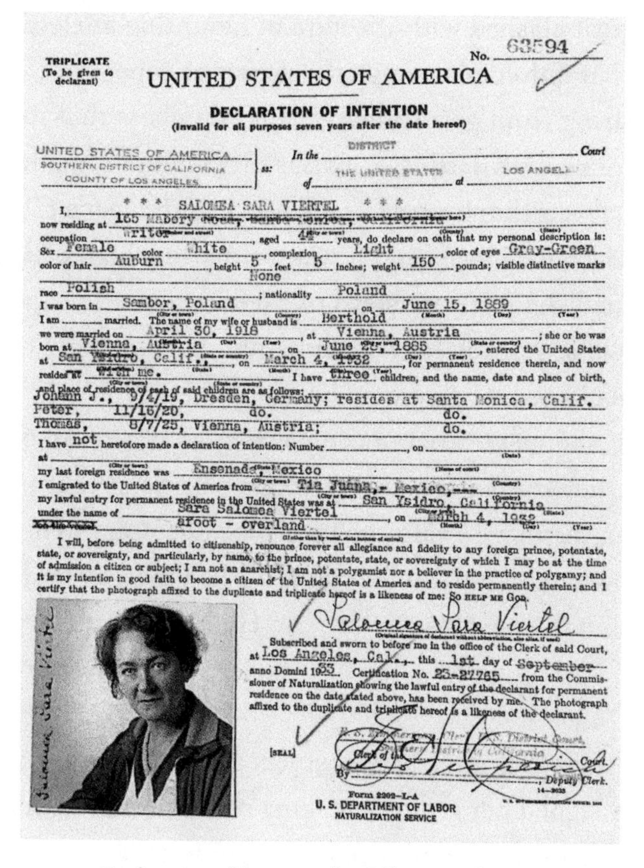

TRIPLICATE
(To be given to declarant)

No. 63594

UNITED STATES OF AMERICA

DECLARATION OF INTENTION
(Invalid for all purposes seven years after the date hereof)

UNITED STATES OF AMERICA
SOUTHERN DISTRICT OF CALIFORNIA
COUNTY OF LOS ANGELES
ss: In the DISTRICT Court of THE UNITED STATES at LOS ANGELES

I, * * * SALOMEA SARA VIERTEL * * *
now residing at 165 Mabery Road, Santa Monica, California
occupation writer, aged 44 years, do declare on oath that my personal description is:
Sex Female, color White, complexion Light, color of eyes Gray-Green
color of hair Auburn, height 5 feet 5 inches; weight 150 pounds; visible distinctive marks None
race Polish; nationality Poland
I was born in Sambor, Poland on June 15, 1889
I am married. The name of my wife or husband is Berthold
we were married on April 30, 1918, at Vienna, Austria; she or he was born at Vienna, Austria, on June 28, 1885, entered the United States at San Ysidro, Calif., on March 4, 1932, for permanent residence therein, and now resides with me. I have three children, and the name, date and place of birth, and place of residence of each of said children are as follows:
Johann J., 9/4/19, Dresden, Germany; resides at Santa Monica, Calif.
Peter, 11/16/20, do. do.
Thomas, 8/7/25, Vienna, Austria; do.
I have not heretofore made a declaration of intention: Number ______, on ______ at ______
my last foreign residence was Ensenada, Mexico
I emigrated to the United States of America from Tia Juana, Mexico
my lawful entry for permanent residence in the United States was at San Ysidro, California
under the name of Sara Salomea Viertel, on March 4, 1932
afoot - overland

I will, before being admitted to citizenship, renounce forever all allegiance and fidelity to any foreign prince, potentate, state, or sovereignty, and particularly, by name, to the prince, potentate, state, or sovereignty of which I may be at the time of admission a citizen or subject; I am not an anarchist; I am not a polygamist nor a believer in the practice of polygamy; and it is my intention in good faith to become a citizen of the United States of America and to reside permanently therein; and I certify that the photograph affixed to the duplicate and triplicate hereof is a likeness of me: So HELP ME GOD.

Salomea Sara Viertel
(Original signature of declarant without abbreviation, also alias, if used)

Subscribed and sworn to before me in the office of the Clerk of said Court, at Los Angeles, Cal., this 1st day of September anno Domini 1933. Certification No. 23-27765 from the Commissioner of Naturalization showing the lawful entry of the declarant for permanent residence on the date stated above, has been received by me. The photograph affixed to the duplicate and triplicate hereof is a likeness of the declarant.

[SEAL]

Clerk of the ______ Court.
By ______, Deputy Clerk.

Form 2202–L–A
U. S. DEPARTMENT OF LABOR
NATURALIZATION SERVICE

Declaration of Intention for Salka Viertel, 1933.

It is difficult to take in this family anecdote and not to recognize it as a mild prequel to the scramble for documents that would determine the fate of the hundreds of thousands who would soon become desperate to escape from Hitler's Europe through other picturesque port cities. In Marseille, in Vladivostok, in Lisbon, in harbors along the Black Sea in Bulgaria and Romania, a drama of life-or-death human migration would gather momentum into a full-blown global catastrophe. It was a story of waiting in festival-themed resort towns whose blithe spirit clashed with the aura of mounting anxiety. It was a story that unfolded through the power of paperwork, its tensions arising from government-issued numbers that might or might not be drawn, from exit visas that might or might not be granted. It was the story of *Casablanca*, of *Surrender on Demand*, of *Hold Back the Dawn*. And it was a story in which Salka, having learned the intricate steps of the bureaucratic paperwork shuffle while waiting for her quota numbers to come through in Ensenada, would play a vital part.

First, she needed one more piece of education in order to perform her role in the largest refugee crisis at that point in European history. To gain the influence necessary to help save her fellow artists and intellectuals, she had to learn how to survive within the power structure of a Hollywood studio.

A FEW MONTHS after Salka returned from Ensenada, Garbo officially signed her groundbreaking new contract with MGM. She then promptly announced her plan to take a trip to Sweden at the end of July 1932. At this time Berthold decided to go to Europe as well, to chase a much-needed business opportunity. The Hungarian film impresario Alexander Korda was establishing a new studio in England and wanted to meet Berthold in Paris to discuss potential projects. From France, Berthold would travel to Vienna to see his father, who had become seriously ill.

One morning, just before Garbo left for Sweden, she took Salka to a sprawling house on Ocean Front Avenue in Santa Monica. She did not tell Salka why they were there. At the entrance to the mansion, a fragile-looking man with soft, sad eyes answered the door. Salka took note of his fine features and delicate hands. "This is Mr. Thalberg," said Garbo.

Salka was caught off guard by the abrupt introduction. At thirty-three, Irving Thalberg was the tireless production head at MGM and one of Hollywood's most powerful and enigmatic figures. When he mentioned that he had heard wonderful things about her, she answered numbly that she had heard much about him as well. "Of course you have," warned Garbo, tacitly asking Salka not to ruin this suddenly very important meeting.

Salka was unaware that Garbo had already given Thalberg the treatment she and Peg Le Vino had recently finished for *Queen Christina*. He was interested. But he told Salka he did not believe in historical films and thought the story needed a lot of work. Thalberg intended, he said, to give it his personal attention: "I would not produce it if I did not think it would make a great picture."

Garbo assured him that she too had a great personal devotion to the story. Nodding toward Salka, Thalberg replied: "I am always open to new ideas and new talent," adding that he'd be in touch and would find Salka a qualified collaborator. Salka protested that she wanted to continue working with Peg Le Vino. Thalberg was unmovable. "I know Mrs. Le Vino," he said. "She is a fine woman but not the person I want on the screenplay." At that moment Thalberg's wife, the actress Norma Shearer, entered the room and invited the women to lunch. Garbo made their excuses and said her goodbyes, with Thalberg once again assuring them that *Christina* would be a great picture.

Salka left Thalberg's house feeling shaken. She and Peg had worked hard on the treatment, grabbing the few available hours when the boys were in school and the cooking and housework were done, and she hated the idea of replacing her cowriter. Her hopes that the picture might somehow be made in Europe were now growing dim. Garbo tried to bolster Salka with reassurances that MGM was the best studio and Thalberg the finest producer. She was confident that Salka could elevate the picture above mere commercialism. A few days later, Garbo left for Sweden and Salka was on her own once again. She was going to have to toughen up, and quickly. As ever in Hollywood, the education she was about to receive would be as unsentimental as they come.

4

THE HOUSE OF METRO

Movies aren't made, they're re-made.

—IRVING THALBERG

LOS ANGELES AND BERLIN

1932–1933

DURING THE 1930S, as the Great Depression slogged on, Hollywood was raining queens. Salka's *Queen Christina* was the first picture in the decade's royal flush, following on the heels of a British production, *The Private Life of Henry VIII*. As always in Hollywood, others of the kind followed. In 1933, Metro was preparing a picture about Marie Antoinette to star Norma Shearer, though the film did not appear until 1938. In 1934, Paramount launched *The Scarlet Empress*, which starred Marlene Dietrich as Catherine the Great, as well as *Cleopatra*, with Claudette Colbert. In 1936, John Ford directed Katharine Hepburn in *Mary of Scotland* for RKO, while Bette Davis finished out the decade in *The Private Lives of Elizabeth and Essex*, for Warner Bros., in 1939.

Why all the crowns? The studio heads were eager to promote the celebrity of their own movie queens, in particular their exotic Europeans, Garbo and Dietrich. They were also tapping into Americans' long-standing fascination with royalty, on whose opulence filmgoers made ravenous by the Depression could visually feast. In fact the Hollywood studios, solid as they seemed from the start, were themselves built as bulwarks against earlier periods of hunger and poverty by men, almost all of them Jews from Europe, who spent every waking breath outrunning the destitution of their youth. The studio bosses built their celluloid fantasies of palaces to eclipse the memories of the hovels in which they were born.

Louis B. Mayer, the cofounder and chief of MGM, endured a childhood of near-mythic harshness. Mayer's father had moved his family to Canada in the early 1890s to escape from a Russian empire so determined to cripple its Jewish population with conscription laws and economic prohibitions that 240,000 Jews had already fled during the previous decade. Life was not much better in the seaport town of Saint John in the Canadian province of New Brunswick where the Mayers landed, with patriarch Jacob Mayer scraping out a paltry living by selling junk from a cart. Louis, his third child, then known as Lazar, learned quickly that survival meant determination and aggression.

Before leaving school at around age twelve, Louis spent his childhood navigating the brutality of his father, fighting off the anti-Semitic taunts of his schoolmates, and peering into the windows of noodle shops, always desolately hungry. In those years he also began his working life. He was a small boy who took to the streets with a large bag, searching for scrap metal to add to his father's salvage pile. "He kept his eyes on the ground," his biographer Scott Eyman wrote. "When he saw something, he would dart forward, grab it and toss it into the bag. It was his now, but he had to have more, so he would keep moving quickly, so nobody else could get to the precious metal before he could. The habit of a rapid pace, almost a trot, would stay with him all his life."

From such beginnings, wrestled into being with the same frantic resolve and some lucky gambles, Louis B. Mayer's house of Metro ascended. MGM had been in business for only eight years by 1932, the year Salka began working as a screenwriter. Yet already Mayer's studio was Hollywood's richest. In early 1933—a nadir year of the Great Depression—while Paramount, RKO, and Fox were declaring bankruptcy or entering receivership, MGM was the only studio to show a profit, its assets holding steady at $130 million.

Mayer had wagered correctly that the cultivation of movie gods and goddesses would be the key to Metro's success. "More stars than there are in the heavens" was the publicity department's slogan, which sprang from a profitable business plan. Single-handedly generating much of that profit was Metro's reigning idol, Greta Garbo, who in the early 1930s was "the greatest money-making proposition ever put on the screen," according to one of her biographers, Barry Paris. Garbo was one of the few survivors from the silent era who became an even bigger star once audiences heard her voice. Her cello-toned cadences with their Swedish inflection perfectly matched her audiences' expectations. Luxury product was what Metro was selling in its feature films, and the Garbo of the 1930s exemplified that luxury: the exquisite face, the erotic physicality, the expensive clothing and furs, the air of androgyne mystery, the European exoticism. Depression-mired audiences could not get enough of her.

Of the period just before Garbo's contract with MGM expired in June 1932, Salka noted: "Other studios made fantastic offers . . . She had only to choose." Mayer was haunted by the prospect of Garbo's defection to another studio, which for Metro would be financially catastrophic. And he understood that more than money would be necessary to keep the Swedish queen in his court. Boldly, he offered her something no star had ever yet been granted: power.

Hollywood stars at that time were tethered to draconian seven-year contracts whose mandates entitled the studios to dictate everything about their actors' careers, including which plastic surgery and dental work they must undergo, which roles they must play under which director, and much of their off-screen behavior. If actors refused to cooperate, they were suspended without pay. But under the terms of Garbo's new two-picture deal, she would have a degree of freedom unheard of since the dawn of the silent era: the freedom to approve film subjects, starting dates, cinematographers, directors, costars, unit still photographers, and portrait photographers. The first film under the terms of her new contract was to be *Queen Christina,* and while the contract did not give Garbo approval for scriptwriters, Mayer made no objection to Garbo's request that Salka, who had already written the treatment, should begin to develop the screenplay.

Like Mayer, Garbo had climbed to her commanding position from the most discouraging origins. The third child of a Swedish laborer and his wife, who were forced to abandon their rural heritage for an attempt at survival in the big city, Greta Lovisa Gustafsson was raised in a cold-water flat on the fourth floor of a tenement in Stockholm's working-class district of Södermalm, surrounded by ugly apartment buildings and dingy shops. She was a dreamy child who liked to sit on the tin roof of the outhouse in the tenement's back courtyard, there to pretend she was sunbathing on an elegant white beach.

By the time Greta was fourteen, in 1920, she had left school and was working for about a dollar a week in a barbershop as a *tvålflicka,* a soap-lather girl. The position nominally involved assistance with shaving chores but more truthfully gave men a socially acceptable opportunity to grope young girls. Fending off grabs and pinches, Greta faced this work with as much dignity as she could muster. When she was not at the barbershop Greta spent much of her time caring for her father, who had become ill and could not work. On one particularly traumatic afternoon, she feared he was dying and went with him to a charity hospital. They waited in a long line while her father blazed with fever, only to be humiliated at the reception window with questions about whether they could pay for treatment. Greta's shame and anger in the face of this callousness remained with her for the rest of her life.

A few days after they were turned away from the hospital, her beloved father died of a kidney inflammation. He was forty-eight. His death threw the family's already grim finances into yet more disarray.

Greta inherited piteously little from her father aside from his willingness to work hard, his love of the outdoors, and his infinitely expressive eyes. She learned to use that expressiveness as she began to pursue a career as an actress. At seventeen she got a scholarship to the Royal Dramatic Theatre Academy in Stockholm, one of the most prestigious drama schools in the world. Through contacts there she met the great Swedish director Mauritz Stiller and became his protégée. It was in Stiller's *Saga of Gösta Berling* that Louis B. Mayer first noticed her and resolved to bring her to Hollywood. Clarence Brown, who later directed seven of Garbo's pictures at MGM, told the film historian Kevin Brownlow: "Greta Garbo had something that nobody ever had on the screen. I don't know whether she even knew she had it, but she did... Garbo had something behind the eyes that you couldn't see until you photographed it in close-up. You could see thought."

When Garbo first arrived in Hollywood in 1925 at age twenty, an unsentimental woman journalist offered a more superficial perspective: "Her shoes were run down at the heels. Her stockings were silk but in one was a well-defined run. As a sartorial masterpiece, she was a total loss." Here during that nativist era was a typically cruel and condescending attitude toward an immigrant—and a famous one at that. Garbo's first year in America was dampened by homesickness, her grasp of English tenuous, her foreignness isolating. In those initial months there was little attempt to welcome her, or to pay much attention to her at all. Her friend the playwright Sam Behrman once asked her why she got involved during her early Hollywood days with the troubled actor John Gilbert, whom she almost married in 1926. Thoughtfully, Garbo replied, "I was lonely—and I couldn't speak English."

Yet Garbo persevered. She had no choice. In the interminable three-month wait for MGM to assign her to a film project, she took a room at the Miramar Hotel in Santa Monica and spent her days walking along the shore. She had found the elegant white beach she had dreamed of as a girl atop the outhouse behind her tenement. Yet no matter how far she ran from her origins, they refused to let her be. The avalanche of fame that followed would not transform or appease her. The restless hunger to outrun her painful childhood would remain during her hardworking ascension to Hollywood queendom and throughout her long life.

These origin stories of Mayer's and Garbo's were the stories, for the most part, of those who built the house of Metro and of almost every one of those who built Hollywood, from its earliest carnival days to the era of corporate efficiency that was now developing. They were the stories of Mary Pickford, Samuel Goldwyn, Charlie Chaplin, William Fox, Joan Crawford. They were the hardscrabble beginnings of people who were scarred by the absence of lost fathers or by the presence of terrifying ones. They had suffered in poverty, vowed never again to endure it, risked all their own money, and were made frantic by the prospect of passing up their shot. The Hollywood pioneers were, as the film historian Cari Beauchamp has noted, almost all women, Jews, and immigrants: outsiders for whom the twin specters of privation and discrimination shaped the ways they behaved and everything they created. Their early miseries inspired the angry resolve they would need to survive in this grueling, misogynistic, fiercely anti-Semitic new world.

ON AUGUST 2, 1932, when Salka walked through the Greek-colonnade gates of Metro's Culver City studio to meet again with Irving Thalberg, she entered an organization teeming with women. Mostly unheralded, all of them were vital to the studio's welfare in large ways and small. Among the women of Metro were not only actresses and secretaries: women populated every corner of its vast campus. They filled the story department, where they read scripts and reported to executives about incoming books and plays. Women taught in the Little Red Schoolhouse, which was the studio's on-site school for child actors, under the supervision of head instructor Mary McDonald. They worked in the commissary, which fed up to 2,700 people daily—where a menu staple was the matzoh-ball soup that was prepared from a Mayer family recipe—and as nurses in the first-aid department, where two doctors and a dentist were always on call. A whole floor of the wardrobe building, it was said, was assigned to hand embroidery and beading performed by immigrant women, like a factory in the garment industry of the time.

"Through their collective efforts, these women were the fuel of Hollywood's large-scale, industrial production process," wrote Erin Hill in a history of women's work in film. True—but also true that more than a few of Metro's female employees had prominent positions at the studio. They had influence, but no authority; responsibility, but no glory. Lofty rewards for achievement went only to men.

Blanche Sewell was a film editor at Metro from the silent era through the 1940s, and would serve as the editor for *Queen Christina*. Even more formidable in the editing department was Margaret Booth, who edited many of the studio's most prestigious productions, also from the silent era onward. Booth's credits include *The Bridge of San Luis Rey*, *Strange Interlude*, and *Camille*, and she was nominated for an Oscar for her work on *Mutiny on the Bounty* (1935). In 1937 she became Metro's supervising film editor, a role she held until the studio collapsed in the late 1960s. The position made her one of the most influential employees on the Metro lot, as she had approval on the final editing of every film the studio released during her tenure.

Nathalie Bucknall, a multilingual polymath from St. Petersburg, began at the studio as a script reader in 1927 and by 1935 had created the research department, overseeing a library of four thousand volumes and supplying period detail for the studio's historical blockbusters of the 1930s, including Garbo's *Anna Karenina*. Kate Corbaley in the reading department was one of Mayer's most trusted story editors, identifying potentially successful scripts and reading their summaries aloud to the boss, sometimes altering plot points to her own satisfaction. Louis B. Mayer's executive assistant, Ida Koverman, was the dexterous traffic controller for all who clamored to see Mayer, as well as his adviser on important acquisition and staffing decisions. She was a forceful fundraiser for the California Republican Party, having previously served as a secretary for Herbert Hoover's presidential campaign. Additionally, and rare for the time, Mayer's personal physician, Jessie Marmorston, and his lawyer, Fanny Holtzmann, were women.

Mayer's head of production, Irving Thalberg, liked women and was not above working with them, though he was quick to withhold his approval or to pit them against one another when those tactics proved useful. Women writers, many of whom had begun as scenarists or as actresses during the silent era, were obedient and discreet. They had been raised to expect much less than men did—less money, less credit, less respect. In one example, Thalberg enjoyed seventeen years of fruitful collaborations with the supremely accomplished screenwriter Frances Marion. She was the winner of two Academy Awards and the writer of more than three hundred pictures of every genre. For many of those she received inadequate credit, or none at all. ("A mouse at the feast" was how she once described her role in Hollywood.) Much of Frances Marion's enormous value to the studio came from her facility with literary adaptations, including Eugene O'Neill's *Anna Christie* in 1929, which Thalberg supervised and which was Garbo's sound-film debut. Thalberg worked profitably with other of Metro's women screenwriters as well, including Anita Loos, Bess Meredyth (the wife of the Warner Bros. director Michael Curtiz), and Lenore Coffee, who once reported that Thalberg had explained to her that writing wasn't hard; it was just putting one word after another. To which Coffee replied: "Pardon me, Mr. Thalberg—it's putting one *right* word after another."

Salka's prospects thus seemed somewhat promising on this summer day, when she ventured onto the studio grounds for the first time to discuss *Queen Christina* with Thalberg. Yet this foray played out even more poorly than had their first encounter at his Ocean Front mansion. This time Salka did not have Garbo with her, as the actress had left for Europe several days earlier. Instead Salka armed herself with Garbo's agent, Harry Edington.

Salka noticed that Thalberg looked even thinner and more ashen than he had only a few weeks earlier. He had been born with a heart defect, as everyone knew, and had not expected to live past the age of thirty; he was now thirty-three. Salka and Thalberg exchanged a few pleasantries, and then his tone turned more businesslike. We have to start working, he told Salka. He asked her what arrangements she would suggest.

Having been coached by Edington, Salka replied that she'd leave it up to Thalberg. To which he responded that he wanted very much to have Salka at the studio and thought it best that she join MGM on a weekly salary.

Bravely, Salka said that she had collaborated with Peg Le Vino and felt that the studio should make a deal with both of them and buy the story.

Thalberg let a long pause go by, then asserted his power. But there is nothing to buy, he told her charmingly. You have no copyright. Anybody can write a story on a historical subject.

Salka was shocked into a rare speechlessness. Without saying it overtly, he was telling her he had every legal right to dismiss her and steal her treatment.

You told me yourself that you wanted to make changes, Thalberg said soothingly. Still, I want to be fair. We'll pay you a thousand dollars now and four thousand when the script is finished.

No, Mr. Thalberg, Salka insisted. You know very well that this is not adequate compensation for a story which demanded a great deal of work and research.

Rounding up her dignity along with the silent Mr. Edington, she said her goodbyes and walked out.

Edington called Salka the next day to tell her that Thalberg was furious but wanted to continue negotiating. Salka asked the agent to tell Thalberg that her treatment was an original, was not in the public domain, and that Thalberg himself had said it was perfect for Garbo. On the advice of Oliver Garrett and her lawyer, she told Edington to ask for ten thousand dollars for the ninety-page story.

A few days later, Thalberg made a counteroffer of $7,500 for Salka and Peg Le Vino, which they accepted and split between them. (Hollywood gossips gleefully inflated their shares to $37,500 each.) Le Vino would do no further work on the script, but would receive a story credit. In later years, in a politically motivated effort to discredit Salka's achievements as a writer, the columnist Hedda Hopper maintained that Peg Le Vino was the sole original author of the *Christina* story. "It serves me right," Salka wrote in her diary in 1959. "I should never have been so generous to Peg as to let her share the credit."

"All during that ordeal I was thinking of you, Berthold," Salka wrote about the negotiation to her husband, who was aboard a ship on his way to Europe. "My first encounter with the world of film business made me very apologetic towards you! But if they don't throw me out, I hope I will learn to cope with it."

Coping meant acceding to the whims of the studio schedule, in which work could charge forward or stop cold during exasperating waiting periods. At Salka's first story conference just a few days later, there seemed to be plenty of momentum. Thalberg introduced Salka to Bess Meredyth, the dimpled, pink-cheeked screenwriter of *Ben-Hur* as well as three of Garbo's hits. A former silent-film actress, Meredyth was prized for her brisk solutions to story glitches and was one of the most highly paid writers on the lot. Over time, Salka grew to become fond of her.

Meredyth smiled placidly while Thalberg outlined his ideas for *Christina*. Also in the room was Paul Bern, his German-born production assistant, who exclaimed admiringly at each of Thalberg's pronouncements about how daring the film must be, but also how human, so that audiences could identify with the characters. Salka intensely disliked Bern, who had supervised the German version of *Anna Christie* in which Salka had appeared opposite Garbo. He was pompous and patronizing toward Salka, all the while keeping up his sycophantic cooing over Thalberg: "Marvelous, Irving... I see! *Now* it certainly makes sense! *Now* it becomes an important film..."

When the conviction arose during the meeting that audiences only wanted a good love story, Salka was moved to remind the men that Queen Christina, being after all the ruler of a powerful kingdom who had inherited a little problem called the Thirty Years' War, was far from some ordinary love-starved woman. Thalberg asked how Salka might portray this fact without making the film dull. Instantly Salka's dramatic instincts came alive. She had composed the *Christina* treatment in the fall and winter of 1931 by acting out each scene for Peg Le Vino to transcribe onto the page. Now Salka again began to act out several incidents from the treatment, careful to make it seem as if Thalberg, with her help, was inventing the scenes à la minute. "My suggestions were pure theater," she later remembered, and she was gratified to see how thoroughly Thalberg the inveterate showman was entertained by her performance. In pitch meetings and in writer's rooms throughout her screenwriting career, Salka would continue to do her storytelling as if it were live theater. Performance was turning out to be her key to survival.

The meeting was breaking up when Thalberg called Salka back. Standing behind his enormous desk, he said to her: "You had a very bad entrée, but if I were not sure that you will be an asset to the studio I would not make you an offer. We need talent, but talent needs us too. You have no experience and I want you to work with Bess Meredyth. She has written great films." They agreed that Salka was to be paid $350 per week on a week-to-week basis. She didn't want a long-term commitment until she knew whether Berthold would be able to get a contract with Alexander Korda in Europe.

Unexpectedly, Thalberg then asked Salka whether she had seen *Mädchen in Uniform*, a 1931 German film about a lesbian relationship between a teacher and a student in a girls' school that had become a great sensation in Europe and more recently in New York. Thalberg recommended that Queen Christina's passionate affection for her lady-in-waiting might be drawn along similar lines, and asked Salka to keep this in mind. "Handled with taste," he suggested, "it would give us very interesting scenes."

Such open-mindedness from an American film producer was a pleasant revelation for Salka, and it was at this point that she decided she liked Thalberg very much. His enthusiasm brought her back to Europe, to the sexual fluidity of the Weimar culture that she had left behind in Berlin. Then she remembered farther back, to the Vienna of the mid-teens, when she had worked at the Neue Wiener Bühne. There she had known an actress named Leontine Sagan who had since turned to filmmaking and was the now-celebrated director of none other than *Mädchen in Uniform*.

Thalberg's comment revealed that he, too, was thinking of Europe, though from a different perspective. He was indeed open-minded about sexuality: he had undergone Freudian analysis and harbored a deep commiseration with—if he did not himself possess—the boundary-pushing impulses of artists. But his suggestion to Salka about the Sagan film was more about business than it was about art or sex. Wildly popular as Garbo was, her success depended significantly on the European market. Thalberg took careful notice as *Mädchen in Uniform* became big box office in Europe, and he sought to replicate that revenue for Metro in any way he could. For Thalberg, the lavish depiction of an enigmatic seventeenth-century European queen portrayed by Metro's most enigmatic twentieth-century movie goddess was a good financial bet at home and abroad. Add to that a suggestive continental embrace or two between women during these freewheeling pre-Code days (the brief period between the advent of sound in 1929 and the imposition of Motion Picture Production Code censorship guidelines in mid-1934), and he calculated that the odds of a hit on both sides of the Atlantic were in Metro's favor.

Every historical drama is as much a reflection of the time in which it is written as the time it attempts to portray. By hiring Salka, Thalberg was building a bridge to the Europe of his own era as much as to the Europe of Christina's. Just as important, he understood that Salka would serve as the bridge between Garbo and the studio.

When the special girl friend
Meets a special girl friend
With great tenderness she'll tell her friend she's special....
Just last week
Her boyfriend had her in a whirl
That romance is over
She's dropped him for a girl...

—"WHEN THE SPECIAL GIRLFRIEND,"
FROM THE 1928 BERLIN REVUE *IT'S IN THE AIR*,
BY MARCELLUS SCHIFFER AND MISCHA SPOLIANSKY;
SUNG BY MARGO LION AND MARLENE DIETRICH

BERLIN AND HOLLYWOOD WERE GAZING AT EACH OTHER, and each sold images of modern womanhood to the other. One after another, the revues in Berlin's packed cabarets marched

American-style kicklines of young girls through their paces. *Girlkultur* was the word for these mechanical parades of often naked dancers, which commented on American consumer culture as well as sexuality. In other revues, pairs of singers warbled teasing homoerotic lyrics to each other as they pretended to go shopping. Women dressed as men, onstage and off, and men as women.

Hollywood was watching, and was drawn to the fluidity and the freedom. Onscreen and off, Dietrich and Garbo helped inspire a fashion trend for men's wear among women, while the films of the comedian Marion Davies took pains to show her in trousers to satisfy the fetish of her patron, William Randolph Hearst. For many in Hollywood, "a knowing, blasé attitude toward lesbianism became a signifier of worldly cosmopolitanism," according to the film historian Laura Horak. "Everyone had to be a lesbian in the thirties, even if they didn't want to be," noted Sam Green, an art dealer who became a good friend of Garbo's in the 1970s. "They certainly dressed up and went to lesbian bars—it was the thing to do."

For the studios, as Thalberg had suggested, the Weimar Republic's spirit of freewheeling sexuality was marketable. Hollywood was happy to impersonate Berlin's lesbian-chic culture as long as it brought a profit. But there were those in Hollywood who were also willing to use it to inflict harm. As was the case with Murnau, innuendo about homosexuality was an industry-wide cudgel, wielded by the jealous and the confrontational. "Interestingly," wrote Patrick McGilligan, biographer of the director George Cukor, "that's the first bit of juicy gossip you hear about *everyone* in Hollywood." When Garbo, with Metro's encouragement, cultivated an aura of ambiguous sexuality to appeal to women as well as men, malicious gossip about her relationship with Salka began to circulate, and continued well after Salka's death in 1978. In fact, if Salka is remembered today, it's not for her screenwriting career or her role in the antifascist emigration; it's most often for her alleged lesbian relationship with Garbo. These allegations are seldom expressed with tolerance or sympathy.

"Salka was AC/DC" (bisexual), Irene Mayer Selznick, Louis B. Mayer's daughter, told Garbo's biographer Barry Paris, years after Salka had died. "Lots of people knew about that. She was quite masculine, I thought—overweight and unappetizing, but charming." Never mind that Salka herself identified as heterosexual publicly, in her diaries, and in her memoir, and strenuously denied that she and Garbo ever had a sexual relationship. There is not a shred of evidence to prove that they did. In pointing this out, however, Barry Paris manages to be just as disparaging toward Salka as Irene Selznick was, writing that Salka, "as everyone, might well have been attracted to Garbo, but the reverse was unlikely, and none of the many claims that they were 'lovers' offers anything but conjecture to back it up."

The truth about whether there was ever a physical expression of Salka's and Garbo's intimate bond is not available and may never be. It's possible that there was, and just as possible not. Yet the kind of casually damaging homophobia and misogyny in Irene Selznick's assertion was not about homosexuality at all, but about fear and power, and it came just as frequently from women as from men. The smaller the portions for ambitious women in Hollywood, the more vicious they tended to be toward other women. An accusation of homosexuality, as the historian Richard Hofstadter wrote about HUAC-era Communism, "was not the target but the weapon," and its real function was "to discharge resentments and frustrations, to punish, to satisfy enmities whose roots lay elsewhere." In Salka's case, the fear and resentment was directed toward a politically progressive foreign woman who had helped to bring in the permissive culture of the Weimar Republic, who had the ear of one of Hollywood's most powerful actresses, and whose influence must be kept vigilantly in check.

IT WAS NOT JUST IMAGES of women's sexuality that Hollywood and Europe were exhibiting to each other as they gazed across the Atlantic. Berlin was pulsing with its best simulation of American jazz. Visiting African-American musicians and dancers imported what Berliners perceived as something primitive and authentic, as "wildness" and "wantonness." Meanwhile, in Culver City, Metro prepared to build an illusion of seventeenth-century Sweden on its backlot, while on Lot Two, a large faux-antique Austrian-style house near the French Courtyard and the London-style Copperfield Street faced an area that would come to be called, for the Garbo film, Christina Court. And back in Berlin, occupying nearly all of Potsdamer Platz was a gigantic proto–Disney World dining emporium called Haus Vaterland, operated by a Jewish family-owned hotel firm called Kempinski, in which eight thousand diners at once could choose among six floors of themed restaurants. On the fourth floor was the Wild West Bar, in which waiters in cowboy hats served American cocktails while jazz bands, showgirls, and minstrels in blackface performed.

Germans co-opted American popular culture for political as well as commercial reasons. National Socialist leaders admired the insouciance of American pictures as they prepared to spread their *völkisch* ideology through the power of film. The frenzied language of Hitler's speeches, the philologist Victor Klemperer noticed, was designed to create suspense in a manner deliberately copied from American cinema. And that language was effective. While Berlin's cabarets were mocking Hitler as a preposterous Austrian clown, by July 1932 his party had won 230 parliamentary seats. Amid more and more dire economic conditions that surpassed the worst aspects of America's Great Depression, within four years the National Socialists had gone from winning barely 1 percent of the vote, in March 1929, to becoming the largest party in the Reichstag.

Salka was getting a few glimpses of the European mood from Berthold, who was in Paris during that summer of 1932. She missed him terribly and wished she could join him, but Berthold's letters provided a corrective. "You ask how Europe is, Salka? It is overwhelming. Impoverished, poisoned by politics, which means by hatred." By November he had moved on to Berlin, where the producers and directors he knew were either hankering for an invitation to Hollywood or hastily adapting themselves to the pervasive influence of National Socialism. Berthold mentioned to Salka that the prostitutes offering flagellation services on the Kurfürstendamm were complaining to onlookers that the police would no longer let them wear their black fetish boots. Despite the new rules, he said, there were more prostitutes than ever. "The Eden bar and other night spots are ultra-chic and full of foreigners and film people," he reported; "an enormous amount of beggars in front of luxurious eating places: Kempinski, Mampe, and new Viennese and Hungarian restaurants—does it give you a picture?

"On every street corner you see youngsters in uniform shaking their collection boxes," Berthold wrote, "opposite them, on the same corner, the Communists. Lately both the young Communists and the Hitler Youth went on strike together. Four dead. The Government reacted with strong measures, but the strike continues."

Immersed in the volatility of Berlin, Berthold was sanguine about Salka's newly influential position at Metro, sending her an essay about Queen Christina he had found ("perhaps it will inspire you") and trying to boost her morale. Not least on his mind were the large portions of her paycheck Salka was cabling to him, some of which he used for himself, while he doled out the rest to family and friends. Sometimes, Salka noted tartly, "he would forget bank notes in hotel rooms or lose them on the streets."

Salka's weekly Metro paycheck of $350—at a time, in August 1932, when the U.S. unemployment rate climbed to 25 percent—shifted the scales of the Viertels' marriage more dramatically than their current geographical separation or their ongoing infidelities. Salka was still involved with Oliver Garrett, but their affair was winding down and both he and his wife Louise had been getting on her nerves. As with all of Salka's liaisons, the situation was nuanced and complicated. Oliver was her film-business adviser and a beloved surrogate father to her sons as well as her lover; Berthold knew all this, and sanctioned most. In the meantime, Salka was sure that Berthold was not sexually faithful to her during what would turn out to be an entire year spent abroad. Life imitated *The*

Marriage Circle; or maybe Lubitsch's bittersweet European comedy was itself reflecting the intricacies of just this kind of European marriage. Even so, beyond matters of extramarital sex the Viertels remained a committed couple. In their letters, each to the other was still "*mein Herz*." When Salka sent Berthold a telegram asking him not to forget her, he replied: "*What* should I say to that? Not only that I *can't* forget you, on the contrary you are even more present to me... I am only planning the future in the 'we' form."

Salka was more than willing to earn the primary income. She was grateful for the chance to send cash to her family in Sambor and to Berthold's family in Vienna, both households pinched by the straitened economic conditions throughout Europe. And her paycheck released Berthold from some of the urgency of securing movie work of his own. He was weighing the offer of a job from Alexander Korda and Gaumont-British Pictures, which would not begin until early the following year, against several other film and theater opportunities on the Continent. But Salka hoped again that Berthold would return to Santa Monica and to his true passion, his own novels and poems. "If you are not making a film or staging a play immediately, you should return as soon as possible," she wrote to him. "Alas, I am sure that you are discussing a hundred projects, talking to a thousand people and dissipating your energy. Now that I am earning money we should consider it as a great chance for you to settle down and finish your books."

Berthold wrote: "In business terms your Greta manuscript is surely the most promising for the future and materially the most promising thing happening right now, more important than any engagement that I might be able to secure. Strangely you do not seem to share my sense of the importance of your work. Are you already so disheartened?"

About her position at Metro, at that point Salka was indeed disheartened. Except for the money, it was impossible for her to attach any importance to her new job, as very little was happening with *Christina*. She spent most of her time waiting to confer with Thalberg, then was told he had to travel to New York. Frustrated, she decided to ask Thalberg for a two-week leave of absence. Oliver and Louise Garrett were taking a trip to Mexico and had invited her along. She put aside her mundane irritations with them and decided to accept. Thalberg was amenable, even offering to keep Salka on the payroll during her absence as a reward for her participation in story conferences. Salka left her sons—now aged thirteen, twelve, and seven—in the able care of her housekeeper, and set off with the Garretts by steamer and train to Mazatlán, Guadalajara, and Mexico City. It was restorative to be in Mexico again, which reminded her once more of Wychylowka, and again she missed Berthold and wished he could be with her, in the *paisaje de campo* that their friend Eisenstein had so loved.

After Salka's return in the autumn of 1932, *Christina* moved glacially forward. No producer had yet been assigned, so she and Bess Meredyth worked on their first draft through November and December without supervision. Garbo remained in Sweden and Salka began to doubt that the picture would ever get made. Toward the end of the year, Salka's usual holiday melancholy was unappeased by the little Christmas trees topping the lampposts along Hollywood Boulevard or the twinkle lights festooning the streets downtown. When she and Bess finally finished their draft and sent it to Thalberg's office, they were told that he was leaving for Europe. Rumors spread that he was unwell, may even have suffered a heart attack, and was going abroad to recuperate.

Disheartened she may have been, but Salka was learning how to stay alive within the studio system. The occasion of her apprenticeship was a high-stakes, extremely expensive, star-powered production which would tolerate no false moves. Much would depend on her recognizing what not to do. After Thalberg left for Europe, having no idea what to work on while she waited, Salka started to write an original story about life in America's Hoovervilles, the encampments built by citizens made homeless by the Great Depression. She was quickly rebuked by a story editor, who assured her that with twelve million people out of work there was little chance that anyone would want to see such a film. Lesson number one: gritty realism was not Metro's style, then or ever. But that didn't mean the studio was impervious to politics. While the presidential election loomed that autumn, the stalwart Republican Louis Mayer asked every studio employee to donate a day's salary to Hoover's reelection campaign. Salka demurred, with the excuse that she was not yet an American citizen. Lesson number two: she saw the futility of suggesting a story about Hoovervilles under a studio chief who happened to be a personal friend of the president. She was stirred by Franklin Delano Roosevelt's speeches and was sorry she was unable to vote.

A secret to studio survival, Salka realized, was refining a talent she already had: the deft management of relationships. She understood that she had been hired to engineer a script that would please its star and generate profits in Europe as well as America. She saw also that as soon as she ceased to contribute measurable financial gains to the studio, she would be dismissed. In the meantime, she would need to develop the skills of a Mata Hari—whom Garbo had played with enormous success for Metro the previous year—to navigate the personalities around her.

Among those skills were diplomacy, tact, charm, subterfuge, strategic compromise, and the occasional targeted aggression. In managing the *Realpolitik* of the studio, these were talents that Salka cultivated more handily than Berthold, who was more inclined to wander off from conflicts, darkly quoting Kant or Karl Kraus, than to dig in and negotiate. It was a different skill set from the one Salka used at home, as the manager of a busy household, and as the host of her Sunday parties, where with uncontested authority she took dominion everywhere. In the studio Salka had to find ways to exert her influence that looked unthreatening but were nonetheless effective. Her authority had to remain a bass note: patiently insistent, but reliable and subordinate.

It was only after Thalberg left for Europe that Salka began to see him as more of a champion than an adversary. This became clear to her at the end of the year when, on December 21, the studio appointed Walter Wanger to serve as producer on *Christina*. Salka found she much preferred Thalberg's arrogance to Wanger's evasiveness. In January 1933, Wanger's first decision was to send Bess Meredyth off to another writing assignment and to take Salka off the script as well, promoting her to his "assistant and artistic advisor." He then hired an obnoxious Hungarian writer named Ernest Vajda, who had worked for Lubitsch, and a countervailingly soft-spoken Englishwoman,

Claudine West. These two proceeded to turn Salka's historical drama into a lurid comedy, full of snappy dialogue and anachronistic "Lubitsch touches." The script was now just the sort of crass Hollywood vehicle that Garbo had asked Salka to avoid.

A fierce battle followed. On behalf of the still-absent Garbo, Salka objected to the Vajda script, while Vajda accused Salka of exploiting her position as Garbo's personal friend. Wanger placated Salka by ordering another draft of the screenplay from a British writer, H. M. Harwood, who refashioned the Swedish monarch into, as he put it, "the prototype of a modern woman, who... shrinks from both marriage and maternity." When Garbo returned from Sweden in April, the trade papers reported that she objected to the current iteration of the script and was demanding changes. With the actress's support, in an impressive show of force, Salka won her battle against Vajda. He and his version were dismissed, and she remained employed. Berthold explained the situation in a letter to Salka's mother in Sambor: "Salka has overcome all these difficulties by her own strength, by her spirit and personality. After some incidents, she is not only personally respected, but she has also achieved a great deal, and the final manuscript has moved closer to her original design... Garbo is superstitious, she knows exactly what she owes to Salka and tells her, too."

While *l'affaire* Vajda played out at Metro, Berthold continued his wandering year in Europe. He had intended to spend Christmas of 1932 with Salka's sister Rose and her husband in Dresden. But Berthold's father became critically ill and he rushed to Vienna instead. Berthold remained at his father's bedside until his father died. Under the burden of this loss, along with more diffuse anxieties about the instabilities of the European moment, Berthold suffered his own health scare. His diabetes worsened dangerously and he checked himself into a Viennese sanatorium, where he purged his diet of his beloved rich desserts and gradually began to recover.

In the meantime, Berthold got an offer from Europa Film in Berlin to write and direct a film version of *Little Man, What Now?*, Hans Fallada's blockbuster 1932 novel about postwar German unemployment. (In Hollywood two years later, Universal would make an American version of Fallada's story, directed by Frank Borzage and starring Margaret Sullavan; not every studio vetoed stories about widespread poverty, as Metro had done when Salka ventured to write about Hoovervilles the previous year.) Berthold arrived in Berlin on January 31, 1933. Newspaper headlines were shouting of Hitler's appointment the previous day as Reich chancellor of Germany. It was, to say the least, a very risky time for Berthold to return. He was an outspoken leftist intellectual Austrian Jew who'd spent the last four years in America. The swiftly consolidating National Socialist regime deliberated over his work permit, seeing no "cultural necessity" for him to be working in Germany.

But the official stance softened after several of Berthold's high-profile friends made entreaties on his behalf, and so Berthold joined the Europa Film production along with the composer Kurt Weill and the set designer Caspar Neher, both of whom had worked with Brecht. While Berthold enjoyed his collaboration with these artists, he acknowledged to Salka that it was "sheer madness to do this film in such times." The picture's producer—"a blond, blue-eyed giant," Berthold wrote—

was falling over himself to please the new Ministry of Culture by working hard to turn the screenplay into ingratiating kitsch.

THE ELIMINATION OF JEWS from every corner of German culture was one of the Third Reich's most immediate priorities. By July 1933, laws prohibited Jews from taking any part in German film production. All Jews were summarily dismissed. As detachments of National Socialists paraded in full regalia and gangs of lesser thugs patrolled the streets with the intent to assault, studio employees from other countries began to fear for their safety. "Foreigner" was already a dirty word. Until recently, for American film representatives Berlin had been a prime posting, fizzing with louche glamour. Now the thrill was turning into fear. Reports drifted back to Hollywood of physical threats hurled at international cinema folk. Metro's Berlin representative, a Dutch citizen and a non-Jew, left for Holland during the first waves of violence, then uneasily returned. According to a front-page report in *Variety*'s April 25 edition, Phil Kaufman, the British branch head of Warner Bros., was beaten by Brownshirts and found his house ransacked. He fled to Paris, then resettled in London, where the studio hastily moved its European operations base.

Berthold wrote to Salka from Berlin: "One can really say that the world is coming to an end in Europe, or at least the biggest part of what was our world." In another letter, he continued: "America is still a kind of luck for us, because if we were to have to go away from Germany now, we would go without any money or knowledge of English and without any international connection and experience. The fate of many immigrants will be a very bitter one, and it will be a question to what degree we saved ourselves from it."

Genuinely terrified for her husband—who was, in the eyes of the National Socialists, a perfect example of the degenerate cosmopolitan Jew—Salka sent cables beseeching Berthold to break his contract and get out of Berlin. But Berthold obstinately held his ground, insisting that Europa Film would not pay him unless he finished the screenplay.

It took no less than the Reichstag fire, on February 27, and the subsequent decree suspending individual rights and due process which triggered a widespread wave of arrests, to pry Berthold away from Berlin. He fled to Vienna, stopping along the way in Prague, where he found himself among an eminent cast of fellow fugitives. Among them were Thomas and Heinrich Mann, Bertolt Brecht, Arnold Zweig, and Berthold's colleague from the Europa Film project, Kurt Weill. Though their politics varied widely, until recently these artists had been celebrated by their fellows and around the world as standard-bearers of the great German artistic tradition, of the lineage of Goethe and Schiller. Now their very existence in Germany was illegal. Their common crime was opposition to Hitler's regime, and all were abruptly stripped of their citizenship and its protections. All these artists, as Salka wrote, were now "expurgated from the culture of the Third Reich."

On March 22, the Dachau concentration camp began to operate on the site of an abandoned munitions factory, ten miles outside of Munich. It was the model for all subsequent Nazi concentration camps and would function continuously until its liberation by American armed forces in 1945.

In April, the first general boycott of Jewish businesses

began in Berlin. Storm troopers raided the boy bars and other night spots, and closed many of them. Speeches by Hermann Goering and Joseph Goebbels poured out of radio loudspeakers in the squares, while people sat in the outdoor cafés and listened without comment.

In May, Nazi-sponsored book burnings began in university towns throughout Germany. On Berlin's Opernplatz, on the night of May 10, among the first to be hurled onto the bonfires were the works of Heinrich Mann and Thomas Mann, of Bertolt Brecht and Arnold Zweig, of Sigmund Freud and of Berthold Viertel's friend Albert Einstein, and of the once-beloved nineteenth-century writer Heinrich Heine, whose 1821 play *Almansor* contained this prophecy: "Where they burn books, in the end they will also burn human beings."

On the Opernplatz, the Reich minister of propaganda, Joseph Goebbels, backlit cinematically by the garish blaze and the chanting mob, was shouting: "The era of exaggerated Jewish intellectualism is now at an end! . . . You do well at this late hour to entrust to the flames the intellectual garbage of the past . . . From its ruins will arise victorious the lord of a new spirit!" A cry rose among the torch-bearing crowd: "See the black souls of the Jews fly away."

Any such writers and intellectuals remaining in Germany—most of them Jewish, but not all—faced arrest and torture in Gestapo basements. They would be lucky to be kept alive, and many would be sent to concentration camps. The linguist Victor Klemperer observed: "regardless of how much worse it was going to get, everything which was later to emerge in terms of National Socialist attitudes, actions and language was already apparent in embryonic forms in these first months."

IN THE CONFIDENT BLOOM of another Los Angeles springtime, Salka wrote to Berthold: "Hitler is the triumph of the German *Spiesser* [philistine] and we will live to see his downfall." Despite her brave words, her own situation felt precarious, if not quite as shocking as the atmosphere in Berlin. To avert a financial panic the U.S. government had declared a national bank holiday, which was in place within days of Roosevelt's inauguration in early March 1933. The bank Salka used in Beverly Hills had already gone out of business. Providentially, she had stashed some of her *Christina* money in a still-solvent savings and loan downtown. It was all that was left of her reserves. In the meantime, Metro had cut salaries in half to manage its Depression losses. Its writers began to organize into a guild, to the extreme displeasure of the studio management.

On the evening of March 10, a 6.4-magnitude earthquake struck Long Beach, about thirty miles south of Santa Monica. It killed 120 people and caused widespread destruction; geologists have recently determined that it might have been caused by deep drilling in nearby oil fields. Salka wrote to Berthold that the aftershocks, which had lasted until dawn, were frightening. The chimney in their living room separated and shifted a full three feet away from the rest of the house.

Early the following month, when Salka went to renew her lease, the estate broker mentioned that she could buy the house at a bargain price because the bank that owned it was under liquidation. 165 Mabery Road could be hers for $7,500, with a $2,000 down payment and a monthly installment of $75.

Berthold suggested that they'd be safer buying a house in an earthquake-free zone, perhaps Austria or Ticino. But Salka decided that Santa Monica Canyon was as close to terra firma as she would find. Hitler's convulsive screaming over the radio airwaves, along with her belief in Roosevelt, had turned her resolution toward the New World. She wanted her sons to become Americans and she herself had just taken out her first citizenship papers. She warned Berthold as well that his visa would expire if he did not return in July. Salka went ahead with the house purchase, using Berthold's power of attorney to add his name to the deed. She took out a loan to repair the earthquake damage and installed central heating and a large guest room over the garage. "I was sure," she wrote about Berthold in her memoir, "that after all his wanderings Odysseus would be pleased to have a home."

Salka knew that Mabery Road was only a facsimile of home, on the strange shore of a foreign sea. Their real Ithaca was receding into a toxic brown twilight behind iron doors. If Berthold was her Odysseus, in buying the house Salka was making a financial decision to cast herself as Penelope. She was putting down roots in Santa Monica for her own safety and that of her family. But just as vital was her obligation toward an extended family of the dispossessed. For them her door would always be open. She was a Penelope whose faithfulness was first to the ideal of refuge, because she knew that houses could be destroyed in a moment, and in her heart she was as much a wanderer as Berthold and nearly everyone they knew.

DURING MILD MAY EVENINGS the whole city of Los Angeles smelled of car exhaust and jasmine. Off the Coast Highway, the sea was a sheet of tinfoil in the cloudy mornings, then a tranquil Delft horizon in the afternoon sun. In the canyon, in their upstairs bedroom, the Viertel boys, dreaming of summer vacation, dawdled over their lessons and stared out the window at their sliver of ocean, visible just beyond the green glass shade of the student's lamp Salka had bought.

On Sunday mornings in the garden, Salka put on her round straw sun hat and tended her roses and tried to train her mostly untrainable dogs. Sunday afternoons were reserved for her at-homes, with a pot of Earl Grey and a cake always at the ready for whoever might drop in—the Garretts and their visiting journalist friends; the Alabama-born actress Tallulah Bankhead; the Viennese novelist Vicki Baum, whose two sons had become friendly with Hans and Peter. Sundays were also reserved for the New York Philharmonic's radio concerts, and, if there was time, for books. Salka read the Yiddish writer I. L. Peretz's "Bontche the Silent" aloud to the boys. The bitter folktale about suffering and helplessness moved them all to tears.

At Metro, in the mouse-infested writers' building, Salka labored away on *Christina*. Her hopes for the picture had risen now that Garbo was back from Sweden. The other good news was that Wanger had summoned the playwright S. N. Behrman from New York to work on yet another rewrite.

Wanger liked to separate his teams of writers, especially after the unpleasantness of the Vajda dispute. But there was no keeping Sam Behrman away from Salka, who had known the playwright casually during Berthold's days at Fox and who now, as she began to collaborate with him on the script, quickly included him within her closest circles. Like Salka, Behrman was an intellectual, an aesthete, and a collector of high-profile friends (Isaiah Berlin, Felix Frankfurter). He was a writer of sophisticated Broadway comedies who made a lot of money polishing Hollywood screenplays. His warmth and wit were among the chief joys of Salka's years at Metro, while Behrman basked in Salka's exuberance. The two writers earned credits together on three more pictures at the studio, gaining a reputation as "Garbo specialists." They remained dedicated platonic friends for the rest of their lives. In their later years they maintained a fond correspondence ("Dear Salk"; "Dearest Sam"), designed to cheer up one or the other during periods of illness or melancholy. "As long as I know that you are well," Salka wrote to Behrman in a 1964 letter, "I shall remain your Griselda, Heloise, Solveig, Penelope and, last but not least, your Jewish girl from Sambor."

Over long weeks, Salka and Behrman rewrote the *Christina* script yet again, reinstating parts of Salka's original drafts which contained more historical fidelity than Vajda's or Harwood's versions. In all—and this was standard procedure for Metro's big-budget pictures of the time—at least ten writers worked on iterations of the script, including the prolific freelancer Harvey Gates and the veteran writer Ben Hecht.

Through the decades, there have been many attempts to discredit Salka's contributions as a writer, not just on *Christina* but on all her subsequent pictures. These include Hedda Hopper's allegations that Peg Le Vino alone wrote the treatment, and film historian Mark A. Vieira's suggestions that Sam Behrman swept in from New York and single-handedly rescued *Christina*'s foundering screenplay with a major rewrite that more or less became the shooting script. Unless one was actually in writers' rooms, it's often impossible to know which writers contributed which lines or scenes to any Hollywood picture from this period. Comparing drafts of scripts is rarely illuminating. There are often multiple names on those drafts, and few records of specific attribution. Such is largely the case with *Queen Christina*.

The assumption has survived that Salka was an inept writer whose script contributions were only marginal, and that the studio granted her screenplay credits in exchange for protecting Garbo's interests. A look at the larger world context shows that the truth is more complicated.

Queen Christina is a study in ambiguity. It's about a monarch with fluid gender identity and sexuality, a girl who was raised as if she were a boy in order to step into the shoes of her dead father, King Gustavus Adolphus of Sweden. As an adult, she counts both women and men as lovers and vacillates between duty and freedom. Ultimately she chooses freedom by refusing to marry and eventually by abdicating the throne. About only a few things is this sovereign unequivocal. She insists on peace in a time of war; she is a globalist among the xenophobes in her court; and she regards the arts and a diverse intellectual culture as more important to a civilized nation than militarism. All these things are true about both the historical Christina and her film counterpart. The Metro story veers from fact chiefly by having the queen abdicate for the love of a Spanish diplomat, when in reality she gave up the throne to convert from Protestantism to Catholicism.

Among the picture's early scenes is the lesbian *frisson* which Thalberg had asked Salka "tastefully" to incorporate, and which appears just as he requested. In fact, the physical interaction between Christina and her lady-in-waiting is nearly identical to two scenes from Leontine Sagan's *Mädchen in Uniform*: a genuflection and a passionate kiss on the mouth. Except for differences in the lighting—Expressionist and erotically enhanced in the *Mädchen* scene but more evenly glossy, as was Metro's style of the time, in *Christina*—the similarity of the sets, camera angles, and action would have been evident to audiences who had seen both pictures. While the lesbian scene suited Thalberg's commercial purposes, it was also a cinematic link—a lifeline, even—to the progressive sexual culture that Salka had left behind in Berlin, a culture which the National Socialists were now intent on destroying.

In other early scenes, the bookish queen reads Molière aloud, admiring his cleverness, and later invokes the work of other such international "men of genius" as the painter Velázquez and the dramatist Calderón. When the nation's archbishop warns Christina not to pollute the university in Uppsala with foreign scholarship ("To admit professors from Spain and Italy might corrupt the purity of our teaching"), Christina reproaches him: "The danger is not so much of corruption, milord, as of staleness. We need new wine in the old bottles." She also makes repeated pleas for the value of the arts above the empty glorification of war. "The people follow blindly," she says to her chancellor; "the generals will lead them to destruction." And when a torch-bearing crowd, encouraged by a bigoted member of Christina's own court, shouts slurs against the ambassador from Spain who has become her lover ("The queen despoils herself with a Spaniard!"), Christina insists on tolerance: "To the unreasonable tyranny of the mob and to the malicious tyranny of palace intrigue, I shall not submit."

Salka may or may not have written these lines of dialogue. But her sensibility is clear in all of them. All are speaking as much to the then-current crisis in Germany as to seventeenth-century Sweden. All decry a Germany dedicating itself to racial purity and anti-intellectualism as Salka was rewriting the script during the first half of 1933. In Salka's memoir, she recalls that *Queen Christina* was one of the last American films to be shown in the Third Reich, and mentions pointedly that, upon its release, "Friends and strangers wrote to me praising it for its pacifist tendency and 'abdication of power.'" Those central themes of the film—the rejection of war and the evanescence of state rule—are no less than a Weimar artist's condemnation of the National Socialists' martial power grab and an expectant prediction of their downfall. They reflect the sensibility of a writer who was receiving eyewitness accounts from her husband about the death threats in Germany to intellectuals, leftists, pacifists, and Jews, and about the thuggish repression of their ideals—the progressive, democratic ideals of the Weimar Republic which had nurtured the artistic missions of Salka and Berthold and their many well-known colleagues.

The "pacifist tendency" that Salka cites in the film was one of the most reviled offenses in Third Reich ideology, which attacked Jewish and Communist revolutionaries for Germany's humiliating losses during the Great War. National Socialists condemned as treasonous the suggestion that German troops might have been disillusioned about the noble cause of defending their fatherland. In early December 1930, a theatrical display of the National Socialists' crusade against pacifism was orchestrated by Joseph Goebbels during the Berlin premiere of Hollywood's adaptation of Erich Maria Remarque's pacifist novel about the Great War, *All Quiet on the Western Front*. Goebbels led a mob of Brownshirts into the theater, yelling "*Judenfilm!*" and other anti-Semitic abuse. Then the mob released stink bombs, sneezing powder, and live mice into the theater. It all sounds a bit farcical until the scene turned violent, with savage beatings of moviegoers who were presumed to be Jewish.

By the time Berthold had reached Berlin, in early 1933, the National Socialists' hatred of pacifism had become even more entrenched. One of the reasons Salka feared so for Berthold's safety was that he was a frequent contributor to *Die Weltbühne* (The World-Stage), a weekly magazine serving as the organ for the pacifist left in Germany, a publication especially despised by the National Socialists and banned after the burning of the Reichstag. *Christina*'s pacifism bewails the crushing of all such opposition to the new fascist regime in Germany. If the picture was, as Salka noted, one of the last of Metro's films to be screened in Germany after Hitler took power, it was also one of the last projections of a democratic-leaning Europe before similar visions and their visionaries were brutally repressed—before their world, as Berthold wrote to Salka, had ended.

More than any individual scene, however, it's *Queen Christina*'s overarching theme of ambiguity that gives it a defiantly antitotalitarian voice. In its final shot—one of the immortals in film history—Christina stares outward from the deck of a ship leaving Sweden, her throne abandoned, her lover dead, her future unknown. In preparing for the scene, Garbo asked her director what she should express, and the reply was: "Nothing... you must make your mind and your heart a complete blank." Such blankness asks us to appreciate the unknowable, to celebrate mystery. It's the opposite of propaganda: by remaining open to interpretation, it insists on freedom. It insists, as art always does, that nobody has total control over the narrative. And controlling the narrative is precisely the mission of every dictatorship. By choking off the free press, by intimidating and chasing out and eventually murdering artists and intellectuals—those "knights of the inkwell," as Hitler derided them in *Mein Kampf*—the National Socialists suppressed all journalism, theater, literature, painting, and film that threatened their stranglehold on the nation.

Christina's ambiguity invites viewers to project their own fantasies on Garbo's blank mask, to see what they want to see. This is what makes the picture a serious work of art and an eternally debatable one. According to Ben Urwand's 2013 book *The Collaboration: Hollywood's Pact with Hitler*, *Queen Christina* played for a robust forty-four days after its 1934 premiere in Nazi-dominated Berlin, earning National Socialist approval as "artistically valuable." The picture's value for the Third Reich lay in its perceived celebration of the *Führerprinzip*, or the "leader principle," a concept applied to Hitler maintaining that the Führer had a direct mystical line of communication with his people, who in turn invested him with absolute authority.

Somehow, the idea that the Swedish queen embodied the *Führerprinzip* was the official National Socialist takeaway from *Queen Christina*. Hitler's propagandists saw what they wanted to see, and ignored the rest. Clearly those officials were not bothering much about the picture's pacifist theme. And if they saw their fascist ideal of blind fealty in the film, their ideological enemies found their own reasons to laud the picture. In 1967, Salka wrote to Sam Behrman that Svetlana Alliluyeva, Josef Stalin's daughter, had mentioned in her own memoir how she had loved *Queen Christina* when her approving father arranged to have it screened for her when she was a child. "Did I ever tell you," Salka wrote to Behrman, "how many people wrote me in the Thirties how deeply affected they were by Christina's renunciation of power and her pacifism." To which Behrman replied: "to think of you and me slaving away in the Thalberg building to provide a thrill for the Stalin girl."

While *Christina* did its best to affirm antifascist values, no case can be made that it is an anti-Nazi movie. Those pictures would come later, under different circumstances. Metro's *The Mortal Storm* is set in Germany in 1933 during the same initial wave of persecution that Berthold had fled. While it was one of the first Hollywood pictures to condemn Nazi anti-Semitism, it did not appear until 1940. *Christina* does not offer any such blistering indictments. But if *Christina* is not an anti-Nazi movie, its pacifist sentiments suggest that it's a pro-Weimar movie, representing everything that Salka mourned and missed, and censuring the regime that suppressed its convictions. Salka deserves more credit for the picture's sensibility than she has received. She was already a passionate ambassador for fleeing European intellectuals and would grow more and more authoritatively into that role.

WHILE *QUEEN CHRISTINA* HOLDS UP A MIRROR to Salka's Europe of 1933, Salka was not the picture's only European influence. There was Garbo herself, who returned from her trip to Sweden with a suitcase full of notes on period architecture and clothing which she had taken in Uppsala and Stockholm. According to Metro's publicity chief Howard Strickling, Garbo was "a daily consultant in matters of historical importance...

In every department, Greta Garbo was technical advisor as well as the star of *Queen Christina*." Garbo's ideas came vividly to life at the hands of the scene designer Alexander Toluboff, who had studied architecture in St. Petersburg in the early 1900s and was responsible for the splendidly aged sets for Christina's castle, the village, and the country inn. There was also the brilliant cinematographer William H. Daniels, who was American but who had learned innovations in lighting from the Austrian director Erich von Stroheim, with whom he'd worked regularly early in his career.

Also influential was *Christina*'s director, hired in May 1933 after Garbo's two first choices proved unavailable. The final candidate, proposed by Salka, was Rouben Mamoulian, whose landmark Broadway all-black production of *Porgy* Salka and Berthold had admired when they first landed in New York in 1928.

Mamoulian was born an ethnic Armenian in 1897 in Tiflis (now Tbilisi), in the Caucasus in imperial Russia. For centuries the city was a sophisticated crossroads for trade and culture between Europe and Asia, its cobblestoned alleys and bazaars and cafés ringing with the languages of many nations. Artists and writers flocked there. Drama societies and orchestras thrived. As a watchful child in this milieu, Mamoulian learned to speak at least five languages and went on to study acting and directing at the Moscow Art Theatre. Eventually he made his way to Broadway, where he specialized in the integration of movement, music, and Expressionist light and shadow, creating a syncopating energy on the stage that was, for its time, brand-new. When Mamoulian got to Hollywood, he translated his theatrical gifts to the screen in *Applause*, *Love Me Tonight*, and *Dr. Jekyll and Mr. Hyde*. Garbo was sold on Salka's suggestion of Mamoulian after the actress saw a rough cut of his picture *The Song of Songs* and noted the tenderness with which he had directed Marlene Dietrich.

Always immaculately dressed in gray flannel, as if eager to trade his foreignness for the demeanor of an East Coast gentleman, Mamoulian was an artist whose power came from the creative tension between his outsider's sensibility and his wish to blend into the American studio system. He was also a tireless perfectionist, his dedication reminding Salka of Murnau. After long hours at the studio Mamoulian would rush through dinner, she said, "to come to my house and go over new problems, prodding, correcting again and again, saying *No* to every suggestion, sure that only he himself could find the solution."

Mamoulian's intensity paid off. Thalberg was fond of saying that every great film must have one great scene, and *Queen Christina* has two. Both are wordless, and both exhibit Mamoulian's genius for soliciting emotion through a theatrical tableau. The film's final shot, scripted by Harvey Gates, is the closing flourish in a picture that fuses Christina's character in the minds of moviegoers with Garbo's. "I'm tired of being a symbol," Christina complains to her chancellor in an earlier scene. "I long to be a human being, a longing I cannot suppress." Yet that final shot of the queen standing at the prow of a great ship and staring into an uncertain future is nothing if not symbolic. It made an indelible image of Garbo as the elusive queen of filmdom.

Mamoulian knew, as he told the film historian Kevin Brownlow, that in this final scene "the audience will write in whatever emotion they feel should be there." We imagine ourselves in Christina's place, and we ask: What will happen to me in an unknown land? What will I lose by abandoning my home and my former self? They are questions every émigré asks every day. They are questions Garbo, Salka, and Mamoulian continued to ask as they assimilated their European perspectives into American film culture.

The other great scene in *Queen Christina* takes place in a rural inn after the queen and her lover, the Spanish diplomat played by John Gilbert, have spent the night together. (The part had nearly gone to the young Laurence Olivier, but Garbo insisted on casting Gilbert, who was at that time down on his luck.) In a wordless reverie, Christina moves around the room, trying to ensure that she'll remember this moment of happiness by touching all the objects in it: the walls, a mirror, a spinning wheel, an icon, a pillow, the bedpost. "This has to be sheer poetry and feeling," Mamoulian told Garbo as she prepared for the scene. He filmed it using a metronome to time Garbo's movements, a method he had used in *Porgy* onstage and in the film *Love Me Tonight*. "I have been memorizing this room," Christina tells Don Antonio. "In the future, in my memory, I shall live a great deal in this room."

As the biographer Barry Paris describes it, Mamoulian and Garbo composed the scene together using Stanislavsky's technique of summoning emotion through sense memory. Four years earlier, after the death of Garbo's mentor Mauritz Stiller, the actress had asked to be shown where Stiller's belongings were stored. According to Stiller's lawyer, Garbo had walked around the room, touching Stiller's effects and making "sad little comments" about them: "This was the suitcase he bought in America," she said; "And those rugs—I remember when he bought them in Turkey."

Together, Garbo, Mamoulian, and cameraman William Daniels made the "memorizing this room" scene one of the most poignant in film history, an anticipation of loss and a premonition of Christina's abdication address later in the film, when she entreats her distraught subjects: "Let me remember you with love and loyalty, until memory is no more." Garbo's fondling of the objects in the room is more erotic than any love scene in the picture, made urgent by the memory and the expectation of grief. In the scene one senses that Garbo's pain over the hardships and losses she endured during her childhood was the sense memory closest to her heart. Her ability to access and convey that pain elevated her art to the very highest level of her time, and perhaps of all time.

GARBO WAS INITIALLY WORRIED that her countrymen would hate the picture. "I am so ashamed of *Christina*," she wrote to a Swedish friend in 1934. "Just imagine [our queen] abdicating for the sake of a little Spaniard." Yet the film was an enormous success in Sweden. Audiences there were thrilled to accept Garbo as the remade image of their monarch. In later years, Garbo felt more affinity for the role, telling Sam Behrman in 1962 that she personally resembled the actual Queen Christina more than any other character she played. As Thalberg had hoped, the picture did very well in Europe, grossing $1.843 million. American profits were a different story. Despite a lavish promotional campaign in the United States—a "talking billboard" on a Hollywood lot, a coloring contest, period fashion displays, and reviews that fused the tantalizing inscrutability of the star with that of the historical figure ("Queen

Christina is entirely Garbo, and Garbo is entirely Queen Christina")—the film brought in a disappointing $632,000 profit in America, marking the first time that a Garbo film earned less domestically than it did overseas.

Even so, as Salka said in her memoir, thirty years later strangers were writing to her to praise the picture and to lament that such films were no longer being made. "The most important critic is time," director Mamoulian was said to have once remarked. *Christina*'s enduring value, Salka believed, was "mainly due to Garbo and her unique personality, talent and beauty, but the film survives also on its own merits." Berthold agreed, writing to Salka in 1934 that the picture was "all in all a decent, coherent work, a clean film. Hollywood instead of Sweden—but skillful and controlled." He continued in a further letter: "You didn't want to make anything of your success with *Christina*, and that is within your . . . character. And yet it was a fine and decent success, and a well-deserved one, for ultimately it was your idea, you fought for it, even Mamoulian . . . was your suggestion . . . God knows you deserve to be admired for it . . . It was a victory for your character, your personality."

About Salka's work on the film, Garbo concurred. She appreciated how hard Salka had labored from the beginning to add sophistication to the script and to prevent it from devolving into a silly romance. Years later, Garbo had this to say about Salka to the photographer Cecil Beaton: "If there was ever any argument about a script I always had this woman to fight for me. She was indefatigable and worked on them to saturation point and always found something good that others wouldn't bother about."

DURING THE FILMING OF *QUEEN CHRISTINA*, from August to October 1933, Salka went to work on the script for Garbo's next film. Ten writers, including Vicki Baum, had already been struggling to adapt *The Painted Veil*, W. Somerset Maugham's 1925 novel about a doctor and his unfaithful wife who travel to China to combat a cholera epidemic. Salka was reluctant to take on the challenge of tailoring this melodrama for the picture's producer, Hunt Stromberg, a former sportswriter. The occasional call back to the *Christina* set to provide rewrites was a welcome interruption.

In the middle of those hectic months, a new romance unexpectedly made its way over her door-sill. Salka got a phone call from her friend Fred Zinnemann, Berthold's former assistant who was just beginning his directing career. Zinnemann told Salka that the Berlin-born younger son of Max Reinhardt was now living in Santa Monica and had asked to meet her. That evening, Salka's ex-lover Oliver Garrett was leaving through her front gate after their customary after-work drink when he passed a young man who'd unfolded himself from a decaying old roadster and was heading to the door. Mildly jealous, Oliver wondered who this could be.

Gottfried Reinhardt was twenty-two years old to Salka's forty-four, a large boy-man with a wry smile, his father's soulful gaze, and a thicket of shiny brown hair. He wanted to work in pictures, was then assisting Lubitsch at Paramount, and he told Salka that it had been Berthold, while in Berlin during the early months of that year, who had persuaded Gottfried's mother to let him make the journey to Hollywood.

Gottfried was funny and shrewd beyond his years, brimming

with political opinions and vaulting ambition. He asked Salka's permission to smoke in an endearing way that reminded her of her former lover, the Viennese art historian Ludwig Münz. In fact everything about Gottfried, as they laughed together that evening, called Salka back to her earlier life—to Berlin, to her days in the Reinhardt theaters, to all the old friends she'd left behind. Where Oliver Garrett had been an envoy to the world of American culture, Gottfried was a filament of her past thrown across the ocean, binding her once again to Europe. There was no resisting him. "I did not jump, but slid into a love affair, which to many people appeared quite insane," Salka later wrote. Salka and Gottfried became an unofficial but unmistakable couple and remained so throughout the next decade, deeply involved emotionally, physically, and eventually professionally. For long periods Gottfried lived in the house with Salka. As often as not he performed the host duties at the Mabery Road Sunday parties, until the day came in 1943 when one of them would break the other's heart.

In July, Berthold at last returned from Europe and folded himself into this complicated household situation. He stayed only until the summer's end, because he and Gaumont-British had at last agreed on the film which he would write and direct in London. It was based on a Viennese novel called *Little Friend*, and it told of the damaging effects of a disintegrating marriage on a couple's young daughter. Once again, the financial dynamic of the Viertels' marriage was shifting: Salka continued to draw her Metro salary, but now in London Berthold would be bringing in a decent paycheck as well. In the meantime their sexual relationship had continued down its regretful but certain path. Berthold's "lost year," so far from home, stood impassably between them. "Odysseus resented bitterly that Penelope had not waited patiently for his return, though he himself had not renounced the Nausicaas," Salka noted. Still, they refused to abandon their marriage. "He was as dear to me as ever," remembered Salka, "but the impulse which had always drawn us to each other, no matter what happened, was no longer there. I felt an enormous tenderness for him but also the sad certainty that never again would we be lovers."

This was the summer of the *Christina* shoot, and of Mamoulian's round-the-clock obsession with every detail. On many midnights, after long evenings when Mamoulian came to Mabery Road to mull solutions to the problems that had arisen during the day's filming, Berthold emerged from the room where he'd been working with his secretary, one of the first refugees to land in Hollywood. Gottfried, whom Berthold liked, would often be there as well, to lament the latest horrors perpetrated in Germany. Salka recalled that "then, exhausted, we all had a nightcap together."

Salka always insisted that her sons were undamaged by their parents' complex relationship. During the day she was a sentimental and demanding mother, alternately insisting on her devotion and haranguing the boys about their studies. But the nights were her own. The boys adjusted to the domestic changes, as children do, disregarding the opera buffa bed-switching among the adults in the house. For them Gottfried was like a genial young uncle in a house that was constantly full of people—in fact increasingly crowded, even during these early years, with refugees. Gottfried was kind and encouraging toward the Viertel boys, offering Peter money for every French novel he agreed to read. But there was never any confusion for the boys about Berthold's primacy for them among the Mabery Road relationships. They were happy to see their father return from his travels, and sorry to see their mother in tears when he left again. Berthold's long absences and the household's shifting emotional alliances affected each of the boys, in different ways, more profoundly than Salka was willing to admit.

When summer slid into fall, Berthold set off for London. Salka packed his suitcases and wrote out the instructions for his diet which she knew he would ignore. Hans, Peter, Salka, and Gottfried accompanied Berthold to the Pasadena train station. Tommy, age eight, was too sad to go with them. As always during farewells, Salka broke down in tears. She ran beside the train for as long as she could, until Gottfried brought her back to the children and they set off for home.

From the *Chief* Berthold wrote to Salka: "remember, never do anything out of your mad generosity. Don't jump head-on into decisions you might later regret. Cable me, phone me, and never give up loving me. Do you hear, never! As for me, only death can cure my addiction to you."

5

FATHERLAND

From the very beginning, the studios gave us Papas.

—LUCILLE BALL

I once had a beautiful fatherland. The oak tree
Grew so tall there, the violets gently nodded.
It was a dream.

—HEINRICH HEINE

LOS ANGELES, LONDON, AND SANARY-SUR-MER
1934–1936

THE ANTIFASCIST EXODUS FROM EUROPE was never homogeneous and never fixed. It evolved constantly, prompted by specific geopolitical events, and caused many different kinds of people with different motivations to move around the globe in different ways. The spirit of the Weimar Republic, the critic Alex Ross has written, "spoke in the meeting of opposites." That clamor was no less dissonant in exile.

In 1933, over 53,000 emigrants left Germany, of whom about 37,000 were Jews. At the time many of those emigrants believed that Hitler's success was unsustainable and that those who had been forced to leave would soon be able to return. Kurt Weill, with whom Berthold had been reunited in Prague after the Reichstag fire, wrote about Germany at that time: "I consider what is going on here so sickening that I cannot imagine it lasting more than a couple of months... But one could be very wrong." Like Weill, most emigrants in this period ventured only as far as the nearest safe place: Prague or Paris, Amsterdam or London. Few were thinking yet of Los Angeles.

Even this early, for many the prospect of exile was so abhorrent that they considered suicide their only option. Paul Nikolaus, one of the leading political comedians in the Berlin cabaret circuit, killed himself in Lucerne at the end of March 1933. From one of his last letters: "For once, no joke. I am taking my own life. Why? I could not return to Germany without taking it there. I cannot work there now, I do not want to work there now, and yet unfortunately I have fallen in love with my fatherland. I cannot live in these times." Others ended their lives with the same despondency in the following months and years, in Europe and around the world.

THE LONDON OF BERTHOLD'S *LITTLE FRIEND* DAYS was not yet overflowing with refugees, as it would be four years later, after the Austrian annexation. (By the end of 1938, an estimated 11,000 would reach England.) But by 1934 plenty had gathered there already, including a convergence of Weimar cinema people. Actor Fritz Kortner emigrated with his entire family, and tried to persuade Brecht and the novelist Leonhard Frank to join him. Conrad Veidt was there, playing the lead in a British adaptation of Lion Feuchtwanger's novel *Jew Süss*. (A second, malevolently anti-Semitic version of the film would be made in Germany in 1940 and would become a wildly successful propaganda tool.) Writers had begun to settle in London as well, for varying periods: Stefan Zweig, Arthur Koestler, Alfred Kerr, Elias Canetti. Yet for Berthold, assimilating into London's moviemaking community came with frustrations. His grasp of English was good, but he had difficulty adjusting to yet another new film culture whose pace was even slower than Hollywood's, with too many long weekends and maddening tea breaks.

Berthold lost his dialogue writer for *Little Friend* when she left abruptly to work on a production of her own play. Through a British cabaret singer named Jean Ross, Berthold heard about a friend of Ross's who had recently published an interesting second novel. Berthold paged through the book and pronounced it "genial," by which he meant in the German sense "gifted with genius." He hired the boyish and handsome thirty-year-old writer, who had no experience in film and whose name was Christopher Isherwood, sight unseen.

Berthold didn't really need a writer. He was lonely, and he wanted an audience. Isherwood had spent five years in Germany before 1933 and was fluent enough in the language to understand Berthold's ironic asides and to listen appreciatively when Berthold recited his poems. "He needed an amateur, an innocent, a disciple, a victim," remembered Isherwood in the 1970s. Berthold admitted as much to Salka in a January 1934 letter. "I need disciples," Berthold told her about Isherwood, "because they give me the necessary illusion that I am working in a community and not for an industry, [an illusion] with which I cannot dispense if I want to be productive."

Isherwood was happy enough to play the amateur for Berthold. He loved movies and was eager to learn what he could.

More important to Isherwood, though, was his determination to record this experience for his own literary purposes, as he recorded everything. He went on to create a memorable portrait of Berthold as the Austrian filmmaker Friedrich Bergmann in one of his best novels, *Prater Violet* (1945). In that book he described Berthold, who was then forty-eight but looked much older, this way: "His head was magnificent, and massive as sculptured granite... I studied the big firm chin, the grim compressed line of the mouth, the harsh furrows cutting down from the imperious nose, the bushy black hair in the nostrils. The face was the face of an emperor, but the eyes were the dark mocking eyes of his slave." "I knew that face," the Isherwood character continues. "It was the face of a political situation, an epoch. The face of Central Europe."

Isherwood was fifteen years younger than Salka, born in 1904. The heir to a once-grand country estate in Cheshire, he was a schoolboy of eleven when his father was killed at Ypres during the Great War. In 1929, at age twenty-five, Isherwood moved to Berlin, eager to escape from a homeland in which his homosexuality was a criminal offense. Because he considered himself a fugitive from a country that rejected him for the ineradicable truth of his sexual orientation, Isherwood came to identify deeply with refugees. In *Prater Violet* the Berthold character delivers a mild objection to this, insisting that Christopher, for all his sympathy, can't really understand what it means to be a refugee. "You have always been safe and protected," he tells Christopher. "Your home has never been threatened. You cannot know what it is like to be an exile, a perpetual stranger... I am bitterly ashamed that I am here, in safety."

When he was living in Berlin, Isherwood fell in love with a German boy named Heinz Neddermeyer, with whom he fled the country in 1933. During the *Little Friend* months, after Heinz's tourist visa expired and he was required to return to Germany, Isherwood spent much of his time seeking permission for Heinz to return to England. Working with Berthold helped to distract Isherwood from this personal anxiety. He became captivated and highly entertained by Berthold's work habits.

These included hours of manic procrastination in the older man's smoky Knightsbridge lair, during which Berthold would expostulate brilliantly about everything except the project at hand: his *Die Truppe* productions in the 1920s, from which he would recite entire speeches; the poetry of Hölderlin; the dark future of the world; the Reichstag fire trial, which was then in the news. Berthold was furiously energetic in some hours and balky in others. There were black diabetic rages if he forgot to eat, and ravenous mealtimes when at last he did. He missed his family in California and talked to Isherwood constantly about Salka and his sons: Hans, tall and thin at sixteen, with a passion for Marxist politics; Peter, a sporty fifteen, with effortless charm and good grades; Tommy, at ten, bewildered by the world, with the soul of a poet. Berthold would show Isherwood their latest photos and letters, and would describe the white house with its green roof, and the canyon and the Pacific shoreline, all of which seemed powerfully exotic and romantic to Isherwood. Berthold told Isherwood that when he came to visit them in California he would meet Garbo, would see her every day, because she came to swim and ride horses with the boys.

About a decade later, this came true. Isherwood would be living over the garage on Mabery Road, and would become one of Salka's dearest friends, perhaps the only one of her famous writer friends to mention her more than cursorily in memoirs and diaries. For now, Isherwood introduced Berthold to an actress named Beatrix Lehmann, a very good actress from a distinguished literary family who was not afraid to transform herself utterly for a role, and who came to meet Berthold for the first time, as Isherwood remembered it, wearing an ensemble made mostly of green feathers. Berthold and Beatrix embarked on a serious romance, a "humanly consolidated" relationship, as Berthold wrote candidly to Salka. By 1935 he had cast Beatrix in the second of his Gaumont-British films, *The Passing of the Third Floor Back*, and was living with her in her Victorian house on the Thames, as he told Salka, largely "in seclusion."

By then Isherwood had moved on, seeking corners of the world where he and Heinz could live together without fear of arrest. But Isherwood called the making of *Little Friend* "a new and absolutely necessary phase of his education as a writer," and he wrote movingly about his friendship with Berthold. "Beneath outer consciousness, two other beings, anonymous, impersonal, without labels, had met and recognized each other, and had clasped hands," Isherwood wrote. "He was my father. I was his son. And I loved him very much."

IN SANTA MONICA, Salka had been writing letters begging her mother to leave Poland for America. But Auguste Steuermann could not imagine starting a new life in a strange land. She would not abandon her home, her husband's burial site, and her three other children who were scattered around Europe. Salka's brother Edward was busy giving concerts in Krakow and Warsaw and teaching piano master classes in Lwów. For the moment he was undeterred by the robust anti-Semitism flourishing under Poland's authoritarian leader, Józef Piłsudski.

Salka's sister Rose—as delicate and reserved as Salka was forthright—continued to live in a now thoroughly Nazified Dresden, where her husband, Josef Gielen, was director of the State Theater. The position was too lucrative for Gielen, a Catholic, to abandon, and secure enough that Goebbels's Ministry of Culture was willing to overlook the inconvenient fact of Gielen's Jewish wife.

Rose had been breathing the reek of National Socialism in Dresden since at least 1930. She had by now retreated from any kind of social life, declining to attend the theater so as not to be forced to hear the compulsory "Heil Hitler." Salka had stopped corresponding with Rose for fear that the Gestapo, which periodically searched the Gielens' apartment, would find her letters and use them to incriminate her sister.

Salka's youngest sibling, Zygmunt Steuermann, whose nickname was Dusko, was a gifted athlete who had been a star player for Sambor's local soccer team. He went on to distinguish himself with other clubs in Lwów and Warsaw, and during the 1920s he played twice, brilliantly, for the national Polish soccer team. He had fathered a child with the pretty housekeeper at Wychylowka named Hania and was doing his best to provide for his family with poorly paid jobs in and around Warsaw. He accepted financial help from Salka, whose weekly Metro paycheck had risen to $550. In addition to Dusko and Auguste, more and more people were now depending on portions of Salka's Metro salary, as were various rescue agencies and causes. Many refugees from Germany were already making appeals to Salka's generosity. "There was not a day," she wrote, "that I did not get letters asking for help, and I besieged my American friends for affidavits."

Affidavits were developed in accordance with the U.S. immigration policies instituted in 1924 and 1930, which denied entrance to anyone who might be "likely to become a public charge." They were sworn testimonies from American relatives or friends that guaranteed financial support to particular immigrants in case of need. The governmental processing of affidavits was complex and time-consuming, and American citizens who agreed to provide them undertook a grave responsibility. Affidavits were neither offered nor granted lightly.

Though he did not emigrate through Salka's auspices, Arnold Schoenberg was among the first refugees from her wide European circle to reach Los Angeles after Hitler's rise to power. The Viennese composer arrived in September 1934 with his wife Gertrud and little daughter Nuria. In October of the previous year, Schoenberg had been abruptly dismissed from the position he'd held since 1926 at the Prussian Academy of Arts in Berlin. Denounced as a Jew and a leading purveyor of "degenerate music," Schoenberg was stripped of his citizenship and any possibility of employment in Europe. As a refugee in Paris, just before his sixtieth birthday, he defiantly reconverted to Judaism (having converted to Lutheranism back in 1898) and departed for America, where he found a teaching position at the Malkin Conservatory in Boston.

Commuting between Boston and New York during the harsh

East Coast winter worsened Schoenberg's asthma, prompting him within the year to head west toward California. Salka looked forward to her longtime friend's arrival. She had known him since 1911, when she was in her early twenties, through an introduction from the pianist-composer Ferruccio Busoni in Berlin. She wasted no time inviting Schoenberg and his family to her Sunday gatherings. On bright afternoons on Salka's terrace, guests could spot Schoenberg, his dark eyes blazing in a finely sculpted head, as he played Ping-Pong and mingled with the likes of Charlie Chaplin and Harpo Marx.

Schoenberg's welcome at Salka's house helped to mitigate the cool reception his dodecaphonic works were receiving from the mostly baffled Los Angeles classical music community. Having been, as he later wrote, "driven into Paradise," Schoenberg felt he had scant support on the West Coast for what many perceived as the too-bizarre evolution of his modernist oeuvre. Nor did he yet have the benefit in America of the talented disciples who were then touring throughout Europe, familiarizing audiences with his latest works. One of the most prominent of Schoenberg's interpreters was Salka's brother, Edward Steuermann.

Among the guests whom Schoenberg met on Mabery Road was the puckish French playwright Marcel Achard, who had arrived from France to work on Maurice Chevalier's pictures. There were the Metro studio composers Dimitri Tiomkin (born in Russia) and Bronislaw Kaper (born in Poland). There was the American pianist and comedian Oscar Levant, whom Schoenberg would take on as a pupil in Los Angeles for a three-year stretch. (Schoenberg was an electrifying teacher; his other Los Angeles students included the cross-cultural maverick Lou

Harrison, the studio composer David Raksin, and a twenty-two-year-old John Cage.) And at Salka's house Schoenberg was reunited with his longtime Berlin colleague Otto Klemperer, the new conductor of the Los Angeles Philharmonic.

A Mahler protégé with a vigorous devotion to innovation during this second phase of his long career, Klemperer had also fled from Europe the previous year. Five days after he arrived in Los Angeles, Klemperer made a thrilling debut with the Philharmonic, after which Salka and Gottfried, along with Charlie Chaplin and the film director King Vidor, went backstage to congratulate him. Klemperer was as disconcerted as Schoenberg was by the casualness of Los Angeles, where audiences clapped between movements and whistled their approval, and where the Philharmonic musicians were known to address their conductor, a stringently formal personage, as "Klempie."

Klemperer met this odd new environment with gusto, declaring in a letter "how infinitely grateful I must be to the great America, which gives me bread and work." Schoenberg took to paradise with similar enthusiasm. He became a UCLA football fan and played tennis with Chaplin and George Gershwin. When Gershwin died suddenly from a brain tumor in 1937 at age thirty-eight, Schoenberg eulogized him in a moving radio address. "Music to him was the air he breathed," Schoenberg said. "There is no doubt that he was a great composer... But may I mention that I lose also a friend, whose amiable personality was very dear to me."

AT CHRISTMASTIME IN 1934, an invitation to Salka's house came to a newly arrived German-Jewish composer in his late twenties named Franz Waxman. Upon entering the living room at Mabery Road, Waxman recognized some of the guests from Berlin, where he'd worked as a musician and arranger for the Weintraub Syncopators—a popular jazz band—and in the German film business as the orchestrator of Friedrich Hollaender's score for *The Blue Angel*. On his way home from work one evening in early 1934 in Berlin, a gang of thugs shouting anti-Semitic slurs had shoved Waxman into the gutter and beaten him. That night he and his fiancée boarded a train to Paris, where they found rooms in a refugee hotel that also housed Peter Lorre, Billy Wilder, and Friedrich Hollaender. The former chief of Germany's UFA studios, Erich Pommer, also in Paris at that time, gave Waxman his first major film assignment, the score for Fritz Lang's *Liliom*. Pommer's next producing job, *Music in the Air*, for Fox Films and director Joe May, brought Waxman to Hollywood.

In Salka's living room that Christmas, Waxman gave his name to a stranger who immediately started out of his chair and proclaimed, "My God! I've been looking all over the world for you! You are the composer for my next film!" This was the British director James Whale, who was then preparing to make *The Bride of Frankenstein* at Universal. Whale had heard Waxman's score for *Liliom* and was impressed by the composer's invention of a "ghost orchestra." In that picture Waxman had put a microphone up in the dome of the theater in which he was recording to give the impression that the music was coming from heaven.

Waxman's film score for *The Bride of Frankenstein* was the debut for one of the most prolific composing careers in Hollywood history. He worked on 144 films, earned twelve Oscar nominations, and won twice, for *Sunset Boulevard* and *A Place in the Sun*. In 1947 he conceived and launched the Los Angeles International Music Festival and piloted it for twenty years, premiering works by Stravinsky, Schoenberg, and Shostakovich and significantly enhancing the city's postwar sophistication. Could one say that Salka, by inviting Waxman to her house on that Sunday, was in some way responsible for his thirty-year career? "Absolutely," said Waxman's son John, who believes that, in Hollywood, talent counts for 25 percent and connections for 75. One could have all the talent in the world, as Franz Waxman did, but without a fortunate link to the right people, one was nothing. As a connector, Salka was more valuable than rubies to a foreign young composer who showed up at her door and was offered the introductions he needed. Waxman paid his good fortune forward by writing affidavits for Jews desperate to leave Europe. Many of those beneficiaries were strangers to him, including an entire family in Vienna named Waxman, to whom he was not related and of whom he had never heard. Their school-age daughter had written to him out of the blue after seeing his name on the credits at the cinema. He saved them all.

AT METRO, preparations for Salka's next picture were not going smoothly. *The Painted Veil* was scheduled to ride along on a wave of Asia-themed pictures, including Paramount's *Shanghai Express* and Columbia's *The Bitter Tea of General Yen*. The production adhered to Metro's formula of lavish spending and compulsive micromanagement, but it was ill-fated from the outset. The newly empowered Production Code

Administration, commandeered by Joseph I. Breen, had begun its enforcement in June 1934, a month before shooting was scheduled. Breen went to war right away against the picture's blasphemies, insisting on diminishing its characters' adulterous misdeeds and ratcheting up their punishments.

But the picture's problems went beyond the imposition of PCA sanctimony. While most of the factors that made *Queen Christina* so successful were present again—a huge budget and promotional campaign, elaborate reproductions of exotic locales, an international supporting cast, a luminescent Garbo—the magic was not. Creative antagonisms sparked by the many screenplay drafts from competing writers, which had given *Queen Christina* both its precision and its depth, in *The Painted Veil* produced an insipid drama with little emotional accessibility. Garbo's costumes, so expressively designed by Adrian in *Christina*, flirted here with the ridiculous. In a 1934 letter, Berthold remarked to Salka of "the abuse of Greta as a mannequin for the tailor Adrian."

Salka's participation as a writer was much narrower this time. After *Christina* she had hoped to expand her credits, complaining in letters to Berthold that she didn't want to write only for Garbo. Salka was consigned mostly to rewrites for *The Painted Veil*, particularly for some of its problematic last scenes, and she collaborated with fellow writers John Meehan and Edith Fitzgerald on the final complete screenplay. But her contributions were fewer than those of Vicki Baum, the Viennese author of the best-selling novel on which Metro's popular 1932 film *Grand Hotel* had been based. Baum changed *The Painted Veil*'s lead character from an Englishwoman named Kitty to an Austrian named Katrin to explain Garbo's accent and to add some Continental glamour. As with *Christina*, a succession of other writers including Salka then reworked the script until the picture began shooting in June 1934.

"I have repressed the memories of *The Painted Veil*," Salka later wrote, perhaps because she shared Garbo's private opinion of the finished picture as "rubbish." While Garbo biographer Mark A. Vieira takes pains to undervalue Salka's contributions toward *Queen Christina*, both he and Barry Paris exaggerate Salka's participation in the inferior *Painted Veil*, pinning the blame for its faults squarely on her shoulders. Writes Vieira: "[Garbo's] reliance on Salka Viertel, who was not qualified to judge literary properties or dramatic values, was undermining the best efforts of producers like Stromberg, directors like [Richard] Boleslawski, and even visual artists like [cinematographer William] Daniels."

In fact, Salka was highly qualified to judge this literary property. She knew Maugham's works well. She had read *The Painted Veil*—which the English critic Lytton Strachey called "a novel at the top of the second rank"—shortly after its publication in 1928. And she appeared as an actress in the German-language film version of Maugham's play *The Sacred Flame* in 1931. Salka had informed opinions about the novel and its prolific author. "He is admittedly imaginative, or better half imaginative," Salka wrote about Maugham in her diary in 1961. "Still I should take to heart the lesson he gives. Hard work can make a writer." The film adaptation of *Veil* was quite faithful to Maugham's novel, thanks in no small part to Salka's familiarity with the author.

For most people in Hollywood, Maugham was a kind of literary avatar of Metro's luxury brand. Multiple versions of his novels, stories, and plays have been made and remade into more than sixty films. Salka was less than enthusiastic about the *Veil* project, which had been kicking around the studio since 1932, and which Garbo herself had chosen as her next picture after *Christina*. Salka called *Veil* "a nightmare of a film," and wrote to Berthold in confidence that she thought Garbo's performance ruinously bad. "The 'mystery-fake' does not work anymore," she said to him about Garbo's acting. "I am sick of it."

Salka's irritation with Garbo was real but momentary. Certainly it was understandable from someone who was on call, day and night, for the actress's every professional and personal need, from redrafting her scripts to meeting her at the boat after her European vacations. Because of the magnitude of Garbo's celebrity, by this point most of the actress's relationships were purely transactional. Salka came the closest among Garbo's few intimates to overriding this dynamic, but even she was restricted by its code. According to Salka's son Peter, Garbo was "not all that great a friend. Actually, she used my mother more than my mother used her, which sounds funny, because she was a star and my mother was an oarsman in the galley." (Peter was making a sly multilingual pun here: Salka's last name, Steuermann, means "helmsman" or "first mate" in German.)

Garbo's enduring relationship with Salka was as complex as a long marriage. By letting go of grudges and combining their strengths, each became stronger. Years later, in her diary, Salka wrote about Garbo's assets with longing: "If I had her position—her looks—her independence—I mean financial independence—what influence would I have in the world." Despite their mutual annoyances, the two women managed for decades to weather the recurring ebbs in their partnership with their loyalty intact.

In any event, Salka would never have confided even a hint of her frustrations with Garbo and *The Painted Veil* to anyone other than Berthold or Gottfried. The stakes were too high. Too many people were relying on her paycheck. Berthold provided his own reminders. "DO NOT BREAK UP YOUR SITUATION OVER THERE," he wrote in a telegram to Salka in June 1934. Berthold respected Salka's role as a champion of the dispossessed and he understood the value of her job and their Santa Monica house as means of providing refuge. In February 1934 he had written to Salka that it was "the instinct of the Mother" that had motivated her to entrench herself in Hollywood and to buy the house. By 1940 he would expand on these thoughts, writing to Salka that "the house is a position, a symbol, it is famous, one must defend it! So many people in our time, the most unfortunate and bewildered in the human migration, look forward to hope in you and the famous house on Mabery Road, a shelter, a place of cordial assistance and a sort of oasis in the ever-widening desert."

At Metro, Salka was next assigned to work on *Anna Karenina* for producer David Selznick, who had joined the studio in 1933 and was turning out a series of elegant hits, including *Dinner at Eight* and *Manhattan Melodrama*. Like most screenwriters, Salka thought highly of Selznick, gratefully remembering the help he'd offered in attempting to finance Eisenstein's Mexico picture when he was RKO's production head in 1932.

Selznick's arrival at Metro came about during a studio shakeup that took the shape, as so many film industry conflicts did, of an Oedipal drama. During the time that Salka wrote her first *Christina* draft, Irving Thalberg embarked on a nine-month absence from the studio, triggered by the heart attack he suffered at the end of 1932 and enduring through a long convalescence spent partly in Europe. In the meantime, Louis Mayer persuaded Selznick, who was married to Mayer's younger daughter Irene, to come to work at Metro. ("The son-in-law also rises" was the quip about these developments around the lot.) In the summer of 1933, while Thalberg was still in Europe, he learned that Mayer had removed him as vice president in charge of production and restructured the studio's organization. Instead of serving as the sole production supervisor, Thalberg would now head one of four production units, along with Selznick, Walter Wanger, and Hunt Stromberg, with a second string of unit producers working for the big four and everyone operating under Mayer's prevailing authority.

Mayer had a few reasons for decentralizing Thalberg's role. There was the legitimate question about Thalberg's fragile health: how much longer could he continue overseeing the studio's punishing schedule of fifty-two movies per year? Mayer was also hoping to prevent the younger man from usurping his sovereignty. In December 1932, the influential business monthly *Fortune* had published a long article that purported to explain why Metro alone among the studios was turning a profit during the Depression. *Fortune*'s answer, without equivocation, was Irving Thalberg. In fact the unsigned article, written in an arch tone that oozed anti-Semitism, did more to burnish the myth of Thalberg as a potent, furtive Jewish genius than anything prior to Fitzgerald's 1941 novel *The Last Tycoon*. "Chattering at lunch," the article wheedled, "Mr. Thalberg and his underlings resemble in their gloomy refectory the personnel of an agitated Last Supper, with Mr. Thalberg as a nervous

Nazarene free, however, from the presentiment that any of his disciples will deny or even contradict him."

Alarmed by the prospect that the protégé he had nurtured might be planning to overthrow him, Mayer acted swiftly to protect himself. "I'll look after him like my own son," he had said in 1923 when he'd hired the twenty-four-year-old Thalberg, who'd instantly been nicknamed the "Boy Wonder." A decade later, the father sought to prevent the son's ascendancy.

All around the studios, in this early age of psychoanalysis, daddy issues were playing out among men and women from broken or wretched homes, among the fatherless or the cruelly fathered, the Hamlets and the Oedipuses, the Cinderellas and the foundlings. Thalberg himself served as a father figure to many. Donald Ogden Stewart, a close friend and writing partner of Salka's, was five years older than Thalberg, yet thoroughly in his thrall. "It was a real father-and-son relationship," Stewart said, "and you wanted to please father." In the meantime, all the Metro actresses honed their performances under Thalberg's paternal gaze.

David Selznick was haunted by a painful love for his own father, Lewis J. Selznick, a high-flying film pioneer brought low by gambling and bankruptcy. The younger Selznick would reprise the same Icarian themes throughout his own career, forever trying to avenge his father's losses. He doubled down on his filial obligations by marrying Mayer's daughter Irene in 1930, then reporting for work at his father-in-law's studio in 1933.

They were all little fatherlands, the Golden Age studios—perhaps Metro most of all. Yiddish-speaking wits maintained that MGM stood for "Mayer's *Ganze Mishpocheh*" (Mayer's Entire Family), a wisecrack that perched on the edge of truth.

Mayer had no problem with nepotism, insisting: "Sure, my nieces and nephews work here, and all my wife's relatives, too. Why shouldn't those with *mazel* in a family help out the others?" He considered himself a father to everyone in the studio, related or not, and was sentimental about his role. His favorites among all Metro's pictures were the Andy Hardy series: sugary comedies in which a small-town judge presides over his orderly family with unswerving rectitude. This was Mayer's perception of his own role as the studio's paterfamilias: confident, magnanimous, and supreme.

Mayer's approach to leadership was a defense against the fear and loathing of Jews that was rampant in Los Angeles and throughout America. In his later years, Gottfried Reinhardt told the German writer Christa Wolf that during the 1930s "even the richest Jews were not allowed to join country clubs and other associations...and they couldn't stay in certain hotels." Gottfried's father had had that happen to him, "his father who was a god in the theater world of Berlin." This bigotry was likely suffered by Max Reinhardt at just this time, in September 1934, when he came to Hollywood to mount his legendary theater production of *A Midsummer Night's Dream* at the Hollywood Bowl.

Certainly Mayer felt the sting of that same humiliation. The 1932 *Fortune* article that had praised Thalberg with such faint damnation had also dripped with disdain toward Mayer, sneering at his immigrant origins and accusing him of sucking up to power as only an avaricious Hebrew could. ("Mr. Mayer's courtesies to U.S. Senators and Vice Admirals make it easier for M-G-M to borrow a battleship for *Armored Cruiser* or a fleet of Navy planes for *Hell Divers*... Mr. Mayer's efforts fall into...the...category...of personal connections, intrigues, and affiliations . . . It is his business simply to get the most and give the least.") In response, Mayer kept his head down, reinforced the coffers of the house of Metro, gave generously to a variety of charities and the Republican Party, and retained his faith in family.

But family did not always keep its faith in him. *Anna Karenina* was one of the last pictures David Selznick produced before he left his father-in-law's studio to start his own production company. As with Thalberg, Selznick's was another bid for independence by a recalcitrant son. Before Selznick left, he was pleased that Garbo asked to work with him and hoped they could settle on a comedy for her, or maybe a new Broadway play called *Dark Victory*—anything other than a historical costume drama. But these failed to materialize, so they acceded to Salka's preference for Tolstoy's ill-fated heroine. Garbo had already played the role once before in a 1927 silent version that had diminished the story with an audience-pleasing happy ending.

In her memoirs, Salka recalled her *Anna Karenina* days as smooth and collegial. She became friendly with her initial cowriter, a tall, full-figured Englishwoman named Clemence Dane, who told Salka that she had never had a love affair. "So we shall rely on *your* experience, my dear Salka," she declared as they began work on the script. Selznick asked for major changes on the draft they turned in, but Dane had a play in rehearsal in London and begged off, so to Salka's delight Sam Behrman was called in once again to cowrite the final script.

During her collaboration with Behrman on the scene depicting Anna's suicide, Salka paced the room, as was her custom, and dramatized the action. The night train approaches; Anna throws herself between the cars; we see her prone figure on the rails as the train disappears; the camera lingers on a woman's handbag on the embankment. Finally, overcome by her own theatrics, Salka cried out, as much to herself as to Behrman: "And that's what's left of a human being." At this Behrman couldn't help but burst out laughing, and the line became a joking catchphrase between them, in later years often serving as the sign-off for their letters. (A sample New Year's telegram from Salka to Behrman: "All good luck for a better 1942 in spite of all predictions. I hope it will bring us peace on earth and bring about a happy reunion on a happier assignment please don't forget what's left of a human being which is still your Salka . . .")

But the *Anna Karenina* production was not as lighthearted as Salka represented it. Selznick became locked in a battle with both the Legion of Decency, which exerted control over the nation's twenty million Catholic moviegoers, and Breen's Production Code Administration. Again the problem was the picture's theme of adultery, without which there would be no story whatsoever, and for which the censors insisted that the characters be roundly punished. As Selznick put it: "We had to eliminate everything that could even remotely be classified as a passionate love scene; and we had to make it perfectly clear that not merely did Anna suffer but that [her lover] Vronsky suffered."

Offended that a classic of world literature might be so boorishly violated, Selznick worked hard with Salka and Behrman to preserve as much of its grandeur as they could. Still Breen continued to order rewrite after rewrite. Throughout, Salka appreciated Selznick's vigorous leadership. Although they never again worked together, the two remained lifelong friends. Selznick would go on to give Salka's son Peter his first job in Hollywood, as a summer filing clerk in his story department when Peter was seventeen, and would later put Peter under contract as a writer just before the United States entered the war.

Neutered as it was by the censors, Selznick's *Anna Karenina* is a solidly good picture but not a great one. Intimate instead of expansive, it's lavishly inoffensive, so as to please the PCA, and impeccably tasteful, so as to please Selznick. The thrills it offers are chiefly visual: Cedric Gibbons's opulent art direction, William Daniels's lambent cinematography. Clarence Brown's directing is reliably on brand, opening the picture with a dazzling reverse tracking shot of a sumptuous banquet table laden with delicacies. Over the unhurried course of the shot, the table appears endlessly elongated, as if to prove that the bounty of the house of Metro goes on forever. Berthold wrote to Salka in October 1935: "I saw 'Karenina' and found the film nicely told...And it occurred to me that every film with Greta has to be more or less the same. As a type, she no longer belongs wholly to our time...Sooner or later you will have to try, independent of her, to shape one of your more contemporary ideas—to make a film of your own invention, and where your story is the main and primary thing—whoever acts in it."

But there was no chance at this moment that Salka could separate herself from Garbo. At Metro the two women were roped together like mountaineers on a dangerous incline. Garbo was still the studio's major revenue producer and every decision about her career was crucial. Thalberg was back at work, his mood much improved, and his production unit was turning out reliable successes. Once Selznick had departed, Garbo came back willingly into Thalberg's fold. As a "Garbo specialist," Salka moved offices from the rickety old writer's building to the newly built Thalberg bungalow, really more of a Moderne villa, with Thalberg's large office and a reception hall on the first floor, the writers on the second, and Thalberg's dining room with a kitchen and pantry on the third.

Salka's next suggestion for Garbo was a historical drama about Marie Walewska, the Polish countess who became the mistress of Napoleon Bonaparte. Thalberg was lukewarm about it, objecting that American audiences would be confused by the complex geopolitical milieu of the First French Empire, but when Salka suggested that her friend Charles Boyer play Napoleon, Thalberg became seriously interested. The French actor's Hollywood career was starting to gather momentum and a starring role for him would earn the studio plenty of prestige. All Thalberg had to do was persuade the Breen office to green-light yet another period piece whose story began and ended with adultery—in this case a double adultery which resulted in the birth of a child.

When Thalberg brought Salka in to pitch the story to the PCA censors in the early summer of 1935, they were far from enthusiastic. "Since the characters and the events . . . are all historical facts and this illegitimate child survived and became a rather important person in France . . . it is not possible to 'clean this story up' under the code . . . The story looks dangerous to me," carped an internal PCA memo. But the Breen office paid grudging respect to Thalberg's reputation and reluctantly allowed him to proceed. Fortunately for Salka, the censors' opposition had the virtue of increasing Thalberg's enthusiasm for the project. He asked Salka how quickly she thought she could write the treatment.

Salka was willing to dive in, but she asked for permission to work on the script while away from the studio. She had not seen her mother and her siblings for seven years, she told Thalberg, and she needed to travel to Europe to spend some time with them and with her London-based husband. Thalberg was sympathetic. The studio allowed Salka a two-month absence on full salary. She arranged to sail for Southampton from New York on June 26. She had never been to England and was eager to see how Berthold was getting along. But personally this voyage was a big risk for Salka, as she could not be sure that her relationship with Gottfried, who was now twenty-four, would survive so long a separation. As always, Hollywood was full of glossy distractions, with newer and younger ones arriving every day. Salka was forty-six years old. Her eldest child would be heading off to college in a year.

The anxiety Salka felt during the ocean crossing did not dissipate on her arrival at Southampton. Berthold was waiting for her at the pier with Francesco von Mendelssohn, the same friend who had seen them off from the train station in Berlin on their way to America in 1928. The three sped toward London in Francesco's new cherry-red convertible, the weather as gray and stifling as a sick headache. At last Salka was back across the Atlantic, and the strangeness she felt was a bitter surprise. In the open car, in her agitated state, hot hazy drizzle mixed with her tears. The city's manicured parks looked hyper-green in the sullen weather and utterly foreign, much more foreign than America had been when she'd first arrived there. It seemed impossible that Berthold could ever feel at home in this rigid and suffocating place.

Nonetheless both Berthold and Francesco were in good

spirits and full of plans, Berthold beginning a third picture for Gaumont-British about Cecil Rhodes, and Francesco off soon to New York to assist Max Reinhardt in a Broadway production of Kurt Weill's and Franz Werfel's *The Eternal Road*. In the lobby of the Dorchester where Berthold had booked Salka's room, she immediately ran into Max Reinhardt himself. It seemed she was forever happening upon Gottfried's father in hotel lobbies in one country or another. A day or so later she also saw Gottfried's producer brother Wolfgang, who was eager to hear her tales of Hollywood.

Everywhere Salka looked in London there were German refugees, many of them her former colleagues. The luckiest among them were starring in West End plays or acting in British pictures. But most were scrounging for work and living in squalid hotels or boardinghouses. All were furiously studying English and hoping for visas to get them to New York or Hollywood. Francesco and his sister Eleonora had abandoned their Grunewald mansion in Berlin and had gone into voluntary exile. Though their family had been Christian for six generations, they were honoring their original Jewish ancestor, Moses Mendelssohn, by turning their backs on their fatherland and joining the antifascist cause. Eleonora had bought herself a castle near Salzburg which she filled with Jewish and Communist artists on the run, and with as much of her family's art collection as she had been able to sneak out of Germany.

Berthold brought his girlfriend Beatrix Lehmann to lunch the following day. Salka liked her instantly. The three spent a weekend at Beatrix's house on the Thames, where Salka was grateful to escape the breathless heat of the city among the imperturbable old trees in the garden. From there, Berthold took Salka to Paris, another city new to her, which was baking through the same hot weather as London. He wanted to show her as many revolutionary monuments as possible as research for her Napoleon picture, but the heat was too exhausting. Instead he and Salka spent three days among the usual tourist spots, reminiscing about their seventeen-year-old marriage. It was a friendly interval and they did not talk about their current liaisons, until Salka candidly asked Berthold if he wanted a divorce. At that point he became angry. "I believe in our marriage as I always have and we will find each other again," he told her. "I know that we will grow old together."

Berthold was pleased that Salka had managed to make this voyage. But from the moment of arrival she was sorry she came, gripped by loneliness and loss. She was filled with guilt for abandoning her fellows who'd been forced out of their fatherland, made stateless, and set to wandering. Writing in her memoir of her black mood in refugee-packed London and Paris, she quoted an old French proverb: *Les absents ont toujours tort.* Berthold's longtime friend Stefan Zweig had used the same quotation in a book about Erasmus which he'd published the previous year, a book that was as much about the rise of Hitler as it was about the Reformation humanist. Zweig had cited the proverb as a stern self-rebuke, in the same way that Salka was bitterly reviewing her own choices now. The absent are always wrong.

SALKA LEFT BERTHOLD TO HIS LONDON LIFE and set off to reunite with her Steuermann family. But to her sorrow she was not going home to Wychylowka. To save money, Salka's mother Auguste had divided the big family home into smaller units which she'd leased to tenants. There was now no room for Salka's sister Rose and her brother Edward to spend summers there with their families as had been their habit. Instead Rose and her husband Josef Gielen, desperate to escape the swastikas and goose-stepping parades in Dresden, found a holiday spot on the shore of Lago Maggiore in southern Switzerland. Joining them along with their two young children would be Auguste, Edward, and Salka. The youngest Steuermann sibling, Dusko, had gallantly offered to stay back in Poland so his mother could afford the trip.

Salka had known that the last two years had been difficult for Rose, but it was not until she saw the worry lines in her sister's face that she began to understand how much stamina Rose needed to live as an internal exile in Dresden. Rose's life "must have been hell," Salka later wrote. Nonetheless, her children looked innocent and happy, and it was good to sit in the garden with them while Edward's piano playing drifted through the open windows of the rented house.

In the warm evenings the family sat and talked on the veranda, sharply aware that their time together was short. Auguste had aged a great deal and had lost much of her hearing. But she was full of stories about her charity work at home in Wychylowka. She went routinely to all the local households and shops of Sambor, asking for old clothes and packages of food for the poor.

Much of the family's talk was about Hitler and whether the world would allow him to carry out his promise to destroy all the Jews. Salka made an emphatic case that Edward should emigrate to America. But he declined for the same reasons

Auguste had given, uncertain that he'd be able to adapt to such a radically new life.

The visit ended too soon, amid tears and promises not to let another seven years go by. "More than ever we are apprehensive about our fate, and our helplessness to interfere with it," Edward wrote to Salka after she had gone. This was her dark mood as well. But she did not set off immediately for the return trip to California. Letters from Berthold indicate that Salka stopped first at a nursing home in England where she underwent a cosmetic surgery procedure, most likely a facelift. "Do not think, *mein Herz*," Berthold wrote to Salka afterward, "that the wrinkles that are gone now are necessary to your face. Go away, damage! You wanted to do it and you have done it, and that's that. Basta! I kiss your new old face."

Cosmetic surgeries were routine among Hollywood actresses by the 1930s, and not uncommon among the general population in Los Angeles. It's easy to imagine that a forty-six-year-old woman with a boyfriend half her age, Greta Garbo for a best friend, and scores of teenage beauties surrounding her on the Metro lot—and one who, in her heart, had not given up the hope of acting again—would be keen to look as young as possible. One also wonders whether medication from the procedure may have exacerbated Salka's depression that had set in when she first arrived in London in June, for during her journey back to America she was dogged by the blackest mood of her life. Her dread worsened when she stopped in Paris to say goodbye to Francesco and a few other friends. There she was confronted by enormous posters on the Champs-Élysées advertising Emil Jannings in a German propaganda picture. To Salka's deep disgust, the great Swiss actor was now one of the

Third Reich's most visible promoters, soon to be designated by Goebbels as a prized artist of the National Socialist state.

IN HER MEMOIR SALKA WROTE that when she returned to California "the homecoming was glorious." Yet letters from 1936 add more somber details. A mutual friend, Gene Solow, wrote to Sam Behrman in September:

> Salka returned from Europe, sick in both body and mind. The joy of seeing her family again barely compensates for the mental depression chaotic Europe generated in her. Many of her friends are refugees from Germany—London and Paris are full of them, and the number of suicides amongst them are appalling—to say nothing of the pitiful circumstances of their present existences. Then, too, the clouds of a new war hang heavy over Europe... both London and Paris are seething with unrest... and she returned to Hollywood so fatigued in spirit that she didn't even have heart to stay an hour in New York on her way back, but entrained directly from the boat.

In her letters to Berthold, Salka's melancholy eroded her confidence in every choice she'd made. "Europe deeply shook me," she told him. "I have a terrible longing for the past, especially for the past that I dealt with in the wrong way... I feel spiritually empty to be back in Hollywood." She asked him: "Why did we separate? Maybe out of egotism and selfishness, but you did not suffer as much as I did... You can write poetry, you can think, whereas inside of me everything is total chaos, sometimes chaos that pins me to the ground. Everybody loves me but they don't know about me. Gottfried is afraid of me..."

She went on to castigate herself for her decision to raise the boys in America: "The children are so strange to me in many ways. I love them more than my life, but after all they have been all these years in America . . . they see and feel so many things differently."

"I'm dramatizing as always, says Gottfried," she reported. "It's true because everything else is so undramatic and incredibly empty, gray and sad." Knowing she was prone to histrionics but unable to help herself, she finally wrote to Berthold: "Once in your life you loved a woman. A very long time ago you saved her. But then you let her fall. And then you saved her again. And then we didn't hold each other tight enough."

Salka had been in the habit of consoling herself that if her American life failed her she could always go back to Europe. Seeing her family scattered so far from Wychylowka, noting Rose's strain under the pall of Nazified Dresden, and besieged by Emil Jannings's propaganda posters on the Champs-Élysées, Salka had seen that this was no longer true. There was no going back. She now had a visceral feeling for the truth of Berthold's letter from early 1933 when he told her that "the world is coming to an end in Europe, or at least the biggest part of what was our world."

On Salka's return to Hollywood she learned that her brother-in-law Josef Gielen had been denounced and dismissed from his post in Dresden. The Nuremberg Race Laws prohibiting marriage between Jews and non-Jewish Germans were being forcefully implemented. Unions such as his to Rose Steuermann were from now on considered a criminal act. It was unclear whether the laws would be applied retroactively. With the help of the conductor Clemens Krauss, Gielen managed to secure a contract at the Prussian State Opera in Berlin, now under the control of Hermann Goering. Fortunately for Gielen, Goering's actress wife knew Gielen from her work on the stage and could offer some protection. But the National Socialists' patience with Gielen wore thin when they discovered that he'd consorted in Switzerland with his Jewish wife's family. They accused him, falsely, of meeting with the "Zionist Berthold Viertel," though Berthold had not attended the Steuermann family gathering. Emmy Goering's support would only go so far, and once again Gielen was dismissed. He was lucky to find a job with the Burgtheater in Vienna, where he moved with Rose and the children, grateful for the moment to be out from under the boot of Hitlerism.

In the meantime Salka's brother Edward at last agreed to emigrate with his daughter Margret, arriving in Los Angeles in June 1936. He stayed for a while in Salka's house, and she rented a practice room with a piano for him from a neighbor across the street. Edward was glad to be reunited with Schoenberg and was invited by Otto Klemperer to play Beethoven's First Piano Concerto at the Hollywood Bowl, which was a success. But he had no interest in film work and recognized that the appetite for modern music in Los Angeles was less than keen, so he arranged to move to New York, which remained his home base for the rest of his life.

SOME MONTHS BEFORE her siblings' latest migrations, in November 1935, Salka took part in a now-legendary encounter between American commercial culture and European high modernism in the Thalberg bungalow at Metro. At the time,

Irving Thalberg was busy negotiating with Charles Boyer's people in Paris to secure the French actor for Garbo's Napoleon picture. He was also immersed in preparations for Metro's adaptation of Pearl S. Buck's blockbuster 1931 novel about China, *The Good Earth*. Thalberg had heard a New York Philharmonic radio concert that featured Arnold Schoenberg's early string sextet, *Transfigured Night*. He thought the music was pretty. Well aware of Salka's friendship with the composer, he asked her to arrange a conference with Schoenberg to see whether he might write the score for *The Good Earth*.

In Salka's often-repeated account, she set up the meeting but first went out of her way to educate each of the men about potential conflicts. She told Thalberg that Schoenberg had long ago abandoned the glittering tonality of *Transfigured Night* for the austerities of twelve-tone technique, which she did not think Thalberg would like. For Schoenberg, who badly needed the money, she estimated that Metro might pay him as much as twenty-five thousand dollars, a lordly sum, but warned of Thalberg's likely interference in every aspect of the composition.

After much fussing over scheduling, the two men at last convened in Thalberg's office along with Schoenberg's wife Gertrud and with Salka, whom Thalberg had asked to serve as translator. The titan of the Second Viennese School leaned forward in his chair, clutched the umbrella he had refused to surrender, and trained his smoldering eyes on the last tycoon, who stood behind his desk and praised the composer's lovely music.

"I don't write lovely music," corrected Schoenberg.

Thalberg changed course and explained that he was looking for Chinese-themed melodies to accompany scenes containing lots of action and not much dialogue. Schoenberg responded in surprisingly eloquent English that all film music was uniformly terrible and that he would not take on the project unless he had complete control over the sound, including all the actors' words, which must be uttered in the precise pitch and key he would compose for them.

Thalberg was fascinated and asked Schoenberg to elaborate. Schoenberg turned to Salka and asked her to recite some verses from his landmark 1912 melodrama *Pierrot lunaire*, which features an Expressionist technique called *Sprechstimme* (spoken voice) that sounds like neither natural speech nor singing—its closest counterparts might be the style of the French *diseuse* or early German cabaret. Gamely, Salka performed some of the work in its original German, using the correct swooping high and low tones and long and short holds: "The wine we drink with our eyes / pours down in waves nightly from the moon."

Thalberg mused on this for a while and then remarked impassively that *The Good Earth*'s director would most likely have contradictory ideas about the dialogue and would want to guide the actors himself. Schoenberg, unbothered, assured Thalberg that the director would be free to handle the actors as soon as they had perfected their lines with Schoenberg.

Still fascinated, Thalberg sent the composer home with a copy of the screenplay and encouraged him to offer more suggestions. When he'd gone, Thalberg declared to Salka that Schoenberg would learn to capitulate and would write the music on the studio's terms, not Schoenberg's. She was doubtful.

The next morning, Schoenberg's wife phoned Salka to let her know that Schoenberg was now asking for fifty thousand dollars for the complete control he would need over the film and its dialogue. At this Thalberg shrugged, telling Salka that the studio had on hand some Chinese folk songs which the sound department was using to write some very lovely music. Credit for the film's score went to the studio stalwart Herbert Stothart, who had served as the composer for *Christina*. Schoenberg, who refused to write lovely music or to compromise on his radical notions about sound in film, was politely cast aside.

It's an excellent story, relayed in *The Kindness of Strangers* with characteristic self-effacement by one of Metro's most literate and engaging storytellers. But self-effacement has its costs, for while the anecdote has been retold many times in different contexts, few bother to mention that Salka played a greater role here than merely recalling the episode. (No doubt much would have been different here had she been a man. And certainly nobody bothered to ask for the perspective of Gertrud Schoenberg, who was also in the room. Surely she too would have had plenty to say.) Salka's position as a cultural broker between the two men shows that Thalberg and Schoenberg, each often portrayed as a stubbornly independent genius, operated as everyone does within a network of connections, without which they could not function.

No one understood this network better, or maneuvered through it more effectively, than Salka. She was the mutual contact who first made it possible for the composer and the producer to meet. She was the diplomat with a firm grasp of the complexities of both milieus, who took the trouble to issue honest warnings about each man's expectations. She was the translator and the trained actress who was able to demonstrate Schoenberg's arcane techniques, doing what she could to make them accessible to Thalberg. She conveyed to Schoenberg what

Thalberg felt entitled to receive from the composer in exchange for the studio's payment. She was the conduit here between two uncompromising sensibilities, and without her mediating presence it is very likely that there would have been no comprehension and perhaps no meeting whatsoever. Instead, after the two famous men had circled each other cautiously, each walked away with a respect for the other that came about completely through Salka's nuanced efforts. Then there is the fact that she recorded the story in her memoir, without which we would not have her amused and amusing account.

It's noteworthy that even during a time of intense personal crisis Salka was able to expand the mission she had begun with Eisenstein and Murnau, softening the boundaries between high culture and commerce in Hollywood for the potential benefit of each. That mission was becoming more urgent as the situation for Jewish artists in Europe worsened. Once, those artists had had a fatherland. But it was a dream. They were beginning to understand that far-flung outposts must be built to preserve the humanist traditions that the National Socialists were destroying in Germany. Salka was establishing one of those crucial outposts, easing the hardship for exiles such as Schoenberg, who struggled to make a living throughout his California years. In bringing Schoenberg to Metro, Salka was not just a fly on the wall of Thalberg's office as the two men tried to apprehend each other. She was a destroyer of walls, a builder of bridges, a welcome among strangers.

THE WHEELS OF TIME AND CHANGE were turning. Salka's boys were growing up and out. Peter asked to have a room of his own, so Salka renovated the first floor of the garage to create separate quarters for him. Hans had been neglecting his schoolwork in favor of reading *Das Kapital*. He then surprised Salka by graduating from high school, and was accepted by the University of California at Berkeley for the fall of 1936. Shy, and impeded by the onset of a serious hearing disability called otosclerosis, Hans had nonetheless found a social life for himself in Marxist study groups, as many young men of the time did, defining himself as a devotee of Trotskyism. Writing of her dismay upon the news of the Moscow trials and "the growing Stalin terror," Salka observed in her memoir that "the Popular Front extended into my family: Berthold had his own personal kind of socialism, Peter was a New Dealer, I was a 'premature anti-Fascist,' Thomas a Democrat and Hans a Trotskyite."

Politics were inescapable in every activity, large or small, on Mabery Road and at the studio. During story conferences for the Napoleon picture, Salka and Thalberg argued idly about socialism, neither expecting to change the other's mind. (A socialist when he was a boy, Thalberg was now an unequivocal pro-business conservative.) Labor unrest had become a major subplot in the daily business of moviemaking. Thalberg had opposed the Screen Writers Guild (SWG) since its inception in 1933; now he was helping to sponsor a rival organization, the Screen Playwrights, made up mostly of affluent right-wing writers including Salka's old nemesis Ernest Vajda. SWG founders Oliver Garrett and Donald Ogden Stewart (Metro's witty "rescue writer of choice" for many a producer, who collaborated briefly with Salka on the Napoleon project and became her lifelong friend) worked hard to defeat the Screen Playwrights, whose efforts to break the SWG would eventually fail.

“These were the days of meetings,” Salka recalled, and rare was the meeting she failed to attend, if not personally to spearhead. Though the word “activist” did not then exist, Salka was among Hollywood’s earliest and most energetic. She joined the newly created Hollywood Anti-Nazi League, cofounded by Don Stewart, who was, unlike Salka, an outspoken Communist. The HANL was a motley assortment of interest groups whose members agreed on little other than their opposition to Nazism. Its members were Stalinists and New Dealers and Republicans, Jews and Catholics, socialists and Trotskyites. Attending the league’s glamorous opening banquet in April 1936 at the Victor Hugo restaurant were the Irish Catholics John Ford and Joseph Breen, the Jewish studio chiefs Jack Warner, David Selznick, Irving Thalberg, and B. P. Schulberg, and a smattering of radicals including Stewart and another of the evening’s organizers, his fellow Algonquin Round Table member Dorothy Parker.

During those early years of the HANL, Ernst Lubitsch mentioned one day to Salka that he was giving up his membership because the league was run by Communists. He recommended that Salka do the same. Salka demurred, arguing that the Popular Front was the only way to fight fascism. Lubitsch repeated that he knew from a reliable source that the Reds controlled the Anti-Nazi League, and he relayed a few names that made Salka laugh. “But Ernst,” she said, “what all these people do is sit around their swimming pools, drinking highballs and talking about movies, while the wives complain about their Filipino butlers.” Still, Lubitsch huffed, he was getting out. And Salka told him she was staying.

Salka’s response to Lubitsch pointed out hypocrisies that have existed among Hollywood’s leftist circles up to this day.

But with the luxury of hindsight one can see that her remark also underestimated the perspicacity of Lubitsch's warning. Membership in the HANL would become one of the House Un-American Activities Committee's first lines of accusation during its hearings in the late 1940s. In denouncing the HANL as a Communist front, HUAC would cast a net wide enough to ensnare not only the actual Communists in the league's midst (there were perhaps three hundred Communist Party members in the film industry from 1936 to 1946, nearly half of these writers), but also many of the other varyingly left-leaning idealists who joined the antifascist cause in its early years.

For Salka's career in Hollywood the consequences would be significant. Many years later, in 1963, Salka reflected in her diary: "It is very necessary for me to be able to see clearly and impartially how they [the Communists] have used me and how I have let them use me during the critical years in L.A. . . . I remember the girl who was [secretary of a Communist group], who always wanted me to get Garbo to sign something, or to give money, or make Charley [Chaplin] do things which would really damage his anyway bad reputation. The ruthlessness was not only stupid, but did not achieve anything." Only decades later would she, who never joined a political party of any kind, understand how vulnerable her openheartedness had been to cynical political manipulations.

AT METRO IN JULY 1936, Salka was writing a first draft of the Napoleon picture with Sam Behrman and musing about world conquest while the newspapers were reporting Hitler's escalating threats, the appeasement policies of England and France, and the outbreak of the Spanish Civil War. Berthold returned to Santa Monica from England that month, again only for the summer, and again most likely to renew his visa. (Gottfried tactfully moved out of Salka's house during Berthold's visits, and just as discreetly returned once the older man was gone.) Berthold had not yet found a new film assignment in England and was missing Beatrix Lehmann. He was anxious and moody that summer, spending much of his time in his upstairs office, chain-smoking and worrying about Europe and writing poetry. Occasionally he emerged to visit with Salka's brother or with Fred Zinnemann. He walked on the beach in the late afternoons with sixteen-year-old Peter, the son deeply tanned from long days of surfing and tennis, the fifty-year-old father pale and drawn.

On these walks Berthold sometimes wore his bathrobe with a kind of eccentric majesty as the shush of the ocean mixed with the cries of the sea birds. Berthold remarked on the beauty of the American bodies that surrounded them in what he called this *Schlaraffenland*, its pleasure-seekers oblivious to the miseries taking place a continent and another ocean away. The seaside exhibition of muscles and bronze skin reminded Berthold of classical Greece, and to Peter's embarrassment his father would perform a clumsy little dance on the sand, his eyes glinting as he chanted, "We are Greeks without brains! We are Greeks without brains! That is the song they sing."

On the indolent American shoreline, the breeze smelling of coconut oil and fried fish, the gulls wheeling blankly against the blue sky, no one was paying the slightest attention to the lone Austrian intellectual, sick with worry about the fate of his homeland and surrounded here by indifference. His only observer was his son, who would later grow to appreciate his father's predicament but at that moment would rather have been anywhere else.

ON ANOTHER SHORELINE, in southern France, an unhappy collection of German-speaking exiles stared out at the sea with an anxiety that mirrored Berthold's. The exiles were gathered in a spot that looked, though they did not know it yet, quite a lot like Santa Monica. Sanary-sur-Mer was a small fishing village on the westerly, less fashionable and cheaper stretch of the Côte d'Azur, near Toulon. It had the same steep rock cliffs as Salka's beach, the same curve to its bay, the same gemstone sparkle to its sea. Where Santa Monica had the sudden bluster of the Santa Ana winds, in Sanary there was the sky-scrubbing mistral. In both places there were rosemary and oleander, palms and pine, yachts and gulls, whitecaps and the wide nets of fishermen.

The Germans who found themselves on this festive coastline after 1933 had little in common with the cheerfully eccentric British expatriates who preceded them. The novelist Aldous Huxley had discovered Sanary in 1930 after visiting the dying D. H. Lawrence in Vence. He went on to live with his wife and son in the hills above the village until 1937. "Sun, roses, fruit, warmth," he wrote serenely. "We bathe and bask." The critic Cyril Connolly, who moved to Sanary to worship at the feet of his idol Huxley, would often bicycle home from the local restaurants with a pet lemur buttoned up inside his jacket, its little head poking out to sniff the wind.

The British writers found the hot weather agreeable, their

mornings spent swimming, the long afternoons reserved for working inside the cool whitewashed rooms of the old houses on the terraced hillsides. Anthony Powell wrote his first novel, *Afternoon Men*, in Sanary, and there too, in 1931, Aldous Huxley wrote *Brave New World*. For them life in southern France was simple and inexpensive, yet lavish in its pleasures. Austere breezes plunged their houseguests all at once, Sybille Bedford wrote, "into the acerbic scent of the Midi: resin, thyme, hot stone." Huxley's wife Maria made potpourri from the local rosemary, geranium, lime, and rose, and kept it in a big urn by the front door. On Sunday nights the town's ramshackle movie theater, converted from a garage, packed with boisterous locals, and blue with cigarette smoke, showed the silent films of Chaplin, Keaton, and Lloyd.

Sybille Bedford was a German-born novelist and travel writer who first arrived in Sanary in 1926 at the age of fifteen and lived there on and off for decades. She recalled that from May to October no rain fell in the region. "Thus nothing changed: the earth was monochrome, the sea reverberated the sky," she wrote in one of her novels about the year 1928. "How permanent they felt, these even summers, how reassuring—this will go on; we shall go on."

Of course there was irony in Bedford's observations, which she published decades later, long after the war, in 1989. The traumatized Germans who came to Sanary after 1933 did not need hindsight to share the irony. They felt it immediately. For them, all reassurances were dubious. As much as they appreciated the beauty of their surroundings, they were unable fully to participate in it. What had been solid in their lives had now melted into air. They had been stripped of their homes, of their money and belongings, and of their citizenship. Without papers to prove who they were, they belonged nowhere and were unwelcome everywhere. Exile put them between worlds, forced them into marginality: they were in Sanary but they were also not in Sanary. "We lived in paradise—necessarily," wrote the Berlin-born Jewish philosopher and theater critic Ludwig Marcuse, who lived in the village from 1933 to 1940. As with Bedford, there was well-earned irony in Marcuse's formulation, and also when he called Sanary "the capital of German literature."

"Rather a dismal crew," Huxley wrote to his brother in 1933 of the growing German colony, "already showing the disastrous effects of exile." As with the British before them, the Germans had landed in Sanary because like called to like. The Jewish playwright Ernst Toller, a friend of Berthold's, had found himself in exile there in 1926 after he was jailed for subversive activity in the Weimar Republic. Julius Meier-Graefe, a brilliant critic attacked by the National Socialists for his promotion of degenerate art, moved to the town next to Sanary in 1930. Others followed. Klaus and Erika Mann, the two eldest of Thomas Mann's six children, got to know the area while smoking opium with Jean Cocteau in Toulon. By 1933 the Mann siblings were no longer *enfants terribles*, turning their energy toward a fierce and long-standing commitment to antifascism.

From Amsterdam and Sanary, Klaus Mann edited an international anti-Nazi journal, *Die Sammlung*, between 1933 and 1935. The publication was the first of its kind and was singled out as especially abhorrent by the National Socialists, whose own leading magazine, *Die Neue Literatur*, trashed it in November 1933: "The communist and Jewish literati who have fled from Germany are now trying to surround Germany with a wall of literary stink-gas from their crevice... Undoubtedly the most dangerous reptile is... the *Sammlung* published by the half-Jew Klaus Mann." (Klaus and Erika's mother, Katia Mann, was a daughter of one of the wealthiest Jewish families in Germany, the Pringsheims.)

After much argument, in June 1933 Klaus and Erika Mann convinced their reluctant parents to abandon their house in Munich for a villa they found for the family in Sanary—a villa called, with a particular sense of disconnection, La Tranquille. Thomas and Katia Mann did not stay in Sanary long, departing for a town near Zurich in September 1933, though Thomas's brother Heinrich, an equally illustrious author whose books were now banned in Germany, remained in a hotel in nearby Bandol.

The Jewish novelist Lion Feuchtwanger, who had once been Thomas Mann's neighbor in Munich, though the two did not then know each other, arrived in Bandol on May 10, 1933—the same day the National Socialists were burning Feuchtwanger's books throughout Germany. A short time later he and his wife Marta moved to Sanary, establishing themselves in a comfortable house above the bay, where they remained until 1940.

During his flight from Germany, Feuchtwanger learned that his Berlin home had been plundered by the National Socialists. All his possessions, from his furniture to his pet turtles, were stolen or destroyed, and his bank accounts were frozen. Perhaps most grievous of all for Feuchtwanger was the confiscation of his large personal library and manuscripts. Like the book burnings this was a deliberately emblematic act, underscoring the National Socialists' contempt for freedom of thought and of the press, for all language and ideas that deviated from their own crude and turgid inventions.

In Sanary in 1935, Feuchtwanger published an open letter in a French exile newspaper to the new occupant of his house on Mahlerstrasse in Berlin. "How do you like my house?" inquired Feuchtwanger. "Do you find it pleasant to live in?... I wonder to what use you have put the two rooms which formerly contained my library. I have been told... that books are not very popular in the Reich in which you live, and whoever shows interest in them is likely to get into difficulties. I, for instance, read your 'Führer's' book and guilelessly remarked that his 140,000 words were 140,000 offenses against the spirit of the German language. The result of this remark is that you are now living in my house."

In the letter Feuchtwanger noted that, though the value of his confiscated house and savings far exceeded the amount of his mortgage, the German government still commanded him to continue the mortgage payments as well as to pay his German taxes from whatever income he might continue to earn abroad. Thus the Nazi authorities were able to siphon off the frozen funds from Feuchtwanger's bank accounts. This was the case for all who fled from Hitler's Reich. Beginning in 1934, those who left were also obliged to pay a "flight tax" that began at 25 percent of their total worth but kept rising as the decade wore on, until nearly all the assets of fleeing Jews and antifascists were seized. In Sanary, burning with anger, Feuchtwanger began to amass a new and even larger library. In his villa overlooking the bay he wrote *The Oppermanns*, a novel about a Jewish family's subjugation under the Third Reich in the Berlin of 1933, and another novel called *Exil* (published in English as *Paris Gazette*), about German refugees in Paris in 1935.

Lion and Marta Feuchtwanger in their library,
Sanary-sur-Mer, 1936.

Unlike Feuchtwanger, many of the German-speaking exiles who passed through Sanary stayed only briefly, including Bertolt Brecht, Erich Maria Remarque, Stefan Zweig, Arthur Koestler, and the Austrian singer Fritzi Massary. But as the 1930s wore on, the smattering of luminaries who had followed Ernst Toller to the Midi became a constellation. As many as four hundred German and Austrian political refugees found themselves in the district of *le Var* up until the end of the decade.

And many of them truly were stars, these "forerunners of catastrophe," as Sybille Bedford called them, who shouldered a highbrow international fame that is hard to imagine of writers today. Thomas Mann had won the Nobel Prize in 1929 and the publications of his books were major events, generating vigorous sales around the globe. His elder brother Heinrich, author of *Professor Unrat*, the novel which became *The Blue Angel* on film, was if possible even more widely read in Germany than Thomas. Lion Feuchtwanger's historical fiction sold in huge numbers in global translation, as did Stefan Zweig's. Bertolt Brecht had come to worldwide prominence as the reigning iconoclast genius of the theater. Franz Werfel's novels and plays made him a well-heeled celebrity whose glamour was increased by the formidable presence of his wife, the magisterial Alma Mahler Gropius Werfel.

Traveling to Sanary with these emissaries of high culture were their entourages—wives and mistresses, secretaries, housekeepers, translators—who called them, with less irony than one might suppose, *Dichterfürsten*: princes of poetry. The princes were imperious and often pompous, but so substantial were their reputations that this moniker was not considered at all ridiculous. Exile did not endear the princes to one another, nor did their wives often do more than abide one another. "We were all victims of intolerance," remembered Marta Feuchtwanger, "and then they were intolerant of each other." Loss and fear made them jealous and disdainful, bristling and bitter. Often all they shared was a loathing for the National Socialists and the certainty of persecution—some of them for being Jewish, all of them for the "degeneracy" of their literature—had they remained in Germany.

And when the princes took flight, leaving behind grand houses and villas and in some cases actual castles, what they took with them was a defiant resolution to *preserve*—not just the values the National Socialists were trampling, but an entire way of life. Thus on Sanary's rocky hillsides they set up provisional households, trying their best to reimagine the homes from which they had been purged. Most of this work, as always, was the province of the women. Katia Mann, Thomas's wife, complained sharply to Sybille Bedford that the *batterie de cuisine* at the Villa Tranquille failed to include a potato ricer. How could she be expected to make the mashed potatoes that must accompany the traditional German Sunday roast of veal?

It was not as trivial a grievance as it seems. The idea of home is built on its details, perhaps most on those of its kitchen. The Manns would not adapt their ways of eating to the local customs of the Var, would not substitute their Sunday veal, as Bedford timidly suggested Katia might, for gigot and flageolets. "Where I am, is Germany," Thomas Mann famously insisted, and by this he surely intended to uphold the sauerbraten of his fatherland every bit as ardently as its tradition of liberal humanism.

What dissonance, for these gloomy Sanaryans, between the Mediterranean shimmer of the Côte d'Azur and the matte substantiality of the homeland for which they grieved, between the menace they had fled and the blitheness of the place in which they found themselves. What a dizzying clash of sensibilities: *Weltschmerz* grappling with *luxe, calme et volupté*. Though some of them managed to work and live well in the bright sunlight of their seaside garden havens, the climate was a peculiar kind of taunt. These were foreign kingdoms where one could never feel at home.

Why were these holiday towns so often the last foothold in the old world, and sometimes the first foothold in the new? Why the grand promenades and casinos of Ostend for Stefan Zweig and Joseph Roth, and why, for Zweig again, the lush emerald forests of Brazil's Petrópolis? Why these insistent reminders of beauty, of pleasure, for those whose dreams of security and permanence had been so carelessly snatched away?

Moments ago, the princes had been the longtime householders, the patrons, the welcomers of strangers. Now dethroned, they were the fugitives, the strangers, the uninvited guests. Through fortunes of timing and geography, when many of them landed in Los Angeles they would be met in the comfortingly continental living room of Salka Viertel—herself a former vagabond, a trouper through a thousand badly furnished European boardinghouses, who in the new world had transformed herself into the very soul of what it means to be a host.

6

MOTHERLAND

There's an old joke. A Gentile says to a Jew:
"The Jews were to blame for everything."
"Yes," says the Jew. "The Jews and the bicycle riders."
"Why the bicycle riders?" the Gentile asks.
And the Jew answers: "Why the Jews?"

—ERICH MARIA REMARQUE, *SHADOWS IN PARADISE*

One does not wander without punishment under palms.

—BERTHOLD VIERTEL

LOS ANGELES AND PARIS
1936–1939

IN 1936, Germany and America were gazing at each other across an ocean, and each offered a reflection of race hatred to the other. The Nuremberg Race Laws had been announced by the National Socialists at their annual party rally the previous year. A codified entrenchment of the Third Reich's white supremacist ideology, the laws had been compiled after a careful study of race-based legal systems around the world. Particularly inspiring to the National Socialists was the American system of immigration quotas, which was designed to accept more "racially desirable" people from northern Europe (whites from Britain and Scandinavia) and fewer undesirable emigrants from eastern and southern Europe (mostly Jews and Catholics) and from Asia.

As the National Socialists created their own system of legal inferiority for non-Gentiles, they also admired America's classification of residents of the U.S. territories of Puerto Rico and the Philippines as "non-citizen nationals." And to fortify their criminalization of mixed marriages, the National Socialists looked to America's Jim Crow laws—in particular those laws in thirty U.S. states which decreed marriage between whites and Negroes illegal. Many of those American states defined a "Negro" as anyone with a black ancestor—with, as they called it, "one drop" of Negro blood. Interestingly, the National Socialists considered the "one-drop" definition too severe. Instead they decreed that a Jew was any person with three or four Jewish grandparents, regardless of whether those forebears had converted to Christianity.

With the Nuremberg Laws in place, the National Socialists now had a legal framework with which to pursue the persecution of Jews in Germany. Jews were no longer citizens and they no longer had most of their former political rights. When the Olympic Games opened in Berlin in the summer of 1936, the Reich momentarily hid these strictures from view, showing off a false spirit of international amity. Once the games were over, for Germany's Jews the situation quickly and systematically grew much worse.

Just as the tightening noose around the rights of Jews in Germany had been partially inspired by the National Socialists' study of American racial legislation, so in turn was the robust climate of anti-Semitism in America directly fueled and abetted by the Third Reich.

ABOUT A FORTY-MINUTE DRIVE NORTHEAST from Salka's house in Santa Monica lay Hindenburg Park, a large public green space in the neighborhood of La Crescenta. There, on a gorgeous summer afternoon in 1936, the annual German Day picnic was under way. Beneath the leaf-laden oaks, a sign draped in ivy bade *Willkommen!* in Gothic script. An enormous bust of Paul von Hindenburg, the former president of the Weimar Republic who had opened the door for Hitler's 1933 stroll into the chancellorship, was adorned with a swastika. Although the Depression ground on and unemployment was still high, the crowds wore their Sunday best and put on a show of easy living. Towheaded boys in neckties ran around waving flags. Babies and toddlers, matrons and courting couples sat at picnic tables dotted with newspapers and snacks. Smiling vendors sold cup after cup of post-Prohibition Eastside Lager ("Healthful Enjoyment"). There was a smattering of lederhosen. There were oompah bands and there was dancing.

But more was in the air on this day than the annual display of *Gemütlichkeit.* The mood grew martial when the speeches and parades began. They took place under banners declaring, in German, "The Enemies of Germany Are Also America's Enemies." The processions featured American flags flanked on both sides by the swastika, and when the speechifiers thrust out their straight-armed Nazi salutes, many among the crowd followed suit.

The Los Angeles branch of the German American Bund, which had rebranded itself that year, staged rallies at Hindenburg Park during the 1930s and had two major goals: to Nazify the German-American community and to sway public opinion toward a positive vision of Hitler's New Germany. The Bund characterized itself as standing for "constitution, flag, and a white gentile ruled, truly free America," and it worked hard, according to the historian Laura B. Rosenzweig, "to recruit as many U.S. citizens as possible into its ranks," "to normalize Nazis into the social fabric of the community," and "to portray itself as a patriotic American defense organization."

To those ends, Bund members visited the tourist steamers docked in the port of Los Angeles, where they received propaganda materials in unmarked packages that came directly from Berlin. They then reprinted the pamphlets to mask their German provenance and distributed them from their local headquarters, the Deutsches Haus on West Fifteenth Street near downtown, a brown stucco mansion that also housed the Aryan Bookstore, a restaurant, and a shooting range.

In collaboration with the Bund was another anti-Semitic organization called the Silver Legion of America, boasting fifteen thousand members at its peak nationwide, many of whom were based in Los Angeles. Local members of the Silver Shirts, as they called themselves in homage to Hitler's Brownshirts, had recently begun construction of a ranch on a secluded fifty-five-acre site in Rustic Canyon. It was said that the land belonged to a Nazi-friendly mining heiress named Jessie Murphy, who had purchased it from the actor Will Rogers. The Silver Legion was working to develop the Murphy Ranch into what they hoped would become a headquarters for Hitler as soon as "*der Tag*," the day of fascist world conquest, at last arrived.

The Silver Shirts and the Bund worked to spread anti-Semitic propaganda around Los Angeles, hoping to attract press attention by picketing Jewish community meetings and by "snowstorming"—dropping leaflets from the rooftops of downtown buildings calling for boycotts of the Jewish-dominated movie business. Many of the Silver Legion's recruits were disaffected U.S. veterans of the Great War who were drowning in the undertow of the Depression, seeing in their mutilated pensions and rejected disability claims the sinister workings of Roosevelt's "Jew Deal." They were glad to pin the blame for their hardships on the Jews, who they were convinced were masterminding an international conspiracy to replace them with nonwhite inferiors. The Silver Legion did everything it could to stoke their anger. The Los Angeles police department was more sympathetic to this homegrown fascism than not, perceiving Communists, not Nazis, to be the real threats to the city's safety. And Communists, for the local police just as for the National Socialists and, later, for the members of the House Un-American Activities Committee, almost always meant Jews.

In the meantime, Bundists and the Silver Legion concocted plans to assassinate Hollywood celebrities, via lynching and execution-style murder, and to firebomb their houses. On the lists of targets for these never-realized acts of terrorism were Louis B. Mayer, Samuel Goldwyn, B. P. Schulberg, Joseph Schenck, Eddie Cantor, Jack Benny, and Paul Muni.

Just outside the fortresses of the picture business, this was the Los Angeles of the 1930s. It was a city churning with anti-Semitism both locally grown and transatlantically inspired, directly targeting as many high-profile Hollywood Jews as possible. The hatred was organized and institutional. It was in government and within the police; in real-estate covenants and in restricted private schools and country clubs; in paramilitary groups performing marching drills in the streets; in oratory swearing allegiance to Hitler in the parks and beer halls.

And it was quotidian: in everyday slurs, in boardinghouse signs warning NO JEWS, in leaflets raining on downtown pedestrians. The hatred sprouted from the same seeds that had taken firm root in Germany, inciting nativist resentment and paranoia.

What would stop the poison trees from flourishing here?

ON THE SAME SUNDAY AFTERNOON of the German Day picnic in 1936, the sun over the bay in Santa Monica was a Klieg light gleaming in the painted blue backdrop of the sky. Below, the surf tumbled over itself like yards of tulle from Metro's costume department, then smoothed to satin as it draped along the shore. Beachgoers baked themselves in the sand or ran after their children toward the merry-go-round on the pier. Through the little tunnel under the highway and up the hill to the canyon, the sea breeze rose to greet the arriving guests as Salka's weekly party was reaching its stride. In the living room the Capehart warbled German songs out into the street as the red front door opened again and again.

If the tone of the German Day picnic was bellicose on that day, the mood on Mabery Road was by necessity restorative. For the American studio folk who attended these afternoon parties, Salka's house offered a respite from a grueling work schedule. Sundays were their only days off, and they looked forward to the refreshment that Salka's house offered. But for the recently arrived Europeans who found themselves there, it was a place of shelter. Sunday open house was a custom transplanted from Europe, comforting and familiar. Here at Salka's was a sense of continuity, an enactment of ritual during an anxious time.

An Improvisation

Indeed, I am a wanderer, a pilgrim on this earth.
But can you say that you are anything more?

Ernst Toch was forty-nine years old, a native of Vienna and a composer of modernist music. Nearly twenty years later he would cite the above lines from Goethe's *The Sorrows of Young Werther* as the motto for his Third Symphony, which would win the Pulitzer Prize, and which he would call his "musical autobiography."

This was how he found himself on the doorstep of Mabery Road in Santa Monica in the summer of 1936. He'd first met Berthold Viertel in Berlin during the frenzied Weimar period before 1933. In 1934, in London, Viertel hired Toch to write the music for the Gaumont-British picture *Little Friend*. Film composing didn't much interest Toch, but the pay was good and he found it a congenial job. When it was done, through a series of fortunate introductions, he seized an opportunity to teach and compose in New York, where for less fortunate reasons (a fight between music publishers, who then refused to publish or promote him) the money wasn't enough to support him and his wife and young daughter.

With further networking help from George Gershwin and others, he landed in Santa Monica, where he'd been holed up in a beach hotel writing film scores for Paramount at $750 per week. Under these palms he hoped to have time for more serious work, and also to resume teaching. But for now his livelihood was composing melodies for films, "a queer step-child," he would one day call that music. And today, as a break from his labors, he decided to impose himself on the hospitality of the wife of his former colleague Viertel.

The front door of the Mabery Road house opened directly onto the living room, with its piano and its many books and a print of Picasso's *Blue Boy* hanging over the fireplace. On the far side of the room there were glass doors leading to a porch, and beyond the porch was a fig tree—a small miracle to Toch, as figs were a personal favorite of his—and a glimpse of some madly blooming rosebushes.

Despite the glorious weather the crowd remained inside, soothed perhaps by the phonograph music and the smell of a just-baked *Apfelkuchen*. Several of Salka Viertel's dogs were inside, too: a pair of unruly Irish setters and an old Alsatian. There was no sign at the moment of the huge German shepherd called Prinz, who was fiercely loyal to Salka but inclined to bite if one leaned in too closely over his head.

The house, practical and unpretentious, packed to the rafters with people, was plainly all Salka's domain, except for an upstairs room which Berthold had conjured into a facsimile of the Knightsbridge flat to which he would return when the summer was over, a furious burrow of ashtrays, newspapers, manuscripts, journals, books and books and books, Aeschylus and Hindu mysticism and modern American poetry.

Salka presently commanded a very good paycheck as a screenwriter at Metro, but whatever she was spending it on did not include fancy embellishments for the house. Some said that she found much of the furniture in the thrift shops in Glendale, where the studios cast off their extra properties. Salka chose instead to adorn her house with people: Sunday guests, houseguests, and a few long-term visitors who clustered around her night and day. There was a feeling of abundance here, but the extravagance was emotional rather than material, and it emanated from Salka herself, was an extension of her.

The Los Angeles in which Toch found himself was discordant, composed in a notation he found nearly impossible to read. By contrast, everything felt recognizable in this Weimar-style ghost house, which was why he and so many others were drawn to it. The prickly conversations throughout the living room brought back the hundreds of hours Toch had spent in the Romanisches Café, arguing about music and art. The books on the Viertels' shelves were written by people he had known in Berlin, the same titles as those the chanting crowds had tossed into the bonfires on the Opernplatz in 1933. The songs on the record player might as well have been Toch's songs. The aromas coming out of the kitchen were the same as those in his mother's house in Vienna.

Some might have blanched at the thought that there might be anything sexual between themselves and Salka Viertel, yet at the same time it's true that there was never *not* a hint of seduction in any of Salka's encounters. In the way she regarded her guests there was always an invitation, a pull toward her that could not be extricated from her reckless generosity, her impenitent laugh, her love of drama. Never an obvious beauty, she had learned during her theater days to use every other asset she had—her intelligence most of all, but also her voice and her glance and her gestures—to assume a forceful presence, to make one pay attention.

Now here was Salka forging toward Toch, a warm smile on her broad, frank face. She took up with confidence her allotment of space in the world. She was not a small woman, but neither would one call her heavy. She dressed in the style of the day, without fuss: that day a tailored pinstripe suit with a longish skirt. Often she added a colorful scarf or shawl. As she crossed the room there was just the slightest hitch in the step of her right leg. It was a distinctive gait and a bit curious for an actress, but if her walk was not as graceful as one might have imagined it was still purposeful, as if she were always leaning slightly forward.

Her hand on Toch's arm, Salka offered greetings in her songful German. Silently he blessed her for the offering of his mother tongue among the harsh English consonants ricocheting around the room. She began to absorb him into the web of connections among the guests. In one corner was Johnny Weissmuller, the star of Metro's *Tarzan* pictures, patiently answering question after question posed by Salka's awestruck eleven-year-old son Tommy. In another was the screenwriter Billy Wilder, Toch's fellow Viennese, who had known the Viertels' close friend Fred Zinnemann since their neophyte filmmaking days in Berlin. At the moment Wilder was laughing with Oliver Garrett, Salka's former lover or so it was whispered. Garrett and Wilder were frequent tennis partners and they had recently coauthored two screenplays for Pioneer Pictures. Toch was hoping for a glimpse of Garbo, but he had heard that she rarely made an appearance at these parties, preferring to come to the house during odd hours when she could have Salka to herself.

Salka directed Toch's attention to a gangly laughing young man. He was pleased to recognize that this was the writer John Huston, whom Toch had met on several occasions in London.

Salka began to entertain Toch with a story about Huston. She had taken an interest in him after hearing of his somewhat wild reputation and had invited him to dinner. When the evening arrived, Huston was less interested in conversing with Salka's adult guests than in talking to her sons Hans and Peter. Once he discovered that the boys were learning how to box with an instructor who came to the house, Huston asked to see the garage, where he wanted to inspect their gloves and punching bag. He himself was serious about boxing and liked to do some sparring whenever he could.

Peter, who was fifteen, was reluctant but too polite to refuse. Soon he found himself and Huston shedding their coats and ties and going at it in the empty garage, with Hans uncomfortably looking on. Huston got carried away and ended up smashing Peter rather too authoritatively in the jaw, after which he apologized as the two, breathless and sweaty, took a break. It was then that they discovered that their shoes were slathered in dog shit, because Salka often locked her dog Prinz in the garage when she had guests and had not had time to clean up after him. The pugilists washed up as best they could and went to rejoin the others at dinner.

Salka laughed richly at her own performance of the story. Toch smiled too, appreciating the harmless little anecdote, understanding that she offered it to him as a balm, as a respite. To an extent she succeeded and for that he was grateful.

Toch knew that Salka understood what he had been through over the last few years, the nature of his exile, its anguish and its costs. She knew that the doctorate he had earned back in 1921 might have saved his life, for it meant that he was eligible for the teaching position in New York that allowed him to emigrate in 1934 after his work on *Little Friend* was done. She well knew Toch's reputation during the Weimar years in Berlin, when he was one of the stars of the International Neue Musik, his concertos and chamber operas in great demand, his contribution to experimentalism as assured as Schoenberg's and Hindemith's. And she knew that this foment of innovation had come to an unambiguous end one day in Cologne in 1933, during a rehearsal of his latest opera, when Brownshirts stomped into the hall and ceremoniously snatched the baton out of the conductor's hand because the music was the work of a Jew. Soon after that, the newly Nazified musical journal *Die Musik* published a special anti-Semitic issue in which reproductions of Toch's face, along with those of the composers Mendelssohn, Mahler, and Weill, were distorted into hook-nosed and dead-eyed caricatures, the Shylockian images festooned with quotations including this from Hitler himself: "*The Jew possesses no power or ability to create culture.*"

Even after all that, Toch was fortunate. He had the good timing to attend a music conference in Florence, where he determined that exile was his only hope of survival, via Paris and London and now Los Angeles. He was lucky to have the chance to work in the picture business, which made him less likely to become a public charge and thus less likely to be expelled from yet another country. He was painfully aware that his sixty-four cousins who remained in Europe did not have this good fortune. He did not know what happened or what would happen to them. What he did know was that *der rote Faden*, the red thread of the narrative of his life, was severed, and that the pain was somewhat like that of an amputation.

He suffered from depression which would stalk him throughout his years in America. His concert music would never find an audience in this country. The studios would cynically recycle his film scores again and again, his orchestrations often going uncredited and without compensation. There would be many years in which he would be unable to produce any serious work.

What could one do under the brutal weight of these times? What could any one person do? Only the smallest of gestures. Salka was in Paris and London not so long ago, she'd seen those cities full of exiles like Toch. She set for herself the mission of personally tending to those who landed here in Santa Monica. She set for herself the mission of creating a *zu Hause*, a provisional home, a familiar place in a strange land, a home that had become more real than the *Heimat* which had been forged into a cauldron of lies, lies that led inevitably to violence, fantasies about blood and soil concocted by thugs who had denied the right to exist to so many thousands of citizens and had expelled them all.

Zu Hause was Salka, and Salka was her house. Laughter and tears came easily to her; her moods were dramatic and unpredictable, just as the house itself was histrionic, layered, complex. The chattering cross-talk of the people at the party registered to Toch's sensitive ears as distractingly and sometimes painfully out of key. The air was jangly and syncopated with nerves. Arguments rose and fell. Insults couched as witticisms punctuated the anxious manners. Near the fireplace, Berthold Viertel was arguing rather violently about pacifism, a position he usually defended but on this occasion considered cowardly. Berthold was as temperamental and dramatic as Salka, and these displays of his volcanic rages were not only about politics. His and Salka's civilized arrangement was sometimes less civilized when Gottfried Reinhardt was present, as he was that day. The undercurrents of the tension were a riptide below the surfaces of the room. The Viertel children made brief appearances at these parties, and Toch wondered how their parents' volatility shaped their lives.

For an exile, a house is a mix of nostalgia and hope, a reminder of what has been lost and what might yet be recaptured. Soon Toch's own beloved wife would arrive in Los Angeles, and she would design for him a home on a hill not far from here with an Italianate view of the mountains, a view intended to lift his eyes and his spirits. His wife would return Salka's hospitality with many a dinner party invitation. And for himself, on a deserted stretch of beach a bit north of here called Malibu, he would construct a shed out of the enormous shipping crate that transported his family's possessions from Berlin. He would outfit the shed with a beat-up old piano, and he would go there to practice and compose, and sometimes he would invite the Viertels and other friends and he would give a little concert. He would name the shipping crate the Villa Majestic.

At the moment Toch was between worlds. His hostess knew that, he could see it in her expression as she handed him a plate of her apple cake and a cup of her excellent coffee. She was rehumanizing him who had been dehumanized, giving him back his name and his reputation. He understood that her act of imagination in creating this stage set of his stolen life was an act of defiance, a refusal to be humiliated or destroyed.

IN EARLY SEPTEMBER 1936, Salka and Sam Behrman finished their draft of the Napoleon picture for Metro, and Hans Viertel left for his freshman year of college at Berkeley. In the middle of that month, Peter and Salka took a driving trip up the coast to see how Hans was settling in. On their way back to Los Angeles, stopping for coffee in a drugstore, they saw a newspaper headline announcing that Irving Thalberg had died. He was thirty-seven years old and his son and daughter were so young that Salka did not think they would remember him.

There were religious imperatives to bury Thalberg perhaps earlier than otherwise, because the Jewish holiday of Rosh Hashanah was to begin that night. Salka and Berthold were among the guests crowding into the Wilshire Boulevard Temple on September 16, 1936, for the funeral. Garbo did not attend, but had sent flowers. Outside, in the slanting light that is peculiar to the hot autumns of Los Angeles, some seven thousand fans gathered as if for a film premiere, hoping to catch a glimpse of movie stars. Inside the synagogue, Rabbi Edgar Magnin, who had officiated at Thalberg's wedding to Norma Shearer, read a tribute from President Roosevelt and offered free publicity for Shearer's *Romeo and Juliet*, which had opened the previous evening. On the ride home with Berthold, Gottfried, and Sam Behrman, Salka made jokes about the pompousness of Rabbi Magnin, over which she and the men all "laughed tears."

Salka was nonetheless affected by Thalberg's death. "To be honest," she wrote later in a letter to Sam Behrman, "he was 'Hollywood' in all its pretentiousness and falseness but he had a certain dignity and talent. I liked him very much but then when I knew him, he was a sick, tired man and I felt sorry for him."

In the early 1960s, when Behrman considered writing a book about Thalberg, Salka was encouraging. "It is a fascinating theme," she told Behrman. "Scott Fitzgerald could not grasp the whole sadness of it. He was anti semitic." Salka's remark about Fitzgerald's portrayal of Thalberg in *The Last Tycoon* is tantalizing. What more would she have said, if asked, about Fitzgerald's failure to capture Thalberg's attitudes toward Jews and Judaism? And, for that matter, how her own nuanced identification with her religion might have contrasted with Thalberg's? Before his marriage, the producer had deferred to his mother's request that Norma Shearer, a Catholic, convert to his faith. Thalberg was a generous supporter of Jewish charities and a big donor, from its earliest days, to the Wilshire Boulevard Temple. He'd been quick to join the Hollywood Anti-Nazi League, as well as to represent MGM in an organization called the Los Angeles Jewish Community Committee, convened in March 1934 to raise funds to expose and combat the active pro-Nazi efforts of the Los Angeles branch of the Bund.

But the primary belief to which Thalberg adhered was in the American film industry, an entity whose health depended on its profits from a quickly Nazifying Germany. It was this fact that caused all the Jewish studio chiefs, at the beginning of the 1930s, to downplay the worst and hope for the best. In 1932, when Thalberg had traveled to Europe to recuperate from his heart attack, he had seen a Jewish couple assaulted on a street in Germany and had tried unsuccessfully to intercede. When he returned to America in 1934, Thalberg predicted that "a lot of Jews will lose their lives." Pressed that perhaps millions, or even all of them, might be murdered, Thalberg responded: "No, not all of them. Hitler and Hitlerism will pass. The Jews will still be there."

If in hindsight Thalberg's equanimity seems strangely buoyant, it was not different from the mood at the time of many assimilated American Jews. New York–based Rabbi Stephen S. Wise, an ardent supporter of the New Deal and an adviser to Roosevelt, admonished against the "hush-hush policy" of those American Jews in 1935 by warning that the Jews in Germany were disastrously adopting the same strategy, naively convinced that if they "devoted themselves to assimilation" and "denied their Jewishness . . . they would escape persecution."

It was only a bit later, as Thalberg was fatally ill and dying, that the studio chiefs began to take secretive action against Hitler's threats, mostly by writing checks to resistance organizations. There is every reason to believe that Thalberg, had he lived, would have done the same. While the studio bosses spent every day trying to fit in as Americans, Germany's well-publicized efforts toward declaring its territories *judenrein*, together with the evident anti-Semitism here in the States, would never let them forget that they were Jews, despised both at home and abroad. The favor was extended to the next generation as well. Budd Schulberg, the son of Paramount founder B. P. Schulberg, wrote in his memoirs that "all through my teens I considered myself un- or non-Jewish. It would take Adolf Hitler to bring me back to a sense of identification with the culture of my forebears."

Many of the newly arrived exiles in Los Angeles were similarly unaccustomed to thinking of themselves as Jews. They had failed to take their heritage as seriously as Hitler did. Until, that is, they were forced into a single community, defined by Stefan Zweig as "the ever-recurring—since Egypt—community of expulsion." Yet these sentiments were far from monolithic. As ever, in Hollywood and everywhere else, there was no one way to be Jewish or to feel Jewish. The condition was as personal as a fingerprint. As ever, it was the work of anti-Semites to universalize and simplify.

Louis B. Mayer and the other studio chiefs were in a precarious position, they who had built their dream cities from the shards beneath their feet. They had managed to survive through the Great Depression and were now faced with death threats from anti-Semites at home in America while worrying about their relatives in Europe and their profits locked up in the fortunes of the Third Reich. But the history of the movies is the history of adaptation in the eye of catastrophe. The chiefs would not buckle under these threats. Quietly they agonized about closing their offices in Germany. While Warner Bros. and Universal shut up shop there in 1934, Metro, which had the biggest German investment of all the studios, maintained its offices in Berlin as late as 1938, staffed by non-Jews, while Paramount and Fox remained in business there until at least late 1940. Quietly they continued to fund the Los Angeles Jewish Community Committee in its battles against the Silver Legion and the Bund. Quietly they issued affidavits for Jews seeking to come to America, and wrote checks to the United Jewish Welfare Fund and other organizations to aid Jewish refugees in Europe. In the meantime, the work of film production in Hollywood clattered on.

At Metro, Salka was also learning to adapt in the eye of catastrophe. She survived the waves of firings as Metro scrambled to rearrange itself after Thalberg's death, then hastened to adjust when Thalberg's Napoleon picture was reassigned to the producer Bernie Hyman. A close friend of Thalberg's, Hyman was an equivocating sort, prone to sentimentality. Gottfried

Reinhardt, who was now rising quickly through the executive ranks at Metro, had once served as his assistant. Hyman seemed at first to be Salka's ally. But he could not abide any screenplay that he had not supervised from the beginning. After much dithering he ordered a total rewrite of the Viertel-Behrman script. Sam Behrman had gone back to New York, so Salka was assigned to work with another Sam, the screenwriter and poet Samuel Hoffenstein. The droll Hoffenstein, born in Russia with, as Salka said, a "Chassidic soul," became her instant friend, and the two worked well together. Nonetheless, as Salka remembered, the Napoleon rewrite "became first a small, then a huge nightmare."

Already hampered by PCA censorship, the story suffered further from a disagreement about where the audience's pathos should lie. Hyman wanted moviegoers to cry for the exiled Napoleon, while the writers preferred to highlight the emperor's ruthlessness, particularly in his treatment of his mistress, the Polish countess Marie Walewska. The historical reality was that Marie, a patriot and a married woman, submitted to be pimped to the emperor in exchange for a broken promise to liberate her country from a repressive Russia. Then she had the misfortune to fall in love with Napoleon and to bear his illegitimate child.

"If you want to feel sorry for Napoleon then let Garbo play him," Sam Hoffenstein offered helpfully to Bernie Hyman. The producer responded in prime Metro style by throwing more money at the problem, hiring seventeen writers in all to try to struggle toward a compromise. At significant expense he brought Sam Behrman back to rejoin the fray, who later recalled: "I wished to convey my personal feeling that the existence of Napoleon... was a disaster for the human race. But it was not easy to get sympathy for this point of view from a group of men who had busts of Napoleon in their offices, since he represented their secret wish-dreams of conquest."

In fact for American audiences the picture was retitled *Conquest*, though it retained its original title, *Marie Walewska*, in Europe. Filming began in March of 1937 but fell months behind schedule, piling up costs. Overall it was Metro's most expensive venture since its 1925 epic *Ben-Hur*. It was the first and only Garbo sound film to finish in the red, incurring losses of nearly $1.4 million, though it did much better in Europe. Salka wrote that it was "an exhausting experience for everyone, especially for Garbo and Boyer, who patiently suffered to the very end (although at doubled salaries)." She also pointed to a personal victory: with Gottfried's influence, she and Sam Hoffenstein were able to reinstate several scenes from her and Behrman's original script in the final version.

Conquest is a somewhat inert contribution to Metro's library of lavish historical dramas, but it is far from a disaster. Boyer, one of the world's most brilliant actors, managed to wring enough Napoleonic bluster from the role to earn an Academy Award nomination, while Garbo, looking beautiful but alarmingly thin after her recent role as the dying Camille, was vulnerable and dignified.

While Metro's simulacrum of European conquest was unspooling on the backlot, Hollywood was transfixed by the civil war in Spain. Its Popular Front deplored the U.S. government's official neutrality and decried the abuses of Franco and the fascist Falange. It organized banquets and receptions to raise money to buy ambulances, food, and medicine for the Republican cause.

In early 1937, the Hollywood Anti-Nazi League sponsored a rally in the Shrine Auditorium downtown, where many thousands gathered to hear the writer André Malraux deliver an impassioned speech on behalf of the Spanish Loyalists. The previous evening, Salka had invited Malraux—whose novel *Man's Fate*, according to Salka's friend Fred Zinnemann, was the bible of his generation—to speak to a gathering of about a hundred film VIPs at her home. In the living room Malraux warned her guests of the support Franco was receiving from Hitler and Mussolini and managed to collect five thousand dollars. After his similar address the following night at the Shrine, Malraux thanked the roaring crowd by raising his fist in the Communist salute. Salka turned around to gauge the response and was surprised to see "ladies in mink rising and clenching their bejeweled hands."

A few months later, in July 1937, Ernest Hemingway and the filmmaker Joris Ivens also made a pro-Loyalist fundraising tour through Hollywood after a stop at the Roosevelt White House to screen their documentary *The Spanish Earth*. Again they stopped first at a private reception on Mabery Road, and again they followed that appeal with another much larger gathering, this time at the Los Angeles Philharmonic Auditorium. Their efforts summoned up about fifteen thousand dollars from members of the film community for ambulances and medicine.

In her memoir Salka mentioned that among the thousands in the Shrine Auditorium crowd listening to André Malraux's address were a mix of "stars, producers, writers, doctors, lawyers, teachers, shop clerks, workers from the studios, the Douglas and Lockheed factories, and practically every German refugee in Los Angeles." It was a hallmark of the Popular Front that the politics of these individuals varied widely, from Salka's vaguely socialistic leanings to New Dealers to Trotskyites. The same was true of those who flocked to hear Hemingway. At that point in 1937, no one among these crowds, and certainly not Salka herself, could imagine that the events would come under suspicion by the Dies committee in 1940–1941 as a rally dedicated to "premature antifascism," meaning antifascist activity that was nefariously controlled by Communists. Nor were they worried that the diverse assortment of German refugees, doctors, and shop clerks in the Popular Front would be as equally damned for attempting to sabotage the ideals of American democracy as the actual Communists in the auditorium that night. The grandstanding ideologues of the Dies committee and its successor HUAC were as eager to demonize as many people as possible with the crime of Communism, most particularly immigrants and Jews.

At this point in 1937, sympathy for the Spanish Loyalists was so widespread that Salka, who was between writing jobs after *Conquest*, was moved to start work on a non-Garbo screenplay about shipwrecked Spanish orphans which she titled *Cargo of Innocence*. She knew that her friend William Dieterle was directing a picture about Spain for Walter Wanger at United Artists called *Blockade* and went ahead with an outline for her own story, with the approval of a left-leaning young Metro producer named Frank Davis.

Salka's continuing attempts to write a story independent of Garbo may have been partly inspired by Berthold, who was back in London trying to drum up work while Salka sent him living expenses of two hundred dollars a month. "Do you think the time has come not to work for Greta any more?" he wrote. "For some time now it has felt like a burden to you." *Cargo of Innocence* did not get far. Even though Salka cowrote the screenplay with the novelist James Hilton, writer of the popular 1933 novel *Lost Horizon*, Metro shelved the picture. Once again she got a refresher course in the lesson of her Hooverville script: Metro opposed any screen story that showed what it considered unreasonable sympathy toward Communism. And regardless of Salka's own ambitions, her value to the studio was and always would be as a "Garbo specialist."

To that end, the studio was eager to have two scripts ready for Garbo when she returned from a long vacation in Europe with her then companion, the conductor Leopold Stokowski. Thus Bernie Hyman asked Salka to find another story for Garbo at the same time that Gottfried Reinhardt was beginning to prepare the comedy that was to become *Ninotchka*. Although Salka's involvement with *Ninotchka* was limited, she was responsible for its inception. Casting around for ideas, she remembered that the Hungarian dramatist Melchior Lengyel had amusing stories to recount among the writers' rooms at Metro. In mid-1937, Salka made arrangements for Lengyel to pitch and sell his idea for *Ninotchka* directly to Garbo from the side of her swimming pool while the film star took a dip.

Gottfried cowrote an early draft of the *Ninotchka* script with Sam Behrman and was originally assigned to direct, though Ernst Lubitsch ended up with the job. Salka also wrote at least one draft, which as usual was reworked many times by a number of writers. Screenplay credits eventually went to Charles Brackett, Billy Wilder, Walter Reisch, Sam Behrman for additional dialogue, and Melchior Lengyel for the original story.

For the second of the two projects, Salka suggested a story about the Nobel Prize–winning physicist Marie Curie, who had died in 1934 and whose daughter Eve had recently written a biography. Nearly everyone at Metro was appalled at the notion that a self-respecting movie queen would consider portraying so boring and sexless a figure as a scientist. But right away Garbo agreed to take on the role. Reluctantly, Bernie Hyman instructed Salka to go ahead with the treatment.

In the meantime, at the house of her fellow screenwriter Anita Loos, Salka met and befriended the novelist Aldous Huxley. In April 1937, the tall, courtly Englishman had left his villa in Sanary-sur-Mer with his wife and teenaged son to travel in the States, where he gave some lectures and stayed for a time at the ranch in New Mexico owned by Frieda Lawrence, the widow of his old friend D. H. Lawrence. By February of 1938 Huxley was in Hollywood writing screenplays, his beloved house in Sanary abandoned—only for the moment, he imagined, but in fact for the rest of his life. By June he found himself sitting at an alfresco lunch at Bernie Hyman's beach house, discussing *Marie Curie* with Salka. Also present was the director George Cukor, who'd been hired for the Curie picture after his great success for Metro with Garbo's *Camille*.

Salka and her new friend Huxley were like-minded about the Curie story, each determined to remain faithful to the details of the physicist's prodigious career which Hyman found dull and unglamorous. The Anglophile Hyman was dazzled by the success of *Brave New World* and the fact that Huxley's family included a number of illustrious scientists. He took Salka off the treatment and hired Huxley to write a scenario on his own. In late August, Huxley turned in a novelistic 145-page treatment highlighting Marie Curie's dedication as she labored with her husband to discover radium in a squalid one-room laboratory and became the first woman appointed to a lecture chair at the Sorbonne, as well as the first to win a Nobel Prize. Huxley was paid twenty-five thousand dollars for his treatment, but he heard no further from Hyman and "it was instantly forgotten," Salka wrote in her memoir. When she later asked Hyman what became of Huxley's work, he confessed that he'd never read it and had given it to his secretary, who told him without hesitation, "it stinks."

Huxley's friendship with Salka took root quickly and lasted till the end of their lives. But close as he was to Salka, the prolific author left behind scant references to their friendship. Christopher Isherwood spoke of Huxley among those of Salka's famous friends who "were sincerely fond of her but perhaps they tended to take her for granted. It is slightly shocking to find that, in the indexes to the collected letters of two of her 'stars,' Aldous Huxley and Thomas Mann, Salka's name isn't mentioned." Huxley's Belgian wife Maria was more voluble, writing in a letter to her sister that Salka was very "us" because "above all she is a European. She loves perfume and takes lovers." For Maria, Salka offered proof that "Europeans can live in Hollywood while retaining their charm and personality."

At Metro other writers, including F. Scott Fitzgerald, submitted versions of the Curie story, all of which were rejected. Among this group was the German-Jewish novelist Bruno Frank, who had strong connections with many who were or would become members of Salka's circle. Bruno Frank had left Germany in 1933 and moved with his wife Liesl to London, where the couple had become acquainted with Berthold. They were former neighbors and good friends of Thomas Mann, who had also recently landed in Los Angeles. The Franks had lived in Sanary-sur-Mer, where Bruno had contributed to Klaus Mann's magazine *Die Sammlung*, of which Aldous Huxley was one of the founding sponsors. Now reunited with Huxley and Mann, among many of their other European friends in Los Angeles, the Franks were living quite handsomely in Beverly Hills after Bruno had signed a lucrative contract with Metro in 1937.

Metro management's indecision over the Curie project wore on, and personalities cycled in and out of the project. Bruno Frank left the studio after spending seven months on the story. Metro producer Sidney Franklin replaced Bernie Hyman. Cukor left to pursue other obligations, including work on *The Wizard of Oz* and *Gone with the Wind*. Garbo was thoroughly occupied by *Ninotchka*. The only constant on the Curie project, it seemed, was Salka, who collected her much-needed paycheck and waited fruitlessly as other writers came and went, hoping without much hope to revive interest in Huxley's treatment. "Like Ariadne's thread, the work on *Marie Curie* was running through the labyrinth of my life, dangling before me, incessantly interrupted, exasperatingly close to my grasp, then suddenly disappearing," Salka wrote. "Months went by... the Hitler menace grew."

In March 1938, the Anschluss, Germany's annexation of Austria, brought the second-largest wave of panic to European Jews after Hitler's rise in 1933. The Jews of Austria and the thousands of refugees from Germany who had recently sought safety in Vienna and its environs—including Salka's sister Rose and her family—now again frantically feared for their lives, and sought any way possible to flee. "[Hitler] hated Vienna especially," said Gertrud Zeisl, the wife of the Jewish Viennese composer Eric Zeisl, in an oral history; "it was a kind of triumph and pleasure for him to enter there with a regime of terror... People were picked up in the street, brought to Gestapo headquarters and tortured there, and imprisoned and shipped off to the concentration camps at night... everybody wanted to leave, and that caused such a storm that the other countries shut off their borders... you couldn't get a visa; you couldn't get out of the country. It was very, very difficult, and you had to try all kinds of things." The Zeisls were among the lucky few, emigrating to the States in 1938 and settling in Los Angeles in 1941.

For Salka, all direct communication with her sister Rose in Vienna had now ended. Salka could only trust that Josef Gielen's connections in the classical music community might somehow help to get the family out of the country.

Salka kept seeking affidavits for the desperate who were trying to leave Vienna and Prague. She also applied for a quota number for her mother in Poland. Gottfried's father Max Reinhardt managed to reach Los Angeles and settled in Pacific Palisades. There he got word that his castle in Salzburg, which he had spent twenty years restoring for use as both a home and an event space, had been confiscated and occupied by Reich Commander Hermann Goering. Salka wrote that Max Reinhardt bore this theft, along with the loss of his entire theatrical empire, "with great dignity." He opened a drama school on Sunset Boulevard and began to give acting lessons to young

Californians, most of whom had little idea who he was. He also hired Salka's son Hans, who had left Berkeley and enrolled at UCLA, to be his assistant and dramaturg. The previous year, Peter had graduated from high school at age seventeen and spent three months at Dartmouth, but he too returned to Mabery Road and continued his studies at UCLA.

Berthold remained in London, sending updates to Salka about family and friends. In Vienna the SS had dragged his sister Paula to their barracks, where they jeered at her as they made her scrub the floors, then forced her to watch while they beat up an elderly Jewish man. Now Paula was searching for any way to leave. "She has written to you asking for an affidavit," Berthold prodded Salka. "Can you do it?" He reported that Rose was unable to write to Salka and that her husband Josef was under constant surveillance; "If only they could get out!" In the meantime, Berthold's hopes for film work had dried up in London and he was keeping himself busy directing for the theater. But he had little income aside from what Salka was sending him, one hundred dollars on the first and fifteenth of each month, and he apologized to her for costing so much. Around the time of the Munich Pact, in late September 1938, he wrote to her: "That you are forced to live and work in Hollywood, whether you want it or not and whether you can stand it, because you are supporting all of us, Mama and others, is hard to bear, first for you, but even more for me."

In addition to begging her studio contacts for affidavits, Salka found jobs for arriving emigrants. She met a non-Jewish German woman, Etta Hardt, who before 1933 had been an executive secretary for a Berlin publishing house. An outspoken antifascist, Etta had been chased by Nazis to the Dutch border, then drove to Spain, only to be forced to leave when the civil war began. Finally she made her way to Los Angeles on a ship via the Panama Canal. Salka engaged Etta to be Garbo's housekeeper, then hired her a year later to be her own majordomo on Mabery Road. At Salka's house Etta applied a Teutonic vigor to sorting out the household's disarray, tackling everything from the Viertel boys' untidiness and Salka's chaotic bookkeeping to the tangled coats of the two Irish setters.

Salka Viertel with one of her Irish setters, Mabery Road.

Eight months after the Anschluss, on the night of November 9, 1938, a forty-eight-hour mass pogrom exploded throughout Germany and Austria that came to be known as Kristallnacht, "Night of the Broken Glass," and marked a turning point in Germany's war against the Jews. The legal, political, and economic harassment of Jews was already paramount in official National Socialist policy. Now the procedures changed to incite physical brutality and, wherever possible, murder. The annihilation of the Jewish people tipped over from rhetorical threats into organized widespread implementation. Kristallnacht marked the night, as the historian Lucy S. Dawidowicz wrote, that "the Jewish community of Germany went up in flames."

During Kristallnacht, with the full encouragement of their government, German citizens engaged in an orgy of terror and violence that destroyed an estimated 7,500 Jewish-owned commercial establishments; killed at least 91 Jews; tortured thousands more; arrested up to 30,000 Jews and sent them to concentration camps at Buchenwald, Dachau, and Sachsenhausen; and destroyed 267 synagogues.

On orders from Hermann Goering and the Gestapo, local police and firefighters did nothing to prevent the destruction. The government blamed the Jews for the riots and fined them one billion reichsmarks to pay for the very destruction that had been perpetrated to harm them.

All these facts were reported in the American press by early December 1938. Information was also abundantly available in U.S. newspapers about the Anschluss and the mounting refugee crisis. Yet Roosevelt and the Congress declined suggestions of any legislation to ease the immigration quotas, not even willing to identify Hitler's victims as Jews, as Hitler did, but referring to them more vaguely as "political refugees." Polls showed that after Kristallnacht 77 percent of Americans opposed an increase in the number of refugees who should be allowed to enter the country. The official government position was "sympathy without hospitality."

By November 29, 1938, the American consulate in Berlin reported 160,000 applications for U.S. visas. Without new legislation to ease the quotas, the consul general declared that none of those who applied could hope to receive permits for at least three years. Yet "flight was both necessary and possible in the weeks and months following [Kristallnacht]," Haskel Lookstein wrote in a 1985 book. "It remained so through 1941. What could not be fully foreseen, however, was the future—the human price that would be paid after 1941 for the failure of the world to open its doors while there was still time."

At some point between the nine months separating the Anschluss and Kristallnacht, appalled by anti-Semitic sentiment in the United States and by the ineffectiveness of the official American response to these atrocities, Bruno Frank's wife Liesl took the first steps toward establishing an American grass-roots response to the Jewish refugee emergency. Liesl was the daughter of an internationally popular Viennese opera star named Fritzi Massary. She became active in refugee work in Europe immediately after 1933. When she arrived in Los Angeles in 1937, she continued to raise money to support Jewish emigration to America. By 1938 Liesl Frank, along with Charlotte Dieterle and a group of like-minded Hollywood folk, had established the European Film Fund in Hollywood.

The EFF asked all Europeans employed by the studios to donate 1 percent of their salaries toward refugee relief. When *Casablanca* wrapped at Warner Bros. in 1942, for instance, the cast and crew—almost entirely European émigrés—gave that percentage of their earnings to the EFF. "You paid in," said the German actor Paul Andor, who played the man without a passport who is shot by Vichy police at the beginning of *Casablanca*, "for the next guys who were coming along." In fact, Jack Warner was the first studio head to arrange for incoming refugees to receive studio contracts through EFF funds. He was urged on by an aggressive young producer on the Warner lot named Henry Blanke, who was born in Berlin and had gotten his start as an assistant to Ernst Lubitsch.

Salka herself was not a founding member of the EFF, though she hosted some membership meetings at her house. In her memoir she made a point to give proper credit to Liesl Frank and Charlotte Dieterle for conceiving the idea and for attending tirelessly to its tedious and frustrating paperwork. Salka was both a contributor to the fund and, in her later years, a recipient of its largesse.

Donations to the EFF helped refugees in two related ways: by collecting the papers that were necessary for them to enter the States and by providing them with the means to survive once they landed there. Although high-profile male members of the fund lent it credibility and prestige (Lubitsch and the agent Paul Kohner in particular), Liesl Frank and Charlotte Dieterle exhibited a superhuman persistence in pursuing and processing the mountains of paperwork required to orchestrate the legal emigration of each refugee. For example, in order to leave France and enter the United States around that time, an emigrant needed the following documents: two notarized affidavits, one for sponsorship and one for support, along with bank statements; a U.S. visitor visa; a transit visa; an exit visa; a "biographical sketch," preferably written by as distinguished a personage as one could muster; and a studio contract or some similar employment document to prove that one would not become a public charge in America.

Aside from contributing part of her weekly salary to the fund, Salka supported it in further ways, primarily by obtaining affidavits. In her memoir, she named the friends whom she personally persuaded to sponsor refugees financially, including Dorothy Parker, Herman Mankiewicz, Donald Ogden Stewart, Miriam Hopkins, and Samuel Hoffenstein. Of these, she wrote that they "generously guaranteed with their bank accounts that none of my protégés would become a financial burden to the United States and I am happy to say that none ever did." And Salka provided sustenance and support by taking refugees into her home, absorbing them into her social and professional networks, and helping to integrate them into American society with its often bewildering language and customs.

In February 1939, Salka herself became a citizen of the United States. Although she hated "flag-waving and patriotic demonstrations," she confessed to being moved as she said the oath of allegiance, feeling immensely grateful toward the country that had done so much for her. Foremost in her mind, though, was what she could do for others as a result of her new status. She expressed her hope that she could somehow get her mother and brother out of Poland as Hitler's threats of war escalated and the panic of the hundreds of thousands trying to leave Europe intensified.

IN HOLLYWOOD, Metro's internal politics ground onward. Salka's participation on *Ninotchka* ended in mid-1939 when Gottfried Reinhardt was fired from the picture after arguing with Lubitsch about a plot point. Until then, Salka had wielded a fair amount of influence on the project, both as Garbo's representative and in consultation with Gottfried. Evidence of her authority survives in a poignant letter to Salka dated March 1939 from the actor Alexander Granach, a former colleague of hers from Max Reinhardt's Berlin theaters:

> Dear Salka Steuermann,
> It is said here that you and Gottfried Reinhardt are preparing a Greta Garbo film, one that takes place in the USSR. Since I worked there (as you know) for almost three years, I could firstly (what could I not?) play any role! And secondly, I could provide you with a bag full of experiences. I intend to go to Hollywood anyway...and without diplomacy. I know it's hard, but I want you to take care of me a little. Salka Steuermann, if your lifeboat is full, I'm not burdened because I row very well. That's all. And now I hope to hear from you soon, so that the ride should be a little easier for me.

Some of Alexander Granach's early life mirrored Salka's. He was born to Jewish parents in Galicia, spoke at least six languages, and played a variety of leading roles in Weimar-era Berlin, including a complex and dignified Shylock in *The Merchant of Venice*. After 1933 he fled to the Soviet Union, where he ran a Yiddish theater in Kiev, then was arrested in 1937 by Stalin's secret police as a suspected German spy. Narrowly escaping imprisonment and death, Granach managed to get to America by way of Switzerland. As he was casting about for a job in Hollywood, Granach wrote his droll entreaty to Salka, imagining her as the pilot of a rescue boat and using her maiden name, Steuermann, to point up its meaning of "helmsman." Salka's lifeboat was indeed full, but by all appearances she and Gottfried were able to make room for Granach. The actor joined *Ninotchka*'s cast in a plum role as Kopalski, one of the three Soviet commissars who become corrupted by capitalism on a visit to the West. Granach went on to play both antifascists and Gestapo agents during his Hollywood career, and during the war he wrote an extraordinary account of his life which was published in English as *There Goes an Actor.* His livelihood in exile would never have been assured without Salka's role in his Hollywood launch.

IN JULY 1939, Berthold returned again to Mabery Road, having failed to renew his British work visa. The overstuffed house now included Salka's brother Edward, who was visiting for the summer, along with all three Viertel boys. Among the steady stream of guests was Christopher Isherwood, who had arrived in Los Angeles in May. Salka wrote that Berthold found the atmosphere "too lively" and moved into the apartment over the garage. "Lively" more accurately meant tense. All the adults were worrying daily about the bad news coming from Europe and Salka mentioned also that she and Gottfried were frequently quarreling. Some of their arguments were large-scale. Gottfried would tell Salka that he wanted to leave her because he wanted to marry and have children; but "he always came back and told me that he could not live without me,"

Salka recalled in her diary in 1963. And others were minor: "Gottfried liked me to get furious at him and then cajole and seduce me afterwards," she recalled. "It made him feel irresistible. And how indignant he would become when I did not wait and either went without him or did something else."

At Metro, the endless disagreements about *Marie Curie* were wearing on her. She had turned fifty in June and was out of patience with "people who considered themselves superior only because they were overpaid." But Salka's salary, which had now reached $650 a week and was supporting a growing network, was indispensable. Back in April, Gottfried and Sam Hoffenstein had convinced Salka to hire the agent Paul Kohner to represent her. They were sure that Kohner would be able to advocate better for her than she could for herself. It was a delicate situation: studios were naturally hostile to agents and were known to bar them from the lot for demanding raises for their clients. But Salka needed to maximize her salary and hoped that Kohner, a fast-rising Czech-born émigré whom she had known since her earliest Hollywood days, could finesse a deal.

At a story impasse on the Curie treatment in Sidney Franklin's office, Salka was still arguing fruitlessly against the producer's conviction that "no pretty girl would ever study chemistry or physics." Finally one of the other writers suggested that Salka might go to Paris to interview Marie Curie's two daughters, one of whom was herself a physicist and might provide some clues about her mother's motivation. In her memoir Salka noted that "this is one of the things the studio adored: sending someone to the Antipodes, to the South Seas, to the Congo, or at least across the Atlantic." But this time it was a good idea. Salka's fluency in both French and Polish (she spoke six languages in all), along with her natural talent for diplomacy, could secure the Curie family's cooperation. Metro was relieved to kick the story problems down the road, while Salka was hoping she could tack on a trip to Poland to see her mother and brother.

On the last day of July Salka sailed from New York on the *Normandie* in beautiful weather. Also aboard the elegant ship was an A-list of vacationing celebrities, all in festive spirits: Norma Shearer, Edward G. Robinson, Charles Boyer, Bob Hope, and the Columbia Pictures chief Harry Cohn. Salka laughed along with them and kept her anxieties hidden. Her brother Edward was worried about the signs pointing toward a new war and feared for her safety. Liesl Frank had asked her to look up and comfort a great many people who were waiting for American visas. Berthold had his own long list of messages for Salka to relay as well. But Salka later remembered that nobody aboard this luxury liner was talking about Hitler. Hoping to see her mother again, she tried to be optimistic. She was glad enough, for the moment, to be on her way.

PARIS WAS EMPTIED for the August *vacances*. The executives in Metro's local offices were off to rest cures in the countryside. Salka was unpacking in her room at the Plaza Athénée when suddenly her friend Marcel Achard bounded in as a surprise, insisting on hearing all the news from Mabery Road. Achard had reestablished his playwriting career in Paris after his stint in Hollywood. When Salka told him why she was in town, he told her that he knew Eve Curie well and would be glad to arrange a meeting. Eve's older sister Irène was more difficult, he said, but he had friends who could try to engage her cooperation as well.

While Salka waited for Achard's help, she and a photographer toured the vacant laboratories and lecture halls of the Sorbonne where Marie Curie had taught. They inspected the exterior of the unprepossessing Institute of Radium, closed now for the summer recess. In the evenings Salka sat at the Deux Magots café in Saint-Germain-des-Prés with her good friends the Viennese journalist Alfred Polgar and his wife, both of whom had left Austria a day before the Anschluss and were now waiting for U.S. visas. At the surrounding tables were many other refugees, some of whom Salka recognized from her Weimar days. All had the same strained faces as the Polgars. All looked worn down by the monotony of their suspended existence. All seemed newly fearful because of Hitler's threats against Poland.

It was now mid-August. Salka learned that both Curie daughters were on holiday separately in Brittany, Irène in the fishing village of L'Arcouëst and Eve about an hour and a half's drive east, in the resort town of Dinard. Salka set off to find them in a studio-hired Renault with a chauffeur who shouted curses at every other motorist on the clotted roadways.

In the end, neither Curie daughter offered Salka much, though the chic and beautiful Eve was indeed friendlier to Salka than her severe older sister. Not even an advance letter of support from Berthold's friend Albert Einstein was able to soften the Curie daughters. Both were certain that their parents' story would be cheapened by Hollywood, with or without Garbo. Nonetheless Salka tried hard to build a bridge between the Curies and the studio, as she had done with Schoenberg and Thalberg. She pledged Metro's commitment to keep the picture dignified and honest, arguing that films about great scientists could educate a vast audience.

In truth Salka found her sympathies more aligned with the Curie women than with the studio. She respected their wish not to simplify their parents' accomplishments and could not even be sure that the final screenplay would reflect the assurances she was making. She had too little power and knew too well that profit, not veracity, was Metro's prime motive. Both daughters declined to participate in the end, refusing even to allow Salka to take photographs inside the Institute of Radium. They explained that if they cooperated with her they would forfeit their right to protest the final product. "Not in a position to take full responsibility," Salka remembered, "I remained silent." She explained the futility of her efforts in a letter to Metro producer Sidney Franklin: "Dear Sidney, when [Irène] refuses it is as if the Rock of Gibraltar were to refuse."

Dejectedly returning to Paris, Salka searched for other scientists she might interview. At the same time she attempted to get a French visa for her mother and brother, but gave up after fruitless hours of waiting in line with all the refugees at city hall. It had been twelve years since she had last seen her brother Dusko. She made arrangements to meet him and Auguste in Warsaw, planning to fly to Poland on August 23.

In her memoir Salka wrote that when she got back to Paris on August 21, the newspapers were announcing the German-Soviet Non-Aggression Pact, and she began to worry about traveling to Poland. Hitler's agreement with Stalin laid the groundwork for the Führer to attack Poland without Soviet intervention. Telegrams began to pour in for Salka—from Gottfried, from Berthold, from Bernie Hyman—insisting that she return to the

States at once. All believed that war was inevitable. But arranging a return was nearly impossible. Ships were crammed to capacity with Americans hastily abandoning their European vacations. Salka learned that no one at Metro was interested in the Curie film any longer, or inclined to instruct her to proceed anywhere other than back to Hollywood. With the studio's influence, Salka was lucky enough to book passage from Le Havre on the *Île de France*, set to sail for New York on September 1.

In the meantime, the telephone in Salka's room at the Plaza Athénée rang and rang with calls begging her for help. Many of the voices were those of people she knew. Others were strangers, acquaintances of acquaintances. People from every stratum of society were seeking affidavits and she swore to do what she could. The desperation besieged her conscience. "My American passport made me feel guilty," she wrote later, "because my heartless adopted country refused entrance to the 'oppressed, persecuted and poor.'" In the evening she walked with Alfred and Lisl Polgar through the Palais Royal, the city blacked out and the columns of the palace glowing in the moonlight. The Polgars were sure that Hitler would attack Poland. Salka tried not to believe them.

In the daylight hours she exchanged tearful telegrams with her mother. Auguste consoled her with a promise to visit the States when her quota number, which Salka had applied for around the time of the Anschluss, at last arrived, and with the good news that Dusko had not yet been called up to the Polish army reserves. On Salka's last night in the city she joined the Polgars for a final dinner at the Deux Magots. "There were the usual intertwined couples on the boulevard," she recalled, "and the refugees, who now spoke in whispers. Those I knew approached our table and again I wrote down addresses and promised help."

The next day, in Le Havre, Salka rushed to send a telegram to her mother from the pier before the *Île de France* set sail. The clerk looked at her quizzically as she wrote out the address. "Poland?" he asked. "The Germans are in Poland, madame. It's war."

In her cabin aboard the ship Salka tried to gather herself, thanking fortune that Auguste and Dusko had not traveled to meet her in Warsaw. Sambor was far away from the Polish capital. Perhaps it would be spared. A steward knocked at her door, found her in tears, and encouraged her to go up on deck. It was oppressively hot. The time for sailing had long passed and the ship remained motionless. There were rumors that it would not sail if France declared war.

The ship was still moored the next morning when Salka was called to attend safety drills. In a moment that would be wildly unbelievable in a work of fiction, she put on her life jacket and gathered with the crowds of passengers, finding herself assigned to the same rescue boat as the renowned cello virtuoso Gregor Piatigorsky and the equally famous violinist Nathan Milstein. Nearby was the Viennese novelist Gina Kaus, whom Salka had known in Berlin and who was emigrating with her husband and sons. In Salka's lifeboat during the drill, all were wondering whether France and England would go to war. No one had heard any news. The ship remained in port throughout the long day, the air stagnant.

At ten that night the siren groaned and the *Île de France* began to move. It docked briefly in Southampton, where the English newspapers were brought aboard. At four in the morning Salka was finally able to grab a copy of the *Times* and read the headlines. England and France had declared war on Germany. To allay her family's fears in Santa Monica, she cabled them that she was on her way home at last. A week later she arrived in New York, where she stayed for a few days to try to expedite her mother's visa. Bernie Hyman phoned to welcome her back to America, overjoyed that she was safe, and then informed her that Metro had decided to abandon *Marie Curie*. (A version was eventually released in 1943, starring Greer Garson, after Garbo had left the studio.) Salka, he instructed, should start looking immediately for another comedy for Garbo. She arranged to take the train back to California.

Poland surrendered within the month and was carved up between Germany and the Soviet Union, which occupied western Ukraine. Sambor and Wychylowka were now under control of the USSR. Communication with Auguste became difficult. Salka heard from the State Department that her mother's visa had been forwarded to the American consulate in Bucharest. There was nothing to do but wait. The massive human logjam that Europe had become, where survival depended entirely on the ink marks of bureaucrats, had never felt more personal or dire. What were Auguste and Dusko enduring under Soviet occupation? And what was happening to Rose in Vienna? Salka heard that Josef Gielen had somehow been able to escape to Buenos Aires. Had Rose and the children managed to join him, or were they still in Europe?

DURING SEPTEMBER IN SANTA MONICA, the eternal sunbathers idled, the fat pelicans skimmed over the milky edges of the surf, and hot Santa Ana winds pummeled the eucalyptus trees. At Metro the extras chatted merrily through their lunch hours and the executives strutted around pompously, flirting with the starlets. Surrounded by blithe indifference, Salka felt half mad with guilt and fear. The disconnect between the terror she had left behind in Europe and the nonchalance on the beach and at the studio wore on her nerves as much as the silence from Sambor and Vienna.

"One does not wander without punishment under palms," Berthold was fond of repeating to Christopher Isherwood, who had moved with his partner, a painter, into a house overlooking the ocean, just above the Viertels. Isherwood was teaming again with Berthold to work on an idea for a film about a young German officer who is seduced into the National Socialist party after the Great War. He recalled that the two men spent hours nearly every day in Berthold's upstairs warren on Mabery Road "in a coma of nicotine poisoning." They were "two aliens from doomed Europe," Isherwood wrote, who "carried our twisted, pain-ridden psyches amongst the statuesque, unselfconscious bodies of California, basking in the frank sunshine. Where would these bronzed and muscular boys be, five years from now?"

Berthold and Isherwood's screenplay had been commissioned by a shoestring producer whose relationship with Berthold deteriorated into bitter arguments over deadlines. The script went nowhere and the writers were never paid. In fact, "after much barking and little biting," Isherwood noted, he himself paid several hundred dollars to settle with the producer out of court.

At Metro, Salka had her own frustrations. She was sidelined in her office while *Ninotchka* hummed busily along without her.

Her desk was groaning with novels and plays recommended by the story department for Garbo's next picture, none of which seemed usable. Meanwhile her old pal Ernst Lubitsch, *Ninotchka*'s director, came every day to tell her which scenes they had shot and what a fabulous job Garbo was doing.

After the outbreak of the war in Europe, the house on Mabery Road was also on edge. Berthold's temper exploded at the tiniest perceived insult. He went around "snorting like a war-horse," in Isherwood's words, at Hans's late hours at the Reinhardt school, at Peter's unseriousness, at the always barking dogs. Tommy wandered through these domestic minefields in a good-humored reverie, a fourteen-year-old compilation of messy red hair and glasses. Salka too was impatient with the boys, berating nineteen-year-old Peter for spending all his time on the tennis court. In the living room one evening Peter brushed by her, racquet in hand, and casually dropped a letter onto her lap. It was from the publisher Harcourt Brace offering Peter an advance for a novel he had written in secret. The book was called *The Canyon* and it recounted his childhood days roaming around the neighborhood with his Mexican friends. Peter's precociously self-assured book, published the following year, ends with a catastrophic flood, about whose aftermath Peter had taken careful note:

> The creek bed had gone. There were many trees, even some of the old ones, that had been torn down by the water. All through the canyon you could see the tops of cars sticking up out of the muddy current. Down to the sea. Down to the sea. It took everything. Telephone poles, toys, furniture, garbage cans, and always mud, heavy and brown, that was the water's brother.

Floods were regular local occurrences in the canyon and Peter was narrating events he had doubtless seen many times. But it's hard to dismiss the ominousness of the passage as a reflection of the foreboding that everyone was feeling at Salka's house that year.

THE SUNDAY PARTIES continued insistently, even frantically, their nervous high spirits creating a soundtrack behind the regular family drama. "I suppose," Isherwood ventured in his diary, "that people of Salka's temperament actually prefer to talk to their intimate friends when they are surrounded by a chattering crowd. She creates huge, expensively fed gatherings of bores as a background to her meetings with Gottfried." This was somewhat unfair. Salka saw Gottfried daily at the studio and nearly as often at home, and even with their frequent spats her alliance with him was strong. She hardly needed to cook for a crowd in order to see him. In any case, Isherwood himself was delighted to be folded into the drama. He basked in Salka's attention as the two became confidants. Isherwood's lifelong sentimental affinity for landladies—from Mrs. Tiggy-Winkle of his childhood's favorite Beatrix Potter books to his own creation of Fräulein Schroeder in *The Berlin Stories*—drew him to Salka as a paragon of the form. He could not get enough of her unconditional acceptance, which Isherwood felt he had never received from his own emotionally withholding mother.

As Berthold had predicted years ago in London, Isherwood and Garbo also became friendly, frequently running into each other when the actress came around to discuss some urgent matter or other with Salka. Garbo delighted Isherwood by girlishly climbing the Viertels' fig tree to pick him the ripest fruit, and they picnicked together at a large gathering that autumn which was organized by the Huxleys in Tujunga Canyon, in the wilds of the Angeles Forest north of the San Fernando Valley. The party of about thirty people also included Salka and Berthold, Anita Loos, Bertrand Russell, and the Hindu spiritual teacher Krishnamurti. At the picnic Garbo wore trousers and her favorite straw gardening hat, with a plaster patch between her eyebrows to prevent wrinkles. She brought her own lunch in a basket. Much of the talk was of the war. When the party hiked toward a wire fence covered with trespass warnings, there was jumpy laughter when Anita Loos jokingly suggested that they tunnel under it like escaping refugees. Few in the party seemed to notice the area's natural beauty. Isherwood remembered that "Berthold—that born city dweller—might just as well have been walking down Fifth Avenue."

EVERYWHERE SALKA WENT IN LOS ANGELES she heard the clamor for affidavits. Every day the stack on her desk of beseeching letters from Vienna, Prague, and Paris grew fatter. Her secretary Etta Hardt stuffed them all into a file and labeled it "Years of the Devil." For many of those who did manage to flee, the costs of exile were high. The previous May, the Viertels' friend Ernst Toller, one of the first German exiles to find a haven at Sanary-sur-Mer, had hanged himself at the Mayflower Hotel in New York. Toller had recently learned that his brother and sister had been sent to concentration camps. He was also despondent over the decline of his playwriting career in exile.

Salka and Berthold would lose other friends to suicide—former Sanaryans all, as it happened—in the years that followed, including Walter Hasenclever in the French internment camp at Les Milles in June 1940 and Stefan Zweig in Petrópolis, Brazil, in February 1942.

What could any one person do? Salka took in Berthold's niece Susan and her eight-month-old baby, who came to stay from England while her husband, a British Navy officer, was deployed abroad. She also welcomed a thirteen-year-old refugee named Andrew Frank, agreeing to look after him until his mother could scrape together a livelihood on the East Coast. Andrew's father was the novelist Leonhard Frank (no relation to Bruno and Liesl) who was then in an internment camp in France. Eventually Leonhard would manage to escape to Lisbon. His life would be saved via passage to the States through a joint effort by the Emergency Rescue Committee, which supplied his visa, and the European Film Fund, which gathered affidavits for him. Andrew Frank was around Tommy's age and a bright, affable boy. Salka had no trouble absorbing him into the household, which at this time also included her niece Margret, Edward's daughter, who lived at Mabery Road throughout the war years.

Salka's salary of $650 per week was thus responsible for the daily care and feeding of Susan and her baby, Andrew, Margret, and the five Viertels. It financed the Sunday parties and paid for the Japanese maid and gardener, the somewhat fearsome German cook, and the indefatigable Etta Hardt. A good portion of that $650 then went to Europe for the refugees, including the percentage of Salka's salary that she donated to the European Film Fund. Large sums also went to anonymous Jewish relief workers who promised to forward the money to Auguste and

Dusko. (Years later, Salka learned that her mother had received only a tiny portion of what she had sent.) And now Christmas was coming, and with it a long list of extra financial obligations.

It was at just this moment that Paul Kohner, the agent who had assured Salka that she deserved twice as much as Metro was paying her, approached the studio's general manager Eddie Mannix to discuss her contract. On the same day, Salka learned that Mannix, who despite a fearsome reputation had until now always been her champion, was infuriated at her gall in allowing an agent to intercede after seven years of the studio's steady and beneficent raises. Mannix summarily fired her. "She should see if Kohner can get her a better job!" Mannix shouted.

There is no evidence to suggest that Garbo did anything to intervene on Salka's behalf. Her attention was elsewhere. *Ninotchka* was finished and an enormous hit, grossing $1,187,000 domestically and nearly as much overseas, even without the now-defunct European market. Yet Garbo did not think the film particularly funny, worried that it was vulgar, and had not enjoyed working with Lubitsch. She was uninterested in talking about future projects. Her time was now devoted almost entirely to the companionship of a popular diet expert named Gayelord Hauser. At thirty-four, she was preoccupied with the specter of aging and was adhering hopefully to Hauser's regimen of a raw-food diet and obsessive skin care.

All during what Salka called "this autumn of tears and anxiety," $650 per week had kept her crowded enterprise afloat. With no more paychecks coming in, how would she and her entire network survive?

7

LIFEBOAT

It is a fantastic commentary on the inhumanity of our times that for thousands and thousands of people a piece of paper with a stamp on it is the difference between life and death.

—DOROTHY THOMPSON

Nay, take my life and all; pardon not that:
You take my house when you do take the prop
That doth sustain my house; you take my life
When you do take the means whereby I live.

—*THE MERCHANT OF VENICE*, ACT 4, SCENE 1

LOS ANGELES, SANARY-SUR-MER, AND MARSEILLE
1939–1942

FOR A WHILE SALKA TRIED TO PRETEND that all would be fine, and made no accommodations to adjust to her vanished income. Isherwood noted in his diary: "Faced by Salka's lost job at MGM, the Viertels are displaying a fatalistic extravagance. Sheaves of cables to Europe. Shopfuls of gifts from an expedition to Tijuana. They are a real Chekhov family." Salka threw a party on Christmas Eve, the tree ablaze with candles. The guests sang "Stille Nacht" and "O Tannenbaum." Edward's daughter played the piano. Peter gave Salka and Berthold the bound manuscript of his novel *The Canyon*, which made Salka cry. She also gave a boozy New Year's Eve party, and got drunk while mixing her own punch. Tipsily she called Isherwood over, telling him, "I want to drink blood brotherhood with you." They drank and embraced, and Salka said: "I am going to tell you a very important secret. If a man wants a woman enough, he can have her. Absolutely. It's only a question of time and place...*Any* man. Any man on *earth*!" A perfectly timed pause, and then: "Except Louis B. Mayer." Later, Isherwood drank so much that Peter had to take him home and put him to bed.

Salka's composure did not last long. She began to consider other ways to make money. Her friends fawned over her cooking enough to make her think seriously about opening a restaurant in the canyon or a goulash wagon on the beach. Her sons assured her that a hot-dog stand would be a gold mine. The idea caused a lot of teasing around the house, with Gottfried predicting that a few weeks as a full-time cook would drive Salka straight back into Eddie Mannix's constricting embrace. The usually generous Ernst Lubitsch declined to finance her, warning her that she'd be feeding all of Hollywood for nothing.

In fact this was most likely true. Joe May, the Austrian film pioneer who'd helped to bring Billy Wilder and Franz Waxman to Hollywood, endured the failures of two Hollywood restaurants after his once-flourishing directing career evaporated. May's second venture, the Blue Danube on Sunset Boulevard, was bankrolled by many sponsors of the European Film Fund but closed soon after it opened in 1949, failing to attract customers outside the émigré community. May spent the remaining years until his death in 1954 in near-seclusion. Formerly a contributor to the European Film Fund, in his last years he lived entirely on its donations.

Salka continued to feed the whole town for nothing in the comfort of her own home. Every Sunday her parties continued, along with frequent smaller gatherings during the week. On a random Tuesday in February 1940, she invited Aldous and Maria Huxley, Christopher Isherwood, Anita Loos, and Gottfried to dinner. Berthold and Isherwood spent much of the meal seeking Huxley's help in convincing a producer to bring Beatrix Lehmann over from England for a film role. Then Berthold started an argument about Russia's war policy, skirmishing first with Salka and then with Gottfried about the Soviet invasion of Finland. Gottfried supported the Finns and happily contemplated the suffering of the Russian troops in the harsh winter cold. As Isherwood reported: "Berthold left the room. Although he isn't jealous in the ordinary, sexual sense, there's no doubt that the friendship between Salka and Gottfried has a lot to do with these fights."

Salka chose to ignore Berthold's outburst and attended instead to Huxley, who was telling her about a scientific advance in which female rabbits could be impregnated by other female rabbits but would then produce only females. He and Salka proceeded to entertain each other with a Huxleyan fantasy about a future era of women without men, imagining a "lesbian tyranny" in Hollywood: the "Warner Sisters, Louisa B. Mayer, United Artistes, Twentieth Century Vixen, etc."

Berthold's ill temper during this unhappy period of his life was not his only emotional key. Just as frequently he was mild and distracted, and often funny. (Peter remembered that Berthold characterized agent Paul Kohner, whom he justifiably regarded at this time "with good-natured distrust," as "the comparative of Kohn.") Berthold was a full participant in Salka's mission to absorb émigrés into the ever-widening Mabery Road circle, generous to every refugee who crossed his path and happy to play host to them whenever he was living at home. And he loved all three of his children, if he did not always sufficiently let them know this, and worried extravagantly about them.

In February 1940 Paul Kohner came through for Salka, selling a story of hers to Warner Bros., an adaptation of an autobiographical novel by Katalin Gero about a woman who goes to heroic lengths to build orphanages in Budapest. Kohner managed to finagle for Salka a whopping thousand-dollars-per-week salary. Among other reasons for celebration, Salka owed money to the bank for back debts on her house and was glad to afford the payments once again. In April Berthold went to New York to stage a Terence Rattigan play called *Grey Farm* starring his former *Die Truppe* leading man Oscar Homolka. He left with relief, glad to have a job and secure for the moment that the family finances were more stable.

About her Warners gig, Salka later wrote, "in the long run the hotdog stand might have given us more permanent security." The job lasted less than three months. There were licensing problems with the story and the picture was shelved. As their cash-flow problems resumed, Salka and Berthold exchanged worried suggestions about putting the house up as collateral to get a new loan. Just as Salka was finishing up at Warners, Gottfried's prediction about her return to Metro came true. Most likely at Garbo's insistence, Eddie Mannix called to ask when she was coming back—without Paul Kohner, he added. Kohner graciously agreed to drop Salka as a client, but advised her to insist on the thousand dollars she'd been getting at Warners. When Salka went in to see Mannix, he enfolded her in his beefy arms, declared his love for her, and insisted that she rejoin the studio at $750 per week. Salka became flustered by Mannix's fast talk and agreed to his terms. "And so," she recalled, in June 1940, "much to Greta's pleasure, I returned to the 'MGM fold' and to the perennial search for a Garbo story."

Salka first suggested a Western based on a novel set in northern California called *Woman of Spain*, by the Los Angeles writer Scott O'Dell. But producer Bernie Hyman was not keen on expensive location shoots. What he and everyone at the studio most avidly wanted for Garbo was a comedy—preferably something like an Americanized *Ninotchka*. Salka halfheartedly proposed the adaptation of an old staple she remembered from the Vienna Burgtheater, a silly bit of fluff by Ludwig Fulda called *The Twin Sister*. George Cukor was assigned to direct, and Garbo gave her assent.

One wonders how many at Metro aside from Salka and Gottfried Reinhardt knew that Ludwig Fulda, *The Twin Sister*'s German-Jewish playwright, had killed himself in Berlin the previous year after being denied entry into the United States. In 1943, Sam Behrman wrote a tribute to Ludwig Fulda in the *New York Times* in which he explained the aging playwright's final days:

> My friend Bruno Frank tells me that he last saw Fulda in Switzerland just after the advent of Hitler. It was impossible for him to assimilate the concept of no longer being considered a German. He was completely bewildered by what had happened both to

> Germany and to him. He was over seventy. He had held high honors in his native country. He was distinguished in philanthropy and in letters and yet here he was in Switzerland—an exile—with his country making a virtue and a slogan of the racial principle that had ousted him. He could not take it in. He was stunned and, I gather, never recovered until he died.

Heedless of fate and cataclysm, Metro invested itself in Fulda's comedy for Garbo. But the continuing bad news from Europe made it hard for Salka to concentrate on writing silly jokes for a mindless farce. When Berthold in New York admitted to Salka in May that "the imminent conquest of Paris does not aggravate my diabetes so much as the bombings of London and Berlin," Salka told him that she "could not write nor work nor think coherently" and "remained glued to the radio in despair."

Isherwood had noted the obsessive dependence on radios among the Hollywood Europeans. "The radio broadcasts claimed large portions of each day," he wrote. "Liesl Frank (wife of Bruno, the writer) carried a portable set about with her, like a sick baby. She nursed it in her arms, bent over it as it muttered its advertisements, tuned it up loud for each new bulletin."

Peter added to Salka's anxieties by trying to enlist in the Canadian Royal Air Force. He was certain that the United States would remain neutral and was frantic that he might never get a chance to fight the Nazis. Salka was relieved when the Canadian draft board rejected him for deficient eyesight. She later wrote: "I dreaded the thought of his being a pilot and my only hope was that my former housekeeper, Jessie's husband, was on the recruiting board. War or peace, the world is rather small when you think of it."

In the meantime, at the Beverly Hills Tennis Club that spring, Peter befriended a twenty-seven-year-old writer who seemed surprised that Peter at nineteen not only played a decent game of tennis but had already written a novel. Peter invited his sporty new acquaintance to the Mabery Road parties, where he became the first of Peter's "tennis friends" to impress Salka with his love of literature and the theater. Always ardent around handsome young men, Salka warmed to his charisma. The Bronx-born Jewish writer, whose name was Irwin Shaw, was dazzled by Salka's Sunday crowds and added many of the émigrés he met there to his own large social circle. Shaw was to become one of the most prolific and popular of the Greatest Generation American novelists, beginning with a spectacular war saga called *The Young Lions* in 1948. He had a Salka-like gift for generosity, nurturing the ambitions of younger writers, including the entire original *Paris Review* crowd. He was Peter's closest friend for the next fifty years and played a key role in Salka's later life as well.

IN SOUTHERN FRANCE during that springtime of 1940, Sanary-sur-Mer had never seemed lovelier to *les Allemands* who clung to its hillsides. After seven years, Lion Feuchtwanger still appreciated the morning views of "the azure coast, the mountains, the sea, the pines," and the nighttime quiet, "broken only by the wash of the sea or by the gentle call of some bird." As dusk fell one mild evening in mid-May, Feuchtwanger was listening to the radio in a little room on the bottom floor of his house, the Villa Valmer, when he heard this report: "All German nationals residing in the precincts of Paris, men and women alike, and all persons between the ages of seventeen and fifty-five who were born in Germany but are without German citizenship, are to report for internment."

Villa Valmer, Sanary-sur-Mer.

Feuchtwanger had already been interned and released the previous year, in the brickworks at Les Milles near Aix-en-Provence. This time, he hoped the edict would apply only to those in Paris and not in southern France. He walked out to his garden, where the fig, cherry, almond, and olive trees cast their shadows in the velvet dark. One of his cats twined playfully around his ankles, wanting her dinner.

Franz Werfel, too, remained under Sanary's spell, writing away in his workroom on the top floor of an old watchtower he had bought in 1938 called the Moulin Gris, "a bright room in the sky," his biographer called it, "on the edge of a precipitous coastline." Almost every day Werfel met Lion Feuchtwanger and other writers in the cafés, where they would argue over the most recent news bulletins. Werfel was plump, rumpled, and excitable ("he smudges so easily," said one of his friends). The compact Feuchtwanger was infinitely more self-possessed.

Heinrich Mann, a lifelong Francophile, had been living a couple of hours up the coast in Nice for the last six years. Though few remember Heinrich today, he once vied with his younger brother Thomas to be the most exalted German writer of the Weimar era. Left-wing readers flocked to Heinrich, while the more conservative leaned toward Thomas. Heinrich's leadership among the writers of the antifascist campaign was so august that Ludwig Marcuse called him "the Hindenburg of the emigration," the president in absentia of their hijacked country. But as the continent began to crumble, so did Heinrich's reputation. His latest novel, *The Last Days of Henri Quatre*, marked the beginning of the end of his international stature, the last to be translated into English. In a letter to friends in 1939, Heinrich had written that the times themselves had become the real novel of the age.

Berthold Viertel had met Heinrich years earlier through Karl Kraus, who considered Heinrich one of the few contemporary writers worth his attention. Heinrich also knew Lion

Feuchtwanger well, having been a frequent visitor to Sanary during and after the brief time that Thomas Mann had lived there, in 1933. Sybille Bedford took note at a party: "Heinrich Mann, even more stiff and formal than his brother, arrived in a high collar and black coat, extending, like Monsieur de Charlus, two fingers to anyone offering to shake hands." Salka later wrote that Heinrich had "the manners of a nineteenth-century *grand seigneur*."

The southern idyll was over for the *Dichterfürsten*, the deposed princes of poetry. It had been a warm and beautiful mirage. That late spring of 1940, after Holland and Belgium fell to Germany, France surrendered as well, signing an armistice on June 22 that ceded the northern half of the country to German occupation. A collaborationist regime now controlled the south, its provisional capital installed first in Bordeaux and then relocated to the abandoned hotels of the spa town of Vichy. An estimated seven million refugees, both French and foreign, took to the roads. They streamed toward the south hoping to cross the border, often penniless and hungry, carrying what they could. Down to the sea. Down to the sea.

Many thousands of German and Austrian antifascists and Jews were apprehended and interned as enemy nationals. French authorities were immediately required to hand over—to "surrender on demand"—every German refugee they encountered. Among those at the top of the Gestapo's long execution lists, for their crime of criticizing Hitler's regime, were Franz Werfel, Lion Feuchtwanger, and Heinrich Mann.

Despite his hopes, in May Feuchtwanger was interned again at the Les Milles brickworks, where sanitation was woeful, food and water were scant, and great clouds of brick dust made him cough up blood. Then he was sent to a military camp called Saint-Nicolas, outside of Nîmes. His wife Marta was interned as well, in the vast camp at Gurs near the Pyrenees, where inmates were confined to windowless, muddy wooden barracks and slept on straw-filled sacks on the floor. The political theorist Hannah Arendt was interned there too, along with thousands of other Jewish women who'd been arrested and detained in the Vélodrome d'Hiver in Paris. To the fugitives on the run through the countryside, southern France now looked like nothing less than an enormous prison.

Lion Feuchtwanger (center) behind barbed wire at the internment camp in Les Milles, France, 1939.

Marta managed to flee from Gurs. She returned to Sanary, then made her way to Marseille. With the help of an American diplomat, she planned a successful but rather comical escape for Lion from Saint-Nicolas. Feuchtwanger was disguised as an elderly Englishwoman in a loose-fitting coat, sunglasses, and a shawl, and spirited into a waiting car. Once he reached Marseille, he was given a temporary haven at the home of the American vice-consul in Marseille, Hiram Bingham IV, who abandoned State Department protocol to offer that hospitality.

Marta joined Lion at Bingham's house after taking some time to return to Sanary to pack up their belongings. Once again, as in Berlin, another Feuchtwanger house, another writing space, another library of several thousand books was dismantled. "I never learned my lesson," Feuchtwanger wrote in a memoir about this period. "I would always begin building over again, then cling spiritually and literally to what I had built, confident that this time I must surely be able to keep it."

Heinrich and Nelly Mann in Nice, 1936.

Heinrich Mann and his wife Nelly, a former Hamburg bar hostess nearly three decades his junior, had made their way from Nice to Marseille and were hiding in a small hotel near the city's railway station. They spent long days waiting for exit visas, hoping that Thomas Mann, then living in a rented house in the Brentwood neighborhood of Los Angeles, could exert his influence. Franz Werfel and his wife Alma had hastily left Sanary with the hope of booking passage on any ship they could find leaving the Atlantic coast. In a grueling and fruitless seven-week pilgrimage that Werfel called their "Tour de France," they passed through Lourdes, where the Jewish Werfel visited the Catholic shrine dedicated to Bernadette Soubiros and prayed for a miracle. He vowed that if he managed to escape from Europe he would write a book to honor the saint. The shops in Lourdes were selling figurines of Saint Bernadette to the pilgrims who joined the swelling tide of fugitives to pray at her shrine. So many images of the saint. Not nearly enough miracles.

Refugees at the U.S. Consulate in Marseille, 1941.

Eventually the Werfels managed to obtain a safe-conduct pass to Marseille, a document issued by the Vichy government that permitted travel within France. In Marseille the consulate supplied the Werfels with American visas, but like the Manns they had no residency permits to allow them to stay, and they still needed exit visas to leave the country. Should they wait and hope to get exit visas, or try to leave illegally? They wrestled with the question as they sat in a hotel on one of the wide streets of the city which was packed with refugees, all bent on their daily hellish missions to petition the consulates. They had awakened from the daydream of Sanary to the nightmare of Marseille, a city that had trapped so many desperate hostages yet could not wait to be rid of them all.

All three of the *Dichterfürsten* and their wives risked arrest and deportation to Germany if they remained in Marseille or if they tried to leave. The hotels in which they hid were filled with German officers. There was a circulating fear that at any moment the borders might be sealed. None of them had the proper documentation they needed in order to stay or to go. They were not young—Mann was sixty-nine, Feuchtwanger fifty-six, Werfel fifty—nor, after their panicky journeys to Marseille, were they emotionally or physically fit. On the waterfront edge of Hades, they joined a chorus of shades who belonged nowhere, who were not quite living and not yet dead, whose swelling voices called across the ocean to the New World. *Save us.*

AT METRO DURING THE EARLY FALL OF 1940, Salka was pulled into meetings to debate whether a Garbo comedy could earn enough domestic returns now that the European market for her pictures was gone. Because of arguments over *The Twin*

Sister's plot, the project had already lost a producer, Sidney Franklin, who was replaced by Gottfried Reinhardt. For the first time at Metro, Salka would be taking orders directly from her own paramour.

Garbo was to play a sporty but unglamorous ski instructor who tests her husband's faithfulness by disguising herself as a more alluring twin of her own invention. The husband falls in love with the counterfeit version, and hilarity, with some luck, ensues. As ever, writers with strongly opposing ideas cycled in and out: Walter Reisch, who had written on *Ninotchka*; the Marx Brothers' stalwart George Oppenheimer; and then, to Salka's relief, Sam Behrman.

The story's selling point was that moviegoers would get two Garbos for the price of one ticket. They could watch her ski and swim as one sister and dance in swanky nightclubs as the other. The risk was that Garbo, now thirty-five and forever an exotic, might not pull off the lighthearted sex appeal the role demanded. She faced comparisons with fresh American actresses like Lana Turner, who was sixteen years younger.

From *Twin Sister*'s beginning, nobody got along. Gottfried was preoccupied with the news from Europe and took out his frustrations on the director, George Cukor. There were arguments over casting (Cary Grant was passed over in favor of *Ninotchka*'s Melvyn Douglas) and costumes (how glamorous for one twin, and how "sweater-girl" innocent for the other?). As the writers skirmished over the best ways to promote Garbo's sexiness, the PCA warned against displaying any carnal knowledge at all. Tensions grew between Salka and Gottfried, though her memoir minimizes the discord. "As nothing divides people more than difference in their sense of humor," she wrote, "it was a miracle that my friendship with Gottfried survived the severe test. Sam Behrman's authority and intervention prevented many bitter feuds."

Gottfried Reinhardt, Wolfgang Reinhardt, and their mother, actress Else Heims, in the garden at Mabery Road, early 1940s.

That August, Salka finally heard from her mother. In a letter dated March 12 and written in French, Auguste reported that Wychylowka had been nationalized by the Soviets, so she was now living in a one-room apartment in Sambor. Life was difficult. Auguste was too old to apply for work and was sharing the cramped apartment with Salka's brother Dusko, his girlfriend Hania, and their little son. Also with them was a young woman named Viktoria who had been born to two of Wychylowka's servants in 1917 and had always been treated as a member of the family. Auguste reported that she was cut off completely from news, had no radio or newspapers. But she was glad to report that Dusko had a job in the "physical culture" sector and was coaching the local soccer team for extra money. "I am thankful that he has become a responsible human being," Auguste wrote.

Salka also heard from the State Department that Auguste's visa had been forwarded from Bucharest to the American Embassy in Moscow. But no emigration would be possible until she received permission to leave Sambor, which could take months. In the meantime, Salka heard that her sister Rose had managed to leave Vienna along with her two children. They were on a Greek steamer on their way to join Josef Gielen in Buenos Aires.

Salka's refugee work was accelerating. She continued to gather affidavits and to make donations to the European Film Fund, which was organizing fundraising events around town. The émigré conductor Bruno Walter gave a concert which raised $1100, while Liesl Frank collected proceeds of $332.42 from a gin-rummy benefit whose participants included many of Salka's friends and colleagues: Alexander Granach, Ernst Lubitsch, Henry Blanke, William Wyler, and Paul Kohner.

Around this time Salka also persuaded Garbo to make a substantial donation to the EFF. Through the years Garbo was criticized for her lackluster participation in aiding the European refugees. Mostly she feared the breach of privacy that these kinds of gestures would require. Yet if Garbo's involvement was much more subdued than that of high-profile Hollywood antifascists such as Marlene Dietrich, she was far from indifferent, having made a five-thousand-dollar donation to the Finnish Relief Fund for its war orphans program in December 1939, under the condition of strict anonymity. There is also some evidence to suggest that Garbo used her influence to help the physicist Niels Bohr escape from occupied Denmark to Sweden and later to America. Salka pulled Garbo into her humanitarian network, persuading the actress to donate $500 to the EFF, the equivalent of nearly $9,000 in 2019 dollars. Garbo's donation put her among the top twenty-eight contributors to the EFF—one of only a handful of women to earn that ranking.

After the United States entered the war, gossip columnists and fan magazines criticized Garbo for refusing to participate in war-bond drives or entertain the troops. Salka rushed to her defense: "If anyone has made the suggestion that Garbo isn't selling bonds because her sympathies are on the wrong side," Salka said, "it's too preposterous even to be discussed. There are some people who just cannot face crowds, no matter for what cause. Garbo is such a person. Instead she buys many bonds herself [and] has done the utmost to help me in my work of rescuing anti-Fascist refugees from Europe."

Salka was correct to point out that Garbo did what she could for the war effort, given the intensity of her social anxiety. The actress's famous aversion to public attention, stemming from a combination of childhood trauma and the intense pressures of Hollywood celebrity, directed much of her behavior. She checked into hotels as "Harriet Brown" and made a trademark of disguising herself with sunglasses and hats. And she hid behind Salka whenever she could.

In October 1940, when Garbo filed a Preliminary Declaration of Intent for American citizenship, she listed Salka's house as her official address, though she had a residence of her own on South Amalfi Drive near the Huxleys in the Palisades. One of Garbo's biographers, Karen Swenson, points to this fact as evidence that "Salka Viertel, her family and friends remained Garbo's anchor in Hollywood," and this is true: for Garbo, as for so many others, Salka's house was a shelter. But the use of the Viertels' address also shows how much Garbo relied on Salka to safeguard her anonymity, to shield her from the fearsome, faceless crowds of everyday Americans who had made her a star.

Everyone was fleeing and everything was temporary.
We had no idea whether this situation would last till tomorrow,
another couple of weeks, or our entire lives.

—ANNA SEGHERS, *TRANSIT*

RESCUE WORK FOR EUROPE'S REFUGEES required coordination among various organizations within a cooperative network. As the European Film Fund was partnering with Salka to integrate those who had already arrived in Los Angeles, it also joined forces with the Emergency Rescue Committee, which had convened in New York in June 1940 after the fall of France. The ERC was the American extension of an international committee founded in 1933 by Berthold's longtime friend Albert Einstein to provide relief for Jews and antifascists trapped in

France. Its founders and supporters included such public intellectuals as the theologian Reinhold Niebuhr and the novelists John Dos Passos and Thomas Mann. It also involved a number of women who were firsthand witnesses to the National Socialists' rise to power, including the German-Jewish banking heiress Ingrid Warburg, the journalist (and good friend of the Viertels) Dorothy Thompson, and Erika Mann, who had been working as a war correspondent.

The ERC's long arm extended to Los Angeles, where much of its fundraising took place. In her memoir, Salka admitted that while she did not remember the first time she met Thomas Mann, it must have been around this summer of 1940 at a meeting or a banquet for the ERC. It was during these summer months, when Thomas and his wife Katia were renting a house up the street from the Schoenbergs in Brentwood, that Salka and Thomas forged a friendship.

Thomas and Katia were regular guests at Salka's Sundays, where Thomas praised the strong coffee and became fanatical about the homemade chocolate cake. Salka took particular pleasure in the little dramas she created by introducing this or that quivering newcomer to the writer many Americans considered the greatest in the world. Mann did not disappoint. Shy or effusive, each person who shook Mann's hand received the benediction of his kindly solemnity. He retained, Salka wrote, "the reserved politeness of a diplomat on official duty."

While Mann and others gave fundraising speeches and wrote affidavits that summer in Los Angeles, the ERC in New York compiled lists of people trapped in France and threatened with arrest by the Gestapo. The committee saw that it needed to focus its initial rescue efforts on high-profile writers, artists, and intellectuals in order to raise money to help the many thousands of others to escape.

Thus the ERC solicited names from the likes of the director of the Museum of Modern Art, Alfred Barr, and the French Catholic philosopher Jacques Maritain. Its initial list of about two hundred refugees included Franz Werfel, Lion Feuchtwanger, and Heinrich Mann, and was entrusted to the care of a volunteer who offered to travel to Marseille to assess the situation. That volunteer was a preppy young American editor with a remarkably impassive demeanor and zero relief-work experience named Varian Fry.

Fry arrived in Marseille in mid-August 1940 with his secret list and three thousand dollars in cash strapped to his leg, expecting to stay for three weeks. In that time he hoped to figure out how to transport the people on the list to Lisbon or Casablanca, which were then the only possible exit points out of Europe. In fact, Fry remained for over a year. Defying both Vichy law and the State Department—which rigorously maintained the U.S. government's nativist immigration policies—he used document forgery and guided escape routes to smuggle more than two thousand people out of France.

Varian Fry's mission would never have succeeded without his expertise in manipulating the ever-shifting visa requirements in Europe and the United States. As with Liesl Frank and the European Film Fund, his was a triumph of paperwork. Though there is no evidence of direct correspondence between Fry and the European Film Fund—neither was eager to leave a paper trail, since much of their activity was illegal—their efforts were coordinated: donations to the EFF were funneled to Fry's operation in Marseille, while EFF members wrote affidavits and arranged for jobs in America for the incoming refugees. In the case of Heinrich Mann, for instance, the EFF secured a screenwriting job for him at Warner Bros. to overcome the "likely to become a public charge" obstacle, and also collected affidavits and travel funds for him. Meanwhile, Fry and the ERC arranged Heinrich Mann's documents in preparation for his escape.

Fry had heard that some refugees had managed to leave France without exit visas by crossing the Spanish border by train and then traveling to Lisbon, where they would hope to find room on a ship. "Up to the last moment," wrote Jean-Michel Palmier, "[refugees] did not know if the expected ship would arrive, and if they would be able to embark, as one of their visas or authorizations might in the meantime have run out." Nonetheless Fry thought this strategy worth a gamble, and he approached the Werfels, Feuchtwangers, and Heinrich Manns with the idea. Feuchtwanger consented to the plan if Fry would agree to go with them.

Fry added a fourth couple, the Czech Jewish graphic artist Egon Adler and his wife Berthe. Then Heinrich Mann asked Fry for one more addition to the group: his nephew Golo Mann, the third of Thomas Mann's six children. Golo had been arrested as an enemy alien after volunteering in France to fight the Germans. Like Lion Feuchtwanger, he was interned at Les Milles and had recently escaped.

Fry planned to leave in mid-September, as soon as he could gather the necessary Spanish and Portuguese transit visas. These were generally available for anyone who had a valid overseas visa, as the Manns, Werfels, Feuchtwangers, and Adlers did. Their journey would still be illegal, however, because they all lacked the impossible French exit visas. And it was still incredibly dangerous: their success depended on the whims of the border guards, who could be generous or vindictive, inattentive or zealous. If the enemies of the Reich were unlucky at the border, they could expect arrest and internment, and possibly execution.

Fry tried to keep his composure so as not to cause panic among the jittery group. The plans kept changing, because the laws kept changing. Word came from the frontier that Spain was no longer letting *apatrides* through: these were Germans who had been stripped of their citizenship because they were Jewish or anti-Nazi. The Werfels and Adlers were Czech and Austrian by birth, while the Manns had been made honorary Czech citizens. But the Feuchtwangers were *apatrides*. Fry was forced to leave them behind, promising that they could follow as soon as possible.

In the early morning of September 12, 1940, the rest of the group met Fry at the Marseille train station. The Werfels had twelve suitcases. Most accounts of the story mention the Werfels' luggage with skeptical condescension: What hauteur! What wifely cluelessness! Yet Alma Werfel, like Marta Feuchtwanger and Nelly Mann, had been responsible for packing up entire lives as quickly as possible, forced to decide what was indispensable in exile. In Alma's suitcases were the artifacts most precious to her, and no one could argue that they were frivolous. They included the musical scores of her former husband Gustav Mahler, the original manuscript of Anton Bruckner's third symphony, and the beginnings of Franz Werfel's novel-in-progress about Saint Bernadette of Lourdes.

The train took the group to the base of the steep linear

ranges of the Pyrenees, arriving just after dark in the border town of Cerbère. Surely the name of the town was not lost on this group: it recalled Cerberus, the three-headed beast from the *Odyssey* that guards the underworld and prevents the escape of the dead. Fry was agonized to learn that the *commissaire*'s supervisor happened to be visiting and was not letting anyone through without exit visas. If they tried to take the train across the border to the Spanish town of Port Bou, the chance of arrest was high.

The group stayed the night at a hotel in Cerbère. The next morning was cloudless and hot. It was Friday the thirteenth, an omen they remarked on with dread. Nelly Mann did not trust Fry. Maybe he was a spy; maybe he would sell them out to the authorities. Yet if they waited any longer, new orders might come in from Vichy demanding their arrest. The best option was for Fry to take all their suitcases on the train to Port Bou while the group hiked over the mountain. Of this scheme everyone in the group was afraid. A fit person could make the climb and descent in about five hours. For these refugees, in the best case, it would take the entire day. Fry did not think Werfel could manage it: "He's too fat," he was thinking, "and Mann's too old." Werfel himself, who had just turned fifty and suffered from serious heart trouble, had his own doubts. But the determination to outrun the Nazis made their decision.

Fry bought them a dozen packages of cigarettes with which to bribe the police along the way, and with great misgivings he said goodbye. An American associate of his who was familiar with the route led the way as their guide. "Half an hour later," Fry wrote, "I could still see them making their way across the rough fields of the hill, following the line of the stone walls, and disappearing now and then behind an isolated olive tree, or resting in its half-shade."

They had tried to dress like tourists on a walking trip, carrying only rucksacks. Alma Mahler-Werfel wore a billowing white dress and a pair of old sandals. She and Werfel walked ahead with the guide, then waited while he went down to help the others. The steep, zigzagging terrain was made up of slippery flat tablets of stone. Some of it could be scaled only by crawling. The paths were spiked with thorny shrubs that tore at the women's ankles and made them bleed. "Mountain goats could hardly have kept their footing on the glassy, shimmering slate," Alma Mahler-Werfel wrote. "If you skidded, there was nothing but thistles to hold on to." The mistral was blowing, whining like an air-raid siren and grinding its grit into the last of their nerves. The air was feverishly hot. For all of Werfel's fears, he managed the climb fairly well. It was sixty-nine-year-old Heinrich who had the most trouble. "Not that he wasn't game," Fry reflected. "He was the gamest of the lot. It was simply that he couldn't make the grade without help." Nelly, Golo, and their American guide took turns virtually carrying Heinrich most of the way over the mountain.

Some hours later, at the shelterless crest 6,500 feet up, they changed guides. "After the march in the broiling sun we felt utterly wretched," wrote Alma. Just then, two *gardes mobiles* spied the party and started toward the desolate little group. They were sure that now they would all be arrested and sent to a concentration camp. But the soldiers only saluted and told them to follow the path toward the Spanish border post rather than the French one, as the Spanish were less likely to check for exit visas. The friendly advice very possibly saved their lives.

The descent was a tiny footpath, worn down by the footprints of smugglers, punctuated with cactus and lavender. The Spanish border sentries examined their passports with anxiety-provoking care, then finally waved them on. Late in the day at the Port Bou railway station the group reunited with Fry, who later wrote: "We almost fell into one another's arms, as though we were old friends who had been separated for years and had met by accident in some strange city where none of us had ever expected to be." There was a subdued meal at the hotel, after which Fry sent a wire to his secretary in Marseille. "Harry can send his friends," it read—code that the route was safe enough for the Feuchtwangers to follow.

Three days later the group reached Madrid, and from there they flew to Portugal. In Thomas Mann's American diary for September 20, 1940, this entry: "Telegram from Golo and Heinrich from Lisbon, where they are waiting [for] a ship. Joy and satisfaction." Two weeks later, in early October, the group sailed on a Greek steamship bound for America. The view of Lisbon as the ship left the harbor was their last image of Europe. "A lost lover is not more beautiful," wrote Heinrich. "Everything life had given us had come from this continent." He had never before ventured away from it, not even across the Channel. Franz Werfel too was pensive about farewells and new beginnings. "Now America lies before us, an entirely unknown continent," he wrote to his parents as the ship sailed. "I hope that it will be favorably disposed toward me."

The Feuchtwangers were aboard, having left Marseille a few days after the others, also via the Pyrenees, with the help of an American Unitarian minister named Waitstill Sharp and his wife Martha. The poet Walter Mehring was there too, along with two other couples who had escaped through the combined efforts of the European Film Fund and the Emergency Rescue Committee: Alfred Döblin, the author of the most influential of all the Weimar-era novels, *Berlin Alexanderplatz*, and his wife; and Alfred and Lisl Polgar, Salka's friends with whom she had walked in the courtyard of the Palais Royal in the days just before the fall of France.

Many others were not so fortunate. Many others whose scraps of paper were arbitrarily rejected ended up in Spanish jails, or were handed over to the Germans, or both. It was impossible to guess which way the dice would fall. That same September, the Berlin-born Jewish historian and critic Walter Benjamin had reached Port Bou with a different group of refugees when he heard that Spain was closing its borders. All of them would be required to go back to France. Benjamin could bear no more. His friend the writer Arthur Koestler had given him a lethal dose of morphine pills. Some have alleged that Benjamin took them; others that he died of a cerebral hemmorhage or an overdose of his heart medication. His body was found the next day. The day after that, Spain reopened its borders and the others in Benjamin's group continued on through Spain and eventually to safety.

From Lisbon, Fry cabled the ERC in New York to report on his journey with the Manns and Werfels and to ask for more money. The celebrity of those he had rescued was a fundraising boon. The ERC was able to send more than twenty thousand dollars to Fry's office during the first four months of his operation. Other donations—most likely raised in part through the European Film Fund—went to support the newly arrived refugees in America.

While there is no evidence that Salka ever met or had any contact with Fry, they were nonetheless united in their work through the EFF and the ERC. Together they formed two endpoints in an underground railroad. He was the American who got refugees out of Europe, and she was the European who received them in California. Both roles were critical. "Some may die on the way," Fry's assistant once said about their work; "Some will never get over it; some will be the better for the experience. But one must get them all out. At least one must try." There was as much peril in adapting to the new world as there had been in leaving the old, and as few guarantees. Without cultural brokers like Salka, the newcomers would have had no chance of success at all.

BY NOVEMBER 1940 the Feuchtwangers, Manns, Werfels, Polgars, and Döblins had all arrived in Los Angeles, and by the following May they were all beginning to acclimate. Different mountains, different sky, different sea—but oh, how like Sanary it seemed. For some, in the early throes of giddy relief, it was even better. Marta Feuchtwanger found the beauty of the Pacific shoreline more informal than the Côte d'Azur. "Here you feel at home in the landscape," she said; "here you live with the ocean and nature; it's part of your life." Franz Werfel wrote to his parents: "The Riviera is just trash compared to this." He and Alma found a house in the hills just above the Hollywood Bowl, where he settled down to finish *The Song of Bernadette*. His garden was full of fruit trees and roses that bloomed in every season. His health improved. He felt ten years younger.

Not everyone was as enthusiastic. When asked how she felt

in America, the German poet Annette Kolb answered, "Grateful and unhappy." Alfred Döblin and his wife moved into a small apartment in Hollywood, where Döblin complained, as Berthold Viertel often did, that "pedestrians had become extinct... people are born as drivers... LA is the opposite of a place I'd choose to live in, since I happen to love walking amongst crowds." Salka did her best to ease the grumbling, taking newcomers to the Farmer's Market on Fairfax and the Grand Central Market downtown, both of which could be ambled through like the European markets to which they were accustomed. Döblin found other reasons to despise his new life. The screenwriting job at Metro which had been secured for him by the European Film Fund was a demeaning distraction from his literary career. He wrote to his fellow exile Hermann Kesten in March 1941 that "the people here don't need our stories, they already have vaults full of them," and, four months later, "I do not believe one can at the same time serve Louis B. Mayer and one's own work."

Thomas Mann was glad to know that his brother Heinrich's first impressions of Los Angeles were encouraging, and that his prospects for success in Hollywood were good. There was even talk that one of his books might once again be made into a film, as had his novel *Professor Unrat*. But the initial optimism did not last long. Salka wrote that Heinrich "appeared an odd figure in the Burbank studio" where Warner Bros., in cooperation with the European Film Fund, had set him up as a screenwriter at six thousand dollars per year. Heinrich himself seemed rather baffled by the position, writing to Thomas about his reluctance to come into the studio "to waste the time between 10 and 1 in consultation and chatter."

Heinrich and Nelly were renting a small house in Hollywood and were soon to move to an apartment on Doheny Drive in Beverly Hills. "Care for the house and the car fall to my wife," Heinrich wrote; "everything is doubtful when it's meant for an uncertain period of time." Salka wrote about her new friend Nelly, "a voluptuous, blond, blue-eyed Teutonic beauty with red lips and sparkling teeth" and a "ribald manner," at least thirty years younger than Heinrich and utterly devoted to him: "She drank secretly, slipping out to the bathroom or kitchen, coyly refusing the drinks offered at parties; then insisted on driving Heinrich home, to which he heroically consented." Nelly's drinking might have been a self-medicating effort to combat a longtime depression, surely not helped by the ordeal of the flight from Marseille. In the years before their escape she had tried several times to kill herself.

There were constant parties for the newly arrived exiles at Salka's house and others. If these occasions were festive, they were not always cordial. Salka remarked on the colony's division into several groups, designating Thomas Mann, who had decided to relocate permanently from Princeton and was renting a house not far from Salka on Amalfi Drive, as "the representative, towering literary figure." "Hollywood could now boast of being the Parnassus of German literature," Salka wrote, "inasmuch as Thomas Mann had become a resident of the Pacific Palisades." In Mann's circle were Bruno and Liesl Frank, William and Charlotte Dieterle, the Feuchtwangers, the Werfels, and the Bruno Walters. But even here there were fissures: Thomas and Katia were publicly polite but privately dismissive toward Nelly Mann, whom they considered hopelessly vulgar, and there was friction between Nelly and Alma Mahler-Werfel as well.

Salka had to take great care to see that Arnold Schoenberg was never in the same room as his rival, the composer Igor Stravinsky, who had arrived in Los Angeles in mid-1940 via Paris and New York. This was never easy, as Stravinsky was very close to many of Salka's friends, particularly Aldous Huxley and Christopher Isherwood. "Only shortly before Schoenberg's death did [he and Stravinsky] mutually acknowledge their importance," Salka remembered. "Later Stravinsky paid great homage to Schoenberg and to his music." If Thomas Mann was the president of this Weimar-in-exile, Salka was its chief ambassador, always trying to soothe the bitterness and jealousy—some of it decades old—that erupted among the factions.

At Metro, conflicts over *The Twin Sister* continued. The Breen office demanded rewrites for a scene suggesting premarital sex, but the new pages drifted in so piecemeal from the writers that the PCA could not make a judgment. Eventually it approved an incomplete script. Filming was scheduled to begin in June and Garbo was impatient to get things going so as to be finished with it as soon as possible. "Nobody's heart was in it," her biographer Barry Paris wrote. Gottfried would come home to Mabery Road from the studio, where he'd been arguing all day with director George Cukor and with Salka. There he would argue with Peter against enlisting for the war in Canada. "If the war comes here, I won't try to dodge," he said to Peter, who was then twenty-one to Gottfried's thirty. "But why should I run after it over there? People talk about the Jews. The Jews! The Jews! The Jews have to fight Hitler! I tell you, the Jews have done enough against Hitler already. Let the others do something. Don't be such a sucker!"

Salka never thought she had done enough to fight Hitler. Her attention was fixed on helping her mother and many more of her friends to emigrate, and on the needs of the refugees who had already managed to arrive. Berthold wrote to Salka from New York, wondering how she was able to work under the circumstances. Isherwood, who was working with the local Quakers in their refugee relief work, observed: "You can't only help people, like a Lady Bountiful, from ten to four. If you want to be of any real use, you must share your life with them. Otherwise, it's probably better to avoid them, and subscribe to charities."

With his usual incisiveness, Isherwood was onto something, attuned as always to the shortcomings and hypocrisies of his own character. It's hard to imagine he wasn't comparing himself here with Salka, who in fact was fully committed to sharing her already busy life with refugees. But being Lady Bountiful had its costs. Stretched between Gottfried, her children, and the legions that depended on her, Salka couldn't possibly please them all.

Birthday Party

Heinrich Mann's seventieth birthday was approaching, and there were many lively arguments among the Los Angeles exiles about how best to commemorate it. In a restaurant or a private home? Whom to include and whom to drop from the unwieldy guest list? The day of honor, March 27, came and went, because Heinrich's younger brother Thomas Mann was out of town. He was receiving yet another ceremonial doctorate and giving lectures in Berkeley and would not return until the end of April. Still, the German colony was determined to mark the occasion, even after the fact. Strenuous negotiations continued.

In the end Salka offered her house, after calling Berthold in New York to get his assent. And in the end, on the Friday evening of May 2, 1941, her house was where the party took place. We don't know why the community chose Mabery Road over a tonier address—Liesl Frank's or Charlotte Dieterle's, for instance—but it was probably the least contentious choice among the colony's discordant factions.

For his part, Heinrich Mann was alarmed by all the fuss. "I'd rather you didn't speak about my birthday," he had written to Thomas in February. "The number, meanwhile, is too high to be mentioned, especially for a *writer* for whose *job* the younger natives are waiting." These were the justifiable fears of an old man looking over his shoulder—fears that were heightened by the trauma of his flight from the Gestapo, and compounded now as he struggled to restart his life as a writer in a foreign language and on a strange continent where he, once so famous, was humiliatingly unknown.

Thomas Mann, in the meantime, was lavishly feted everywhere he traveled in America. He had just spent two days visiting personally with President Roosevelt at the White House. He was enjoying a particularly fertile period in his writing life and was soon to complete the finest work of his career, his *Joseph* tetralogy. Both Heinrich and Thomas profoundly appreciated the gift of being alive after the expulsion from their stolen homeland, where the hoodlum regime loudly continued to wish them dead. But the fortunes of the exiled brothers, born four years apart and locked in a lifelong competition fueled equally by reverence and resentment, had never seen so wide a gap.

The Germans in Los Angeles often played the game of debating which of the Mann brothers was the greater writer. The brothers' rivalry had begun long ago, when they were children in the 1870s, with the unoriginal sin of vying for their mother's attention. Thomas and Heinrich had been raised in the stolid old Hanseatic port city in the north of Germany called Lübeck, which was encircled by a river called the Trave. They were the eldest of the five children of a wealthy grain merchant who had become a senator at age thirty-six. The father's hopes that his sons might follow him into the grain-importing business were quickly dashed. Early on, both Heinrich and Thomas elected to dwell in the artistic world of their mother, Julia da Silva-Bruhns Mann, rather than in the world of commerce inhabited by their father. "I sat in a corner and watched my father and mother as though I were choosing between them, deciding whether life would best be spent in the dream world of the senses or in deed and power," wrote Thomas. "And my eyes rested finally on the quiet features of my mother."

As little boys they watched bashfully as their mother presided over Thursday salons in the ballroom of the family home and gracefully encouraged conversation among her guests about literature, music, and art. On other evenings, both boys snuggled close to Julia Mann as she read them fairy tales by Hans Christian Andersen and Charles Perrault. She also filled them full of stories from her earliest childhood that must have seemed as fanciful to the little Lübeckers as any of the fairy tales she recited. She was the daughter of a German-born planter and his Portuguese-Creole-Brazilian wife and had been raised in the tropical lushness of the Costa Verde in Brazil's Rio de Janeiro state, where her maternal family had lived for three generations. Her memories teemed with monkeys and parrots and boa constrictors and rang with the songs of the slaves on the plantation.

The tales the Mann boys heard in their mother's mellifluous, *saudade*-tinged voice became the seeds for their art as they rejected their father's path of "deed and power" to pursue careers in literature. To the end of his life, Thomas never lost his faith in what he called the "primal simplicity of the fairy tale." He insisted that he undertook in all his novels and stories merely to dream—up to and including his latest work, about the biblical Joseph, with its fairy-tale themes of sibling betrayals, forgiveness, and, yes, exile. Similarly, Heinrich admitted, "There is no sharp boundary in my memory between children's games and the practice of art."

Now in their sixties, these renowned models of dignity and decorum had not abandoned their childhood selves, not at all. Yes, their external appearances were rigid with responsibility: Bertolt Brecht referred to Thomas Mann as "the Starched Collar." But internally they grew ever more playful, inventive, ironic. "He looks wonderfully young for his age," Christopher Isherwood had noted of Thomas Mann when he first met him in July 1940, "perhaps because, as a boy, he was elderly and staid." The brothers shared a ritualistic devotion to their birthdays, which Thomas had once called, in a 1931 sixtieth-birthday address to Heinrich, "the childlike big moments, times of celebration and honors."

Since 1925, every five years on their birthdays the brothers had hired a hall, summoned a crowd, and delivered speeches to each other. The declarations were part homage to the other and part rivalrous bid to grab away the attention. As the biographer Nigel Hamilton put it, speaking about Heinrich: "there behind him, his entire life, was a brother who revered him, but stole the limelight." In fact, when one reads their letters, in which each brother routinely confesses his impatience to receive this or that new book by the other so as to deliver his feelings about it, one begins to understand that they wrote their works in counterpoint, and to a large degree for the half-admiring, half-envious eyes of the other.

In 1925, for Thomas's fiftieth birthday, the brothers' speeches had taken place before an audience in Munich's town hall. In 1931, for Heinrich's sixtieth, they spoke in front of hundreds at the Prussian Academy of the Arts in Berlin, where Heinrich was then serving as president of the poetry department. By 1936, when Heinrich turned sixty-five, both brothers had been driven out of Germany and had found separate places of refuge, Thomas in Zurich and Heinrich in Nice. But they published their homages to each other that year in *Die Neue Weltbühne*, where, as in all their other birthday speeches, they invoked their childhood years together. Thomas, quoting Goethe, remarked that "he is happiest who can forge a connection between the end of life and its beginning." Then they protested vigorously against their current condition of exile.

On that occasion, Thomas's birthday wish for Heinrich was that in five years, when Heinrich turned seventy, "our people and our country might once again have need of us." For his part, Heinrich also invoked Goethe, asserting that if Goethe were alive today he "would also have had his house and possessions taken from him; he shares his exile with all of us." Heinrich went on to condemn the "new Europeans" who had cast aside all pretense of the "essential work" of the development of the individual. "They know nothing," Heinrich said of this young generation, "which would be bad enough; but they arrogate their ignorance to themselves as a preference. Work on their own improvement, personal responsibility and effort, all of this gets short shrift when they are allowed to seek it by joining together in groups to follow 'leaders'... they pursue their egotistical enjoyments, intoxicate themselves with subordination, march in step, singing all the while the headlines from the propaganda ministry."

By 1941, Thomas's wish for Heinrich's seventieth birthday had not come true. The Mann brothers remained among the most reviled of those expelled by the Reich. This time they would not deliver their valedictory speeches to each other in a formal German hall before a large audience, but in a California living room among a bedragglement of fellow outcasts.

Even so, it was no ordinary living room. No host was better equipped to rise to this occasion than Salka Viertel. No one was more attuned to the poignance and the drama of the moment. In fact, Salka's triumph is that her staging of this Santa Monica birthday party and her account of it in her memoir have fixed the event in the collective memory more firmly than any of the Mann brothers' earlier speeches in the august Weimar-era halls of Munich and Berlin.

With her usual improvisatory spirit, Salka brought the Ping-Pong table inside and added it to a makeshift collection of seating that could be covered with tablecloths and then taken apart quickly once the dinner was over. "Decorated with flowers and candles it looked very festive," she said. She arranged places for the forty-five guests who, after many disagreements, had finally been invited. Every person in the house that night was an émigré. In addition to the guests, there was the young Viennese couple, Walter and Hedy Herlitschek, who kept house for Salka and agreed to do the serving. Toni Spuhler, Salka's Swiss-German friend who sometimes catered for parties, took over the kitchen. Also crowding into the kitchen was another collection of refugees who had gathered to witness the event under the pretext of helping to cook and serve.

Salka had asked Berthold to send a telegram of welcome from New York for Heinrich Mann, and was hoping to receive it before the dinner began so she could read it aloud. Mindful of the current feud between Nelly Mann and Alma Mahler-Werfel, she put Heinrich Mann next to herself on one side and Thomas Mann on the other. "Nelly was opposite us, towering over the very small Feuchtwanger on her right; on her left was Werfel," Salka noted. Marta Feuchtwanger and Alma flanked their husbands, while "everyone else was seated strictly according to age and prominence." These included the Alfred Polgars, Alfred Neumann, the Alfred Döblins, Walter Mehring, Ludwig Marcuse, and Bruno and Liesl Frank. All of them, Salka noted, "represented the true Fatherland to which in spite of Hitler they adhered, as they adhered to the German language."

Walter and Hedy served the soup. Berthold's telegram had not yet arrived, so Salka made a short toast to Heinrich. As she motioned for Walter to begin serving the next course, he alerted her to Thomas Mann, who was rising from his chair and pulling out a manuscript from the inside pocket of his tuxedo jacket. Thomas put on his glasses and began to speak.

Writing about the moment years later, Salka admitted that she no longer remembered exactly what Thomas Mann had said. But, she went on, "it gave one some hope and comfort at a time when the lights of freedom seemed extinguished in Europe, and everything we had loved and valued buried in ruins. At the open door to the pantry the 'back entrance' guests were listening, crowding each other and wiping their tears." In fact, Mann's birthday speech, which was eventually published, was a thundering denunciation of Hitler's Reich, a shout of rage against its death cult, its vacuous ideology, its desecration of language, its exaltation of ignorance, its gleeful erasure of Germany's long-treasured humanist canon. As Heinrich had remarked years earlier that Goethe, were he alive that day, would join them in exile, on this evening Thomas made the same claim about Nietzsche, asking: "Who doubts that he would turn over in his grave if he found out down there what has been made of his philosophy of power? He, who already under the Kaiserreich lived as an émigré—where would he be today? He would be with us, in America."

Thomas offered thanks that Heinrich had managed to reach America safely, "that in the last second we succeeded in opening the way for you to join us just before poor, broken France, a nation estranged from itself, was forced by those vile torturers, those defilers of humanity now ruling Europe, to fulfill its monstrous obligations." He recalled how Heinrich's literary sensibility had developed through his love of French culture, and acknowledged how "here in this young land you necessarily feel yourself to be foreign. But, ultimately, what is the meaning of foreign, the meaning of homeland? Lübeck on the Trave we left, in any case, long ago. When the homeland becomes foreign, the foreign becomes the homeland.

"Most profoundly foreign to us today is Germany," Thomas went on, "and, compared to its fatal foreignness, every foreign place seems familiar." He proceeded to outline his hopes for a unified world, in which nationalism would have no dominion, in which the "universal slavery" and "absolute cynicism" of Hitler would never again be tolerated. Thomas invoked the weapons against Hitlerism that he believed would ultimately prevail over it—"freedom, truth, right, humanity"—and praised Heinrich for his prophetic political essays which had anticipated that epic battle, decades before the present moment. He commended the "moral phenomenon" of Heinrich's writings, which, "in their blend of literary brilliance and—I would almost say: a fairy-tale simplicity, a popularity on the scale of humanity," were the greatest examples of moral expression. Finally, he praised Heinrich's invention of the doomed Professor Unrat from his early novel, remarking that *Unrat* means garbage. "Hitler is no professor—far from it," he said. "But *Unrat* he is, nothing but *Unrat*, and soon he will be the rubbish of history." Addressing Heinrich: "If you, as I trust you do, have the physical patience to endure, then your old eyes will see what you in your bold youth described: the end of a tyrant."

When the homeland becomes foreign, the foreign becomes the homeland. How deeply that formulation must have pierced everyone in Salka's house on that gentle California evening, as the sun floated downward toward the horizon and the sea exhaled its steady soothing breaths over the shoreline. Salka gathered her emotions and tried once again to proceed to the main course, an expensive roast of beef. Bruno Frank and Lion Feuchtwanger were scheduled to speak once the meat course was done and she was hoping to keep things moving. But no sooner had the guests toasted Heinrich's health than Heinrich himself also rose, put on his glasses, and produced a manuscript.

As Thomas had spoken of Nietzsche, Heinrich now brought up Shakespeare, declaring that if the Bard happened to return to earth in these times, "the enemy would have to die of shame." Echoing Thomas's defiance, Heinrich noted that all intellectual talent, even if lesser than Shakespeare's, "is justified in concluding from ancient experience: as long as the forces of destruction are active, so long do we persist in our efforts. We have often survived the late after effects of the destructive and the ignorant." With the prerogative of his advanced years, he took the long view and vowed that good would outlive evil: "We must preserve the hope of growing older than virulent hatred . . . moral centuries follow centuries of barbarism."

Heinrich thanked Thomas for his tribute and verified the strength of their bond, noting drily that "the bullets that come flying are aimed at both of us." Acknowledging his younger brother's superior reputation, he said: "Our life and our thinking have always remained fraternal, and it is not only my birth, but my heart and knowledge, that justify the pride I take in your greatness, your fame—'as if it were a piece of myself.'" He concluded with the only other word of thanks in either of the brothers' speeches that was directed toward someone outside their circle of two. "I rendered honor where it was due," he said, "and offer it today to our dear hostess. This glass is for Frau Salka Viertel."

When the homeland becomes foreign, the foreign becomes the homeland. While the *Dichterfürsten* had undertaken to carry their forebears Goethe and Nietzsche with them into exile, Salka had dedicated herself to housing them on alien soil. Understanding that this house was in many ways all that remained of their homeland, Heinrich honored the fact by raising his glass to Salka. And Salka, in wordless acknowledgment, went on with hosting the evening. The beef was grievously overdone, but nobody cared. The remaining speeches were short. Before dessert was served, Marta Feuchtwanger offered an impromptu toast to Nelly Mann, applauding her for saving Heinrich's life by carrying him over the Pyrenees. Nelly responded with several waves of embarrassment, first hiding her face in her hands, then erupting with laughter as she pointed to the bodice of her red dress. Somehow it had come undone, exposing her ample décolletage barely contained within a lacy bra.

After this little tableau, because after all it was a birthday party, there was a cake. It was Salka's own recipe: a simple flourless cake, a brisk mix of butter, sugar, eggs, and chocolate. Some called it a *Sachertorte*, though this is not exactly right. Salka called it her "speciality of the house." But for her family and friends it was more than that. Just as her house was a representation of all the lost houses, for a great many people her cake also had symbolic powers, nostalgic depths, Edenic traces of mystery and memory. If anyone else had baked it, it would not have been the same. Its secret was that Salka somehow imbued it with her own spirit. Adam Shaw, Irwin Shaw's son, remembers many boyhood afternoons he spent devouring the cake after hockey practice in Salka's tiny kitchen in Klosters, Switzerland, in the 1960s. "Perhaps one had to live her life to make it," he said. "The density of it, the hint of bitterness buried in the rich, moist, slightly undercooked core."

He is happiest who can forge a connection between the end of life and its beginning. So devoted was Thomas Mann to Salka's *Sachertorte* that, as another family member recalled it, some years after this evening he showed up at a wedding reception in Beverly Hills for a couple he did not know, because he heard that Salka was bringing the cake. For Thomas and for Heinrich, the party, the cake, the sense of being looked after and cared for, the comforts of this book-lined living room—all brought back their childhood and their mother, brought back the first sense of freedom their mother had encouraged in them to improvise and play and dream and create, brought back her fierce championship and eternal love. Salka and her house gave the Mann brothers permission on this bittersweet evening to forge the connection between the past and the present, to inhabit their ends and their beginnings all at once: to be at the same time the august statesmen in exile, eloquent in their anger and their survivors' guilt and their gratefulness to the country that took them in; but also to be the little boys, avidly licking up the last crumbs of the homemade chocolate birthday cake. It would not have been the same at a restaurant or even at someone else's house. In grief, in confusion, in relief, the brothers' souls cried out to the soul of the house, and the motherly soul of the house embraced them. After Berlin, after Sanary and Nice, after Zurich and Marseille, after all the stations of their expulsion and their long separation, the brothers found themselves reunited at a table sharing a child-like big moment, in what must have seemed like the last safe place. Which was in so many ways a copy of the first safe place, in Lübeck, all those years ago.

"I'VE STARTED WORK ON A FILM, which probably won't amount to much," Garbo wrote to a Swedish friend on June 23, 1941. "It's strange that I should be writing about films when war is on our doorstep."

The film was the twin-sister comedy, retitled that summer as *Two-Faced Woman*. It was Garbo's twenty-sixth picture for Metro and had begun shooting on June 18. Most of the filming was done on the lot, except for ski sequences which were shot on location at the Sugar Bowl Lodge near Donner Summit, a 475-mile drive from Los Angeles.

The script was still incomplete when filming began. Salka, Sam Behrman, and George Oppenheimer churned out new scenes, still trying to appease the censors, who continued to veto the faintest hints of premarital or extramarital sex, while hoping somehow to maintain the airiness of Ludwig Fulda's farce. Meanwhile, Gottfried argued with director George Cukor over the script. Toward the end of filming Garbo wrote again to her Swedish friend: "I'm only very sorry that the story has changed so much. Salka had a much better story to begin with. But since I would rather go walking in the country than fight for stories, it will have turned out like it has."

Two-Faced Woman is often accused of failing so completely that Garbo was unable to recover from the humiliation and consequently abandoned her career. Often the blame went to

Salka: for suggesting and then botching the story, for meddling in the reshaping of Garbo's image, for the fact that the picture was not *Ninotchka.* While it's true that Garbo never appeared in another film, the actress had no plans to quit acting at the time. Once *Two-Faced Woman* was finished, with another picture remaining under her current contract, Metro again enlisted Salka to continue searching for Garbo vehicles. And in fact *Two-Faced Woman* earned reasonable box office returns, with a foreign and domestic take (minus a full release in Europe and Japan) of $1.8 million. This was in spite of the Catholic League of Decency's "condemned" rating and its decision to ban the film in Boston and Providence. Urging Catholic filmgoers to boycott it, the league condemned the picture for its "immoral and un-Christian attitude toward marriage and its obligations; imprudently suggestive scenes, dialogue and situations, [and] suggestive costumes."

No matter how hard Gottfried, Salka, and Behrman had tried to please the censors, decency remained implacable. No less a personage than Cardinal Spellman, archbishop of New York, was drawn into the controversy while visiting with his personal friend Louis B. Mayer in Los Angeles. Mayer screened the picture for Spellman before its release and asked him to make an assessment of its wickedness. Salka wrote that Spellman gave his blessing after suggesting that the writers add a scene showing that the husband could not be committing adultery with the twin sister because he knew all along that she was actually his wife. "This change did not improve the film," Salka noted acidly.

So aggrieved was Gottfried over these indignities that he was still complaining about them in a memoir he published in 1979. "More incensed than his minions," he wrote, "[Spellman] took time off shepherding X-million souls to wage a one-man crusade—in a world torn by strife, with his own country on the brink of it—against my sinful *Two-Faced Woman*." Salka had battled with Gottfried throughout the production, straining their relationship at home. But she was in total agreement with his sentiments about censorship and the war. Both of them felt hard-pressed to care much about the moral rectitude of a featherweight comedy "at the time," Salka wrote in her memoir, "when each day brought news more horrible than one could bear."

In fact, if most of Salka's "indecent" lines never survived the censors, the preoccupation with the war in Europe does emerge in the finished picture. In a ritzy Manhattan nightclub during a scene full of the sort of fizzy repartee that made Sam Behrman such a sought-after screenwriter, Garbo makes an appearance in a low-cut sleeveless black gown and loads of diamonds. She is pretending to be Katherine Borg, the sophisticated twin sister of Melvyn Douglas's unglamorous wife Karin. Asked where she has come from when nobody had previously known of her existence, she concocts a quick explanation. But it is not just any flip answer. "From Lisbon," she says gaily. "I caught the last boat out—I'm a penniless refugee." And then, responding to a sensible follow-up question—did you escape in evening clothes?—Garbo laughs it off: "Oh, these! I just slipped into these."

Knowing the context within which that snippet of dialogue emerged, it's impossible to watch the rest of the scene, if not the entire picture, without channeling the mood of its European makers: its producer Gottfried Reinhardt, its star

Garbo, its Polish composer Bronislaw Kaper, and Salka, who, immersed as she was in refugee work, quite probably wrote the line. What follows is the picture's centerpiece—an attempt at Thalberg's "one great scene"—in which Garbo causes a sensation on the dance floor by improvising a Latin-inspired rhumba, the "chicachoca," transporting the nightclub crowd into a unified ecstasy. Again knowing the context, the group dance feels not so much euphoric as frantic, even desperate, a frolic on the lip of a volcano. This was not only the last glimpse of a still-radiant Garbo that moviegoers would ever see. It was the last glance at an America that was still gazing in isolation across the ocean toward a blood-red Europe—an America that was soon to be pushed, in these waning days of 1941, headlong into the conflagration.

METRO NEXT ASSIGNED SALKA to write a crime drama based on a novel called *The Paradine Case*, which the studio had bought nearly a decade previously as a possible Garbo vehicle. Salka did her best to spark Garbo's interest in the lurid murder-and-seduction plot. But the actress was not keen to play another femme fatale, so Salka labored on without her. In October 1941, through events worthy of Franz Werfel's prayers to Saint Bernadette, Salka's relentless efforts to rescue her mother yielded a miracle. When seventy-four-year-old Auguste Steuermann emerged from a Pullman car at the train station in Los Angeles, she was barely recognizable to Salka, who had last seen her as a still-vigorous woman during their family reunion in Switzerland six years before. At the end of a months-long journey from Sambor via Lwów, Moscow, Vladivostok, and

Seattle, Auguste looked ancient, emaciated, and tremulous. She was dressed in rags, the pitiful "new" shoes she had bought in Moscow an emblem of the hardships she had endured.

Hitler's armies had invaded the Soviet Union in June, just after Auguste had arrived in Moscow to try to obtain a visa. She was alone and knew no one in the city. Salka had cabled infusions of money and with Garbo's help had secured promises of intervention from the U.S. ambassador. Still the Soviet government denied Auguste permission to leave. Salka had also received pleas for money and help from her brother Dusko in Sambor, but after the Germans conquered the area no money or communication was permitted in the war zone in West Ukraine. Distraught about Dusko, Salka could only pray that he had fled Sambor with the retreating Soviets. She reread *War and Peace* to steady her nerves as the Nazis advanced on the capital.

Through the ambassador's efforts, Auguste's visa was finally approved. In early September she left bombed-out Moscow on the Trans-Siberian Railway to Vladivostok, there to catch a steamer bound for America. Six weeks later, on her birthday, she arrived in Seattle, where she was received with a hospitality that would have been unthinkable toward a Soviet citizen just a few months earlier. A quirk of history had led to her good fortune: with the Nazi invasion the Hitler-Stalin pact was shredded, and Russia was suddenly America's ally. So eager were the immigration authorities to welcome Auguste that they threw her a birthday party, after which they put her on the train that would take her to Los Angeles.

"I could not wait to feed and dress and pamper her," Salka wrote. She happily made room for Auguste in the crowded house on Mabery Road, and took great pleasure in mothering her mother. As with the other refugees in Salka's care, Auguste recovered much of her energy, expressed her admiration for the beauty of her new surroundings, and began to learn English. And Salka did what she always did to mark such occasions: she threw a party. "Everyone brought friends," she recalled, but as the afternoon wore on she noticed that the Hollywood ladies who flocked around Auguste had evaporated. "Old age even gallantly borne frightened them," she wrote. By the party's end, only Bertolt Brecht and his wife Helene Weigel were attending to Auguste. The Brechts had arrived in California in July, along with their two children and Brecht's translator/lover, Ruth Berlau. Alexander Granach and Marta Feuchtwanger met them at the train station. The Brechts' exodus from Finland, Moscow, and Vladivostok was similar to Auguste's but had taken even longer, their Swedish ship forced to dawdle through the Panama Canal. Their emigration was financed by many people, including the journalist Dorothy Thompson and Brecht's longtime friend Lion Feuchtwanger, who, while never a major donor to the European Film Fund, quietly supported the evacuation of Brecht and a number of other refugees through its bureaucratic channels.

Salka's joy in her reunion with her mother and with the Brechts was challenged daily by her fears for those who remained in Europe, especially Dusko. In fact, the truth was unfathomably bad, much worse than her nightmares. Along with most Americans, she would not learn of the scope of the atrocities in Eastern Europe until the release of the Molotov Report in 1942: the advancing German armies turned the Eastern Front into a sea of flames, while on their heels came battalions of SS units into the occupied territories. The German police brigades served as mobile killing units, or *Einsatzgruppen*, slaughtering entire Jewish communities through mass shootings or by shoving people into sealed vans which were then pumped full of carbon monoxide gas. Because the SS contingents did not have enough manpower to carry out the massacres, their officers recruited local collaborators.

From this time in 1941 until the Germans evacuated the Soviet Union in 1944, they slaughtered between 1 million and 1.5 million of its Jews by shooting them or poisoning them in gas vans. It's estimated that 40 percent of Jewish victims of the Holocaust were murdered in mass shootings. It was a turning point in the National Socialists' push for *Lebensraum* that had begun with the invasion of Poland: eviction of the Jews had now officially turned toward genocide. As of late October, it was unlawful for Jews to emigrate from Germany or any of its territories. Since the previous summer, nearly all who looked to America for asylum were rebuffed. In June the U.S. State Department had further tightened its already stringent restrictions to include those refugees with close relatives in Nazi states. In July all the American consulates in German territory were closed. To implement "a complete solution of the Jewish question," three centers dedicated to the obliteration of the Jews were established in German-occupied Poland: Bełżec, Sobibor, and Treblinka II. Orders came for mass deportations of Jews from the seized territories to the killing centers. In these camps and through further shooting operations, up to 1,700,000 Jews were murdered in Eastern Europe. Many more camps opened and followed the same orders.

In Santa Monica, in the dissonant calm of this same autumn, all Salka and Auguste could do was pray that their former servant Viktoria might be sheltering Dusko's girlfriend Hania and their little son. Viktoria was not Jewish, so unlike Dusko she had some measure of protection against German persecution. From Dusko himself Salka had had no word in months.

On a quiet Sunday morning, a few weeks before the release of *Two-Faced Woman*, Gottfried Reinhardt was sitting in a dubbing room at Metro, mixing soundtracks and listening to the New York Philharmonic broadcast. At that same moment, after another fraught week at the studio, Salka was taking her mother for a drive along the Pacific highway in her open car, basking in the freshness of the sea air. Mother and daughter also had the radio tuned to the Philharmonic concert from New York. Salka remembered: "Arthur Rubinstein was just finishing the first movement of the Tchaikowsky Piano Concerto no. 1, when the broadcast was interrupted and the announcer said that early in the morning Japanese airplanes and submarines had attacked and sunk the American fleet in Pearl Harbor." All at once, the United States was at war.

8

ILIUM

Moral communities are fragile things, hard to build and easy to destroy.

—JONATHAN HAIDT, *THE RIGHTEOUS MIND*

In Hollywood there are only two categories of writers, those who are loaded and those who are penniless.

—ALFRED DÖBLIN

LOS ANGELES
1942–1945

EVERYTHING WAS CHANGING, more bewilderingly than ever before. Immediately after Pearl Harbor, President Roosevelt issued proclamations designating citizens of Japan, Germany, and Italy as enemy aliens, restricting their movements and authorizing their arrest. Salka wrote: "All the Japanese living in California were sent to concentration camps or, as they were politely called, 'internment centers.'" German refugees in Los Angeles were required to register as enemy aliens and to observe a curfew, confined to their houses every night from 8 p.m. to 6 a.m. Policemen warned that it was forbidden to speak German on the street. They could not own or use short-wave radios, and—in the earliest days of the restrictions—could not travel farther than five miles from their homes.

Everywhere there was the fear that Nazi spies and fifth columnists were lurking, and often they were. The FBI rounded up many of the prominent Reich sympathizers who had marched so proudly in Hindenburg Park, and sent them to federal prison on Terminal Island in Los Angeles harbor. While it seems preposterous to suppose that those refugees in Los Angeles who had fled Nazi persecution might now be working as agents for the Reich, the paranoia of the times made this a reasonable assumption. Wartime suspicions were especially hysterical in Los Angeles, with its easy access from the Pacific and its large concentration of military sites. Interestingly, Salka noted, "there was no curfew in the East, where the 'Bund' and the 'Silver Shirts' had an impressively large membership of racists and pro-Nazis of German origin. In Hollywood," she continued, "most refugees goodnaturedly accepted the restriction of their liberty. They observed the blackouts and spent their evenings at home, convinced that a 'fifth column' existed and caution was necessary."

Gottfried, just turning thirty, was in uniform immediately. He went through basic training and was sent to New York to make training films for the Signal Corps. Hans Viertel, now twenty-three, was unhappy to be excluded from the draft because of his hearing impairment. He left Max Reinhardt's workshop for a job in the shipyards at the Port of Los Angeles, fulfilling a proletarian dream and seeking, as he wrote to Berthold, "to build my place in life so that I do not have to reproach myself." Tommy, at seventeen, was too young to serve. But twenty-one-year-old Peter, now a screenwriter at Warner Bros. on a loan-out from David Selznick, saw his chance at last and enlisted with the Marines. The news filled Salka with dread.

Berthold wrote to Salka from New York that Peter "is compelled to face the monster, man to man, as in a duel, otherwise his own existence will become worthless to him." Hitler's war was a referendum on the manliness of all America's men. Participation or avoidance told you exactly who you were. In Peter's case, becoming a Marine was a way of separating himself from his European parents while also fighting on their behalf. It was proof to himself that he was irrefutably an American, whose patriotism in helping to defeat his parents' greatest enemy could never be doubted.

All the same, Salka wrote, "it tortured me to think that Peter had become a tiny, passive particle in an immense, grinding mechanism... I loathed people who said: 'The Marines will make a man of him.' The training alone: this teaching of killing, of brutality, the drill sergeants demanding that it be done enthusiastically, was amply gruesome." But Salka kept her misgivings to herself. They would not have been warmly received in the court of public opinion at the time. Hitler's war was a referendum on America's mothers as well as its men.

Just before Peter left for basic training in San Diego, he invited Salka to dinner at a restaurant on Sunset Boulevard, where they sometimes met when he had something important to discuss. When Salka arrived she was pleased to see Harold Clurman already seated at their table. The theater director was a friend of the family and a frequent guest at Salka's parties. When Peter appeared, Salka began to understand that he had invited Clurman to soften the edges of an awkward moment, for Peter had brought a young woman with him. She was someone Salka already knew slightly, because she was married to Peter's friend Budd Schulberg. It was obvious that Peter wanted Salka to know that he and Virginia Ray Schulberg were in love.

In a city with an ever-replenishing stock of beautiful people, it was difficult for any woman who was not a movie star to stand out. But Virginia Schulberg did. Half of Hollywood was besotted with her, particularly the brainiest screenwriters. It was not just that she was exquisite, though she was: effortlessly graceful and slender, with thick, shining dark hair that she pulled back with a velvet ribbon or twisted casually into braids, and a perpetually flushed complexion that suggested good health and outdoorsiness. It was that her beauty accompanied a searching intelligence—she was never happier than with a stack of books under her arm—and a quick, acerbic wit. She was the daughter of a working-class American family ruined by the Depression, and grew up roller-skating around Beverly Hills when it was still a sleepy village. She graduated from Fairfax High, where one of her best friends had been Marian Edwards, now married to Peter's friend Irwin Shaw. She'd appeared briefly as a dancer in a few Hollywood pictures, but her passions were more literary than cinematic. She hated the name Virginia, preferring the childhood nickname her sister had given her: "Jigee" (pronounced JIE as in pie, GEE as in gee whiz).

Jigee and Budd Schulberg had been married since 1936 and they had a two-year-old daughter named Vicky. Nineteen thirty-six was also the year that Jigee joined the Communist Party. In the Benedict Canyon house of Budd's unsuspecting father, B. P. Schulberg, she and Budd hosted Marxist study groups of Hollywood's up-and-coming writers, among them Dalton Trumbo, Ring Lardner Jr., Albert Maltz, Robert Rossen, and Maurice Rapf. But unlike, say, Hans Viertel, by the time Jigee met Peter she was no longer an ideologue. Her political convictions grew from her sympathy for the victims of the Depression, and she had believed in and worked for the cause of early Hollywood unionizing. But she found Marxist texts tedious, and for her the meetings were largely social: they were the arenas in which the chic young people of her milieu drank and flirted and jousted. Nonetheless, for a time she was an active Marxist and became something of a romantic advertisement for the American Communist Party, the magnet through which many a lonely young man in Hollywood became drawn to its bright, empty promises.

In 1941 Budd had published a provocative critique of the picture business in a novel called *What Makes Sammy Run?* At the same time he was enjoying the benefits of a thriving screenwriting career. The Schulbergs' marriage crumbled not long afterward when Peter and Jigee began their romance. Five years younger than she, Peter was already at twenty-one a dashing personality, athletic and handsome, with his mother's social ease. Salka later wrote that Budd's mother Ad Schulberg had had "strong reservations" about Jigee and Budd's marriage and had warned Salka, shortly after they broke up, about Jigee's "destructive character." The Schulberg family naturally had its reasons for feeling protective of Budd and bitter toward his unfaithful wife. But Salka confessed that at the time she saw little to dislike about Jigee. Over the next few days the women established a quick intimacy as they accompanied Peter on errands before he left for basic training. Salka's reservations about the relationship centered on Peter: she doubted that he'd be able to support Jigee and her daughter on a Marine private's salary. In Jigee she saw a lovely, intelligent, but brittle young woman who, she guessed, "would need a lot of courage to face the future." "We both knew," Salka wrote, "that once Peter was gone we would need each other." And so they did, then and for many years that followed.

Jigee brought joy into Salka's life through her daughter Vicky, a shy child with great dark eyes and a halo of curls who was content to entertain herself for hours with simple toys or her little collection of baby turtles. While Peter was at boot camp near San Diego, Salka drove down frequently with Jigee and Vicky to visit him. "We spent Sundays on the beach," she wrote. "When I was taking a walk Vicky would usually appear at my side and silently slip her hand into mine, trying to keep step with me; with this handclasp she also took hold of my heart."

Virginia ("Jigee") Viertel and her daughter Vicky in the fig tree at Mabery Road, 1945.

When his basic training ended, Peter shipped to the South Pacific on the *Lurline*, a former luxury cruiser that chugged off to war in a sea teeming with enemy submarines. Before he left, Salka gave him a copy of *War and Peace*, hoping he would find in it the wisdom and solace that she did. She forwarded any scant news of him to Berthold in New York, who was staging a few plays and had published a new book of poems. Salka made a brief trip to visit Berthold in New York and to see Gottfried and her brother Edward. On that occasion she also met the new woman in Berthold's life, a Viennese refugee actress named Elisabeth (Liesel) Neumann, of whose cheerful attentiveness Salka approved. With Liesel, "Berthold was much more at peace with himself," Salka remembered of him during this time, "and also with me and Gottfried."

Back in Hollywood, Christopher Isherwood was angling for a job at Metro, armed with recommendations from Gottfried and Salka. He saw Salka there frequently and described in his diaries the studio in wartime: "A surprisingly large number of elevator boys and messengers were still at their jobs, despite the draft. There are now exits to air-raid shelters at the ends of the corridors." Isherwood himself had thus far avoided the draft, first as a conscientious objector and now as a theological student. He had established himself as a disciple of Swami Prabhavananda, founder of the Vedanta Society of Southern California in Hollywood, and was helping the Swami write a translation of the *Bhagavad Gita*. Salka was interested in Isherwood's adventures with Vedanta and told him she would like to try yoga. Berthold was less impressed. Still wrestling with his filial emotions toward Berthold, Isherwood complained that the older man was not nearly as open-minded as Salka, and prone to grumpy interrogations: "What am I doing with this old, unfashionable Indian stuff? What relation can it possibly have to America?"

With Gottfried and Salka's influence, Isherwood was eventually assigned to a yearlong contract at Metro. He had time there to observe Salka dispiritedly searching for a new story for Garbo. The studio was doing little to move the process along. Two years had gone by between each of the last several Garbo pictures, so this was not yet cause for concern. But Metro was concentrating its energies on a younger generation of stars, including another extraordinary Swedish actress named Ingrid Bergman. "For Garbo and her contemporaries," the film historian Mark A. Vieira notes, "1942 was the Twilight of the Goddesses."

Nonetheless Salka kept at it, enduring the tedium of her nearly impossible job. The long hours gave her too much time to worry about Dusko in Sambor and Peter in the South Pacific. With England the only remaining European market for Metro's pictures, the studio was brimming with wartime Anglophilia and tea breaks were a daily studio ritual. On a November afternoon Salka had tea with Isherwood and the British filmmaker Victor Saville, whom Berthold had befriended during his Gaumont-British days. Saville had come to Hollywood in 1939 and had coproduced Metro's first anti-Nazi picture, *The Mortal Storm*, in 1940. Though quite good, the picture was a failure at the U.S. box office. It was much more effective in Germany, prompting Goebbels to shut down Metro's Berlin office and to forbid the screening of its films in all German territories. On this autumn afternoon the excitable Saville was energized by the latest war news, particularly the favorable reports from

Egypt. He looked forward to seeing Italy invaded and pulverized by bombs, and hoped for the shooting of French collaborators. Isherwood later made Saville the model for the character called Chatsworth in his novel about Berthold, *Prater Violet*.

Salka managed to interest Garbo in a new project, the remake of a Russian film called *The Girl from Leningrad*. It was the story of a wounded soldier and a nurse, originally set during the Russo-Finnish war but now updated to the Soviet-German conflict. With Garbo's consent, Metro bought the rights and Bernie Hyman told Salka to start developing the script. But in early September, Hyman suddenly died of heart failure at the age of forty-five. His death marked the end of an era for Garbo and Salka. He had been Thalberg's close friend. He had given Gottfried his first job at Metro as his assistant. And Hyman had overseen many Garbo projects, from *Conquest* to *Ninotchka* to the ill-fated *Marie Curie*. Despite Salka's complaints about his chronic indecision and his corny taste, she never doubted his sincerity, and she believed that he had Garbo's best interests at heart. His death provoked much anxiety about what would come next.

What came next was bad. Metro decided to pull the plug on *The Girl from Leningrad* and chose to make *Song of Russia* instead, a terrible picture starring Susan Peters and Robert Taylor that would have the distinction, after the war, of forcing Louis B. Mayer to defend Metro against HUAC's allegations that the film fostered Communist propaganda. For now, Mayer told Garbo he did not want to make another picture with her, citing the loss of the European market. He offered to buy her out of the $80,000 left on her *Girl from Leningrad* contract, but Garbo refused the money, saying she had not earned it.

A gaggle of Metro employees boxed up the contents of Garbo's dressing room to accommodate its new and much younger occupant, Lana Turner. Metro continued to employ Salka for the moment, asking her to keep looking for stories that might bring the studio and Garbo back together. Salka was grateful for the paycheck. But she wasted no time trying to convince herself that her job was secure.

FOR MANY OF THE LOS ANGELES EXILES, the gap between sufficiency and penury was ruthlessly wide: you got everything, it seemed, or you got nothing. In May 1942, Franz Werfel's *Song of Bernadette* was published in the United States to blockbuster sales and was chosen in July as a main selection for the Book-of-the-Month Club. Werfel sold the film rights to Twentieth Century Fox for the huge sum of $125,000. Lion Feuchtwanger and Thomas Mann likewise saw no interruptions in their sturdy international earnings and each prepared to move into large houses in the Pacific Palisades.

Alfred Döblin, once considered along with Thomas Mann the finest Weimar-era German novelist, had no such good fortune. Döblin's book sales dwindled to nearly nothing. The screenwriting contract at Metro which had secured Döblin's escape from Europe expired in the spring of 1942 and the studio did not renew it. Döblin had hated the job, but losing it was worse. Although he had trained as a physician in Germany, his medical license was not recognized in America and his prospects for employment were dim. It was only the continuing financial assistance from the European

Film Fund, he admitted, "that prevented us from destitution." He narrowly survived a heart attack. His wife had a nervous breakdown.

Depression lurked everywhere among the émigrés. The community was still absorbing the shock of the February suicide of Stefan Zweig and his wife Lotte in Brazil, just as it had struggled to bear the suicides of Ernst Toller in New York and Walter Hasenclever in Provence. Heinrich Mann's contract at Metro had been revoked and he too faced mounting debts. He fell behind on the rent. The monthly hundred-dollar check he received from his brother Thomas, issued through the European Film Fund for tax purposes, was his only lifeline. His wife Nelly began to take a series of low-paying odd jobs. Despondent, she continued to drink and drive. She dreamed of a rural life, maybe somewhere in the sunny San Fernando Valley, where she and Heinrich might one day rent a house with a bit of land and support themselves with what they could grow. They had moved several times in the past year to economize. In their small house on South Swall Drive, which sat yearningly just outside Beverly Hills, Nelly wrote out her will, leaving everything to her husband. At the time, she was forty-four.

In late 1942, restless in exile, Klaus Mann joined the U.S. Army to join the fight against the Third Reich. He enlisted as a private, with an ordinary soldier's duties, then became a staff correspondent for *Stars and Stripes*.

The Hollywood Canteen opened its doors on Cahuenga Boulevard, offering free food and entertainment for members of the armed forces who were headed overseas. It was run entirely by industry volunteers, many of them movie stars and many of those émigrés who frequented Salka's parties, including Paul Henreid and Paul Muni.

On Mabery Road, Auguste and Salka shared the housework, with Salka complaining to Berthold that "Mama is no expert in the treatment of technical implements." There was still no news of Dusko. Salka hid the details of the Molotov Report atrocities from her mother, still trying to believe that Dusko had escaped from Sambor with the Soviet garrison.

In Los Angeles, a for rent sign hung on the Deutsches Haus, the headquarters of the Bund. Its leaders had been arrested by the FBI and were currently in jail, awaiting trial for sedition. There were no more pro-Nazi rallies in Hindenburg Park, whose picnic grounds were occupied by U.S. troops on the day after Pearl Harbor. The wartime clampdowns on homegrown fascism did not come with declining anti-Semitism. In fact, since the country entered the war there had been a rise in open hatred against Jews. Much of it was inspired by nationwide campaigns, including Charles Lindbergh's speeches for America First. But plenty was local, fomented in part by a radio broadcaster named G. Allison Phelps, whose anti-Semitic diatribes attacked the Los Angeles refugee population for stealing jobs that ought to go to American citizens, and who vowed to expose immorality in the film community. Terror plots continued to fester underground. There were plans for lynchings, for vandalizing storefronts in imitation of Kristallnacht, for developing new ways to murder Jews.

From nearly the moment of their arrival in Los Angeles, the exiles, Jewish and not, were under surveillance by the FBI, the Immigration and Naturalization Service, and the Office of Strategic Services, all looking for evidence of both Nazi and Communist infiltration. The agencies were concerned as well that, once the war was over, Germany might institute a pro-Soviet government, with high-profile exiles returning as heads of state. The FBI began to compile lengthy dossiers for Brecht, Feuchtwanger, Erich Maria Remarque, Heinrich and Thomas Mann, and the composer Hanns Eisler. The antifascist organizations they supported were suspected of being Communist fronts. Their homes were watched; their telephones were tapped; their correspondence was intercepted. Heinrich Mann sometimes went outside to find his mail scattered on the street or in a neighbor's yard. The National Socialists had used these same tactics when they came to power in 1933, as the historian Fritz Stern remembered from his German boyhood: "We learned to speak freely only at home or with our closest friends. It became an ever more controlled life."

Beginning in January 1942 and continuing for four years, Salka's telephones were tapped and her mail opened and censored. Berthold's and her FBI files—numbering over two hundred pages—contain opened correspondence from Brecht, Isherwood, the Joint Anti-Fascist Refugee Committee, which the FBI considered a Communist front, and others. The files note that "for many years the motion picture actress Greta Garbo received a great deal of mail at...165 Mabery Road." In September 1942 Salka's name was added to the FBI Watch List. Her participation in the Screen Writers Guild and the Hollywood Anti-Nazi League and her humanitarian efforts on behalf of the refugees were deemed "anti-capitalistic and communistically-inclined." In 1943, an FBI report admitted that there was "no indication that either [Berthold or Salka] has important Communist Party connections." Yet the agency continued to monitor Salka's activities, keen to gather information about her many red-tinged friends.

Salka willingly opened her door several times to FBI agents, "strong, handsome young men," she recalled, "who would have served their country better in the Marines rather than in harassing the refugees." As an American citizen she generally shrugged off these intrusions. But on one occasion, when answering questions about her friend Annie von Bucovich, she lost her temper. Von Bucovich was the daughter of a wealthy Jewish family in Berlin who had been scraping by in a low-paying job at Warner Bros. Now Annie was seeking a position with the Office of War Information in Washington, where the producer John Houseman, a friend of hers and Salka's, was coordinating the radio programming that would become the Voice of America. When the FBI agents inquired about Annie, they repeatedly asked Salka whether Annie was a Communist, a Russian, an antifascist. Salka answered truthfully—no to the first two, yes to the third. Whereupon one of the agents sighed, "Oh, you people. You are anti-fascist but I have never heard one of you say: I am anti-communist."

At this Salka exploded. "Whom do you mean by 'you people'? The refugees? They were the first victims of the Nazi horror, the first enemies of the regime with which the U.S. is at war. And aren't the Russians our allies?" Then just as quickly she took hold of herself. "I realized that my outburst was a waste of time and energy," she wrote later, "so I assured him once more that Annie was not and had never been a communist and had never read a word of *Das Kapital*."

Since the human capacity for empathy is very small, it must be nurtured.

—HEINRICH MANN, IN A LETTER
TO EGON ERWIN KISCH, JUNE 18, 1945

MOST OF THE EXILES lacked Salka's equanimity, haunted by the possibility that soon, right here in Santa Monica, they could be reliving their recent waking nightmares in southern France, or in Germany during 1933. Fears about the war, about their trapped families and friends, the daily revilement they endured as enemy aliens and Jews, the growing sense that they would never again belong anywhere, the unrecoverable loss of their homes, their occupations, their languages: all this took a serious toll.

In their distress they looked for acts of kindness, and in many instances they found it. The British actor Charles Laughton, perhaps the finest film actor of his time, befriended many of the exiles he met at Salka's. Recognizing that their nights under curfew were long and lonely, on many evenings he would visit one or another of them, and sit with them deep into the night, and read to them in his marvelously pliant West End voice. Thus he made those anxious hours more tolerable, playing chess with the curfew-bound Austrian director Henry Koster, reading Shakespeare to Salka's friend Jean Renoir and his wife Dido. He also read regularly to recuperating GIs at Birmingham General Hospital in the San Fernando Valley.

AS 1942 BARRELED INTO 1943, Salka's already tenuous composure collapsed when Gottfried, who was still serving with the Signal Corps in New York, announced that he was leaving her. He wanted children, as he had often told her, and he had met someone, a divorced former actress from New York named Silvia Shapiro, and he was planning to marry her.

Salka would soon be turning fifty-four. Although the tensions between her and Gottfried had escalated and she could hardly expect to be surprised, she felt his rejection as the cruelest of blows and the end of their relationship as no less than a bereavement. "The death of this love is horrible," she wrote to Berthold. Decades later in her memoir she wrote with some understatement that "it was difficult to extricate myself from an involvement which, for ten years, had been a vital part of my life." She also noted with characteristic perspective that "it is senseless to compare one's own grief with the enduring horror suffered by millions, but the consciousness of unspeakable tragedy makes sudden loneliness even more desperate and hopeless."

In truth she had found that she liked Gottfried less and less the older he got. She had thought him more mature in the first months of their romance, when he was twenty-two, than he was today. Nonetheless she had continued to pour her love into him, an investment that now left her—still ardent, still willing—with nothing. None of the power, the prestige, the socially approved support that coupledom conferred on women of her age. Women in their fifties without men were degraded creatures, sexless and irrelevant, objects of pity and scorn. After Garbo's exit from Metro, Hollywood had been warning Salka ever less subtly of her disposability. Now Gottfried was confirming it. She staged a mighty pretense of superhuman cheerfulness and industry, and told no one aside from her closest family of the news.

Her difficulties multiplied when Berthold returned from New York at the beginning of the year. He had moved around so frequently that his U.S. citizenship could not be finalized until he established residency for six months, so he decided to wait it out on Mabery Road. There he confronted the inconvenience of a front-row seat to Salka's depression. "Just as he had resented my happiness," she wrote in her memoir, "he now resented my sadness." His girlfriend Liesel Neumann followed from New York and took a room across the street, in a house also occupied at the time by Salka's brother Edward. Hans was back living at the house, along with Auguste and Tommy, Berthold, his niece Susan and her little son, and Edward's daughter Margret. Salka continued to cook and clean for all, arranged her Sunday parties, and ventured off daily to her ever-more-precarious job at Metro.

Isherwood came to Mabery Road on occasional lunchtimes during this period. On a golden afternoon in May, "the air full of spray and falling light," he walked on the beach with Garbo and Tommy as Garbo chattered away about her interest in Vedanta and her intention to visit Isherwood's Swami Prabhavananda. This was no new fad for Garbo; she had expressed similar attractions to Indian philosophy as far back as 1939, when she and the Viertels had attended the all-star picnic in Tujunga Canyon with the Huxleys and Krishnamurti. And indeed in July Salka brought Garbo to pay a visit to Isherwood at the Swami's temple on Ivar Avenue in Hollywood, where Garbo "played up outrageously, sighing about how wonderful it must be to be a nun, and flirting with Swami, telling him about his dark, mysterious, oriental eyes." The Swami was equally infatuated.

Isherwood also mentioned meeting Hans's good friend Stefan Brecht, the son of the playwright, "a spotty boy with glasses" who bowed stiffly from the waist upon being introduced and was fond of playing chess with Edward Steuermann. "Everything in the household was just as usual," Isherwood noted with satisfaction in July. "Berthold and Hans got into one of their heated arguments. It might easily have been 1939—except that Peter is in the Pacific war zone with the marines, and Tommy will shortly have to register for the draft. Salka came home around three o'clock, attended by collaborators, secretaries, etc. She is writing two stories at once—one about Iceland, for Garbo; the other about refugee domestic servants."

In fact Isherwood was wrong about the household proceeding as usual. In early July, Metro had canceled Salka's contract for good. Its producers had rejected every project Salka recommended for Garbo, while Garbo in turn declined every screenplay they suggested. Of Salka's old champions only Eddie Mannix remained, and swore that as soon as Salka found a good story for Garbo he would welcome her back wholeheartedly. "I am convinced he meant it," Salka said sadly. From Hollywood executives, then as now: the more emphatic the yes, the more resolute the no.

As in 1939, when Metro had last fired her, Salka was not unduly worried about her finances. That same July she sold a treatment for a domestic comedy to Paramount for three thousand dollars, and around that time she also sold a love story for Garbo set in Iceland for ten thousand. Neither was produced, but she was grateful for the income, which went toward paying her taxes and relieving her mortgage worries. There was still plenty of interest in Garbo from around the industry, even at age forty, even without the European market. And Garbo was interested in making pictures as well, as long as she approved of the scripts and directors. But without the backing of a major studio, both Garbo and Salka were cut adrift from the resources of the filmmaking apparatus. The actress was spending more and more time in New York. She didn't need the money. Salka was tethered to her family and the refugee community, and she very much did. Donations to the EFF had been declining since the United States had entered the war. The fund declared itself in dire financial straits by 1943. Its coordinators began asking recipients to repay their loans. Few were in a position to do so. As ever, they continued to rely on whatever Salka could do to help.

In early August, an FBI informant reported on a meeting that took place at Salka's house to discuss a proposal suggested by the Free Germany Movement, an anti-Nazi organization that operated in the Soviet Union during the war. The movement was hoping to install Thomas Mann as the leader of a German government-in-exile. The FBI considered the movement's American iteration to be a Communist front, claiming that its aim was to establish a postwar German government under the strict auspices of the Soviet Union. Brecht's participation in the movement earned him a place on the U.S. National Censorship Watch List.

At the Mabery Road meeting were Salka and Berthold, Lion and Marta Feuchtwanger, Thomas and Katia Mann, Heinrich and Nelly Mann, Ludwig Marcuse and his wife Sascha, Bertolt and Helli Brecht, Bruno and Liesl Frank, and Hanns Eisler. The next day, Thomas Mann decided to withdraw, rejecting any possibility of his becoming a president-in-exile.

Bruno Frank and Ludwig Marcuse likewise withdrew their signatures. The event sparked a bitter disagreement between Thomas Mann and Brecht: Mann believed that the entire German nation was at fault for Nazism and should be uniformly punished, while Brecht argued for less draconian measures and grew angry with Mann for declining to serve as a leader. As in Weimar, as in Sanary, as in Marseille, as in Hollywood's Popular Front, the umbrella of antifascism covered a broad range of political sensibilities—from Brecht's Marxism to Salka's pro-Roosevelt liberalism to Thomas Mann's democratic humanism—many of them in conflict with one another.

A Wedding, a Funeral

The positions on the lifeboat kept shifting. Etta Hardt moved to New York, abandoning Salka to her own deplorable bookkeeping. Liesel Neumann also returned to New York, having been cast in a play, and Isherwood moved into her room across the street for a few days' furlough from the Vedantans on Ivar Avenue. He mistakenly supposed that the Viertels would be free to devote themselves entirely to his entertainment. "They are quite pleased to see me," he wrote, "but they're all working hard, or busy with their own problems. Berthold has his play, Salka her movie stories, Edward his music... Salka's mother her housework. Hans his sleep. Only Tommy is nearly always available."

Isherwood and Tommy continued their walks on the beach, the boy pelting the older man with questions "about politics, Buddhism, literature, everything... listening very carefully and earnestly to my replies." At night Berthold read to Isherwood some of his poetry, along with some Hölderlin and Brentano, both men happily reenacting their London days. There was a big party at the Viertel house on August 23 which featured a lot of yelling about world affairs. Hanns Eisler ("the Red composer," Isherwood wrote, "a little moon-faced man with peg teeth...who talks very rapidly in a loud unharmonious voice, with whirring wittiness") made a spirited attack on the role of religion in politics, while Isherwood was called upon to defend pacifism. "They were all very apologetic about this," he said, "as though they'd been guilty of bad taste in even mentioning the subject—rather as though a Negro had been dragged into a discussion of race prejudice. It was silly and futile. I felt like a fake."

Villa Aurora, Pacific Palisades, with the Santa Monica Bay in background.

At the Villa Aurora, Lion Feuchtwanger's rambling Spanish house on a hill in the Palisades which he and Marta had bought that year with his book earnings, his exile friends gathered to wait for the radio news broadcasts from Europe that came at midnight. Observing the curfew, the exiles passed many nighttime hours by throwing darts at a board painted with Hitler's image.

Max Reinhardt had gone to New York to stage a play by Irwin Shaw called *Sons and Soldiers*. He celebrated his seventieth birthday there in September, in excellent health. Next he was planning, with less enthusiasm, to stage Offenbach's *La Belle Hélène* on Broadway; he had recently told Salka that he would have preferred not to have the reputation in America of "a specialist in musicals." Quite suddenly, while still in New York, he suffered a series of strokes, and by the end of October he lay close to death. Gottfried and his brother Wolfgang were with him, while in the living room on Mabery Road the Viertels held their own vigil.

As they waited for news, Salka reflected on the elder Reinhardt's influence in her life. "To be 'discovered' by Reinhardt had meant more to me than the best contracts at royal theaters," she wrote. His ideas about spectacle had revolutionized Western drama and had generated endless imitators—had even influenced, unmistakably, the ultra-theatrical propaganda pageants of the Third Reich. The National Socialists had expelled him all the same, eager to grab his theaters and personal property and glad to be rid of his pernicious Jewish influence on the purity of German entertainment.

In California Salka's heart had hurt to see Max Reinhardt's fortunes reduced to the staging of student productions in a humble auditorium, to hear affable young amateurs, their feet draped over the theater seats, thoughtlessly addressing him as

Max. Yet he had been no less hardworking in exile as he had been in his former life, when he ran eleven stages in Berlin and founded the Salzburg Festival on the grounds of the castle in which he lived. "He once called himself a 'negotiator between dream and reality,'" Thomas Mann said of Max Reinhardt. "With these words he not only characterized himself and the essence of his art, which was to render thought palpable, but he defined the essence of *all* art." The master was lofty, but could be gently prosaic too: it was his custom, before the curtain rose on an opening night, to give each of his actors a little bag of candy.

Max Reinhardt's death was a deeply personal loss for Salka. It entrenched her grief for the death of her relationship with Gottfried as well as for the lost world of German culture that Reinhardt represented. To her son Hans he had been an important mentor, the first outside the Viertel household to give him creative encouragement. Hans went on to do translation work for Brecht and to distinguish himself as an intellectual and a linguistics scholar.

As the curtain closed on the life of Max Reinhardt, Salka's sorrow at being so recently abandoned by his son Gottfried must have felt especially raw. The grief she could not share took its place among the somber community in her living room on the night of October 31, 1943. "We jumped when the telephone rang," Salka recalled. "It was Gottfried to tell us that his father was dead."

WITHOUT WARNING, just before Christmas, Peter returned to Mabery Road. He was off soon to officer training at the Marine base in Virginia. The news was a bright spot in Salka's dark year. She was relieved to know Peter would be out of combat for the next six months. He had participated in the Allied landing at Bougainville in the Solomon Islands. The destroyer on which he'd sailed toward home had been hit and slightly damaged by a Japanese bomb. He was thin but otherwise buoyant, appreciative of his good luck. And he would waste no more time: Jigee had gotten her divorce from Budd Schulberg and Peter intended to marry her right away.

Peter Viertel en route to Officer Candidate School in Quantico, Virginia, 1944.

In early February of 1944, in Salka's living room, a local judge performed the wedding. Only the families and a handful of friends attended. Berthold loved Jigee from the start and was happy to welcome her as a daughter-in-law. Jigee teased Salka for crying during the ceremony, then cried a little herself. Then they both burst into laughter, determined to grasp the moment of joy while it lasted.

It seemed that a tinge of bitterness always tempered the sweet, for the war effort demanded that Salka immediately trade the safety of one son for another. The morning after the wedding, at dawn, eighteen-year-old Tommy left the railroad station downtown for the Fort MacArthur induction center in San Pedro. From there he would be sent to basic training in Alabama. Salka and Berthold drove to the station to say goodbye, queuing on the platform among a nervous scrum of parents and sweethearts. Salka watched her youngest son marching in a long line of boys in poorly fitting uniforms, looking undefended and lost. She broke ranks and ran up to him, engulfing him in a final hug and kiss, then retreated as the sergeant yelled. Tommy waved briefly and disappeared into the tide of uniforms. Salka could barely drive through her tears on the way home.

No more young people remained at Mabery Road. Hans left for San Francisco to train as a machinist so he could work in the aircraft industry. Jigee and Vicky went to the East Coast to be closer to Peter at Quantico. Edward's daughter also went east to continue her studies, and Berthold's niece Susan rejoined her husband in England. The house's lightheartedness went with them. Now the breakfast room where Salka, Berthold, and Auguste had their meals was thick with tension.

Salka felt weighted by depression, and Berthold was prone to snap at every provocation. He was working late into the nights on a play which he was determined to show to Manhattan producers, and in the middle of March he departed for New York in a furious haste, his study a blizzard of papers and manuscripts for Salka to wade through as she packed his suitcases.

Berthold's letters from the train were as fond toward Salka as they had ever been, perhaps more so in the relief of leaving. With physical distance he was able to grow emotionally closer. He was planning to return to California the following month, unless by some luck his play was produced. His impatience with Salka evaporated and his sentimentality returned as he wrote to her of his appreciation for her financial and emotional support. "For many years you have given me the possibility to do my literary work: in the drawers of the bureau in my room, on tables, chairs and in cupboards, among newspapers and books, are manuscripts and loose papers containing the lyrical output of my whole life, which one day will justify me before my children." His mood improved as well with the prospect of returning to Liesel Neumann.

March 1944 was also the month that Gottfried married Silvia Shapiro. The finality was a blow for Salka, even as she had known it was coming. In the early 1960s, she looked back at her grieving self from this time and wrote in her diary: "At that time, and this is now twenty years ago, I thought I could not live without his love... Now I wonder, why he had such a grip on me. Because he needed me?" Publicly, though, she said nothing, and distracted herself by looking after the house and the people who still needed her. "Why didn't I let the house go dirty, neglect the garden, the dogs? I could not," she wrote later, invoking the memory of her nurse Niania. "It was Niania's heritage, her tidy peasant mind that had a firm grip on me and made me loathe disintegration."

Salka Viertel and her dog Prinz at Mabery Road, 1944.

She continued to scrub, wash, iron, cook, and tend the garden. She drove Helli Brecht to the Grand Central Market, where for ten or twelve dollars they could buy food for an entire week. "At the stalls previously owned by Japanese," Salka wrote, "Mexicans and Filipinos now stood behind mounds of fruit and vegetables. If only one could send some of it to Europe."

During a time of private heartbreak, Salka kept providing what Arnold Schoenberg's grandson E. Randol Schoenberg has called "the social glue that made the exiles into a community." It was a job without end. Fissures opened constantly throughout the German colony, its old and new feuds made more stinging and less forgivable under the particular conditions of the southern California exile. In 1943, a trio of Salka's friends—Arnold Schoenberg, Thomas Mann, and a youngish German philosopher and music theorist named Theodor W. Adorno—entered into a simmering confrontation that erupted five years later and produced lifelong bitterness among them. A significant portion of the drama took place on Mabery Road.

That summer, Thomas Mann had begun work on a new novel. It was a reimagining of the Faust legend in which a modernist composer named Adrian Leverkühn sells his soul in exchange for twenty-four years of otherworldly artistic inspiration. To help Mann understand the more abstruse details of avant-garde music, he turned to what he called "benevolent connoisseurs" of his acquaintance, including Schoenberg, Stravinsky, Ernst Toch, and Hanns Eisler. The most eager of these connoisseurs was Theodor Adorno, whom Mann had met at the Pacific Palisades home of Adorno's colleague Max Horkheimer in July.

Adorno was a Frankfurt-born musical prodigy who had studied piano with Salka's brother Edward and composition with Alban Berg in 1920s Vienna. He was a champion of modernist music and his characterizations of Schoenberg's twelve-tone method caught the attention of Schoenberg himself, at least in part through Adorno's continuing friendship with Edward Steuermann. After Adorno's ejection from Europe in 1934 and eight frustrating years of exile in England and New York, he arrived in Los Angeles in 1940. He made the journey on the heels of Max Horkheimer, his fellow Frankfurt School philosopher, on whom he was dependent for financial support. Adorno settled with his wife in a duplex apartment in Brentwood and went about trying to resurrect his professional life in the alien environment of Los Angeles. He brought with him an as-yet-unpublished manuscript called *Philosophy of New Music*, which contained a critique of Schoenberg's twelve-tone method and which he gave to Thomas Mann, who saw in it much that might be helpful for the novel he had titled *Doctor Faustus*.

Throughout that year and over the next four, Adorno became deeply involved in the manuscript for *Doctor Faustus*, advising Mann on its many composition-related technicalities and even writing some descriptions of Leverkühn's fictional music. In January 1944 the two men met at Salka's house, where according to Mann's diaries they discussed "the musical problematic of the novel." Adorno also showed Mann a collection of essays about Alban Berg to which Adorno had made several contributions. Those essays of Adorno's became important source material for the book. Many similar meetings followed. Mann made use of Adorno's writings on Wagner and Kierkegaard, early versions of his critical-theory work *Minima Moralia*, and the sections of his *Philosophy of New Music* that featured Schoenberg. Adorno accepted no payment for his efforts, but he clearly hoped his relationship with Mann would open doors toward the relaunch of his career.

When *Doctor Faustus* was published in 1948, Schoenberg was deeply insulted by Mann's portrait of Adrian Leverkühn as the creator of a twelve-tone system that mirrored his own.

He was especially distressed that Mann, with whom he was casually friendly if not especially close, had portrayed the Schoenberg-like protagonist as syphilitic. Schoenberg fumed and fulminated over what he saw as an intolerable character assassination. He startled Marta Feuchtwanger when he ran into her one day at the Brentwood Country Mart and began yelling in German that he did not in fact have syphilis.

When Mann agreed to append a note to future editions of the book attesting that a real-life contemporary composer named Arnold Schoenberg was the true creator of the twelve-tone system, Schoenberg was only partially mollified. And when he learned the extent of Adorno's contributions to the book, Schoenberg transferred much of his anger from the older man to the younger. He had never much liked Adorno, and now he despised him. As if to highlight Adorno's abiding deceitfulness, Schoenberg insisted on calling him "Wiesengrund"—the surname of his Jewish father which he had changed to his Italian mother's name upon his arrival in America. In 1950, Schoenberg added a codicil to his will in which he made a list of potential advisers who could be trusted to safeguard his reputation. He took care to note: "Wiesengrund should be excluded altogether."

Katia and Erika Mann were also offended by Adorno. They found him pretentious and self-aggrandizing, and sought to minimize his role in the creation of *Doctor Faustus*. The controversy spilled into the press. Everyone was eager, even gleeful, to take a side. In her memoir Salka recounted the frequent "excited discussions" that took place on Mabery Road. "There were impassioned arguments about 'Geistiges Eigentum,'" she remembered, translating the German as "spiritual ownership," though today we would call it intellectual property. Then she attempted to smooth over the unpleasantness, writing: "But everything was amicably settled when Thomas Mann, in a short note in his book, explained that despite all his respect and admiration for Schoenberg he had never intended to use him as a model for his hero."

In truth nothing was settled. The discord went deeper. It could only have emerged from the circumstances of this exile, and it was exile—not injured feelings about intellectual property, and not even personal dislike—that lay at the conflict's bitter root. In *Minima Moralia*, Adorno's 1951 philosophical reflection on his "damaged life" in California, he wrote: "Every intellectual in emigration is mutilated without exception." Adorno had been a young man of twenty-nine when he was expelled from Germany and had struggled ever since to regain a toehold in three foreign environments. There is more than a touch of autobiography in his musings about "every intellectual in emigration," of whom he writes in *Minima Moralia*: "He is always astray . . . His language has been expropriated, and the historical dimension that nourished his knowledge, sapped." If Katia and Erika Mann disdained him for his sycophancy, his behavior was motivated at least in part by desperation and loss. He had hoped that his alliance with Mann might restore what was taken from him when *der rote Faden* of his career was severed in 1933. When instead his efforts fostered outrage and contempt, he could only have felt again the pain of the original amputation.

For Schoenberg the pain was even greater. In his mid-seventies by the time *Doctor Faustus* was published, he perceived as under attack not only his livelihood but also his legacy. That the perpetrators were his neighbors and his fellow exiles rather than an external enemy was particularly galling. He had no trouble imagining a future in which his cultural contributions would be erased worldwide—as the National Socialists had erased his "degenerate music" in Europe—while Thomas Mann and *Doctor Faustus* endured. He agonized that generations would believe that Mann, and not Schoenberg, had invented the twelve-tone method. While he himself suffered no lack of self-worth, he repeatedly expressed his fears about the marginalization that he believed the *Doctor Faustus* episode encouraged. He wrote as much in a letter to Mann, lamenting: "To the Germans I am a Jew, to the Latins a German, to the Communists I am bourgeois, and the Jews are for Hindemith and Stravinsky."

The National Socialists' expulsion had forever ruined the security of even so indomitable a figure as Thomas Mann, who unlike Schoenberg and Adorno did not suffer the stigma of being Jewish, endured no financial hardships, and seemed assured of a legacy as unshakable as that of Goethe or Nietzsche. Yet the determination of Mann's wife and daughter to minimize Adorno's role in the creation of *Doctor Faustus* suggests a keen vulnerability. Their exertions in shoring up the Nobel Prize–winner's reputation at every turn were impulses born of the trauma of 1933, from which there was no recovery, only vigilance and suspicion.

Salka knew she could not heal these wounds. She took no public side in the conflict among the three men, all of whom were her close friends. But her compassion for each of them was a position and a principle. It attempted to shift the climate of the drama, at least within the confines of her living room. Despite her ministrations, nothing was "amicably settled." But without the tone she set through the constancy of her community-preserving efforts, the damage undoubtedly would have been worse.

SALKA TRIED TO HIDE HER ANXIETIES about the war and the absence of news about Dusko. But "it was impossible to conceal from Mama the pictures of the concentration camps, which appeared in newspapers and *Life* magazine," she remembered, and sometimes Auguste was so overwhelmed that she remained in her room all day, pretending to read. In the evenings they listened together to the Southern California Gas Company concerts on the radio, and Salka put Auguste to work as her sous-chef in the kitchen. As she chopped and peeled vegetables, the older woman shared her memories of Polish and Russian recipes from Wychylowka, and of Salka's father's favorite foods. And then, wrote Salka, "after a while we would cease talking and plunge into our separate gloom."

Salka Viertel and her mother, Auguste Steuermann, at Mabery Road.

Thomas Mann wrote his daily five hundred words of *Doctor Faustus* and then took his standard poodle for a walk, or napped in his backyard with a napkin over his face. Bertolt Brecht sat in the garden of the old wooden house he and Helli had rented on 26th Street in Santa Monica and worked on his poems and plays. Helli, an excellent actress and later a stage director, stayed up into the late hours to serve homemade cake to the visitors who came to discuss the war with Brecht.

Heinrich and Nelly Mann were both unwell. He had attacks of bronchial asthma and worried about his heart. She was hounded by depression and suffered through migraines so painful that they made her cry, and continued to soothe herself with alcohol. In the spring Nelly went to stay at Ananda Ashrama, a spiritual community founded in 1923 by Swami Paramananda, a rival of Isherwood's guru. Still operating today, the ashram sits in the La Crescenta foothills, a ten-minute drive from Hindenburg Park and its erstwhile Nazi rallies. Alfred Döblin's wife Erna also stayed there around that time and in fact many of the ashram's guests were émigrés, who must have sensed in the pine-scented air a therapeutic reminder of the magic mountains of their homelands. Nelly liked that she could stay for free, as she had no money to pay. She was treated with abundant kindness by the sisters, whose belief in life after death was a comfort to her, and who gave her lessons in English. Heinrich came to join Nelly later in the summer and stayed until October, finding as Nelly did a refuge from his fears about money and his health. Thomas and Katia drove over to see them in late September, glad to see Heinrich looking improved.

Dim the lights,
Wait for information,
Most of all, obey your air-raid warden.
Stop the panic,
Don't get in a huff,
Our aim today is to call their bluff.
Follow these rules and that is enough.
Obey your air-raid warden.

— "OBEY YOUR AIR-RAID WARDEN,"
PUBLIC-SERVICE ANNOUNCEMENT SONG PERFORMED
BY TONY PASTOR AND HIS ORCHESTRA, 1942

ONCE THE UNITED STATES ENTERED THE WAR, Salka's Sunday gatherings grew rowdier. No longer confined to the house and back garden, they spilled out onto the front lawn and the street and lasted all day and into the night, like a neighborhood block party. The Vienna-born director Fred Zinnemann, one of the Viertels' dearest friends, lived a few houses away. His son Tim was a little boy at the time and remembered the parties as unruly, with lots of drinking. To him Salka seemed grandmotherly and strikingly European in dress and manner, and always the center of the show.

Fred Zinnemann was the air-raid warden for the block during those years, and Tim would often accompany his father on his rounds. On one Sunday evening they were patrolling the blocks around their street to make sure the neighbors complied with the rules during a drill.

The Zinnemanns could hear the music booming out of Salka's house from all the way down the block. Her windows were wide open and German songs roared at full volume. As father and son approached, it seemed as if all of Santa Monica Canyon was sitting around on Salka's front lawn. More people spilled out of the crowded interior.

Fred Zinneman was serious about his responsibility as an air-raid warden. His government-issued handbook stated: "When the warning sounds after dark, the blackout will be enforced. You will warn householders at once of any light showing and if it is not at once turned out or covered, report the fact to the nearest policeman." Zinnemann yelled at Salka in German through the open window to draw the blackout curtains and stop the noise. In German, Salka yelled back at him that she would do no such thing. The music kept blasting. The windows remained open. There was no way Salka was going to shut the party down, the Office of Civilian Defense be damned. This was Los Angeles in wartime: two Hollywood notables arguing in German about U.S. government blackout rules, while a houseful of enemy aliens who had barely escaped their deaths in Europe let off steam. It must have been, from Salka's point of view, a thoroughly successful evening.

Out of the fervency of the parties, partnerships continued to bloom. In the Mabery Road living room that March, Charles Laughton met Brecht. Salka reported that Laughton was "completely hypnotized" by the playwright. The two men arranged to work together on a new version of Brecht's 1938 play *Galileo*. The actor Simon Callow observed in his book about Laughton: "The very fact that their meeting took place at the Viertels' salon might have suggested to Brecht that Laughton was not like the common run of American actors; but Laughton, though not easy socially, always wanted to be near artists—painters, composers, poets, playwrights; and Salka Viertel had somehow created a space where that most un-English and largely un-American phenomenon, the community of artists, could flourish."

Brecht spoke little English and Laughton no German at all. During their collaboration on *Galileo* the two men communicated in French, in which Laughton had become fluent during a 1936 stint at the Comédie-Française. The large, mobile-faced actor and the crop-haired little playwright worked in the garden of Laughton's house on Corona del Mar in the Palisades, perched high on an unstable cliff with views of navy warships and oil tankers in the sea below. Brecht's mind was fixed on erosion—of Laughton's hillside and of civilizations in general—and he wrote a poem about it called "Garden in Progress," in which he compared Laughton's transplanted fuchsias to immigrants. The poem ends with a warning: landslides had already sent parts of the garden tumbling down the hillside. Brecht cautioned that there might not be time enough to see it repaired.

A YOUNG INDEPENDENT PRODUCER named Lester Cowan had approached Salka with a film project called *Woman of the Sea*, with a role for Garbo as the captain of a Norwegian steamer who becomes a heroine of the Resistance. Garbo was interested but would not sign an agreement until she approved the final script. In the summer of 1944, Cowan put Salka to work on a week-to-week contract at a thousand dollars per week. To help her he hired a Warners screenwriter named Vladimir Pozner as well as Joris Ivens, the Dutch documentarian who had made the 1937 antifascist film *The Spanish Earth* with Ernest Hemingway. The writers had completed two-thirds of the script when Garbo suddenly backed out of the project. She gave no reason and no one could change her mind.

Garbo had been convinced by her agent that this type of war story was dated and that Pozner's and Ivens's Communist sympathies were box-office poison. Her desertion was calamitous for Salka, who was now jobless. There was no studio infrastructure to cajole Garbo into continuing. Toward Salka, Garbo was unmoved. "I have done enough for you," the actress told Salka. "I cannot do more." Only Ernst Lubitsch, at whose house the two women had first met all those years ago, came to Salka's defense, writing a reproachful letter to Garbo: "I haven't read the script, but I must tell you that if it's good, you behaved badly. If it's bad, you behaved even worse. You threw an old friend to the wolves. You have been in Hollywood long enough to know how much damage you have done to Salka."

Garbo was furious at Lubitsch's reprimand, but more so at Salka's disloyalty. Although the women eventually reconciled, they did not speak for a number of months. Salka was too emotionally preoccupied—not just with Garbo's betrayal, but also with her worries about Dusko, and Tommy in the army, and her depression over Gottfried—to heed the lessons of the Cowan debacle. Only with hindsight would she come to understand that her chances for independence from Garbo were dimming, and that her fortunes were tied to an unaffiliated actress with dwindling ambition and little self-confidence. Worse, Salka shrugged off the growing vilification of left-leaning filmmakers such as Pozner and Ivens as inconsequential. She underestimated her own financial jeopardy within the red scare that was beginning to engulf Hollywood.

If adaptation in the eye of catastrophe is the key to survival in the picture business, the day every insider dreads is the day when adaptation is no longer possible. Obsolescence is the great Hollywood equalizer. Eventually it happens to everyone, from Louis B. Mayer and David O. Selznick all the way down the line. During her years at Metro Salka had proved herself to be more adept than most at diplomacy. Outside the studio she had built her personal reputation on remaining proudly uncompromising. Would that resolve prove to be her ruin or salvation?

THAT AUTUMN, Tommy was honorably discharged from the army. He had survived two grueling bouts of basic training when his superiors decided that his slow coordination made him unfit for combat. To Salka's relief he returned to Santa Monica and enrolled at the local junior college. Berthold remained in New York, having made some progress toward a production of his play. Liesel Neumann came to Hollywood for a few days to make a film test. After spending time with her, Salka wrote to Berthold suggesting once again that they get a divorce. He'd be happier married to Liesel, she told him, and "as far as both of us are concerned, we will remain the same to each other as long as we live." But again Berthold refused.

By late October, Heinrich and Nelly Mann had returned from Ananda Ashrama to a mountain of bills. Nelly had taken another odd job at a hospital, but the debts were overwhelming. She had been arrested twice for drunken driving over the past two years, the first of which had led her to a failed suicide attempt. Now she was scheduled to appear in court for a probation hearing and the prospect filled her with panic. On the night of December 16 she tried again to kill herself with an overdose of pills. This time she was successful.

In the days following Nelly's death, Heinrich's stoicism abandoned him. He was exhausted by grief, and wrote to a friend that he dreaded the loneliness he now faced. He admitted that this was the fifth time Nelly had set out to end her life: twice in France, twice in California, and now the final achievement.

Salka had run into Nelly shortly before she died. Pleased to see her laughing and joking, Salka arranged a lunch date, but the next day Nelly called to cancel. Katia Mann called Salka a few days later to tell her the terrible news.

Salka arrived for Nelly's funeral at Woodlawn Cemetery on Pico Boulevard on December 20, a sunny winter day. There she found herself alone with the newly dug grave, covered with a lurid green carpet of artificial grass, she remembered, "such as they use on movie sets." The hearse arrived. Its two attendants off-loaded the casket, chatting about baseball. Salka in a folding chair and Nelly in her coffin waited companionably together until the other guests assembled: Thomas and Katia, the Feuchtwangers, Helli Brecht, Ludwig Marcuse, Liesl Frank, and Salka's Swiss friend Toni Spuhler, who had been helpful to Nelly during many personal crises. Heinrich Mann came last, a hulking shadow. He shook his head violently at the undertaker's call for speeches. The polite young man read one psalm, shook Heinrich's hand, and withdrew. The ceremony was over. The coffin would not descend into the grave until after the mourners had gone.

Heinrich groaned, held a handkerchief to his face, and staggered blindly away. "It was gruesome," wrote Salka. Katia redirected Heinrich to her car and he rode back to the Palisades with her and Thomas. In his diary entry for that day, Thomas mentioned the funeral of "Heinrich's unhappy wife, who had brought him a lot of trouble." Possibly Thomas was thinking more of himself than of Heinrich. He had never quite seen the point of Nelly. He saw her as an unfair burden on the family and blamed her for Heinrich's descent into debt. In 1941 Thomas had refused to provide an immigration affidavit for Nelly as he had for Heinrich, insisting that Nelly appeal to her own relatives in America to act as her sponsors, which she did.

When he heard the news of Nelly's death, Klaus Mann, then serving in Italy with the U.S. Army, wrote to his mother Katia: "What an embarrassing, superfluous, *ugly* tragedy! . . . What deplorable, objectionable lack of consideration and self-control! . . . She should have stayed in Germany with people of her own kind."

Heinrich did not believe that Nelly had brought him trouble. He knew that Nelly's depression and alcoholism were illnesses and not moral failings, not occasions for shame. He praised Nelly's steadfastness in the face of her challenges. He was completely diminished by his loss. "We were together, she and I, and now I'm alone," he wrote to the novelist Hermann Kesten in New York.

Doubly exiled, Nelly never found a place among the intellectuals with whom she had fled to California. Her ribaldry and her anguish, both extreme, made them all uncomfortable. "But even those she shocked had no doubts about her devotion to her husband," Salka wrote in her memoir. Nelly had carried Heinrich over the Pyrenees, had ventured onto a strange continent with its baffling language to create a new life for them both. Marta Feuchtwanger had been right to raise a glass to Heinrich's wife at his seventieth birthday party. Nelly was as brave as any of them, maybe more so. She could have used more kindness.

Mrs. Tiggy-Winkle

"Dearest, dearest Berthold," Salka wrote to her husband at that Christmas of 1944, "Nelly's death was the last, sad event of this depressing year. The new one must be better."

With her straitened finances, Salka could no longer make contributions to the EFF or anywhere else for refugee relief. She recognized that her house was now her most effective asset and she used it for whatever amenities it could supply: the Sunday parties went on, and houseguests occupied every available sleeping space. Before long Salka took a necessary next step in order to pay the mortgage and began to charge several of her guests a fee for room and board. One of them was Sonya Schulberg O'Sullivan, who was Budd's sister and who had remained close to Jigee after Budd and Jigee divorced. Sonya's husband, a lawyer, was serving overseas. In early March Sonya moved to Mabery Road along with her eighteen-month-old son Johnny, taking the upstairs bedroom next to Salka's. Among the other paying guests, at thirty-five dollars a month each, was the actor Hurd Hatfield, who had recently starred in *The Picture of Dorian Gray* for Metro. Brecht's Danish girlfriend, Ruth Berlau, moved into the room next to the garage, also as a paying guest. She was young and lively and could make Auguste laugh, lightening some of the dark hours.

Sonya remembered that Salka's house "was a marvelous home for homeless people." Salka treated her paying guests as if they were family, with everyone gathering for meals around the dining-room table. Salka had no money for clothes but managed to dress well, throwing a vivid scarf around her shoulders to disguise a ratty sweater. At the time Salka was without household help and did everything herself with outward good cheer. She drove twenty-five minutes to Beverly Hills to do the food shopping, as there were no decent grocery stores in Santa Monica. Sonya noted that on many afternoons Salka and Garbo spent hours alone in the master bedroom, with Salka's German shepherd Prinz guarding the closed door.

Prinz was temperamental and Sonya remembered that if one leaned too close, as she once watched the actress Fay Bainter do, he would bite. One day Prinz bit Sonya's son Johnny when they were walking with the dog through the little tunnel that led to the beach. Prinz was forever causing trouble for Salka but she loved him lavishly anyway. In the house at that time there was also another big dog named Sherry and a fat, moody dachshund named Frieda that belonged to Jigee. Frieda was a former show dog and had nothing but scorn for everyone except for Brecht, to whom she was amorously devoted.

In the mornings Johnny would wake early and Sonya would hear him toddling into Salka's room, where they would romp on the bed for a while. "She was darling about it," recalled Sonya, the sweet moment no doubt a bright spot at the beginning of Salka's chore-filled day.

Sonya wrote letters to her mother Ad Schulberg that spring with the news from Mabery Road. She recalled a visit from the writer Gina Kaus, and a little dinner party with Thomas

Mann and Ernst Lubitsch—"it was fun," Sonya told Ad. She reported that she was helping Salka with the Americanisms in her scripts. "There is much to admire in her," Sonya said to her mother about Salka. "I'm particularly impressed with her handling of her terribly bad luck and terrible prospects at the moment. She has nothing—no job no dough no husband no lover—only bills and dependents. Yet she manages to stay cheerful and scrubs the kitchen floor as if she enjoyed it."

The war in Europe was in its last months. Sambor had been liberated by the Soviet army the previous August, and during January of 1945 the Russians launched an offensive that liberated western Poland. But there were still no responses to Salka's attempts to locate Dusko.

Peter had finished his officer training and was now a second lieutenant with the OSS, the precursor to the CIA. He was sent to Germany, where his language skills enhanced his service in tactical intelligence operations. Peter's letters home described the wholesale destruction as the Allies bombed Dresden, American troops crossed the Rhine, and the Russians marched into Berlin. "The well-known streets were now a bloody, senseless battlefield," Salka wrote. "But to prevent one from having pity for the German people, new concentration camps and Gestapo murders with their infernal gruesomeness were discovered. When finally Hitler and Goebbels killed themselves in the bunker, a British newspaper quoted Shakespeare: 'The day is ours, the bloody dog is dead.' Still, the day is not ours and bloody dogs were still on the loose."

As the war in the Pacific continued and the draft boards stepped up their recruitment, Hans showed up at Mabery Road with the news that he at last had been declared fit to serve in spite of his hearing disability. "I had never seen him so happy," wrote Salka. Hans persuaded a recruitment officer that the benefits of his excellent German and decent French far outweighed the encumbrance of his awkward hearing aid, which some soldiers at the induction center had mistaken for a new sort of walkie-talkie. He was immediately sent to the East Coast to train for the Counter Intelligence Corps, and a few weeks later, as Peter had, he shipped out to Germany. All three of Salka's sons could now call the army their proving ground as U.S. citizens in the fight against fascism.

Jigee and Vicky came to join the household after Peter left, and their presence lifted Salka's spirits a bit. But anxiety and sadness plagued her still. In letters to Berthold, Salka called her depression "combat fatigue," which worsened with the reports of Roosevelt's death in April 1945. "I know we are winning the war," she wrote to Berthold, "and I know Roosevelt's death will not affect its outcome, but it is as if one had suffered a great personal loss."

Brecht tried to cheer up Salka by suggesting that they write a film story together, as highly commercial a story as they could manage, to make a quick and profitable sale. Confidently he asked her: "Why shouldn't we be able to do as well as any Hollywood hack?"

Salka immediately set him straight with a dose of timeless Hollywood wisdom: "what the producers want is an original but familiar, unusual but popular, moralistic but sexy, true but improbable, tender but violent, slick but highbrow masterpiece," she told him. "When they have that, then they can 'work on it' and make it 'commercial,' to justify their high salaries."

Every day for some months Salka and Brecht worked

faithfully on their story, about a modern-day Joan of Arc. But they failed to meet the breezy criteria that Salka had articulated, as no studio offered to buy it.

That summer marked Berthold's sixtieth birthday, which he observed in New York among a gathering of émigré theater folk. "At the end I had to speak and said that I consider this celebration a symbolic homage to all who are in exile," he wrote to Salka. "It is a shame you were not there... Garbo came and was much noticed but not bothered." Berthold was moved by letters of congratulation from Thomas and Heinrich Mann, Albert Einstein, Vicki Baum, Hanns Eisler, Lion Feuchtwanger, Jean Renoir, Alfred Döblin, Brecht, and others, and was most touched by a poem from Bruno Frank. Then Berthold reported: "Next morning at breakfast Liesel and I wondered where to get the housekeeping money for the coming week. Please don't be alarmed, there are all kinds of prospects." In questions of finances, there was little that alarmed Salka more than when Berthold begged her not to be alarmed. At some point before June 1945, Salka accepted a donation of two hundred dollars from the European Film Fund, when not so long ago she had been one of its chief contributors.

In June, Bruno Frank died in his sleep of heart disease. He'd been among the most stalwart of the exiles since his Sanary days, when he'd joined weekly reading circles with Thomas Mann and Aldous Huxley, and had remained a faithful champion of refugee causes. Bruno's death saddened Salka, but she "was comforted by the thought that he had lived long enough to see the crumbling of the Nazi power."

Then, in August, Franz Werfel died, at age fifty-four. The faulty heart that had worried him as he crossed the Pyrenees had at last given out. Werfel's biographer Peter Stephan Jungk wrote that the author's enormous success with *The Song of Bernadette*—which Thomas Mann called "a well-made bad book"—had offered Werfel a "restitution of justice" after his expulsion by the National Socialists, and Salka was glad to see that Werfel, like Bruno Frank, had survived to see the Germans surrender. But Werfel's was a justice, Jungk continued, that "had not been evident in the fates of his fellow writers in exile who, almost without exception, lived at subsistence level," and inflamed in many of them a lasting resentment.

Alma Mahler-Werfel, who made a point of never going to funerals, ostentatiously declined to attend her husband's. Salka kept her own counsel, but years later, after Alma published a memoir in the late 1950s, Salka unloaded her feelings about Alma's book into her diary. "I find it disgusting," Salka wrote. "Only the part from Werfel's diary she quotes is fascinating and wonderful writing. Though in translation the vulgarity of her style is less offensive than in German, the difference between her writing and Werfel's is enormous and revealing. It could have been a wonderful book... if she would not have been determined to glorify and purify herself. The men in her life were extraordinary artists. Mahler and Kokoschka geniuses, Werfel an enormously talented poet and writer, but ruined by this monstrous bosom engulfing him and choking his heartbeat. She is the most Wagnerian non-singer one could imagine... What a monstrous self-adoration Alma has!"

Though she barely mentions it, Salka's antipathy toward Alma was probably not assuaged by the fact of Alma's lifelong anti-Semitism, which in spite of her marriage to a Jew included frequent expressions of admiration for Adolf Hitler and tirades about Jewish inferiority and unattractiveness. As was not unusual then or since, Alma recognized no contradiction in her own opinions and behavior. Her loud objections to the Jews as a people coexisted alongside her willingness to join them in exile.

BY AUGUST, Salka found she had been mistaken to think that the end of the war would bring her some long-awaited satisfaction. For her, the nuclear obliteration of 120,000 civilians at Hiroshima and Nagasaki was yet another dimension of the boundless capacity for cruelty in these years of the devil. "Some people," she mused later,

> among them my own friends, whose humanity and compassion I had never doubted, thought that the thousands of burned bodies . . . were less terrible than a prolonged war, and the sacrifice of thousands of American lives. Some saw the great promise that the channeling of atomic energy held: warmth to the Arctic, cooling of the African desert, abundance for barren countries. Mercifully the future, although menacing, is unknown to us. Fumbling, we try to cope with the sins of the past and their reverberations upon the present.

9

UN-AMERICANS

The ultimate logic of racism is genocide.

—MARTIN LUTHER KING JR.

Tyranny is the absence of complexity.

—ANDRÉ GIDE

LOS ANGELES
1946–1953

SHE HAD KNOWN, and she had not known. She had known some, and she had not wanted to know all. She had known, but now she lost the luxury of pretending not to know, because the enormity of the truth had begun to assault her.

"The Nuremberg Trials were coming to an end," Salka remembered of the time around October 1946, "and the pitifully small groups of survivors of Dachau and Auschwitz began to arrive in the States. The tattooed numbers on their wrists, the eyes which still reflected the horror, haunted me in sleepless nights." Like every Jewish émigré in the States, Salka in Los Angeles and her brother Edward in New York were trying to get information about what had happened to their loved ones. There was still no word from Sambor about Dusko. Every morning Salka intercepted the mail before her mother came downstairs, hoping to shield Auguste from bad news. On one of those mornings Salka opened a letter from Sambor that was addressed to Auguste and scrawled in pencil from a torn notebook page. It came from Viktoria, the woman who had been raised at Wychylowka as if she were part of the Steuermann family. Salka had bottle-fed Viktoria and changed her diapers. Her father had doted on Viktoria from the time of her birth in 1917 until his death in 1932.

Now twenty-nine, Viktoria had gotten through the war more or less intact. Her letter reported that she and her Ukrainian husband were well. She had four children, and she wondered whether Salka, "who had always been a sister to me," could send them a package of food. She was sorry to mention some bad news: that Dusko had come to her house begging her to hide him in 1943, "but as we are living in a rented place I could not do it, and since the last German *Aktion* I have not heard from him again." She was no longer in contact with Dusko's girlfriend, Hania, who had left Sambor with their son Adam. She had no idea where they had gone.

The blithe tone of Viktoria's letter shocked Salka to her core. She did not know which to feel first, grief or fury. She wrote in her memoir: "The German word '*Aktion*,' the only one clearly written and correctly spelled, killed all my hope that Dusko was alive."

An *Aktion* was the National Socialists' name for each of their campaigns to obliterate the Jewish population of Europe, through the hunting, assembling, and mass shooting of Jews, and through the deportation of Jews to slave-labor or death camps. In Sambor all those efforts had occurred at regular intervals. As preliminaries, the conquering Germans had forced the Jews of Sambor to wear a white ribbon with a blue Star of David on their sleeves, and to hand over their possessions, beginning with their silver and gold, furs, and radios. Anyone who refused was shot. Then, in January 1942, the Germans established a ghetto just outside the city. By autumn, all Jews living in the town and in neighboring villages were forced into the ghetto. There the cramped houses were frequently searched, a shoot-on-sight curfew was imposed, and many suffered from hunger and typhus.

The first *Aktion* in Sambor began on August 4, 1942. In the early morning hours the Gestapo hounded thousands of screaming Jews to the sports square near the railway station. From there they were pushed into cattle cars headed for the gas chambers in the death camp of Bełżyce near Lublin, about four hours away. The operation, which lasted until August 6, was directed by the Gestapo with the help of local Ukrainians, whom the Germans had incited to a frenzy of hatred against their Jewish neighbors.

The second *Aktion*, at the end of October 1942, repeated the deeds of the first, with another several thousand Jews forcibly removed to Bełżyce. Here too, local Poles and Ukrainians contributed to the efforts, patrolling the areas around the railway station and turning over to German authorities any Jews who tried to run away. For their trouble, the Germans promised to give anyone who caught a Jew or provided information for one's whereabouts a liter of vodka and five kilograms of sugar.

The last *Aktion* in Sambor took place in April, May, and June of 1943. Hundreds of German soldiers from battalions returning from the Russian front remained in the town to help the Gestapo surround and enter the Jewish ghetto. They broke into houses and dragged out Jews who were hiding in cellars, cupboards, and chimneys, and herded them into prison cells. On April 14, they brought somewhere around twelve hundred Jews from the prison to the cemetery, first taking away their clothes. Then they led the Jews on foot, under heavy guard, toward open graves which had been dug by Ukrainians and Poles.

The shooting began around one in the afternoon and continued until sunset. The Ukrainians loaded the clothing they had taken from the Jews onto German trucks and hauled it away.

In early June, the final liquidation of the Jews of Sambor took place. The Gestapo and Ukrainian police destroyed and burned the houses of the ghetto, where many men, women, and children had already died from disease and starvation. They dragged remaining Jews from every conceivable hiding place and shoved them into the prison, along with a number of Jews who had been retained as slave laborers. From there the Jews were loaded onto trucks, on which they were ordered to kneel with their hands over their heads, the Ukrainian police ready to strike with their rifle butts anyone who dared to move. The trucks arrived at a wood near the town of Radlowicz, five kilometers away, where all the Jews were shot and killed.

SINCE AT LEAST THE NINETEENTH CENTURY and probably long before that, Jews had coexisted in Sambor among their Ukrainian, Ruthenian, and Polish neighbors. In 1889, out of a total population of 13,586, there had been 4,427 Jews. In a 1931 census, Jews had comprised nearly 29 percent of the population of Sambor. In the early years of the twentieth century, when Salka's father had served as Sambor's mayor, he had dedicated his efforts toward integrating the Jews into the general culture. In 1908, he went so far as to oppose the establishment of a Jewish orphanage, issuing a proclamation that Jews should not separate themselves from the general population, insisting that the town's welfare institutions ought to be nondenominational. He won the debate, and the Jewish orphans of the town continued to be accepted into the city orphanage.

Thirty-five years after its Jewish mayor succeeded in that ecumenical mission, every Jewish citizen of Sambor was murdered. With immense satisfaction the Germans declared the town of Sambor *judenrein*, cleansed of Jews.

. . . as we are living in a rented place I could not do it, and since the last German Aktion *I have not heard from him again.*

BEFORE THE WAR, Salka's brother Dusko had been a star player for Korona, the football club in Sambor, one among at least five Jewish competitors on the Polish team. He then played for a variety of clubs in Lwów and Warsaw before returning to Korona in Sambor before the occupation. He had played many times in the sports square near the railway station where Sambor's Jews were hounded to their deaths. Unlike his older siblings, Dusko had struggled to find his place in the world, had just begun to establish himself as a spouse and a father, when the Gestapo sealed his fate. After reading Viktoria's letter, Salka could no longer pretend that Dusko was not among Sambor's murdered. She was never granted the dignity of knowing whether he had been shot during the last *Aktion* or sent to the crematoria at Bełżyce, though she hoped that he had been spared the gas chamber. For the moment she was consumed with rage at the offhandedness with which Viktoria had described her betrayal of Dusko. She began to compose a letter in response. "I wrote her," Salka said in her memoir, "that she had forfeited the right to appeal to my sisterly feelings. She had cruelly denied shelter to a hunted Jew, whose father and mother had given her love and devoted care since she was born, and that she had allied herself with murderers and torturers."

But then Salka stopped. She began to wonder if she had the right to rebuke Viktoria, who would have been shot without hesitation by the Gestapo if she had been found hiding a Jew. Untold numbers of people far more powerful than Viktoria were behaving with far more indifference. Salka had dedicated herself to saving Jewish lives with every resource she could gather. But Viktoria was in a vastly different position. She was uneducated, poor, and cowed by authority. Salka decided she would be wrong to judge her according to her own principles of *Zivilcourage*, a universe away.

It was not so simple. It never was. In truth you could never be sure how you would behave, what choices you would make, when forced to gauge the chances of your own survival. Salka could not directly accuse Viktoria of cowardice in failing to save Dusko. She never sent her letter and she never told her mother what Viktoria reported. She arranged to send a CARE package to Sambor, as Viktoria had asked.

Salka herself was haunted by guilt. She had failed to prevent the slaughter of her brother. How had she allowed that to happen? And why was she herself spared, by a lucky stroke of early timing? Here again she was hardly alone in her suffering. Everyone was hearing unimaginable news. There was not even a vocabulary at that time with which to speak about it, and often they did not. In 1938, Fred Zinnemann's parents, Oskar and Anna, had bought their passage for a ship leaving from Spain and were waiting for visas when they were arrested and deported. Oskar Zinnemann was shot in the Warsaw ghetto, and Anna Zinnemann was killed in Auschwitz. Franz Waxman's brother died in a Nazi camp. Alfred Döblin learned that his brother had been murdered in Auschwitz along with his family, while Döblin's son Wolfgang, who had fought for the French, had killed himself so as not to be captured by the Germans. Three-quarters of Billy Wilder's family were murdered in Auschwitz, including his mother.

The genocide claimed one individual life after another, each with its vast network of connections. "How can one possibly stand what has been stood by millions and millions of suffering people?" Ernst Toch wrote to a friend in June 1946. Deeply depressed by the reports from Europe, he left California to seek psychiatric treatment in Illinois.

On the evening in 1942 after Salka had first learned from the Molotov Report of the massacres of the Jews that were taking place in Poland and Russia, she had sat with Brecht and Ruth Berlau by the fireplace on Mabery Road, and Salka had confessed her guilt to them. The next morning she found that Brecht had slipped a poem under her door, which he dedicated to her. Called "I, the Survivor," it's a four-line cry of self-excoriation for remaining alive through sheer luck, when so many of his loved ones were dead.

SALKA PRETENDED to be her usual brisk and vigorous self, but grief wore her down. A lesser worry was the fact of her dwindling finances. She had to have the house painted and repaired, which cost her dearly, and she began to imagine renting it out and moving to someplace where she could live debt-free. At fifty-six, for the first time, she was feeling her age. Only to Berthold would she confess this: "I don't want to cook or wash for strangers again because I don't have the strength any more," she wrote to him. "I would like to be alone and work for myself in peace... Oh, how I would like to have two hours without worrying about anybody."

Auguste's health had deteriorated in the last year. Salka suspected that her mother guessed the truth about Dusko without ever mentioning it. If so, the torment was taking its toll, as Auguste's trembling from Parkinson's disease had increased and she could no longer write to Rose in Buenos Aires or Edward in New York. She was also quite deaf but refused to use her hearing aid, so that Salka had to shout to make sure she understood. Despite these frustrations Salka tended to Auguste zealously. She found friends to stay with her mother whenever she had to leave the house.

As much as Salka wished for solitude, the demands on her attention were as great as ever, and the house was just as crowded. Peter had been demobilized and was back at Mabery Road with Jigee and Vicky. Irwin Shaw had also returned from the war. He and his wife were inveterate New Yorkers, but during Irwin's screenwriting gigs they spent part of the year in California and they visited often at Salka's house, accompanied by a good friend of Irwin's, the Hungarian photographer

Robert Capa. Altogether the next generation brought welcome high spirits into the Sunday group of Huxleys, Manns, Brechts, Hanns Eisler and his wife Lou, and Charlie Chaplin and his wife Oona. They introduced a young Hollywood crowd, including Ava Gardner, then an MGM starlet, her bandleader husband Artie Shaw (no relation to Irwin), and the director George Stevens. Peter later wrote that he and Jigee and Irwin and Marian "were united in a common front against the European regular guests, who, no matter what innovative American play, or even film, was mentioned, would dismiss it with the words 'Oh, that was done in Berlin in the twenties,' or 'We've seen that done before.' Jigee said: 'I suppose if fascism ever comes to America, they'll say, "Oh, we had that in Germany long ago,"' a flippant remark that provoked only polite laughter at the tea table."

Salka's long days were sweetened by the presence of little Vicky—"my great joy," she wrote to Berthold. Vicky entertained herself by lying under the piano while someone or other was playing fortissimo, or by mixing potions of bath soaps in the upstairs bathroom sink. She went to kindergarten at the same elementary school that Salka's boys had attended. Hans and Tommy gave her piggyback rides around the neighborhood, and her roller skates clack-clacked on the pavement up and down the incline of Mabery Road. Her collection of pets had the run of the house; on one unfortunate occasion, Auguste stepped on one of her baby turtles. Every night Salka brushed Vicky's hair with one hundred strokes before bedtime, and counted out the numbers for her in different languages.

Peter and Jigee were longing to become homesteaders. They found a parcel of nine acres in Zuma Canyon, eight miles north of Malibu, where the land was unspoiled and cheap. In 1946 they decided to buy the plot in partnership with a young film editor named Robert Parrish, with whom Peter had served in the OSS, and his wife Kathy. Together with other willing friends and a plumber and carpenter, the two couples built a small board-and-batten house. Jigee sat up on the roof hammering down shingles, with Vicky by her side holding handfuls of nails.

Soon after the house was finished, Peter got an offer to write a screenplay for a picture Fred Zinnemann was directing called *The Search*, which would star a new actor named Montgomery Clift and film in Switzerland. It was to be Jigee's first trip to Europe and she could barely contain her excitement. Without any complaints, Vicky ended up again in Salka's care. In Switzerland Peter and Jigee learned to ski in the mountain villages near Zurich. Their passion for the sport eventually led them to spend as many ski seasons as possible in the little town of Klosters near Davos, not far from the locale where Thomas Mann had set his 1924 novel *The Magic Mountain*.

Hans was still in Germany, immersed in postwar work with the Counter Intelligence Corps. Tommy had gone off to college at the University of Vermont, wanting to be near Berthold in New York and eager to spend his holidays with him. Berthold did not have the money to travel back to California, so he and Liesel Neumann spent their vacations at the country homes of friends, most often at Dorothy Thompson's Twin Farms in South Pomfret, Vermont.

In the meantime, in the spring of 1946, Christopher Isherwood moved into Salka's garage apartment with his photographer boyfriend Bill Caskey. Isherwood loved the cheerful little upstairs rooms with the view of the garden and a glimpse of the sea. He was especially fond of sunbathing on the balcony, which offered plenty of privacy if one lay on its floor, as he loved having sex outside.

"Salka was always glad to see you and she usually had visitors," remembered Isherwood. She was "the most perfect landlady-hostess imaginable," inviting him and Caskey to use her kitchen and borrow her books. He spent plenty of time at the Sunday parties. And on weekday mornings he often came to have coffee with Salka on his way down to the beach for a swim, "thus reviving," Salka wrote, "the old Wychylowka breakfast tradition." Garbo was spending more time in New York but was back in California that summer, and came around often in the daytime looking for Salka. If she found that Salka was out, the actress was content to pal around with Isherwood and Caskey. "Being unemployed," Isherwood wrote about Garbo, "with the whole day on her hands, she was ruthless in her demand to be talked to and walked with... At first [we] both quite enjoyed her visits; she was lively and campy and easily entertained. Then she became a nuisance." One day, Isherwood was bemused to find himself whispering to Caskey: "Imagine—if someone had told us, six months ago, that we'd be hiding under this bed, to avoid going for a walk with Garbo!"

Salka and Garbo were still discussing story ideas. In 1946–1947 alone, three Garbo projects went fairly far in negotiations before the actress backed out: a biopic of the French writer George Sand for producer Walter Wanger and director George Cukor, with a follow-up picture based on Alphonse Daudet's 1884 novel *Sappho*; and a romantic comedy about the love affair between the Parisian salonnière Madame Récamier and the writer Chateaubriand. A friend of Garbo's suggested that Salka ought to cowrite the Récamier script with a French playwright named Sacha Guitry. Salka firmly declined, because Guitry had been a fascist sympathizer during the war. "As Mr. Guitry's previous collaborators from 1940 make it impossible for me to collaborate with him, I refused," Salka wrote to George Cukor. She went on to speculate that Garbo would keep making excuses and declining opportunities, telling Cukor in confidence: "Greta is impatient to work and on the other side she is afraid of it. I understand this very well after all these years of idleness. Work is a habit and she lost it."

In the meantime Salka accepted a screenwriting job at Warner Bros., offered by an influential old friend, the producer Henry Blanke. Grateful to be working again, she immediately hired a Viennese woman named Anna to run the house in her absence. Optimistically, she also hired a gardener.

For a brief time at Warner Bros., Salka at last had some professional independence from Garbo. The picture for Henry Blanke, *Deep Valley*, was "a strong and simple story," as Salka described it, a doomed romance between the daughter of a poor California farmer and a road-gang fugitive. Warners was rushing it into production for the actress Ida Lupino, whose contract stipulated that she be paid a fixed amount whether she was filming or not. After the actress had collected a twenty-thousand-dollar paycheck for doing nothing in the early months of 1946, the studio was anxious to get her working again. So it wedged *Deep Valley* into its already bustling schedule.

Versions of the screenplay had been around since 1942, when Warners bought the rights from a San Francisco novelist named Dan Totheroh. The studio hired at least half a dozen writers to work on various drafts, including William Faulkner, who delivered an unfinished script in March 1943. (Faulkner's version has since disappeared.) Two other screenwriters who wrote drafts of the screenplay, Robert Rossen and Albert Maltz, would become prominent players in the HUAC hearings that began in October 1947.

Blanke was keen on *Deep Valley* because it resembled Warners' 1941 hit, *High Sierra*, a Western noir about gangsters on the run in which Lupino had starred with Humphrey Bogart. This time the role of the anguished tough guy would go to first-time leading man Dane Clark, previously a supporting player in *Hollywood Canteen* and *Pride of the Marines*.

Henry Blanke paired Salka with a veteran screenwriter named Stephen Morehouse Avery ("very nice but deadly boring," Salka wrote to Berthold). "This is practically a first draft," Blanke wrote to Jack Warner. "I know that you are trying to rush this picture into production, and I have already gotten busy with Salka Viertel this morning on improving it all the way through." Salka wrote to Berthold: "Blanke is nice and not hurrying me but I would like to do it quickly and well. It's a very difficult story and there are many scripts."

From March to June 1946, Salka, Stephen Avery, and a writer named James Gray reworked the script. Again it's impossible to determine the precise contributions of each writer, yet there is evidence that Salka took a lead writer's initiative. Archives show that Salka was paid $21,992, Avery $14,167, and Gray $3,000, and are full of Salka's research questions: What procedure would be followed in disciplining a prisoner working on a road gang in California? Has the labor union put a stop to convict labor building roads in California? Would reward notices for Folsom escapees be posted in a small-town post office?

In the meantime, Salka wrote to Berthold about her anxieties about the job, worrying that her paycheck "only goes from week to week . . . difficulties have already started but this time I don't have a Garbo behind me . . ." Worse still was the news that the government had placed a lien of six thousand dollars on her salary for tax debts.

If Salka lacked Garbo's support at Warners, neither did she have Thalberg's firm stewardship or Sam Behrman's bon mots to sparkle up the dialogue. She swallowed her pride during arguments over the script, complaining only to Berthold that Blanke "will not do anything that requires any courage," and that the picture's director, Jean Negulesco, "is also no pleasure but a big star here in the studio." Soberly, Salka told Berthold that, of the twelve hundred current members of the Screen Writers Guild, only three hundred had jobs. She had no choice but to try to keep hers.

Salka gave no hint of these fears in her memoir, remarking only that "work in the studio was pleasant," and praising Blanke for setting a tone of culture and intelligence. Blanke had been the coproducer, with Hal Wallis, for Max Reinhardt's production of Warners' *A Midsummer Night's Dream* in 1935 and had helped establish the studio's biopic library with his supervision of *The Story of Louis Pasteur* and *The Life of Emile Zola*. His reputation for good taste made him one of Warners' most enduring producers. *Deep Valley* was his sixty-eighth production for the studio, and he continued to make movies there until 1961.

Born in Berlin, Blanke had begun his filmmaking career at UFA at age twenty. He arrived in Hollywood as personal assistant to Ernst Lubitsch in 1922, then returned to Berlin to supervise Warners' operations in Germany. When Blanke returned to the Burbank studios in 1931, he brought with him the distinguished director William Dieterle, a friend from his Berlin theater days, who went on to direct *A Midsummer Night's Dream*, along with many other films for Warners. Through affidavits, Dieterle was instrumental in getting Lion Feuchtwanger and Brecht to the States, and it was his wife Charlotte Dieterle who with Liesl Frank was the coordinating force behind the European Film Fund.

Blanke himself had persuaded Jack Warner to arrange the first studio contracts for refugees when the EFF was originally established. And Blanke was a significant benefactor to the fund, a top-twenty-eight donor who contributed $2,260.50 between November 1938 and June 1945. When the EFF reinvented itself in September 1948 as the European Relief Fund, Blanke served as a founding board member, along with Walter Reisch, Gottfried Reinhardt, Robert Siodmak, Billy Wilder, Henry Koster, and Paul Kohner. The reconfigured fund's mission was to support relatives and friends of Hollywood's émigrés who were now suffering under difficult postwar conditions. The ERF coordinated the distribution of CARE packages and raised money to help insolvent refugees in the States to return to Europe.

Thus Blanke and Salka had long traveled in the same circles when he hired her to write the script for *Deep Valley*. As with *Queen Christina*, a majority of others who worked on the film were also Europeans. Yet unlike *Christina*, *Deep Valley* derived from a homegrown story about longtime inhabitants of the American West. "They were the descendants of pioneers," wrote the novelist Dan Totheroh about his characters, "turned in on themselves, imprisoned by sea and hills, dead traditions and ethics long since discarded by the world outside."

Salka's first Hollywood screenwriting credit and her last were women's pictures and star vehicles, the first featuring a regal Garbo, the second a destitute Lupino. Just as the two indelible scenes in *Christina* conveyed apprehensions about leaving much-loved places and people behind, *Deep Valley* is suffused with yearning representations of a dream of home. Lupino plays Libby Saul, the twenty-two-year-old daughter of embittered parents who treat her like a servant. Numbly she caters to her bedridden mother, who has commandeered the upstairs portion of their ramshackle house, and serves meals to her churlish father, who rules the rooms downstairs. The Sauls' house and farm lie in a remote valley, hemmed in by mountains and the sea. But big changes loom. Amid a postwar building boom, a road gang of prisoners arrives to construct a portion of the coastal highway that will connect the valley and the Sauls to civilization.

Libby's only loving relationship is with her devoted dog, Joe, with whom she roams the nearby woods in her free time. There she has found an abandoned cabin, and it's in this makeshift refuge that she hides the convict Barry Burnette after he makes a run for freedom. With a wood-burning stove, a pallet, and the loyal dog, the place becomes a fragile representation of domesticity for them, an ideal of home—much as the snowbound room at the inn had been for Queen Christina and Don Antonio, and as Mabery Road was for so many of Salka's refugees.

During the time that Salka was writing *Deep Valley*, her emotions about home and domesticity were more heightened than ever. Worries about maintaining her house and caring for her mother were always on her mind. She recognized her importance as a sustainer of her family and friends, but was growing weary from the long hours at the studio and the longer hours of housework. By January 1947, when *Deep Valley* was wrapping, she wrote to Berthold that she was completely broke, and that if she failed to get another screenwriting job she would have to rent out the house. "I've worked 14-16 hours a day in the last 3 years," she told him. "I am simply dead tired."

Salka knew what it would mean to lose the house, not only for her dependents but for herself. In the thirteen years since she had written *Queen Christina*, her identity had dramatically shifted. She was now an American citizen and a settled Californian. Plans to return to a Europe that lay in ruins had begun to take shape for many of her friends, but she wanted no part of them. The house had rooted her. Mabery Road was as close to belonging somewhere as she had felt since she was a child. In 1962, she wrote in her diary of her upstairs bedroom in Santa Monica, where every night she'd been "rocked to sleep by the waves" on the shoreline below: "That room in which I have been so miserable and so happy and which I loved so much. When I think back now it was my 'home.' This and Wychylowka."

The psychic distance Salka had traveled between the years of *Christina* and *Deep Valley* was almost as far as her journey from Europe to America. In her first Hollywood picture she was a European writing about Europe, explaining it to Americans. In her last picture she was a Californian of European extraction, illustrating the postwar evolution of the Western landscape for an American audience. Her continental perspective was still there, but it had become grafted into a hybrid sensibility that was no longer purely European or American, but some of both. The aspirations and concerns of émigré filmmakers such as Salka—themes of isolation and belonging, of home and away—were now so fused into the language of Hollywood pictures as to be indistinguishable from it. In American moviemaking, Europe and Hollywood were no longer looking at each other. Out of a cauldron of global catastrophe, they had become each other.

Film noir, born in Germany, was finding American iterations in a variety of contexts, including the pastoral neo-noir of *Deep Valley*, with its deeply shadowed Expressionist palette. Europeans' infatuation with the American West had evolved from a distant longing—interpreted through the novels of Karl May and the Haus Vaterland's Wild West bar—to a close-up cinematic embrace.

As with *Queen Christina*, Salka was not *Deep Valley*'s only reinterpreter of these points of view. There was Henry Blanke, who contributed his own Berlin-born sophistication. There was the director Jean Negulesco, who had studied painting in Paris with his fellow Romanian Constantin Brancusi and had been working in Hollywood since the early 1930s. When *Deep Valley* fell forty days behind in its production schedule as 1946 drifted into 1947, Negulesco caught much of the blame for his painstaking slowness and his insistence on location shooting in Big Sur. Yet the picture's drama owes much to his artistry with light and shadow, a style that possesses, as the film critic David Thomson has noted, "the entrancing, velvety quality of a dream world brought to life."

Most distinguished of all of *Deep Valley*'s European-born artists was the film's composer, Max Steiner, a former child prodigy in his native Vienna, classically trained by Gustav Mahler, and known throughout Hollywood as "the father of film music," nominated for twenty-four Academy Awards and winner of three. Steiner's music for *King Kong* (1933)—one of the first American films to use music as "commentary sound" to enhance the story—made his reputation. But it was Steiner's sumptuous (some say saccharine) orchestration for *Gone with the Wind* in 1939 that cemented it. It was he who so memorably incorporated the "Marseillaise" and the "Deutschlandlied" into *Casablanca* in 1942, along with "As Time Goes By." Max Steiner was so busy in the 1940s that he wrote and supervised the music for *Deep Valley* and another Warners production, *Woman in White*, at the same time, using a large ensemble for the first and a smaller for the second, finishing both projects in six weeks.

Steiner's brassily orchestral score, Negulesco's Expressionistic tableaux, Lupino's vulnerability, and the sensitivity of the script combine to make an affecting melodrama. Offsetting the moody lyricism of the Sauls' house and the woods, the location shots in Palos Verdes, the Angeles Crest, Big Bear Lake, and Big Sur offered panoramic views of the ambitious road-construction expansions that were continuing up and down the state on Highway 1, using convict labor from the San Quentin and Folsom prisons.

Most important, *Deep Valley* offers proof that, however unwelcome F. W. Murnau and Sergei Eisenstein had been when they made their early Hollywood forays, their influence and that of scores of other émigrés entrenched American filmmaking in European sensibilities. *Deep Valley* is deeply American, but it is just as sincerely German and Polish and Romanian and Austrian. The critic Clive James wrote in 2008:

"European and American cultures have always been a two-way interchange and to talk about either of them exclusively is like trying to cut water in half with a knife."

There is no better example of the contributions of immigrants to American culture than their enhancement of the motion picture business of the 1930s and 1940s. It is profound and it is enduring. Without immigrants, there would be no Golden Age of Hollywood.

IRWIN SHAW TO SALKA VIERTEL, December 9, 1946:

> Dear Salka,
>
> How are you? What happens with you and Warner Brothers? How's the large, insanely hospitable house near the beach? What new argumentative guests do you have for dinner? Have you solved the problems of the theatre, the motion picture industry, and the world over coffee in the living room this week? Have your dogs bitten anybody yet? Do you plan to come to New York? Does Vicky read Proust yet? How are things in Zuma Canyon?

Peter and Jigee returned from Europe, gathered up Vicky and her menagerie of animals, and settled into their house in Zuma Canyon. Peter had finished a novel and was casting around for screenwriting jobs, hoping to do what he could to help with Salka's financial problems.

Shaw's question about Salka's dogs must have stung. Her big dog Sherry had fallen ill and had to be put to sleep, and Prinz had become so unmanageable that she finally had to give him away. Feeling bereft, she happened to see a notice about an English sheepdog puppy that needed a new home.

She drove to a North Hollywood bungalow where she fell in love with the dog, whose name was Timmy. At four months he was already so huge and shaggy that he looked, Salka wrote, "like a medium size haystack." Timmy rode back to Santa Monica with the majesty of a visiting dignitary, his paw on Salka's shoulder and his mane rippling in the breeze. Neither Anna the housekeeper nor Auguste were thrilled with the new addition, but Salka and Timmy were inseparable. He parked his massive self upstairs in the hallway between Salka's room and Auguste's, where he alerted Salka every time he saw that her mother needed her attention.

Salka Viertel and her dog Timmy, mid-1940s.

SALKA HAD NEARLY COMPLETED the *Deep Valley* screenplay in late September 1946 when the set decorators, carpenters, painters, story analysts, and cartoonists went on strike, preventing the use of the studio backlot. The picture's shooting schedule was pushed back while the production scrambled to move locations from the Warner Ranch to Palos Verdes. This latest outbreak of labor unrest at Warners was the continuation of a bitter, violent ongoing war for power between two unions: the conservative, management-aligned International Alliance of Theatrical Stage Employees (IATSE) and the radical Conference of Studio Unions (CSU).

Reflexively sympathetic to progressive young people, Salka contributed to the CSU strike fund and argued with her cowriters against crossing the picket lines. She asked a group of secretaries about their allegiances. At first, they told her, most of them sympathized with the CSU strikers. Then one of the secretaries, who worked for the anti-Communist screenwriter Ayn Rand, "swayed them by insisting that the strikers were just a bunch of communists and that a decent person had to be against them."

Blanke diplomatically suggested that the *Deep Valley* writers work at home and meet at his house for story conferences. The strike continued for many more months, well after Salka's work at the studio was done. The chairman of the Motion Picture Association of America, the trade organization representing the six major Hollywood studios, blamed its slow resolution on continuing Communist agitation on the shop floor, though he was careful to insist that no Communist ideology had ever infiltrated scripts or the screen. In June 1947, the strike was resolved in IATSE's favor through federal legislation in the form of the Taft-Hartley Act, which restricted the power of labor unions and required union leaders to sign loyalty oaths disavowing any Communist sympathies.

As was also the custom with Louis B. Mayer at Metro, when a picture wrapped and was ready for previews Jack Warner invited the producer, director, and writers to have dinner with him in the executive dining room. Salka compared the suck-uppery at such functions to "the *Gemütlichkeit* when Stalin's staff was dining with their boss," but she attended anyway, and got into an argument with Jack Warner about anti-Semitism in Soviet Russia. Warner averred that thousands of Jews had been killed by the Communists there, and asked Salka how her mother had managed to escape. Salka told him that her mother had lived for two years under Soviet rule; that in her hometown Jews were treated decently during the Soviet occupation; and that there had been no official anti-Semitism there.

Salka may have believed this, but the truth was more complicated. In fact the Soviets did trust the Jewish population of Sambor more than the Ukrainians and the Poles, and they appointed Jews to higher positions in city and government services. But life was often difficult for the Sambor Jews under Soviet occupation. Jewish refugees who declined to accept Soviet citizenship were deported to the interior. Some wealthy Jews were sent to Siberia. Under Soviet nationalization in Sambor a grim deprivation prevailed. There were long lines for inadequate supplies of food.

After Salka finished her pro-Soviet defense in the executive dining room, her cowriter jokingly jumped in to say, "Salka is a Communist, Mr. Warner." Blanke objected: "She is not!" Salka replied evenly: "One need not be a Communist to say that Soviet anti-Semitism is not to be compared to the horrors the Nazis committed. It is just as unconstitutional in Russia as it is here, but uncontrollable in individuals." She commented in her memoir: "As no one could deny that anti-Semitism existed in America, the discussion ended." But the accusation was a sign of troubling times ahead in Hollywood for premature antifascists.

Jack Warner was pleased with *Deep Valley* and told Salka he was especially satisfied with the screenplay. The picture did a modest box-office business of $1.4 million, with postwar audiences less inclined to be in the mood for noirish gloom. Still, the paychecks allowed Salka to pay off some debts and part of her mortgage. Her financial situation was looking a bit rosier.

That is, until the IRS informed her that Berthold owed money for delinquent back taxes. Salka took out a second mortgage and in May 1947 decided to rent her house to a New York playwright named Eddie Chodorov, who had signed a big studio contract. Since Isherwood was vacating Salka's garage apartment for a trip to South America, Salka moved into the upstairs section of the garage and installed Auguste in the pine-paneled room downstairs, which Isherwood's partner Bill Caskey had used as a darkroom. Salka cooked on an electric hot plate that Garbo had bought for her and hoped that her agent would find her another job. After her bills were paid each month, she had $150 left for herself and Auguste.

"The two of us need very little," Salka wrote to Berthold. "We can live wonderfully on milk and fruit. Recently we have eaten meat once a week at most." She went on: "I am going to plunge into another story and perhaps I will even dare to try a book." For the first time she was thinking of writing a memoir, though it would be years before she began.

Salka later wrote that her *Deep Valley* days were "the last time I was to work at a major studio, but it took me several years to realize why." There was no way for her to imagine how ruinous the red-baiting in Hollywood would become for her tenuous screenwriting career.

SALKA TUNED IN EACH NIGHT THAT FALL OF 1947 to the radio broadcasts of the U.S. House Un-American Activities Committee investigation in Washington, which NBC and KNX recorded during each day's events. Ever the actress, she fixed on their theatricality. "The Un-American Committee is giving a great performance and poor Hanns Eisler is still the target of the Inquisition," she wrote to Berthold. "If the Communists had spent lots of money on propaganda they could not have done it better and more successfully." Salka joined a fundraising committee in Eisler's defense, along with Charlotte Dieterle and Lisl Henreid, the Vienna-born wife of *Casablanca*'s Paul Henreid. The proceedings were disastrous for Eisler, who submitted to three days of questioning in late September as a preliminary for the main show in October.

After denying Eisler the right to read an opening statement, the Committee established that the composer had lied on a visa application in 1941 when he claimed he was not a Communist. There was evidence that he had rather desultorily joined the party in Germany back in 1926. No help to Eisler was the fact that his brother Gerhart was perhaps the most notorious Communist spymaster in America. Two years later, in 1949, Gerhart Eisler was arrested, jumped bail, and made a brazen escape aboard a Polish ocean liner. But the Committee was after bigger fish than Gerhart's mild-mannered and jocular brother Hanns, whose refugee life in America had been dedicated to composing music, largely for the works of Brecht, and to the social consolations of Salka's parties. HUAC's goal in interrogating Hanns Eisler was to expose those who had petitioned the State Department to allow him admission to the country in 1941, an illustrious group that included Dorothy Thompson, William Dieterle, and—its white whale—Eleanor Roosevelt. The former first lady's recommendation on Eisler's behalf offered proof to the Committee of the Roosevelt administration's pink-tinged lenience toward the anti-Nazi (and thus, to their minds, pro-Communist) infiltrators who took advantage of American hospitality during the war.

For violating U.S. immigration law, Eisler and his wife Lou were forced to leave the country and to sign a declaration that they would never return. The Hearst columnist Westbrook Pegler viciously cheered Eisler's exit, lamenting only that it was "too late for Hitler to gas him." (Eisler was not Jewish.) Eisler himself made this statement upon his departure: "I could well understand it when in 1933 the Hitler bandits put a price on my head and drove me out. They were the evil of the period; I was proud at being driven out. But I feel heartbroken over being driven out of this beautiful country in this ridiculous way."

Eisler eventually settled in East Berlin. He died in 1962, his later years mired in depression.

After its gleeful manipulation of Eisler, the Committee was less successful with its one other European quarry. Answering a subpoena, Bertolt Brecht testified for about an hour on the ninth and last day of the hearings, on October 30, 1947. "I am a guest in this country and do not want to enter into any legal arguments," Brecht told the Committee smoothly, and denied that he had ever been a member of the Communist Party. "The Committee was utterly unprepared for this," wrote Salka, "and even some of Brecht's friends were surprised." When asked if he knew Gerhart Eisler, Brecht remarked that they had played chess together in Los Angeles; when asked about Hanns Eisler, Brecht said that he was an old friend and his musical collaborator.

Of Brecht's elliptical performance before the Committee, Salka wrote: "The Chairman could do nothing else but thank him for having been a cooperative witness." She reported that immediately after the hearing Brecht boarded an airplane and left the country for Switzerland, one step ahead of political storm clouds that looked very much like those that had propelled him out of Nazified Europe in 1941. A few weeks later, Helli Brecht packed up the house on 26th Street in Santa Monica and left with their children to join him. They ended up in East Berlin, where he received a hero's welcome.

Brecht was nowhere near as sorry as Eisler to leave America, having gotten what he wanted out of his Hollywood exile: a splashy American production of one of his plays. Three months earlier, during a July heat wave, the production of *Galileo* over which he had labored for two years with Charles Laughton premiered at the Coronet Theatre on La Cienega Boulevard. The weather was so hot that Laughton ordered trucks loaded with ice to park against the theater's exterior walls, and fans to be kept whirring "so that the audience can think." Among the graciously perspiring attendees on opening night were Ingrid Bergman, Gene Kelly, Frank Lloyd Wright, Billy Wilder, Igor Stravinsky, and Charlie and Oona Chaplin.

The play's brief run sold out, after which the production was set to move to Broadway. Salka wrote to Berthold: "I saw Galileo. I find the play quite beautiful, Laughton too private, the epic theater unbearable and the production a mixture of megalomania and rank dilettantism."

Public reaction was equally skeptical. The Hollywood folk were confused by Laughton's underplaying, which seemed to them a willful lack of engagement. They could not understand the absence of high drama when Laughton as Galileo recanted his scientific principles to avoid being burned at the stake. Hanns Eisler's music created no emotional swoon, and director Joseph Losey's "living-newspaper" staging was monotonously episodic. Both Los Angeles and New York audiences felt cheated of big moments and of the kind of outsized performance they had come to expect of a larger-than-life movie star.

With the influx of the refugees in the '30s Hollywood became
a kind of Athens. It was as crowded with artists as Renaissance Florence.
It was a Golden Era . . . It had never happened before.
It will never happen again.

— S. N. BEHRMAN, *PEOPLE IN A DIARY*

THE BAFFLEMENT THAT GREETED *GALILEO*, with the HUAC hearings on its heels, signaled a loosening of the embrace between Hollywood and the exiles. Ernst Lubitsch and Samuel Hoffenstein both died that fall, taking with them a universe of European-Jewish sophistication. ("No more Lubitsch," Billy Wilder lamented at the great director's funeral. "Worse than that," replied William Wyler, "no more Lubitsch pictures.") After the anticlimax of *Galileo* and the exits of Eisler and Brecht, the remaining refugees in Los Angeles saw the earth below them shifting in familiarly unsettling ways. They felt the welcome in their place of refuge growing weary, their freedoms every day becoming less free.

In December 1947, the Screen Writers Guild magazine put out a defiant special edition devoted to arguments against HUAC's impingement on free speech. Among the contributors was Thomas Mann, who offered a statement about the Committee's "ignorant and superstitious persecution" of proponents of the First Amendment. "I testify that this persecution is not only degrading for the persecutors themselves but also very harmful to the cultural reputation of this country," Mann wrote. "As an American citizen of German birth, I finally testify that I am painfully familiar with certain political trends. Spiritual intolerance, political inquisitions, and declining legal security, and all this in the name of an alleged 'state of emergency'... this is how it started in Germany. What followed was fascism and what followed fascism was war."

Salka contributed a longer essay which she titled "Sorcerer's Apprentice." Like Mann, she offered a Continental perspective to the subject of censorship in American films. Her essay performed a star turn in what the historian Thomas Doherty has called "the ritual enactment of a great Constitutional conflict" in American civic life: the clash between civil liberties and national security.

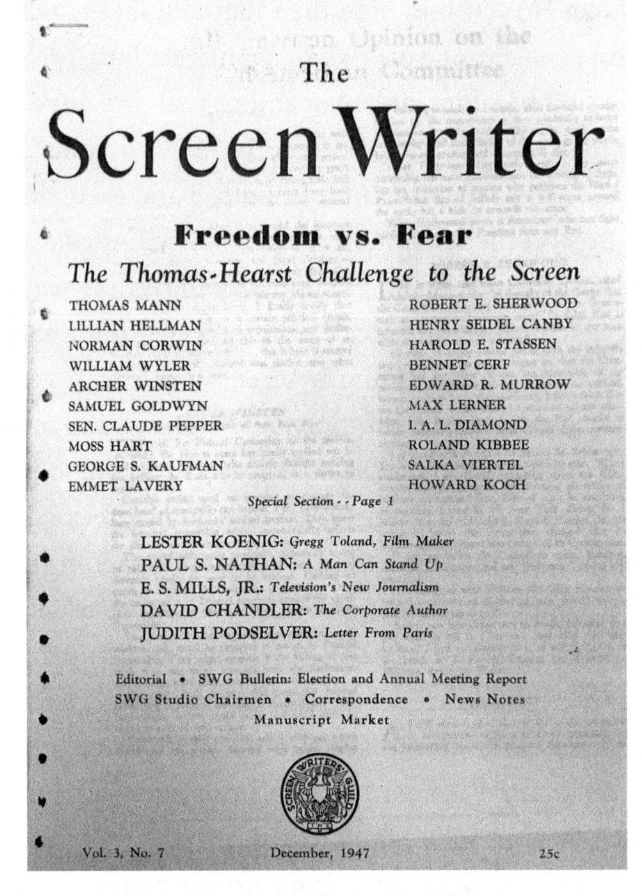
The
Screen Writer

Freedom vs. Fear

The Thomas-Hearst Challenge to the Screen

THOMAS MANN
LILLIAN HELLMAN
NORMAN CORWIN
WILLIAM WYLER
ARCHER WINSTEN
SAMUEL GOLDWYN
SEN. CLAUDE PEPPER
MOSS HART
GEORGE S. KAUFMAN
EMMET LAVERY
ROBERT E. SHERWOOD
HENRY SEIDEL CANBY
HAROLD E. STASSEN
BENNET CERF
EDWARD R. MURROW
MAX LERNER
I. A. L. DIAMOND
ROLAND KIBBEE
SALKA VIERTEL
HOWARD KOCH

Special Section - - Page 1

LESTER KOENIG: *Gregg Toland, Film Maker*
PAUL S. NATHAN: *A Man Can Stand Up*
E. S. MILLS, JR.: *Television's New Journalism*
DAVID CHANDLER: *The Corporate Author*
JUDITH PODSELVER: *Letter From Paris*

Editorial • SWG Bulletin: Election and Annual Meeting Report
SWG Studio Chairmen • Correspondence • News Notes
Manuscript Market

Vol. 3, No. 7 December, 1947 25c

Cover of The Screen Writer, *December 1947.*

Salka's essay is a pungent recitation of her political convictions and points out historical nuances which the HUAC committee was opportunistically reducing to one suspicious shade of red. Like Thomas Mann, she located the signposts of fascism which she believed the House Un-American Activities Committee was erecting. She told about the clampdowns on progressive artists that she had witnessed in Germany during meetings of the Actors Guild in the 1920s, when "the first ones to be denounced and verboten as 'Kulturbolsheviks' were Stravinsky, Arnold Schoenberg, Remarque, James Joyce, Picasso, Sigmund Freud and many others, some of whom have since contributed their great gifts to the cultural life of the countries which gave them refuge." She reminded readers of the stink bombs the National Socialists tossed into theaters during showings of *All Quiet on the Western Front*, and of the Composers League complaints against Brecht and Eisler ("it seems it always starts with Hanns Eisler," she noted). "As in the tone poem *The Sorcerer's Apprentice*," she wrote, "uncontrollable forces were released; and no sorcerer has been able to banish them."

Salka then turned her attention to the current climate in American filmmaking, in which such great pictures as William Wyler's *The Best Years of Our Lives* were being labeled subversive, and she called on citizens to guard against a culture determined to follow the same dangerous path. "Democracy is a precious thing," she wrote. "So is freedom. But in wartime both are the first casualties." She expressed her faith in the American people, whom she praised for continuing stubbornly to think for themselves: "Neither yellow journalism nor hysterical gossip columnists will make their minds up for them." But she ended more soberly:

> ...being free from political affiliations, I still cannot forget that twenty million Russians died in the fight against fascism, that to the Soviet occupation of Poland in 1939 I owe the life of my mother, and that the Nazis murdered my brother. These are my politics: they are simple enough, and I am not afraid to state them. And after having lived through two world wars and seen the destruction of my home and native land and mourned my

dear ones, I dare to express the hope that the screen shall remain free of the censorship of moronic haters.

Salka sent her essay to Berthold, telling him: "It is the beginning of my journalistic career. But I can only do this as a sideline, since I have to look around for a more lucrative occupation. I will probably work in a restaurant if our film project does not come to fruition."

"Our film project" was the George Sand story for Garbo, which she and the actress were hoping to make abroad with Pathé in France and Laurence Olivier's production company in London. Salka's new agent, an up-and-comer named Irving Lazar, was tireless in his advocacy. But over the next couple of years the financing for the picture unraveled, then pulled together, then unraveled again as the property hopscotched from one producer to another. Salka wore herself out with draft after draft of the screenplay, only to be sidelined when other writers were brought in. After finally signing a contract, Garbo balked at the last minute, and the picture never happened. Neither did a handful of other projects that producers tried to dangle in front of the actress.

Nor, despite dogged efforts, were other offers coming Salka's way. The recitation of her political beliefs in *The Screen Writer* did not help her cause. It turned out that moviegoing audiences were more fearful about Soviet totalitarianism than incipient fascism, which, after all, America had already defeated. The studio chiefs, again forced to adapt, took action. At the Waldorf Conference in November 1947 they capitulated to HUAC, agreeing to fire the writers the Committee had condemned as the Hollywood Ten—which included Salka's friends Albert

Maltz and Ring Lardner Jr.—and to make this pledge: "We will not knowingly employ a Communist or member of any party or group which advocates the overthrow of the government of the United States by force or by any illegal or unconstitutional methods." The years of the blacklist had begun.

What did this mean for Salka's career? Despite the FBI's determined efforts, it failed to establish through its surveillance of her house and activities that she was or had ever been a Communist. Salka herself consistently denied ever being a member of any political party, and there is no evidence to refute her claim. She leaned toward a vaguely imagined kind of socialism, with an emphasis on equal rights and helping the poor. It was a politics that hewed slightly to the left of Roosevelt's New Deal. But her most ardent dedication was always to the cause of antifascism.

Salka was no longer a studio employee, and thus not important enough to be summoned during the HUAC hearings. At the same time, because of her friendships with Hollywood Ten members and her alliances with Brecht and Eisler she was considered guilty by association, so her name was never officially cleared. As Garbo's biographer Karen Swenson put it: "Technically she avoided the blacklist, but not J. Edgar Hoover's unofficial 'pink' list of suspected Communist sympathizers; the FBI remained in the background as long as Salka remained in Hollywood."

What the blacklist represented for Salka, as for so many others in Hollywood, was a convenient excuse for the studios to close the door on those whom they no longer considered useful. To be "graylisted" meant that the reasons for Salka's professional rejections were thenceforth shifting and vague. In 1950, Salka's friend Jean Renoir was concerned that preview audiences were struggling to understand the narrative of his picture *The River*, which he had adapted from Rumer Godden's 1946 novel and filmed in India. When he appealed to Salka for help, she suggested a narration, "something like a nostalgic recollection which would tie the story together." Renoir liked the idea and asked Salka to write it. The budget was small and she was paid little, but she loved Renoir and enjoyed working with him. In the end she was stunned to learn that her contribution would not be acknowledged. She explained in her memoir that Renoir's investor refused to add her name to the credits; that the filmmaker was in France and could not help her; and that her SWG contract stipulated credit for "additional dialogue" but not for a narration, "even," she wrote, "if it represented 25 percent of the screenplay."

Salka's letters to Berthold tell a different story. "I don't have any credit in the Jean Renoir movie, political reasons," she wrote to him in July 1951. It's possible that she was talking about the intransigence of her SWG contract, but just as possible that she was hinting at Renoir's wish to distance himself from a friend who was under suspicion as a Communist sympathizer. After Renoir hired Hanns Eisler to provide the music for his 1947 picture *The Woman on the Beach*, he had begun to act more circumspectly in his alliances, avoiding political organizations that might cost him work. In a letter to Berthold in March 1953, Salka said that she and Renoir had talked about working together on another unnamed project, but that it had come to nothing. She needed the work: she told Berthold that she had no money to go to the grocery store or buy gasoline. "Financially it is bleak. My work with Renoir fell through; in the last moment he pulled out, not very nice, not very friendly,

I don't know why but I do think it has something to do with my situation. That I'm on the list there's no doubt. If this will spread into television work I'm going to starve to death."

The graylist meant that Salka could not even trust her good friends to tell her why they were turning down her story ideas. But she had every good reason to suspect that the answer was political fear.

IN NEW YORK, Berthold was receiving offers for directing jobs in Europe, and he decided to go. Salka said that leaving America seemed to him "like a second emigration, or like a return to somebody once very dear but now disfigured and scarred by a horrible disease." Berthold hoped eventually to direct at the Burgtheater in Vienna, but there were rules there against his cohabiting with Liesel Neumann without the benefit of marriage. So at last Salka got from him the decision she had long pursued: the amicable dissolution of their marriage. On December 20, 1947, Salka took Renee Zinnemann as her witness to the courthouse in downtown Los Angeles and stood before a judge to obtain a divorce. Telling Berthold about it a week later, she wrote: "Thirty years ago, when I married you, I was convinced that our relationship would be exceptional in our absolute truthfulness toward each other. I loved you and I shall always do so. We have held each other and belonged to each other through all the storms. Nothing will ever change that." Berthold responded: "You must know that I consider this formality an act of your kindness and utmost generosity and it makes you more lovable than ever. It moves me deeply as it only strengthens our bond... If only you were happier."

Berthold Viertel, 1950.

Salka was surprised by his last line, as she did not consider herself unhappy. “I was exhausted, impatient, frustrated, often desperate, overworked,” she wrote in her memoir, “but my life still had moments of joy, of sensuous and intellectual pleasures. Even getting old was no threat. I never had the temperament nor the leisure to become aware of it.”

Berthold and Liesel went to London. There Berthold was to direct German programs for the BBC, who sent him to Germany to report on the postwar situation of the cities along the Rhine. From Düsseldorf he wrote to Salka, remembering their long-ago life in that city together:

> There are no words to describe what this place looks like. No words, no photography can give you a glimpse of the total destruction. That's what totalitarian total war looks like, and that's how the whole world will look after the next one... I saw our old colleagues and friends; no one has changed much... the most amazing thing is that the Hitler years have left no mark: it seems they have not existed. Only *we* know of the millions dead, murdered and martyred, of the unspeakable horrors. The people here pick up exactly where they left off in 1928.

From London, Berthold accepted a position at a theater in Zurich, then returned to his hometown of Vienna for a directing contract at the Burgtheater. The sumptuous old institution on the Ringstrasse had recently appointed as its director none other than Salka's Viennese brother-in-law Josef Gielen, who had moved from Buenos Aires to take the job. Rose was not happy to leave her children and a grandson in Argentina, but she acquiesced, unable to deny her husband this prestigious chance to return to the theater where he had last worked in 1935. Berthold, who married Liesel in September 1950 in Vienna, settled into a part-time job at the Burgtheater, translating and directing the plays of Tennessee Williams among others. He tried to persuade Salka to relocate there to pursue her own theater work, but she would not consider it. She hated Vienna, telling Sam Behrman that her allergy to the city "was the major disagreement between Berthold and me," calling it "the anti-semitic, false, corny city of Gemütlichkeit."

THE CHODOROVS' LEASE EXPIRED and they moved out of Mabery Road. Salka returned to the house with Auguste and rented the garage apartment to a young couple who could not find housing because they were intermarried. Carlton Moss was a pioneering African-American screenwriter who had made recruitment films for the army during the war and was now directing educational films for black schoolchildren. His wife Lynn, who was white, was a blacklisted actress. Ignoring the suspicious glances of some of Salka's neighbors, the Mosses became her irreplaceable friends, with Carlton stepping in as a diligent father figure to twenty-four-year-old Tommy, who was sorely missing Berthold.

Both Hans and Tommy were living in the house, each trying to finish the college courses that their army duties had delayed. In late July 1950 Salka wrote to Berthold from her bed, felled by the flu and depression, "terribly tired and too poor to call a doctor. Oh this daily constant struggle for a dollar is so crushing." Feverishly she railed to him about the corruption of the Truman administration and the futility of the newly launched Korean War. Her friends Albert Maltz and Ring Lardner Jr. had gone to prison in June to serve one-year sentences for contempt of Congress. She declared to Berthold with certainty: "Fascism is here." "I couldn't give a damn about freedom of the press and thought in a world and in a country where lies and brutality are tolerated," she wrote. "Today I am convinced that only in a socialist community, a communist one if you will, which aspires to anarchy, can humanity be cured of the damage done to it. One thing is clear to me, no government is worth a human life. But any government is preferable to the one we have here."

In the same letter Salka complained to Berthold about Hans and Tommy, who she felt were taking too long to assume financial responsibilities. "The house is a sort of Shangrila for everyone who enters it, built on my enslavement," she told him. She asked for help with the boys. "I can't carry this burden all alone. From the minimal money I earn as a boarding house mother and what I get from Peter I can scarcely feed everybody and pay off the mortgage." Two years earlier she had mentioned to Berthold that she would have liked to move to New York, to "seek my fortune or my living there but Mama is weak and in need of care and is too old to be transplanted. It isn't easy with her now. Her memory has declined greatly. Sometimes I think, Thank God!"

There was no hope of moving anywhere. Edward was contributing some money toward Auguste's care, and whenever Peter was on a studio payroll he helped Salka if he could. But the expenses were crushing her. Twice during this time the house was threatened with foreclosure, bailed out at the last minute by loans from Donald Ogden Stewart and Charlie Chaplin.

Parties at the house were subdued now, often staged to help those who needed professional introductions: for the novelist Norman Mailer, touchingly young and polite; for the critic and screenwriter James Agee, who sat at the piano and played Schubert; for a trio of Peruvian performers—the soprano Yma Sumac, her guitarist husband, and her dancer cousin—whose avant-garde recital in the living room became an informal audition in front of the Chaplins, Hedy Lamarr, John Huston, and John Houseman. For the actor Montgomery Clift, off-putting to many who met him socially but solicitous toward Salka, who thought Clift resembled her old friend Francesco von Mendelssohn. ("He always presses his sex towards me when he embraces me like Francesco," she wrote about Clift in her diary.) Salka retained her ardor for beautiful young men; was not above kissing them impetuously on the lips during her parties; had been spotted by the actress Shelley Winters "necking in a rather sexual manner" with Monty Clift in a convertible late one night after a party at Gene Kelly's house.

To make money Salka began to give drama lessons. Among her students were Susan Kohner, the daughter of Paul Kohner; Margo Thomas, the daughter of comedian Danny Thomas, later to become famous as Marlo Thomas in the television show *That Girl*; and Arianne Ulmer, the daughter of the director Edgar G. Ulmer. Once a week Salka picked up fifteen-year-old Arianne from the bus stop, fed her a snack of stuffed cabbage or some other European delicacy, and did her best to improve what she deplored as the girl's hopeless American diction. She taught Arianne all the gestures she had learned from her Reinhardt theater days—the same gestures she had once taught Garbo—and together they rehearsed scenes from Shaw's *Saint Joan* for Arianne's upcoming audition for the Royal Academy of Dramatic Arts in London, which was successful, earning the teenager a spot at the school. Jigee and her sister Anne balked when Salka tried to teach them elocution, privately smirking at her accent when she conveyed the finer points of projection to them: "Now say *faaaaaaahzer*," she would instruct, meaning "father."

Salka had stopped dyeing her hair to match its original reddish-brown color. It was now a soft white cloud framing her face, on which worry lines had become engraved. Age had added bulk to her upper frame but her legs remained shapely. Housework and determination kept her strong. At sixty-three she still drove recklessly around the canyon in her Packard convertible, Timmy beside her, his paw on her shoulder, while the ocean coruscated to her west. In those moments it seemed, as John Cheever once wrote in his journals, as if all the days were mornings. As if now, even after all that had happened, goodness was still possible.

Beware, oh wanderer, the road is walking too.

—JIM HARRISON, AFTER RAINER MARIA RILKE

ALFRED DÖBLIN HAD RETURNED TO GERMANY in October 1945, trying to outrun the poverty that embittered his Hollywood exile. Carl Zuckmayer had followed in 1946, as had also, some years later, Ludwig Marcuse. All three of these writers surveyed the ruins of their birthplaces and felt the same radical disorientation that Berthold had described to Salka. Klaus Mann returned to his hometown of Munich as a soldier with the U.S. Army and found that the house where he had been born was now an empty shell. A young woman squatting there told him she thought the house had once belonged to a famous writer. Klaus searched for people his family had once known and came upon Emil Jannings, Goebbels's acclaimed *Staatsschauspieler*, who was full of resentment at being taken for a Nazi when anyone could see he was very nearly a martyr.

Klaus Mann had been suffering through decades of depression and drug dependency. In May 1949 he died of an overdose of sleeping pills in Cannes, after writing in his diary the previous January: "I do not wish to survive this year."

Ten months later, in March 1950, Heinrich Mann died. He had been planning to move to East Berlin with the hope that he could recover his lost literary reputation but also with dread that he might become a propaganda tool of the German Democratic Republic. Six weeks before his scheduled exodus, he suffered a fatal brain hemorrhage in his sleep in his Santa Monica apartment. For his brother Thomas it was "the most merciful outcome." Salka's mother was moved by Heinrich's death and asked Salka to take her to his funeral. Auguste's trembling had worsened so badly that Salka had to bathe and dress her, but they managed the trip to Woodlawn Cemetery, with memories of Nelly's funeral no doubt in Salka's mind. Lion Feuchtwanger and a minister from the Unitarian church offered eulogies. The Temianka quartet played Debussy. "He would have approved," Thomas Mann wrote of his brother. Their bonds of love and rivalry were now undone, at least in this life.

In September, Arnold Schoenberg died. He had been weakened by advanced asthma, his tall frame turned gaunt. "Only his huge, burning eyes remained the same," Salka noted of his final months. "To the last," she wrote, "Hollywood did not recognize his genius and only very few attended his funeral."

AS IT HAPPENED, coaching skittish young actors was not the key to Salka's financial salvation. She continued to hustle for screenwriting jobs. She had a new agent, Ilse Lahn, who worked for Paul Kohner and who encouraged her to write for television. Ilse managed to sell two of her scripts, refusing to acknowledge that Salka was on any kind of blacklist.

In the meantime Salka noticed that Peter and Jigee were behaving with increasing irritation toward each other. Peter had early on established a pattern of infidelity, and Jigee had retaliated with affairs of her own. Their mutual recriminations kept mounting. Desperate for a change of scene, they sold the house in Zuma Canyon and returned to Klosters for the ski season, joined by Irwin and Marian Shaw, who now had a baby son named Adam, and Robert and Kathy Parrish. Vicky enrolled in a Swiss school and sent Salka and Auguste adorable little notes in German.

The tensions between Peter and Jigee grew worse as they became stuck in a spiral of separations and reconciliations. The last of those resulted in a pregnancy, and in late April 1952, on the day of Salka and Berthold's wedding anniversary, Jigee gave birth to Salka's first grandchild, a girl named Christine. The baby was the very image of Salka from her first minute and continued to resemble her throughout her life, blue-eyed and sturdy-shouldered, with a similarly zestful energy and charm.

But Salka's joy at the news was inextricable from sadness, for from the moment of Christine's birth Peter and Jigee's marriage was dead. Peter took up with a celebrated French fashion model named Bettina Graziani and thereafter with a series of high-profile women, including Ava Gardner and Joan Fontaine. While he accepted screenwriting jobs throughout Europe and in Hollywood, Jigee decided to remain in Klosters, where she had friends and where Vicky was happy at school.

Berthold wrote to Salka: "I am terribly sorry for Peter and

Jigee. I knew for some time that the marriage wouldn't last and it is difficult to say that one or the other was at fault... Our tiny Christine has just started. I hope and trust, Salka, that she has inherited your lioness's strength."

IRWIN SHAW TO SALKA VIERTEL, Klosters, January 19, 1953:

> Dearest Salka,
>
> I just heard that grandmother died and I want to tell you how sad I am and how much I admired the gallantry and strength of heart of both mother and daughter in these last trying years.
>
> I will always remember your mother for the fortitude and cheerful avidity for life which nothing, not even these horrible times, could extinguish, and which she passed on to you in such splendid measure.
>
> I'm sorry I couldn't be with you, to help in whatever small way I could.
>
> We never cease to think of you and talk about you and love you—and we are constantly reminded of you by little Christine, who is a miraculous small image of you—and a certain promise that this line of powerful and valuable women will go firmly on—
>
> Love, Irwin

Auguste Steuermann had contracted pneumonia and faded away as 1952 slipped into 1953. At her funeral that January, a light rain fell on Woodlawn Cemetery, which now seemed as crowded with Salka's dear ones as had the house on Mabery Road. Among the pallbearers were Hans, Tommy, Fred Zinnemann, Carlton Moss, and Christopher Isherwood, who had attended Salka's Christmas Eve party with a new and as it turned out a permanent partner, an aspiring young painter named Don Bachardy. At Auguste's funeral the rabbi, unknown to all, spoke of Auguste's courage throughout a long life upended by wars and mourning. He tried to guide Salka and her sons through a recitation of the Kaddish, but their voices were stifled by tears. Salka wrote to Berthold and Rose: "At the horrible moment when one had to leave her in this foreign earth, we found ourselves surrounded by people ... not only those who were fond of her: the Renoirs, Feuchtwangers, Dieterles, Gottfried ... but many Negroes and German refugees and young Americans ..." Always thinking of others, Salka submerged the personal loss of Auguste, her moral compass, her role model in *Zivilcourage* and hospitality, her motherland.

Hans and Tommy persuaded Salka to give up the house, worried about the toll on her of the physical labor and financial worries. In April 1953, Salka's old friend John Houseman and his wife Joan offered to rent it for a six-month period with an option for another six. Carlton and Lynn Moss would continue to occupy the garage apartment. Tommy moved to Hollywood, where he had gotten a job cutting film, and Hans to Burbank, where he was working at the Lockheed plant and hoping to earn enough to return to his studies at the University of London. Salka hauled her giant dog and a number of suitcases around to the homes of a series of friends, a houseguest now, where for so long she had been the host. She was planning to go to Europe, with Peter agreeing to finance the trip. There would be a family reunion in Salzburg with Rose and Edward, Berthold and Liesel, and Peter, who was then in Paris. She would visit Jigee and Vicky in Switzerland and was pining to meet Christine.

Berthold at age sixty-eight had recently been hospitalized with a number of serious ailments including bronchitis, asthma, and a circulation disorder. He was slowly improving, but his letters had taken a tone of finality that alarmed Salka. She lost no time in applying for her passport in June, expecting to receive it in a couple of days. But as the summer came and went, her letters and telegrams to the passport office went unanswered. In August a letter arrived from the State Department in Washington notifying her that her application was denied. "It has been alleged that you were a Communist," it read, and "it is further alleged that you have been closely associated with known Communists."

With her lawyer's advice, Salka signed an affidavit stating that she was not and had never been a Communist. She wrote that her views occasionally coincided with the Communist Party line, "because it supported the fight against fascism." She admitted that she had friends who had been mentioned as members of the Party. She emphasized that her reasons for travel were not political, that she only wanted to visit her family. Again there was silence from the State Department.

Timmy became ill, would not eat or follow Salka into the car. The veterinarian, suspecting a tumor, performed an operation. Waking from the anesthetic, the dog tried to put his paw on Salka's shoulder and failed. He died a few hours later. "He had been my constant companion and my comfort for seven years," Salka wrote in her memoir. "He understood everything and he truly loved me. Now no one seemed to need me any longer. The shackles of love were falling off."

Salka allowed Hans to convince her that she needed a change of scene, should go to New York to stay with Edward and his wife Clara while she waited for her passport to clear. Hans even had a way for her to get there: he knew a man who wanted someone to drive his station wagon across the country, and Hans thought Salka could do it. Outlandish as the plan seemed, Salka in her vulnerable state agreed. She found an acquaintance to travel with her, a fortyish writer named Jay Leyda who had once studied with Eisenstein and who urged her, as she recounted some of her personal history to ease the tedium of the drive, to publish an autobiography. She reached New York on September 25, exhausted by car trouble and bad weather, and told Edward that she was going on immediately to Washington to fix her passport situation. "I *have* to go to Europe; I *have* to see Berthold," she told him. Her brother looked away, then took her hand. Simply, almost sternly, he said, "Berthold died last night."

Berthold Viertel was buried in the vast Central Cemetery in Vienna, the city from which he had been exiled for all the years of his prime. Before his interment there was a religious service in a synagogue, and think for a minute of that: a public Jewish ceremony in the same city that, only fifteen years before, had sponsored the burning of its synagogues in full view of the fire departments, followed by the deportations of thousands of Jews to Dachau and Buchenwald. "Vienna excels in funerals," Salka wrote years later to Sam Behrman. "A Hapsburg legacy for pomp and celebrations of the dead, especially when they were badly treated as long as they were alive."

Hans arrived in Vienna from London and Peter from Paris. They came too late to say goodbye at their father's bedside, but in time to carry him to his grave. For Salka there would be no farewell at all.

She had cried at every one of Berthold's leave-takings, and now, over the next few days in Edward's apartment on West 73rd Street, the tears came in torrents. She had last seen Berthold nine long years ago, in March 1944, when he had dashed out of the house in a fury of impatience to go to New York, leaving Mabery Road for what neither of them had imagined would be the last time. "He was the mainspring of my life," she wrote to Sam Behrman in 1964, when she was writing her memoir and wrestling with the impossibility of summing up her marriage. "I loved him more than anybody else and I am catching myself writing *to* him and *for* him."

Berthold's last apartment with Liesel had been on the Zedlitzgasse in Vienna, next door to the house in which he and Salka had first met and where he had declared with absolute certainty that he was going to marry her. Though she had been alone now for many years, she remained bound to Berthold by their mutual respect for each other's work, by their children, and now by a grandchild. For decades, all of Salka's decisions had been made with an eye toward what Berthold might think. The years had bestowed on them a dynamic intimacy that separation and divorce could not dissolve. Only death could do that.

IN MANHATTAN, as autumn deepened into a cheerless November, Salka left Edward's apartment and moved in with her old friend and former secretary Etta Hardt on East 73rd Street. Ghosts from her past flickered around her. In the house next door to Etta's, Salka's friend Eleonora von Mendelssohn had killed herself a year earlier after spending much of her emigrant life mired in a morphine addiction. Eleonora's brother

Francesco, who had entertained Salka in his Grunewald villa another world ago, was locked in a deep depression in a hospital in White Plains, with no visitors allowed. Eleonora and Francesco were among the staunchest exiles Salka had ever known, refusing categorically to return to Berlin. They had told Salka: "The name Mendelssohn obliges."

Garbo was living in New York then. She was a lifeline for Salka when she came sometimes to visit, "compassionate, unchanged, and very dear." Their fondness played out in their longtime nicknames for each other: Salka was still "Salka lilla" (little Salka); Garbo was "Gruscha" or "Miss G."

Salka had never felt so unmoored. Her passport difficulties continued. Through some Hollywood connections she found an influential lawyer, identified in her memoir only as "Ernest C.," who agreed to represent her at a hearing he arranged for her in Washington. They flew down together, and in a faceless office building two State Department bureaucrats confronted her with the FBI's dossier of years of surveillance of Mabery Road: "the list of my sins," as Salka described it, "as thick as the New York telephone book." A litany of questions followed. What was her political association with Hanns Eisler? Had she signed an amicus curiae brief for the Hollywood Ten? A clemency appeal for Ethel and Julius Rosenberg? Had she said that she'd prefer *any form of government* to the one in the United States?

While Salka admitted to signing her name on behalf of the Hollywood Ten and the Rosenbergs, she strenuously denied that she'd ever made that last statement. The interrogator only smiled. He knew she had written those very words to Berthold in July 1950, when she'd been sick in bed and despondent about the state of the nation. FBI agents had been opening her mail since the early 1940s, and did not mention to her that they possessed records of sentiments she had long ago forgotten or dismissed.

As the functionaries deliberated over Salka's case, perhaps they were influenced by the reputation of her high-powered lawyer, for they granted her a temporary passport that was valid for four months. Or maybe they had seen the final two documents in Berthold's FBI file, which stated that there were no grounds to institute revocation proceedings against him, despite his "political indiscretions," and noted that he had regained his Austrian citizenship before his death and was thus no longer a U.S. citizen or a threat to the nation.

Salka decided she would use her temporary passport to travel to Ireland on December 26, where she'd been invited to stay at John Huston's country house. She'd then go on to Klosters to greet the new year with Jigee and Vicky and Christine. When she returned to Los Angeles in early 1954 she would apply for a regular passport, and it would arrive without a fuss. In the spring of 1954 she would give up her home by the Pacific for good, selling it to John Houseman. Before she left for Ireland she wrote to him: "It would be wonderful to know that 165 Mabery Road, which has seen so much of life and love, struggle and happiness, and which was the 'port of entry' for so many stranded souls, is a happy home for you and your family."

ON CHRISTMAS EVE, her favorite time of year, Salka was alone in Etta Hardt's ground-floor apartment. She had tried to phone Tommy in Los Angeles to wish him a merry Christmas, but there was no answer. Glumly she contemplated her prospects for a moribund evening. And then came a most welcome coup de théâtre in the form of a knock at the door: all at once there was Garbo, her face appearing just as it had in the cutout window of Salka's red front door on a sunny afternoon in 1929. Salka scraped together a bare supper to serve them both. The two women lit the candles on a tiny Christmas tree, and they raised a glass of vodka into the silence to say *skål.*

Not so long ago both of them, in different ways, had commanded multitudes. Now here they were on the other side of the continent, still standing, still vital, somehow still hopeful. But they were two Prosperos in exile on a cold steel island, playing to an empty house. The audiences had moved on.

10

HOME

In the future, in my memory,
I shall live a great deal in this room. . . .

Let me remember you with love and loyalty,
until memory is no more.
— *QUEEN CHRISTINA*

LOS ANGELES, NEW YORK, KLOSTERS
1953–1978

SALKA LIVED FOR ANOTHER QUARTER CENTURY, one year longer than her twenty-four years on Mabery Road. It was to be a fractious exile, its joys muted, its losses ascendant. First came seven years of itinerancy in Los Angeles and New York, followed by eighteen years in Switzerland. When Salka had complained to Berthold that her Mabery Road house was "a sort of Shangrila for everyone who enters it, built on my enslavement," she could not yet imagine how grave would be the cost of giving it up. Just as she had imbued the house with her spirit, so had the house become a symbol of her sense of self. As for so many women, it was the only stable seat of power she could expect to inhabit. More than that, within the house she had built an intentional community that was as passionately committed to social support as the local ashrams, the

Quaker cooperatives, and the Hollywood Canteen. Without the house, all those who sheltered there were once again set to wandering, including its helmsman. Who would take her in, hand her a cup of tea, soothe her *mal du pays* as she had done for others all those years? The loss of the house was as grievous to her as losing a lover, a mother, a husband.

She rented an apartment on Veteran Avenue in Westwood from 1954 to 1956, cramming it with as many of her books and papers as she could. She gave drama lessons and hustled for scripts, eventually earning credits on two more pictures, both European productions: *Loves of Three Queens* (1954), starring Hedy Lamarr, and *Prisoner of the Volga* (1959). In early 1956, having at last received a permanent passport, she sublet her apartment to an actor named Jack Larson—who along with his life partner, the director Jim Bridges, was among the closest friends of her late life—and went to London, where she was reunited with Hans. She had not seen her firstborn son for half a decade, and was delighted to meet his wife, a young Frenchwoman named Violette Poulain-Salveton, whom Hans had married on December 31, 1954. Salka ever after expressed admiration and love for Violette, and later for her and Hans's daughter Valérie, born in Paris in 1957.

After she left London, Salka traveled to Munich with Hans and Violette, there to attend meetings about *Prisoner of the Volga* and to see Rose, who came to meet them from Vienna. It was Salka's first trip back to Germany since 1928. In Munich she announced her determination to see Dachau. Hans refused to go, but Violette reluctantly agreed to accompany her. When the two women arrived in the town after the half-hour train ride, their taxi driver insisted he did not know where the site was. Salka and Violette spoke to him harshly. He suddenly seemed to remember the route and took them without asking anybody for directions. At the time Dachau was operating as a center for homeless German refugees. The grounds were open to the public, but they were in a state of flux amid an impassioned debate over how much evidence to display and how much to conceal of its mass murders of the Jews. Fierce arguments erupted over how many people died there—a number that most likely will never be known.

Violette chose not to enter the camp, waiting outside while Salka went through the wrought-iron gates emblazoned with the Nazi slogan ARBEIT MACHT FREI. After some time Salka came out alone. If she said anything, Violette did not report it.

Salka reflected on what she had seen in Dachau a year later, when she was living in New York. She had got to chatting with a neighbor who hailed from the city of Tarnopol in Poland. What a small world, the neighbor had said after learning that Salka came from nearby Sambor. In her diary, Salka reflected on the subjective notion of a "small world," writing: "The world is certainly not big enough for the Jews—especially the Polish Jews. Millions had to die because there was nowhere a place for them. Israel is also much too small—only the gas chambers were big enough..."

She continued to grapple along with the rest of the world with the impossibility of comprehending the breadth of the genocide.

In the meantime, yet another personal heartbreak entered Salka's life. A family tragedy ripped a hole in her American life and sent her off to a more isolated exile in Switzerland.

When she returned to the States from Munich, Salka

became more and more devoted to her granddaughter Christine, who had moved with Jigee and Vicky from Klosters back to California in 1954. In 1956 Jigee decided to move to Manhattan to work at a literary agency, and Salka went also, to stay close to Christine. Vicky, who was then sixteen, remained in boarding school in California. In 1958, when Christine was six, Salka followed Jigee and Christine back to Los Angeles, where Salka returned to the Westwood apartment she had sublet, and Jigee rented a house on Monte Grigio Drive in the Palisades, paid for by Peter. (Vicky had gone off to college by then, and married at age eighteen.) Salka spent much of her time with Jigee and Christine at the Monte Grigio house and the three of them formed "a small female family," Salka's diary notes, "held together by our love for Christine." The little girl who looked so much like her was "the last grand passion of my life," she had written to Sam Behrman the previous year.

By 1959, when Salka turned seventy, she noted: "I am an old woman. I don't look it and don't feel the burden of my years... I love as deeply and wildly as I used to in my youth. But now I love Christine. Let's face it: It is all my present life." Part of Salka's devotion came from fear for the little girl's welfare, and that was because Jigee had developed an increasingly debilitating addiction to alcohol and sleeping pills. When she could, Jigee did her best to be a mother to Christine, and tried to hold jobs—at the literary agency in New York and then as a story editor in Hollywood—but she spent more and more of her days incapacitated in her bedroom. In the meantime Peter had fallen in love with the British actress Deborah Kerr and was pressuring Jigee for a divorce. He visited Christine when he was in town and paid the household bills. But all that was left of his relationship with Jigee was a bitter mutual rancor. He had broken her heart and she, unable to tolerate his current happiness, could not forgive him. Nor could she manage to save herself. Her addictions came to dominate her, with Salka and Christine as intimate witnesses.

Salka stepped in to care for her granddaughter, staying over at the Monte Grigio house, taking Christine to the beach, giving her dinner, putting her to bed. In Jigee's better moments, Salka found that she preferred her company to that of any other adult, and she believed that when Jigee was sober she was an excellent mother. But she watched Jigee's decline with helpless horror, reminded painfully of her late friend Eleonora von Mendelssohn's enslavement to morphine. Salka wrote in her diary, "my heart bled. Nothing is so terrible to watch than the human degradation of an addict."

In July 1959, Jigee yielded to Peter and went to the Los Angeles courthouse to obtain a divorce. Christopher Isherwood went as her witness and noticed a bad bruise on Jigee's temple—sustained, he supposed, "from falling down when drunk." Jigee's torment grew worse as the year wound down. One night in mid-December, she went into her bathroom late at night where, fumbling with a cigarette, she set her nylon nightgown on fire. Suffering massive burns, she was taken to Cedars of Lebanon Hospital, where she lingered between life and death for five weeks.

"I went to see her at the hospital Sunday the 24th of January," Salka remembered in her diary. "She was swathed in bandages, the upper part of her face strangely austere and beautiful. She could not hear well and I had to shout, but she smiled when I said that the doctors praised her courage and admired her. Still, there was that faraway look and that estrangement, which I noticed in Mama's eyes before she died."

Before dawn on February 1, 1960, at age forty-four, Jigee died. She was cremated and her ashes buried, or so Salka remembered, at Woodlawn Cemetery in Santa Monica.

In her grief Salka was disturbed by how quickly and carelessly the world seemed to move on, by how few people seemed to be missing or even remembering Jigee. "She was such an audience for me, such a responding interested audience, when she was not in her destructive mood," Salka wrote in March. "And now there is nothing left of her." Plans for eight-year-old Christine's care were quick to take shape: the little girl would move immediately to Klosters to join Peter's household, which included Deborah Kerr and her two young daughters from her previous marriage. Salka moved to Klosters as well at the end of June, leaving California with reluctance but no longer able to survive in Los Angeles with no work, and too deeply invested in Christine's welfare to abandon her. In July Peter married Deborah Kerr in a large and showy Swiss ceremony, with Irwin Shaw and the director Anatole Litvak as witnesses. Salka attended and wished the newlyweds well, but wrote in her diary that if Jigee were still alive, "she would have suffered beyond words, reading about this wedding in 'her' Klosters. The whole population turning out to wish Peter happiness with another woman."

Salka moved into an apartment an easy walk from the town center. She saw Christine whenever she could, submitted gratefully to the hospitality of Irwin and Marian Shaw, and began to work in earnest on the autobiography she had first thought seriously about writing in 1947. She had begun a diary in New York in 1957 which was an early part of the effort: she wrote it in English rather than in her more instinctive German as practice for the memoir which she intended for American readers. Occasionally she noted that the diary might itself make a fine book, were it not so hurtfully full of the "utter honesty" of Jigee's decline. Clearly she perceived all her writing during this time—her diary, her brisk correspondence with family and friends, and the memoir—as writerly performances, worthy, she dared to hope, of publication.

The Israeli writer Moshe Pearlman, Irwin Shaw, and Salka Viertel at Shaw's house in Klosters, 1960s.

In 1962, Peter and Deborah sent Christine to boarding school in England. Salka missed her terribly in the long months between school holidays, though there were some distractions.

Klosters came alive at Christmas, when such Hollywood stars as Gene Kelly, Audrey Hepburn, and Orson Welles piled into parties at the town's most charming hotel, the Chesa Grischuna. Salka also managed to travel throughout the 1960s and into the 1970s, in Europe and a few times back to the States. There were trips to see Edward perform in Salzburg, to the Chaplins in nearby Vevey, and with Peter to Biarritz, where he showed her his favorite surfing spots and took her to the bullfights. In Klosters in the late summers Garbo came for weeks at a time, with Salka setting up a favorite apartment for her, cleaning it and filling it with flowers. Garbo relished her walks around the hills and meadows, the townspeople respectful and not bothering her much.

Salka Viertel in the snow at Klosters, 1970s.

But in the dreary times between the ski and summer seasons, with Christine away at school and Peter and the Shaws often out of town, Salka felt depressed and unwell, bothered by arthritis and a worsening deafness that made socializing difficult. She was lonely, and told Sam Behrman in confidence that her purpose for moving to Klosters—to influence Christine's upbringing—had been crushed when the girl was sent away to school. In letters to Vicky, she confessed that if she could afford it she would move back to California, telling her: "I never ceased regretting that I sold 165 Mabery Road."

There was little for Salka to do but to read and work on her own writing. Her reading tastes were wide-ranging and intellectual, and often they fueled her diary entries. While making her way through the second volume of Simone de Beauvoir's memoirs, Salka remembered an afternoon in March 1947, just after *Deep Valley* had finished shooting, when de Beauvoir had dropped in at Mabery Road. The thirty-nine-year-old French philosopher had been traveling through the States on a lecture tour and was staying at the Westwood house of a mutual friend of hers and Salka's, the screenwriter Ivan Moffat. Salka reminisced: "I remember how she sat in my kitchen while I was making a salad and when I asked her if she likes cooking she was quite indignant. I said that I think everybody should do some physical work, or at least know how to do it and she disagreed violently. Not really violently, but with great irony. BUT she has courage and this I admire..."

Such memories of her kitchen and her competence there may have increased Salka's melancholy. That same diary entry records "another one of those desolate lonely Sundays" in Klosters, "which make me think constantly of death and my not being wanted anymore." She fought against depression by working on draft after draft of her memoir. "The first sentences I put on paper are always horrible but then, once I said what I wanted to say, I can 'translate' it into quite decent English," she noted in her diary. She wrote to Sam Behrman that she spent much of her time correcting her own prose, telling him: "I don't want you to think, darling, that I was kissed by the Muse ten to twelve hours a day." She had a title, she told him: "The Kindness of Strangers," from the not-yet-clichéd line in Tennessee Williams's 1947 play *A Streetcar Named Desire*, but she warned Behrman: "This is a *secret*, don't mention it yet to anybody." Behrman in turn suggested "The Incorrigible Heart," which later became the title of the German edition. But Salka stuck to her original title for the American version, nostalgic perhaps for Berthold's adaptations of Williams's plays and more generally for the glamour of the theater.

Daily she was plagued by her poverty, lamenting that she could no longer support herself or others, humiliated by constantly having to ask Peter for money, fearing that she would not be able to pay her medical bills as she aged. Selling the memoir was her last hope, though on her worst days she feared that nobody would buy it. She wrote to Behrman: "The only thing I can leave to my granddaughters are the dedications of great men in the books they have given me; other girls get mink, but those decrease in value."

In March 1962, Knopf and Random House rejected the memoir, based on 120 pages and an outline which Salka had sent. "The content is not gossipy enough. They don't give a damn about the person who writes the book, they only want anecdotes of famous people. To hell with them," Salka fumed in her diary. That November a German publisher called Rütten & Loening Verlag (a "politically irreproachable" firm, Salka reported to Sam Behrman) made an offer of three thousand deutsche marks for world rights—all countries outside North America. The offer was disappointingly low, but Salka hoped it would generate interest among American publishers. She was to deliver each chapter as she finished it so that the firm could translate it into German—a decision she later regretted, as she thought their translation inadequate.

By 1966, three other U.S. publishers had turned down the book or made unacceptably low offers. At the time Salka was without U.S. representation and was dejected when Carol Brandt, a leading New York agent, assessed the first half of the manuscript as too long and uninteresting for American readers. In early 1967 the Berlin-born agent Robert Lantz, who represented James Baldwin, Carson McCullers, and a slew of movie stars, agreed to take on the memoir. By August Lantz had submitted Salka's complete manuscript to a young editor at Holt, Rinehart & Winston. His name was Tom Wallace and he was interested enough in the book to pay Salka a visit in Klosters in October.

When Wallace arrived, Salka told Behrman she'd been expecting an "American, martini-addicted Madison Avenue editor" but met instead a most sympathetic Viennese-born Jewish intellectual who was impressed that she was reading Malraux's *Antimemoires* in the original French. (She loved Malraux as a writer, she told Behrman, "although he himself is not a pleasant man.") Salka and Wallace agreed that she should cut the first half of her manuscript and then, if he decided to buy it, they would work on the second half together. Behrman had read several drafts and insisted that Salka delete passages about Wychylowka's servants and anything about menstruation or puberty and the births of her children. "Couldn't you have had those three in one day?" he shuddered. Irwin Shaw, too, had warned her that she included too many of her lovers; "he is such a Puritan," Salka wrote to Behrman. But she told Behrman that she had dutifully relented: "One governess and the menstruation are already out."

By January 1968 Tom Wallace agreed to publish the book. It would join a collection of Holt titles that were known around the office as "Wallace's Follies"—books by authors he considered culturally important but who would not be recognizable names at his sales conferences. On her own in Klosters, Salka labored doggedly to cut down the manuscript. She thanked Sam Behrman for his editing help, joking that "although I don't think I will get rich on 'The Kindness of Strangers' I am still young enough to write 'The Unkindness of Lovers' and make it a best seller." She was seventy-nine years old.

Salka asked that bound galleys be sent to Isherwood, who praised the book for maintaining a clear narrative line, like a good novel, and for avoiding the pitfalls of most memoirs, which in his view tended to dissolve into crowds of people. *The Kindness of Strangers* was published on April 17, 1969. Salka used the opportunity to travel to Boston and New York for the book's debut. She was delighted with the attention and glad to be back in America, telling Sam Behrman that "in spite of the filthy young people with long hair and beards, in spite of Nixon and cemented spiderwebs spreading over the cities, there is a lot I love and cherish in my 'adopted country.'" She was both amused and disgusted by hippies, writing that "the middle-aged ones go around dressed in such fantastic costumes that they reminded me of Purim in Sambor. Only the Jews in Sambor always washed for the holidays. Really unbelievable how dirty people are."

On that trip Salka visited Hans, who was living with his family in Massachusetts and had become a colleague of the linguist Noam Chomsky. Salka suffered her first attack of Parkinson's disease while she was at Hans's house. It was the same disease her mother had endured. Even so, on that visit she directed her attention toward her twelve-year-old granddaughter Valérie, asking her to show her where she went with her friends for a treat. Valérie took her to the local diner, a hilly twenty-five-minute walk away, where they shared an order of fries and each drank a lime rickey. "She was not a person of pretense," Valérie remembers. "She was a person of great generosity, who was able to really be present with you, no matter what age, and make you feel important."

The novelist Carl Zuckmayer, in his foreword to the 1971 German edition of *Kindness*, fixed on the same egalitarian ability to honor each person's humanity that Valérie appreciated in Salka: "Everyone, even only fleeting acquaintances, felt himself understood by Salka Viertel, just as he was, even in his weaknesses." Nor did Zuckmayer consider Salka's merits to be exclusively feminine, pointing out that "willpower, tenacity, constructive deliberation, spontaneity and especially generosity" are no less aspirational qualities for men than for women.

The publication of *Kindness* brought all kinds of correspondence to Salka, from forgotten Hollywood colleagues to complete strangers. Many warm letters came from Israel, where survivors from Galicia told her how in their youth they had admired her brother Dusko, "the football champion." A lawyer in Tel Aviv who had grown up in Sambor wrote that he went to the town after the war to investigate what was left, and found "all the Poles and Ruthenians had been deported (or killed) during the Stalin era and [were] replaced by Tartars, Gruzinians, Kirgizians, and [a] completely Mongolian population. There is only one Jew there, a party functionary of course . . ."

Holt printed no more than four thousand copies of *Kindness*, and the book was out of print within five years. Nonetheless Salka was energized enough to plan for a second volume of memoirs as well as a novel. She gathered her store of papers, hired a secretary, and continued to write for several hours on most days. She finished neither book, though "the tenacity is there," her son Tom wrote to Vicky in 1975.

Reviews of *Kindness* were few but complimentary. In *The Nation*, Harold Clurman summarized it as a chronicle of its author's limitless capacity for "this gift of love, this passion for life which sustains and ennobles all the artistic, intellectual, social and political events which her book narrates . . . Without that core of warm humanity all the rest would be vanity." In a private letter to Salka, Marta Feuchtwanger offered her admiration. "What a great gift you have to make a human being just with a few words," she wrote, and went on to praise Salka's discretion. What Marta admired most in the book, she told Salka, "is what you did *not* say."

Yes, *Kindness* displayed its author's capacity for love, and yes, it was discreet, but these are not the qualities that make it a great memoir. Its importance lies in what Salka *did* say, which nobody else before or since has said as thoroughly or convincingly. Alexander Granach poignantly evinced the texture of life in the Galicia of his childhood and his Reinhardt theater years in his 1945 memoir *There Goes an Actor*, but its narrative ends long before his time in Hollywood, where he portrayed in movies both Nazis and Jews. The marvelous actor S. Z. Sakall wrote about Europe and America in *The Story of Cuddles: My Life Under the Emperor Francis Joseph, Adolf Hitler and the Warner Brothers* (1954), but as its title suggests he was reduced to playing his story for laughs. As for most books about Hollywood published before Salka's, Carl Zuckmayer was correct to point out that, from those, "One knows the working world of Hollywood only from the perspective of glorification or satire, of worship or disgust." Salka's Hollywood, Zuckmayer wrote, was infinitely bigger and more nuanced. Through her own life story, she connected the dots between Granach's Galicia and Sakall's Warner Bros., mapping Hollywood's global origins and its webs of connections, identifying her role as a bridge between cultures. Through her experience as a woman, an immigrant, and a Jew, she charted Hollywood's role on the twentieth-century world stage, from the mass migrations triggered by Hitler's rise in Europe through the war and its aftermath into the early 1950s. She showed that women's influence in the picture business was not limited to that of movie stars. Zuckmayer again: "Without Salka's mind and bravery, a film like Queen Christina of Sweden—I mention only this one—would never have been made."

During the many times she had been cast adrift throughout her wandering life, Salka had always been able to steady herself by creating a refuge in a house. Wychylowka was her first touchstone, followed by its reincarnation on Mabery Road. Each of her houses contained the imperative to open its doors to strangers and absorb them into a community. Now, in her memory, she lived a great deal in those rooms. During her final exile in this vapid Swiss resort town, she sat at her desk and built one last house, a house of leaves, the house of the story of her life, and invited readers inside, adding them to her circle. It's a house infused with her confidence, her compassion, her generosity, and yes, her love: kindergarten virtues that one might deride as boringly earnest. They are not. They combined into nonviolent resistance against mass expulsion and genocide, a cultivation of life to resist the National Socialist cult of hatred, cruelty, violence, and death.

IN MAY 1971, Tom Viertel came to visit his mother in Klosters accompanied by his wife Ruth, whom he had married the previous November. Salka told Sam Behrman that Tommy "was two years old when he left Europe and you can imagine what this trip means to him and his wife." At twenty-six, Ruth Jenkins Viertel was twenty years younger than Tom and had met him at work. Both were employed by the city of Los Angeles in the Department for Social Services, Ruth as a social worker and Tom as an administrator. Salka was relieved to see her son looking so happy and settled after she'd worried for so many years about his waywardness. In his leisure hours he remained a poet, with an abiding devotion to his poetical father. He and Ruth went to Vienna after their visit with Salka. Tom was as keen to commune with Berthold's milieu as Peter had been to cast it off.

At Christmastime in 1973, at age eighty-four, Salka traveled once more to Los Angeles, where she stayed with Jack Larson and Jim Bridges, who had visited her over the years in Klosters. Again she saw Tom and Ruth and met their baby son Andrew, her third grandchild (though Salka would have included Vicky, and counted four). And she ventured to visit Mabery Road. Her house had changed hands several times after John Houseman had bought it. It was now owned by Houseman's former theater protégé, the director Gordon Davidson, and his wife Judi. They threw a little party for Salka with remnants of the old Sunday crowd: Billy Wilder, King Vidor, Marta Feuchtwanger. Salka was pleased to see that the Davidsons had kept the feeling of the house, though she was taken aback to see that a swimming pool had replaced her rose garden.

On that trip, Jack Larson took Salka to dinner at Isherwood and Don Bachardy's house in the canyon. Isherwood reported in his diary that Salka was "so shaky and deaf and it is sadly dreary and exhausting being with her. You have to shout and she takes forever understanding what you're saying." It could not have been half as exhausting for him as it was for Salka, who was showing remarkable grit in traveling internationally while suffering from advancing Parkinson's disease, arthritis, and deafness. "The intricate tortures of old age make me indignant," she had written to Sam Behrman earlier in the year.

By 1975 Peter was obliged to hire a full-time nurse for Salka, whose doctor had prescribed powerful drugs to combat her shaking and prevent strokes. Jim Bridges and Jack Larson spent time with her in Klosters in February, and Jim wrote to their mutual friend Katharine Hepburn to apprise her of Salka's health. Salka had reacted badly to the drugs, Jim reported.

She had hallucinations, telling him and Jack that she had just seen Rose, who said they were going to make a garden together. Rose had died in 1973.

Then after two days Salka rallied, "her mind as clear as a bell," Jim wrote to Hepburn; "she is weak and shaky, but she is full of piss-and-vinegar." Peter made a big pot of spaghetti at his house and brought it to Salka's apartment and she ate heartily. "Forgive me," she told Jack and Jim, "for being so dilapidated that I can't do anything for you." Jim ended his letter to Hepburn: "At her weakest, the second day, she woke up when she saw Jack and me come into the room. She asked for her comb and slowly and painfully she combed and brushed her hair to receive the gentlemen."

Salka's health continued to vacillate but her mind was lucid. She wrote to Vicky in January 1976: "The new medication seems to work and I am less shaking and stronger. I am also determined to vote for U.S. President which the Congress has made possible for Americans living in foreign countries." But slowly she continued to decline, the exuberant sprawl of her signature with its voluptuous *S* reduced to a spidery blotch. She could no longer read and she had more and more despairing moments. "The mere fact that I need a nurse is depressing beyond words," she wrote to Vicky. "What a dreary way to wait for death," she had said to Jim Bridges.

In April she wrote to Vicky and Violette about their gardens, and wondered if their fruit trees were in bloom. In October she praised Vicky's description of her harvest, which "made me homesick for my youth. I remember well the harvests in our garden. My father liked apples very much and had all kinds of them."

ROSE WAS HERE, *and we are going to make a garden together.*

No, Rose died in 1973.

The sunsets at Wychylowka were blue and golden in summer, and purple-red in winter.

There were hundreds of fruit trees in the orchard.

Papa is feeding Viktoria corn kernels out of his palm as if she were a little bird.

Darling Vick, when I think of my youth in Sambor, I remember vividly and with great pleasure when I worked in the gardens and in the fields under the supervision of my Niania. I also remember the peacocks promenading in the garden.

When I remember the beach in Santa Monica, I see the millions of little silvery young gulls covering the shore and melting into the foam of the waves.

Little Vicky has climbed into the fig tree but Jigee won't let her fall. They both look so happy.

In 1921 I was bringing the children to Dresden from Wychylowka. Peter was only ten months old and Hans was two. We had to change trains at the Poland-Czechoslovakia border and I did not have enough money because of the changing currency and the inflation. A young woman recognized me from the stage, she said she was a cabaret singer, and she paid for our third-class tickets. We shared a crowded car with Transylvanian peasants. My children were hungry, they had not eaten since the previous evening. An old woman took pity on them and fed them home-baked bread with so much jam that my boys were covered in raspberries.

The kindness of strangers.

Please don't forget what's left of a human being.

I filled Grusha's apartment with flowers.

Rose is here and we are going out to the garden.
Rose and Mama are inviting me into the garden.

TELEGRAM TO FRED ZINNEMANN in London from Klosters, October 27, 1978:

DEAREST FREDDY SALKA DIED PEACEFULLY IN HER SLEEP LAST NIGHT LOVE PETER

Footpath over the Landquart River in Klosters named in honor of Salka Viertel.

ACKNOWLEDGMENTS

MY DEEP THANKS to Salka Viertel's family, who were abundantly generous with memories, stories, letters, photos, and patient answers to questions: Ruth Viertel, Violette Viertel, Valérie Viertel, Andrew Viertel. Eternal thanks to Vicky Schulberg, Adam Shaw, Elizabeth Frank, and Christine O'Sullivan, each of whom extended multiple kindnesses toward a stranger. Additional thanks to Vicky, Adam, Valérie Viertel, and Rachel Slade for reading early portions and/or later drafts of the manuscript.

For sharing personal and family memories of Salka Viertel and her milieu, thanks to Sonya Schulberg O'Sullivan, Don Bachardy, Jack Larson, Norman Lloyd, Chester Aaron, Lawrence Weschler, Ricky Pecker, Francine Schoeller, Sam Schoeller, Beatrice Siebenmann, Arianne Ulmer Cipes, Barbara Zeisl Schoenberg, Ronald Schoenberg, Nuria Schoenberg Nono, E. Randol Schoenberg, Tim Zinnemann, John Waxman, David Wyler, Pancho Kohner, Danny Selznick, Monika

Henreid, Francesca Robinson Sanchez, Regina LeBorg, Diana Soltesz, Dan Ford, Anne Edwards, Diane Leslie, Dr. Christian Grote, Ben Woythaler. Grateful thanks to Gordon Davidson and Judi Davidson for giving me a tour of the house on Mabery Road and for their reminiscences. Additional thanks to Ren Weschler for reading part of the manuscript and for engaging me to write the Afterword for the 2019 NYRB Classics reprint of *The Kindness of Strangers.*

For assistance with permissions and for their valuable comments on the manuscript, thanks to the executors of Salka Viertel's estate, Thomas Kuhnke and Katharina Prager. I extend a respectful salute to Katharina Prager for writing the first biography of Salka Viertel, published in Austria in 2007, and for her ongoing scholarship on the lives and achievements of Salka and Berthold Viertel.

For enlightening and amusing conversations about his experience as the original editor of *The Kindness of Strangers* and about his friendship with Salka Viertel, thanks to Tom Wallace.

For help from writers, scholars, and artists whose work intersects with one or several themes of this book, thanks to Noah Isenberg, Cari Beauchamp, Farran Smith Nehme, Glenn Frankel, Emily D. Bilski, Jan-Christoph Horak, Helga Schreckenberger, Katherine Bucknell, Michael Shnayerson, George Cotkin, Henry Slucki, George Prochnik, Mark A. Vieira, Alex Ross, Olivia Kaferly, Terry Teachout, Nancy Riegelman, Louise Cullman, Donna Kanter, Neal Brostoff. Particular thanks to Andrea Simon for sharing her knowledge and her inspiring film, *Every Sunday.*

For their guidance during my visits to the following institutions, thanks to the following:

Deutsches Literaturarchiv Marbach: Thomas Kemme, Hildegard Dieke, Elke Schwandner
Villa Aurora: Margit Kleinman, Friedel Schmoranzer
USC Special Collections: Michaela Ullmann, Marje Schuetze-Coburn
UCLA Special Collections: Ernst Toch Papers
United States Holocaust Memorial Museum: Nancy Gillette, Daniel Greene, Rebecca Erbelding, Nancy Hartman
Skirball Cultural Center Los Angeles: Adele Lander-Berk
Margaret Herrick Library: Sandra Archer, Stacey Behlmer, Genevieve Maxwell
New York Public Library: S. N. Behrman Archives; Yizkor Books
Warner Bros. Archive
Gesher Galicia website and organization: Shelley Pollero
Los Angeles Public Library, Studio City Branch: heroes all

For extraordinary assistance, encouragement, and collegiality, thanks to Doris Berger, formerly of the Skirball Cultural Center, now at the Academy Museum of Motion Pictures in Los Angeles.

For their excellence as translators and for the content of their good character, my thanks go to Pamela Selwyn and Friedel Schmoranzer.

For reading portions and drafts of the manuscript, for offering suggestions, and for general bolstering, thanks to Diane Arieff, Diana Wagman, Lienna Silver, Kerry Madden-Lunsford, Ella Taylor, Ellen Slezak, Susan Caggiano, Tod Mesirow, Jeffrey Silver, Kiffen Madden-Lunsford, Todd Porterfield, and MJ

Witt. Special appreciation goes to Joseph Epstein, my long-time teacher and friend, for his comments on the "Birthday Party" section; to Heather Dundas for her gimlet-eyed sense and sensibility; and to Denise Hamilton, one of the first people to imagine what this book could be, whose participation in discussions and book borrowings was an ongoing pleasure.

For lending books and/or talking with me about subjects and themes, thanks to Hillary Heydle, Tom Astle, Saralee Melnick, Bryan Berkett, Ellen Lancaster, Meryl Friedman, Steven Totland, Rod McLachlan, Sudi Khosropur, Ruth Cushner, Jeanette Miller, John McDole. Extra thanks to Meryl Friedman at CAP UCLA for organizing the panel discussion on émigré musicians at the Villa Aurora in January 2017.

Thanks to the following friends for their professional expertise: Craig Semetko, Bob Boorstin. To Debi Frankle, for the words. To Niki Saccareccia, for the breath.

To Jess Rifkind, Thelma Rifkind, Julie Rifkind, David Rifkind, and Arthur Purdy, whose incarnations of loving enthusiasm I'll always remember and sorely miss. To Carol Steinberg, who gave me many important books, shared her abundant knowledge, and cheered me on. To Leonard Steinberg, Leslie Steinberg, Diane Kopit, Neal Steinberg, Helen Rifkind, and their families. To Dale Russakoff, for writing advice, everlasting kindness, and a thousand other things. To Thelma Purdy, Matthew Purdy, Amy Purdy, and my extended Purdy clan including the Kurtzes and Ari Holsten, thanks to you all.

For their belief in this project from the beginning and for good-humored support throughout, my fond gratitude goes to my literary agents, Georges and Anne Borchardt.

For her early and continuing faith in both the idea and the

reality of this book, for her rigorous patience, keen editing, generous care and feeding and walks on the beach, deepest thanks to Judith Gurewich. My appreciation goes also to the smart, kind professionals at Other Press, with particular thanks to Alexandra Poreda, Yvonne Cárdenas, Janice Goldklang, Jessica Greer, Kevin Callahan, Julie Fry, and Gage Desser, and an additional note of thanks to Walter Havighurst for his thoughtful copyediting, and to Andreas Gurewich.

And finally, thanks to my husband, Joseph Purdy, and my sons, Ben and Noah Purdy, for the sustenance and joy they bring me every day.

NOTES

INTRODUCTION

2 "the most complete migration of artists and intellectuals in European history": Kevin Starr, *The Dream Endures: California Enters the 1940s*, p. 367.

6 "systematically omitted from the accounts of the past . . . as though only men have participated in the events worthy of preservation": Martin Sauter, *Liesl Frank, Charlotte Dieterle, and the European Film Fund*, p. 60.

6 Salka Viertel has the double distinction . . . of being both maligned and dismissed: The most salacious of these portraits of Salka appear in *Here Lies the Heart* by Mercedes de Acosta; *The Girls: Sappho Goes to Hollywood* by Diana McLellan; and *Ich liebe dich. Für immer: Greta Garbo und Salka Viertel* by Nicole Nottelmann.

6 ". . . and a horrible witch": Kurt Weill to Lotte Lenya, from *Speak Low (When You Speak Love): The Letters of Kurt Weill and Lotte Lenya*, p. 7.

8 "the history of Hollywood, which is not yet written": Gottfried Reinhardt, *Der Liebhaber. Erinnerungen seines Sohnes Gottfried Reinhardt an Max Reinhardt* (München: Droemer Knaur, 1973), p. 269. Cited

in Helga Schreckenberger, academic lecture, "'They Say Hollywood Is a Paradise!': Salka Viertel's Perseverence During Hollywood's 'Inquisition,'" p. 5.

1: THE WISHING SEASON

11 The Wishing Season: SV to S. N. Behrman, 12/21/70; calls the Christmas season "the wishing times": SV to S. N. Behrman, Behrman Archives, NYPL.

11 she ordered the cheapest new dresses she could find: Salka Viertel, Tagebuch 1957, 6/24/61, DLAM: "terribly expensive though I chose the cheapest."

12 even a tiny step-great-grandson now: Vicky Schulberg's son Tom.

12 Christine, her darling, her Puck and her Ariel: SV to S. N. Behrman, 1957: "she is the last grande passion of my life. Puck—Ariel—simply enchanting"; Behrman Archives, NYPL.

14 for the Ukrainian servants: Salka Viertel, *Kindness of Strangers* (hereafter *KOS*), p. 164.

14 to the distress of her American-born neighbors: ibid., p. 165.

14 Forever uprooted: Tagebuch 1957, 2/17/61. "I am homesick for California and when I am there I long for Europe. Uprooted that's what it's called."

14 She thinks of this time as her exile in the Alps: "Darling Sam, you don't know what you mean and have meant to me during all these years of exile in the Alps": SV to S. N. Behrman, 9/16/67, Behrman Archives, NYPL.

14 The rye and wheat fields; the orchards and the little forest: Tagebuch 1957, 6/16/57; *KOS*, pp. 2–3.

15 The Committee had already succeeded in wrecking her livelihood: SV to Berthold Viertel, 10/3/47, Deutsches Literaturarchiv Marbach

(DLAM): "Please don't be alarmed if you hear my name. I have been warned that it may happen. But I don't really believe it because in my case they have already succeeded in ruining my livelihood."

15 How strange to find herself... rosy-cheeked tourists: insights courtesy of Adam Shaw.

16 likes to regale her with tales of her dead father's Nazi past: Tagebuch, 7/9/61.

16 approached to be kissed by every man in the room: ibid., 1/1/63: "Irwin kissed me first..." While married to Berthold, Salka was the romantic partner of director Gottfried Reinhardt from 1933 to 1943. Reinhardt married Silvia Hanlon Shapiro in 1944.

17 For some reason she thinks of a time: ibid.,1957, 6/22/58.

17 She has demonstrated it all her life: ibid., 6/8/62.

17 with a slight hesitation in the step of the right leg: conversation with Elizabeth Frank.

18 "the foreign family up the street": *KOS*, p. 24.

18 Peter sent a copy of *The Canyon* to Ernest Hemingway: Peter Viertel, *Dangerous Friends*, p. 33.

19 Peter has found himself another *Ersatzpapa*, Orson Welles: Tagebuch, 12/20/62: "I know Peter likes Orson now with the same intensity as he loved Hemingway... Orson is an *Ersatzpapa*."

19 More recently they worked together on a doomed film: P. Viertel, *Dangerous Friends*, pp. 388–391.

19 his bulk draped in acres of soft dark clothing: observations by Adam Shaw.

19 he was loud and to her mind not terribly interesting... with a better education: Tagebuch, 12/27/62.

20 He has recently finished making a film of Kafka's *The Trial*... when no one else was interested: Orson Welles and Peter Bogdanovich,

This Is Orson Welles, 244–248. The "blithe Russian" was Michael Salkind, an uncredited producer on *The Joyless Street*, whose grandson Ilya would later marry Charlie Chaplin's daughter Jane.

20 even as they praised him to the skies as a great genius of the cinema: Viertel, *Dangerous Friends*, p. 391.

20 Orson told Salka.... the haunted hopelessness of refugees: Welles and Bogdanovich, *This Is Orson Welles*, pp. 244–247.

20 Peter who seemed bored and impatient with his guests: Tagebuch, 12/27/62.

21 It was the spring of 1918... the Eastern Front: *KOS*, pp. 79–81; Viertel, *Dangerous Friends*, p. 119.

22 a shopkeeper's attention: *KOS*, p. 82.

22 a profusion of cherries to the markets... the Castle District: ibid., p. 82.

22 They had rented a furnished room... and so he only stared: ibid., pp. 81–82.

24 It is too depressing: Tagebuch, 2/12/63.

24 At one point he'd been after Salka... Greta and Charlie Chaplin: Welles and Bogdanovich, *This Is Orson Welles*, p. 137.

24 This took place after Charlie's *Monsieur Verdoux* unpleasantness... for all kinds of reasons: ibid., p. 135. Chaplin's *Monsieur Verdoux* is a 1947 black comedy based (Welles claimed) on a true story about a serial wife killer, a Frenchman named Henri Landru. (Chaplin suggested it was also inspired in part by another man, Thomas Wainwright, a nineteenth-century British forger.) The idea for the picture originated with Welles, who approached Chaplin about playing the lead. Chaplin decided he would rather write and direct his own version, and paid Welles $5,000 for the rights. Welles consented, with the stipulation that he be given a screen credit, to read "Idea suggested by Orson Welles." The film was a box office flop in

America, though more successful in Europe, and was praised by the likes of James Agee and Evelyn Waugh. Welles was sure he would have done a better job as its director, while Chaplin claimed Welles had little to do with the picture. Chaplin regretted giving Welles the screen credit, and neither man was thrilled with the other in the aftermath.

25 Ah, Charlie... helping to save her Santa Monica house from foreclosure: *KOS*, pp. 290, 313.

25 She last saw him... enchanting: Tagebuch, 9/27/62.

25 Even Charlie thinks... is pretentious: Charles Chaplin, *My Autobiography*, p. 477.

25 that frames the mountains and the lake: ibid., p. 476.

25 and has always so hated to lose: Lillian Ross, *Moments with Chaplin*, p. 48.

25 in their white cotton dresses and their pigtails: ibid. p. 43.

25 "Bonjour, Charlot!": ibid., p. 36.

25 so that they look like feet: ibid., p. 48.

25 Oona is unchanged: Tagebuch, 9/27/62.

26 and they revel in the private indulgence: Ross, *Moments with Chaplin*, p. 37.

26 He has asked her to read his memoirs... impress the reader with his vocabulary: Tagebuch, 9/27/62; and Ross, *Moments with Chaplin*, p. 50.

26 But his philosophy... pompous and often wrong: Tagebuch, 9/27/62.

27 When she visited him she did not have enough money to tip his servants: ibid., 9/27/62.

27 She is flattered: Chaplin, *My Autobiography*, p. 434.

28 She would like to be remembered for her courage: Tagebuch, 2/17/51: "The greatest achievement of my life is probably to have

created the image of a very courageous woman. Nobody will ever know what it has cost me."

28 "And meet the time as it seeks us"...his own haunted memoir: George Prochnik, *The Impossible Exile*, p. 8.

2: CARRIED ACROSS

29 The party Salka remembered...among the celebrated collection of Corots: Salka's description of the party at the Mendelssohn villa appears in *KOS*, p. 125.

30 *Beware, oh wanderer, the road is walking too*: This line from Rilke's diary, in Stephen Mitchell's translation ("protect yourself wanderer / with the road that is walking too") was changed into this formulation by the American poet Jim Harrison. The latter version appears as the epigraph to Joseph Kertes's 2014 novel, *The Afterlife of Stars*, and in Harrison's poem "After Ikkyu."

31 while singing the *Horst Wessel Lied*: *KOS*, p. 119. Most sources cite the song as having been written around 1929, which does not match Salka's chronology, as she was in Düsseldorf in 1926 or 1927. She may have conflated it with other songs from the *National Socialist Anthology* songbook, cited by Lion Feuchtwanger in his 1933 novel *The Oppermanns* ("When Jewish blood spurts from the knife / Then all goes well again," p. 158). Hertha Pauli cites similar lyrics in *Break of Time*; it seems evident that these anti-Semitic chants were common on German streets in these years.

31 a weekly salary of $600...a travel allowance of $1,200: Katharina Prager, *"Ich bin nicht gone Hollywood!": Salka Viertel—ein Leben in Theater und Film*, p. 98.

31 their "great adventure" would pay off: Berthold Viertel to Salka Viertel, undated (sometime before 8/20/27), DLAM; also ibid., p. 96.

31 Peter had nearly died of pneumonia: *KOS*, p. 108.

32 Hans had contracted scarlet fever: ibid., p. 115.

32 "I would have stayed in Berlin": ibid., p. 126.

32 maybe they would stay longer: Berthold Viertel to Salka Viertel, 8/3/27, DLAM.

32 while she spoke all the parts: *KOS*, p. 4.

32 only slightly less vulgar than prostitutes: P. Viertel, *Dangerous Friends*, p. 118.

33 sometimes she appeared in playbills as Mea Steuermann... for others Viertel-Steuermann: Prager, "*Ich bin*," p. 31.

33 "It saddens me deeply... But fate calls us and we must follow": BV to SV, undated (before 8/20/27), DLAM.

34 "*Garçonnes*... the Eldorado": Steven Bach, *Marlene Dietrich: Life and Legend*, pp. 66–67, quoting Stefan Zweig in Otto Friedrich's *Before the Deluge*, pp. 128–129, and Zweig's *The World of Yesterday*.

34 "I was always hungry and cold... any money at all": Friedrich, *Before the Deluge*, p. 122.

34 that reflected the hurly-burly of contemporary Berlin: *KOS*, p. 104: *Die Truppe* would "bring back great but neglected plays of the past, and introduce meaningful ones of the present."

35 far too intellectual even for Berlin's sophisticated audiences: *KOS*, pp. 106–108.

35 *Die Truppe* continued its frail existence: ibid. p. 107.

35 "We got paid every day... swept away by the value of the old ones": ibid.

36 But its death knell came in March 1924: Prager, "*Ich bin*," p. 74.

36 a currency speculator seeking cultural cachet: Friedrich, *Before the Deluge*, p. 125, and Prager, "*Ich bin*," p. 72. The speculator was a Viennese Jew named Richard Weininger, whose philosopher brother Otto Weininger became famous before his suicide at age twenty-three for

publishing a crackpot thesis called *Sex and Character* that was both misogynistic and anti-Semitic and was later taken up as propaganda by the Nazis. Richard Weininger wrote to Salka on May 17, 1969, after her memoir had been published (Prager, p. 72), angrily refuting her version of the demise of *Die Truppe* and denouncing Salka's abilities as an actress, and invoking his brother Otto's name ("the glory of Die Truppe could have been multiplied by mentioning the name of the man who has a brother who wrote a work that's translated into 18 languages") as a way of defending his own actions.

On April 24, 1954, Irwin Shaw published a short story in the *New Yorker* called "Instrument of Salvation" in which the main character is based on Salka during the period of *Die Truppe*'s demise. It's likely that the story was inspired by an anecdote Salka herself told Shaw; according to Michael Shnayerson, Shaw's biographer, Shaw rarely made up the situations on which his stories were based. In this one, the character based on Salka, here named Inge Clavered, reminisces about rejecting the sexual advances of the patron of her theater company, which caused him to revoke his financial support. Decades later, Inge reflects that this fateful decision saved the lives of her and her husband because the ensuing bankruptcy forced them to leave Germany before Hitler's rise to the chancellorship in 1933.

36 The Viertels declared bankruptcy: *KOS*, pp. 108–109.

36 at the Volksbühne in Leipzig: ibid., 88 and 91.

36 and to murder her make-believe children offstage: ibid., pp. 86 and 96–98.

36 Mary Stuart in Düsseldorf: ibid. p. 118.

36 Judith in Berlin: ibid., pp. 100 and 105.

37 Romanisches Café: ibid., p. 101.

37 all the important composers: ibid., p. 56.

37 Berlin's wild young things: ibid., p. 113.

37 hoping the waiters would turn out the lights: ibid., p. 111.

37 *Nora*, based on Ibsen's *Doll's House* for UFA in 1923: ibid., p. 102.

37 F. W. Murnau asked Berthold to be the writer for his pictures: ibid., p. 116.

38 and she a saucy Amazon . . . able to soften his Prussian inflexibility": ibid., p 116.

38 In November of 1927: www.tcm.com biography of F. W. Murnau.

38 just after staging *Peer Gynt* for Reinhardt's theaters in Berlin: *KOS*, pp. 124–125.

38 and the great Swedish director Mauritz Stiller: ibid., p. 102.

38 a very young Greta Garbo: ibid., p. 111.

38 Chaplin's Little Tramp: ibid., p. 102.

39 Salka had written a film treatment of her own: ibid., p. 111.

39 the first new form of storytelling to come along in five hundred years: observation by William de Mille, quoted in Kevin Starr, *Inventing the Dream: California Through the Progressive Era*, p. 310.

39 "an immense political tool of the future": "*ungeheures politisches Mittel der Zukunft*," Katharina Prager, lecture on Berthold and Salka Viertel from "Quiet Invaders Revisited: A Workshop on Biographies of Austrian Immigrants to the United States in the 20th Century," Vienna, June 18, 2015.

40 "I often wish you had a worthier man . . . with all of my failings": BV to SV, April 30, 1927, DLAM.

40 twenty cigarettes a day . . . his frequent raging: BV to SV, August 3, 1927, DLAM.

41 Ludwig Münz . . . Luise Dumont: Prager, "*Ich bin*," p. 87. In her memoir Salka mentions that Luise Dumont saw in Salka "what she had always longed for: a daughter" (KOS, p. 114), and tells the story of their alliance from first infatuation to later disenchantment. Letters between Salka and Berthold indicate that the relationship was

complex, but it's unclear whether there was a sexual component. Katharina Prager points out that several of these letters hint at the possibility of an actual love affair; in one, Salka links Ludwig Münz and Luise Dumont in a way that suggests she's listing them together among her marital infidelities. SV to BV, September 4, 1928, DLAM; Prager, "*Ich bin*," p. 87.

41 a holiday week in Venice: Prager, "*Ich bin*," p. 95; *KOS*, p. 121.

41 sailed from Cuxhaven on the *Albert Ballin*: *KOS*, pp. 125–126.

41 "mountainous heights" of first class . . . a stay at a spa: BV 1928, DLAM.

42 stowaway, dead soldier, canaries: *KOS*, p. 127.

42 "They were emigrants first of all": Lion Feuchtwanger, "The Grandeur and the Mystery of Exile," quoted in Anderson, ed., *Hitler's Exiles*, p. 170.

43 Salka had never heard of her: *KOS*, p. 127.

43 "the Barnum of world theater": Bach, *Marlene Dietrich*, p. 47.

43 she'd had major roles on his stages for over a decade: Prager, "*Ich bin*," p. 37; the author notes that Salka had acted in Reinhardt theaters since 1911.

43 The performances the Viertels saw: Salka's descriptions of New York, the theater productions she saw there, and her encounter with Max Reinhardt appear in *KOS*, pp. 127–128.

44 would continue to bewilder her: ibid., p. 124.

44 Murnau's anxious telephone calls . . . and the impressionistic mounds of sagebrush: Salka's descriptions of the train ride west appear in ibid., p. 129.

45 roofs shaped like mushrooms, a restaurant shaped like a hat: ibid., p. 130.

45 NO ACTORS, NO JEWS, NO KIDS OR PETS: observation by Winfred Kay Thackrey in Cari Beauchamp, ed., *My First Time in Hollywood*, p. 196.

45 Autopia: term coined in Reyner Banham, *Los Angeles: The Architecture of Four Ecologies,* p. 213.

45 too many Karl May novels: Karl May was an immensely popular German novelist who wrote about cowboys and Indians in the American West. He had never been to America. Among the many who were huge boyhood fans of May's books were Billy Wilder, Peter Viertel, Fred Zinnemann, and Adolf Hitler.

45 "I went to Hollywood... a gigantic traffic jam made the city alive": Prager, "*Ich bin,*" p. 97.

46 her father had been obliged to find a map: *KOS*, p. 122.

46 a fancy way station for visiting film folk: Rosemary Lord, *Hollywood Then and Now*, p. 88.

47 Murnau's insufferable arrogance: *KOS*, p. 131.

47 a German journalist of their acquaintance: this was Richard A. Bermann, a well-known journalist and travel writer who wrote dispatches from Hollywood for the *Berliner Tageblatt* under the name Arnold Hollriegel.

47 as if it were a vast sheet of mother-of-pearl: *KOS*, p. 132.

47 the yellow hippodrome and the merry-go-round inside it: from Fred E. Basten, *Santa Monica Bay: A Pictorial History*, p. 83.

47 telling fortunes out of a shack: *KOS*, p. 132.

47 Salka had been raised near a river... that she sometimes heard: Salka's memories of the Dniester River are from ibid., p. 1.

48 She pleaded with Berthold to let them find a house in Santa Monica: ibid., p. 132.

48 Those people... had thrived on it for more than seven thousand years: Information about the Tongva is from the website of the Gabrielino/Tongva tribe: www.gabrielinotribe.org/historical-sites-1.

49 that extended north toward the canyon: from Ernest Marquez, *Santa Monica Beach: A Collector's Pictorial History*, p. 51.

49 gates and garages fronted the street: see www.la.curbed.com, "How Old Hollywood and Starchitecture Built Santa Monica's Gold Coast," July 22, 2014.

49 In six weeks . . . at a cost to Mayer of $28,000: Details about the construction of Louis B. Mayer's beach house are from Scott Eyman, *Lion of Hollywood: The Life and Legend of Louis B. Mayer*, p. 134.

49 recurring bronchitis and gout: *KOS*, p. 132.

50 climate-controlled, double-windowed, and sound-proofed: see www.la.curbed.com above, and also *Milwaukee Journal*, September 18, 1939, "Cinema's Big Salaried Stars Fill Homes with Expensive Playthings": "Norma Shearer's beach house is soundproof to shut out the rumble of breakers, air conditioned to shut out the heat and shutter equipped to shut out the light."

50 the mad rush her husband would have to endure: *KOS*, p. 132.

50 a pleasant mock-Tudor . . . the foothills of Laurel Canyon": Airgram, BV to SV, September 13, 1928, DLAM.

50 The interiors shone with onyx . . . mahogany": www.allenellenberger.com, "Hollywoodland," October 27, 2012.

51 among the swanky parlors of film folk: *KOS*, p. 133.

51 "a warning to European directors": ibid.

51 "sheer blasphemy": ibid. pp. 128–129.

52 a welcome jolt . . . glum expatriates: ibid., p. 133.

52 Calamities at "the Jinx Mansion": "Hollywood's Peyton Hall Had Drama, Glamour," *Los Angeles Times*, September 3, 2006.

52 Jannings would be dismissed from his contract with Paramount: Scott Eyman, *The Speed of Sound*, p. 260.

52 with rococo displays of his vanity: Karen Wieland, *Dietrich and Riefenstahl: Hollywood, Berlin, and a Century in Two Lives*, p. 164.

53 traveling from one dangerous war zone to another to entertain the troops": ibid., pp. 171, 380.

53 Jannings as "artist of the state": www.imdb.com, biography of Emil Jannings.

54 for his foreign intellect and originality: *KOS*, p. 135.

54 the globetrotter of his world . . . the American driver of their luck: BV to SV, May 16, 1928, DLAM.

56 and coaxed her into a grudging politeness: *KOS*, p. 134.

56 She was glad to be able to send fifty dollars here or five dollars there: Auguste Steuermann to SV, May 1, 1928, call # 80.1.322/12; and May 30, 1928, call # 80.1.322/30, DLAM.

56 "Are there snakes on the beach?" . . . "Are the film stars interesting?": Auguste Steuermann to SV, May 1, 1928, call # 80.1.322/12, DLAM.

56 to be able to buy things she didn't need: *KOS*, p. 134.

57 "and to survive in Hollywood we had to work": ibid., p. 135.

57 There were disagreements about the story: ibid.

57 "a tale about wheat": quoted in Janet Bergstrom, "Murnau in America: Chronicle of Lost Films," *Film History* 14: 450.

57 Berthold wrote three drafts in all: This is according to Janet Bergstrom; others have said he wrote two drafts.

57 including Murnau's hospitalization for appendicitis in early July: Bergstrom, "Murnau in America," p. 443.

57 during the summertime miseries of his army duty: BV to SV, August 30, 1928, DLAM.

58 once the harvest was in and the picture was done: Bergstrom, "Murnau in America," p. 443.

58 "the illusion of my existence as a prisoner is perfect": BV to SV from Hotel Pendleton, date unknown, DLAM.

58 "and I understand every word she says": *KOS*, pp. 135–136.

58 back pain that had emerged from an operation she'd had several years ago: Prager, "*Ich bin*," p. 102, for mention of back pain; and

various letters between SV and BV to and from Oregon in September 1928, DLAM.

59 Berthold tried to deny that he'd written such a thing: Prager, "*Ich bin,*" p. 102.

59 "too late, my dear!": BV to SV, September 1, 1928, DLAM.

59 "where we represent home to each other": BV to SV, September 9, 1928, DLAM.

59 "while you are able to create with writing": SV to BV, September 10, 1928, DLAM.

59 "I'm not one iota more in a foreign country here . . . California is not a bit more alien to me than Germany": SV to BV, September 1928, call # 78.907-4, DLAM.

60 at the time he was married to somebody else: *KOS*, p. 74.

60 the looting and burning it had sustained during the Great War: ibid., p. 71.

3: A GREAT HOUSE FULL OF ROOMS

63 the suave screen idol Rod La Rocque: Mordaunt Hall, "A Romantic Fantasy," *New York Times*, June 10, 1929.

63 and doubled his salary: *KOS*, p. 138.

63 as long as they rented it only for the summer: ibid., p. 137.

64 she drove straight to Santa Monica: ibid., p. 137.

65 in the popular "English style," painted white with a pitched green roof: Christopher Isherwood, *Christopher and His Kind*, p. 155.

65 $900 for the three summer months: *KOS*, p. 138.

66 as a leading lady on the world's stages: ibid., p. 3.

66 "moving swiftly like a figure in a puppet show": ibid., p. 10.

66 during her parents' frequent and sometimes violent quarrels: ibid., p. 12.

66 including a dread of Friday the thirteenth: Tagebuch, September 14, 1957, DLAM.

67 gathered to light the Sabbath candles: *KOS*, pp. 2–3.

67 and sent out meals around the clock: ibid., p. 5.

67 skating and sleigh rides in the winter: ibid., p. 24.

68 "A woman from Lemberg . . . and will not disturb us too much": Auguste Steuermann to SV, May 21, 1929, call # 80.1.322/33, DLAM.

68 three hundred dollars to pay the coal bill: Auguste Steuermann to SV, December 31, 1929, call # 80.1.322/49, DLAM.

68 all soldiers, not just officers, would be fed: *KOS*, p. 64.

68 a bowl of cabbage and potato soup that Niania had cooked for them: ibid., p. 72.

68 on any day they pleased: ibid., p. 13.

68 "They were a nightmarish procession of misery . . . whom they cursed and beat with sticks": ibid., p. 13.

69 but she did not specify what kind of God she had in mind: Prager, "*Ich bin*," p. 19. Also: "Mother believes in God," P. Viertel, *Bicycle on the Beach*, p. 187; "May God whom you believe in bless and protect you," BV to SV, April 30, 1927, DLAM; "She [Salka] says she has always believed in God and prayed to him. She can't even imagine what it would be like, not to have faith . . . And she said, 'Doubt is just fear—that's all it is.'": Christopher Isherwood, *Diaries, Volume One, 1939–1960*, p. 290.

69 "I have no ties . . . when they wanted to talk to the world": Tagebuch, July 16, 1957, DLAM.

70 the only arenas in which they exercised any power: Emily D. Bilski and Emily Braun, *Jewish Women and Their Salons: The Power of Conversation*.

70 a professor from the university in Lemberg: *KOS*, p. 22; "an eccentric . . . Kissingen": *KOS*, pp. 26–27.

71 lieder by Schumann and Brahms: ibid., p. 20.

71 to apply for immigration visas: ibid., pp. 138–139.

71 "counting the days till [her] return to Europe": Prager, "*Ich bin*," p. 53, quoting a letter from SV to Camil Hoffman; *KOS*, pp. 139, 143.

71 all their books that had been sent from Berlin: *KOS*, p. 139.

72 they still had a bit of savings for a return trip to Germany: ibid., p. 130.

72 They renegotiated their rent...and resolutely began again: ibid., pp. 139–140.

72 an "all-talker" called *Seven Faces*: Mordaunt Hall, "The Screen," *New York Times*, November 16, 1929, and "Short Subjects," *Film Daily*, November 17, 1929.

72 born in Lemberg, not far from Salka's hometown: Lemberg changed names many times as it became variously occupied: it was Lwów in interwar Poland, Lvov in the Soviet Union, and Lviv in Ukraine today.

72 continuingly unhappy about the interruption of her acting career: *KOS*, p. 140.

73 "My face, my neck, my whole upper body": Salka Viertel, *Das unbelehrbare Herz: Ein Leben in der Welt des Theaters, der Literatur und des films*. (This is the 1970 German edition of Salka's memoirs, which she had published in English as *The Kindness of Strangers* in 1969. There are some differences in the texts.)

73 "Salka Stenermann": Hall, "Short Subjects," *Film Daily*, November 17, 1929.

73 "Salka Stensrmann": Hall, "The Screen," *New York Times*, November 16, 1929. See above.

73 "like drinking from an eyedropper when you are parched": *KOS*, p. 140.

74 She hated her makeup and her costumes: ibid., p. 151.

74 “I got excellent reviews and fan mail from Germany”: S. Viertel, *Das unbelehrbare Herz*, p. xx.

74 “It made me miserable”: *KOS*, p. 152.

74 “She greeted newcomers warmly...that she had been a great actress”: Christopher Isherwood, *Lost Years: A Memoir, 1945–1951*, pp. 70–71.

75 as feminist scholars have noted: Bilski and Braun, *Jewish Women and Their Salons*, p. 145.

75 Some film scholars believe it took place in the spring: Karen Swenson, *Greta Garbo: A Life Apart*, p. 206.

75 or around Christmas: Barry Paris, *Garbo*, p. 186.

77 Berthold agreed, saying it was a high price to pay: *KOS*, pp. 142–143.

78 “a kind of deus ex machina...and kept me in America”: SV to S. N. Behrman, October 5, 1966, Behrman Archives, NYPL.

78 from the time of her arrival there on March 31, 1930: Wieland, *Dietrich and Riefenstahl*, p. 226.

78 “Mary Dietrich”: *KOS*, pp. 55–56; Prager, “*Ich bin*,” p. 54.

79 Dietrich frequently showed up: Wieland, *Dietrich and Riefenstahl*, p. 233; also see P. Viertel, *Dangerous Friends*, p. 10.

79 “my mother thought [Dietrich] something of a *poseuse*”: P. Viertel, *Dangerous Friends*, p. 10.

79 the newcomers who were flocking to Hollywood: *KOS*, p. 150.

79 who’d been summoned from New York to the West Coast: ibid., p. 139.

80 William Dieterle...Charles Boyer: ibid., pp. 139–140.

80 had accepted a six-month contract with Paramount: Marie Seton, *Sergei M. Eisenstein: A Biography*, p. 157.

81 “a colorful film symphony”: Scenes from Eisenstein’s film are available on www.youtube.com, as *Que Viva México!*, via Gregori Alexandrov, 1979.

81 a gift of two pounds of Malossol caviar: *KOS*, p. 139.

81 she proceeded to offer advice: Prager, "*Ich bin*," pp. 115–116.

82 to help pay an advance to the film's composer: *KOS*, p. 146. The composer was Hugo Riesenfeld.

83 sandwiches for his motoring trip up the coast: Lotte Eisner, *F. W. Murnau*, p. 222.

83 It fell to Salka: Prager, "*Ich bin*," p. 116; letter from Ottilie Plumpe to SV, March 15, 1931, DLAM.

83 The boy allegedly lost control of the car: Swenson, *Greta Garbo*, p. 243; and Eisner, *Murnau*, p. 222.

83 with an indelible stylistic legacy: Seton, *Eisenstein*, pp. 117–118.

83 Its enormous sets were used again and again: Scott Eyman, *Print the Legend*, pp. 107, 111.

84 and Werner Herzog: Gerd Gemünden, *German Exile Cinema, 1933–1951*, p. 190.

84 "I am never at home anywhere": quoted in Milestone Film & Video Press Kit for "F.W. Murnau's Last Masterpiece: Tabu: A Story of the South Seas," www.shopify.com.

84 and their group of Pasadena investors on November 24, 1930: Seton, *Eisenstein*, p. 188.

84 "they would have been horrified had they ever seen one of his films": *KOS*, p. 146.

84 In December 1930 . . . as they departed for Mexico: Seton, *Eisenstein*, p. 190.

85 "decadence and blight wrote a last chapter to history": ibid., p. 191, quoting *Theatre Guild Magazine*, February 1931.

85 in an attempt to justify what they saw as his needless extravagance: *KOS*, p. 154.

85 "Use your Medea flame": ibid., p. 157.

86 "a mutilated stump with the heart ripped out": ibid., p. 159.

86 As his friend Léon Moussinac remarked: Seton, *Eisenstein*, p. 155.

86 a right-wing agitator named Major Frank Pease: ibid., p. 167.

86 Eisenstein's father's family ... his mother was not Jewish: ibid., pp. 17–18.

87 hate speech that greeted Charlie Chaplin ... "Jewish film clown": J. Hoberman and Jeffrey Shandler, *Entertaining America*, p. 37; other Internet sources for "Jewish film clown" as well. The year was 1931.

87 decided the Russian director was more trouble than he was worth: Seton, *Eisenstein*, p. 186.

87 Upon his farewell ... the only films he had managed to make in America: *KOS*, p. 144.

87 his idiosyncratic views of art and film ... of Stalin's regime: Neal Gabler, *An Empire of Their Own: How the Jews Invented Hollywood*, p. 320 fn.

88 "You have helped me in the most difficult years of my life": *KOS*, pp. 159–160.

88 These men were cruelly derided for being homosexual: Eisenstein identified as heterosexual. Some historians have concluded that his sexuality was inchoate but probably homosexual. He was nevertheless demonized for consorting with homosexuals. Upton Sinclair told Marie Seton that Eisenstein "was simply staying in Mexico at our expense in order to avoid having to go back to Russia. All his associates were Trotskyites, and all homos ..." Seton, *Eisenstein*, p. 231, from a letter from Sinclair to Seton of April 5, 1950, in Appendix 6 of Seton's book.

88 by its "others"—that is, by Jews and immigrants: Cari Beauchamp in the documentary *The Story of Film*, PBS, 2011.

88 Salka's sister Rose wrote from Dresden to report: Rose Steuermann Gielen to SV, call # 80.1.146-12, DLAM.

89 the *New York Times* was still dismissing him as a buffoon: *New York Times*, October 20, 1930: "Germany has no idea of delivering herself over to a madcap Austrian."

89 "I became aware that we were constantly explaining ourselves to our American friends": *KOS*, p. 143.

90 Budd and Sonya: Salka does not mention the youngest Schulberg child, Stuart, who was born in 1922.

90 "WE HAVE A NEW DOG NAMED DUKE": Tom Viertel to BV, 1930, DLAM.

90 whose families had once owned all the land in the canyon: P. Viertel, *The Canyon*, p. 21.

90 to swim and ride their bikes and go fishing in mud ponds: ibid., pp. 18–19.

90 to stage Western scenes from their favorite Karl May and Fenimore Cooper tales: P. Viertel, *Bicycle on the Beach*, p. 349.

90 She sprinkled lavender in the linen closet and pine oil in the bath: memories of Vicky Schulberg, as are the details of what Salka cooked and baked.

91 During the Halloween evenings of those years . . . the Mexican boys from the neighborhood: Tagebuch, November 1, 1957, DLAM.

91 Christmas Day gift exchanges: *KOS*, p. 165.

91 "My life with Berthold was always predominant": ibid., p. 193.

92 All the important New York journalists: ibid., p. 161.

92 "part of that ancient, baffling continent . . . an unappeased longing": ibid., p. 161.

92 educated her in his left-leaning belief in democracy: ibid., p. 193.

93 "I don't feel guilty about . . . Oliver . . .": Tagebuch, June 17, 1959, DLAM.

93 "in love with [X] or [Y]": In her diary, Salka names these women only as "Toni D." and "Ehmi."

93 "You would bear Hollywood much better if you worked": *KOS*, p. 143.

94 She began to think about adapting it as a picture for Garbo: According to Salka's papers at the Margaret Herrick Library, the biography was *Sibyl of the North* by Faith Compton Mackenzie (MGM reader report by Jessie Burns, July 29, 1932; 2346.f-Q-7); but in *KOS*, p. 152, Salka says it was a biography that had appeared in Germany. Several biographies of Christina were published around this time.

94 $250,000 per picture . . . her own director and costars: Swenson, *Greta Garbo*, p. 285; Paris, *Garbo*, pp. 284–285. Garbo signed the contract on July 9, 1932.

94 "masculine education and complicated sexuality . . . contemporary character": *KOS*, p. 152.

95 recently founded the Progressive School . . . Bertrand Russell: memories of Christine O'Sullivan.

95 the last time in Piłsudski's Poland that Jews and Gentiles would mourn together: *KOS*, pp. 167–168.

96 "The Depression was at its worst . . . was sure that the misery would not last": ibid., p. 164.

96 the Viertels would need to apply for an Immigration Quota: ibid., p. 168.

97 often proved so daunting that many were too discouraged to apply: Erik Larson, *In the Garden of Beasts: Love, Terror, and an American Family in Hitler's Berlin*, pp. 31–32; www.ushmm.org, "Roosevelt and the Refugee Crisis."

97 Berthold and Tommy were applying for an Austrian quota number . . . and Salka for a Polish: *KOS*, p. 168.

97 they could then reenter as legal immigrants who had declared an intention to become permanent citizens: P. Viertel, *Bicycle on the Beach*, p. 7.

98 reminded him of the joyless streets of Berlin: ibid., pp. 7–10.

98 "yet I felt frightened at the thought of losing America forever": ibid., p. 9.

98 "that I was safe again in the land of the free": ibid., p. 10.

100 to see his father, who had become seriously ill: *KOS*, p. 170.

101 "This is Mr. Thalberg," said Garbo: ibid., p. 169.

101 "I would not produce it if I did not think it would make a great picture": ibid., p. 169.

4: THE HOUSE OF METRO

103 "Movies aren't made, they're *re*-made": Thalberg quoted in Vieira, *Irving Thalberg: Boy Wonder to Producer Prince*, p. 63.

103 though the film did not appear until 1938: Gavin Lambert, *Norma Shearer*, p. 197.

104 240,000 Jews had already fled during the previous decade: Scott Eyman, *Lion of Hollywood: The Life and Legend of Louis B. Mayer*, p. 18.

104 Before leaving school at around age twelve: ibid., p. 24.

104 always desolately hungry: ibid., pp. 21–22.

105 "The habit of a rapid pace . . . all his life": ibid., pp. 22–23.

105 its assets holding steady at $130 million: ibid., p. 170.

105 "the greatest money-making proposition ever put on the screen": Paris, *Garbo*, p. 284.

105 "Other studios made fantastic offers": *KOS*, p. 152.

106 the freedom to approve film subjects . . . portrait photographers: Paris, *Garbo*, p. 285; Vieira, *Greta Garbo*, p. 7.

106 The first film under the terms of her new contract: Vieira, *Greta Garbo*, p. 174.

106 surrounded by ugly apartment buildings and dingy shops: Swenson, *Greta Garbo*, pp. 22–23.

107 to pretend she was sunbathing on an elegant white beach: ibid., p. 25.

107 a soap-lather girl: Paris, *Garbo*, p. 21.

107 A few days after they were turned away from the hospital: Swenson, *Greta Garbo*, p. 33; Paris, *Garbo*, p. 18.

107 one of the most prestigious drama schools in the world: Swenson, *Greta Garbo*, pp. 42–43.

108 "Greta Garbo had something that nobody had ever seen on the screen . . . You could see thought": Kevin Brownlow, *The Parade's Gone By*, p. 148, quoted in Vieira, *Greta Garbo*, p. 237.

108 "Her shoes were run down at the heels . . . she was a total loss": Vieira, *Greta Garbo*, p. 11.

108 John Gilbert, whom she almost married in 1926: Swenson, *Greta Garbo*, p. 123.

108 "I was lonely—and I couldn't speak English": ibid., p. 313, quoting S. N. Behrman, *People in a Diary*, p. 151.

108 she took a room at the Hotel Miramar . . . walking along the shore: Paris, *Garbo*, p. 90.

109 as film historian Cari Beauchamp has noted: Beauchamp quoted in *The Story of Film*, PBS, 2011.

109 when Salka walked through . . . to meet again with Irving Thalberg: Vieira, *Greta Garbo*, p. 175.

109 They filled the story department . . . Mary McDonald: Stephen Bingen, Michael Troyan, and Stephen X. Sylvester, *Hollywood's Greatest Backlot*, p. 77.

110 a Mayer family recipe: Louis B. Mayer's mother's matzoh-ball soup: "Take nine fat, two-year-old kosher hens for every three gallons of liquid, stewing them overnight, then separating the broth from the chicken. Add chunks of chicken and delicate matzoh balls": ibid., p. 62.

110 where two doctors and a dentist were always on call: ibid., p. 78.

110 A whole floor of the wardrobe building: Erin Hill, *Never Done: A History of Women's Work in Media Production*, p. 4.

110 she had approval on the final editing of every film the studio released during her tenure: Obituary for Margaret Booth by Ronald Bergan, *The Guardian*, 2002.

111 Kate Corbaley in the reading department: Eyman, *Lion of Hollywood*, p. 301; and biography of Kate Corbaley on www.imdb.com.

111 Louis B. Mayer's executive assistant, Ida Koverman... Herbert Hoover's presidential campaign: Bingen, Troyan, and Sylvester, *Hollywood's Greatest Backlot*, p. 27; and Hill, *Never Done*, p. 145 onward.

111 Mayer's personal physician... were women: Eyman, *Lion of Hollywood*, pp. 64 and 562.

111 or to pit them against one another when those tactics proved useful: Lenore Coffee, *Storyline: Reflections of a Hollywood Screenwriter*, quoted in Eyman, *Lion of Hollywood*, p. 93.

111 "A mouse at the feast": Cari Beauchamp, *Without Lying Down: Frances Marion and the Women of Early Hollywood*, p. 11.

112 "Pardon me, Mr. Thalberg—it's putting one *right* word after another": Bob Thomas, *Thalberg: Life and Legend*, p. 183.

113 Rounding up her dignity... she said her goodbyes and walked out: Salka's recounting of this episode appears in *KOS*, pp. 172–173.

114 "I should never have been so generous to Peg as to let her share the credit": Tagebuch, June 21, 1959, DLAM.

114 "All during that ordeal... I hope I will learn to cope with it": *KOS*, p. 173.

114 three of Garbo's hits: Meredyth's screen credits for Garbo pictures at Metro were for *The Mysterious Lady* and *A Woman of Affairs*, both 1928, and *Romance*, 1930.

114 Paul Bern: The forty-two-year-old Bern was found dead the following month, under suspicious circumstances. He was said to have committed suicide, but there were hints that he may have been murdered. The studio threw itself into damage control, anxious to downplay the scandal to protect its investment in Bern's widow, the sexy blond actress Jean Harlow, whose new film *Red Dust* was about to be released. Thalberg was deeply shaken by the death of his close

friend and colleague, which could only have underscored his fears about his own ill health and mortality.

114 had supervised the German version of *Anna Christie*: Eyman, *The Speed of Sound: Hollywood and the Talkie Revolution*, p. 295.

114 "Marvelous, Irving... becomes an important film": *KOS*, p. 174.

115 She had composed the *Christina* treatment... to transcribe onto the page: Prager, "*Ich bin*," p. 150. ("Peg LeVino is an excellent audience and her excitement when I play a scene enlightens me and makes me suffer at the same time": SV to BV, November 12, 1931, DLAM.)

115 "My inventions were pure theater": *KOS*, p. 175.

115 "You had a very bad entrée... She has written great films": ibid.

116 "Handled with taste... very interesting scenes": ibid.

116 it was at this point that she decided she liked Thalberg very much: ibid.

118 "a knowing, blasé attitude toward lesbianism": Laura Horak, *Girls Will Be Boys: Cross-Dressed Women, Lesbians, and American Cinema*, p. 16.

118 "Everyone had to be a lesbian in the thirties": Swenson, *Greta Garbo*, p. 260.

118 "Interestingly... that's the first bit of juicy gossip you hear": Patrick McGilligan, *George Cukor: A Double Life*, p. 346.

119 "Salka was AC/DC": Irene Mayer Selznick quoted in Paris, *Garbo*, p. 263.

119 and strenuously denied that she and Garbo ever had a sexual relationship: conversation with Tom Wallace.

119 Salka, "as everyone, might well have been attracted to Garbo": Paris, *Garbo*, p. 263.

120 "was not the target but the weapon... to punish, to satisfy enmities whose roots lay elsewhere": William J. Mann, *Behind the Screen: How Gays and Lesbians Shaped Hollywood, 1910–1969*, p. 41,

quoting Richard Hofstadter, *Anti-Intellectualism in American Life* (1963).

120 "wildness" and "wantonness": review of Josephine Baker from *Berliner Tageblatt*, January 4, 1926, quoted in Peter Jelavich, *Berlin Cabaret*, p. 171.

120 would come to be called, for the Garbo film, Christina Court: Sylvester, *Hollywood's Greatest Backlot*, pp. 172–173.

120 a gigantic proto-Disney World dining emporium... and minstrels in blackface performed: Erik Larson, *In the Garden of Beasts*, p. 54; "Cabaret Berlin" blog, www.cabaret-berlin.com, April 3, 2012.

121 The frenzied language of Hitler's speeches... copied from American cinema: Larson, *In the Garden of Beasts*, p. 134, citing Klemperer's *The Language of the Third Reich*.

121 "You ask how Europe is, Salka?": *KOS*, p. 177.

121 the pervasive influence of National Socialism: ibid. p. 179.

121 "The Eden bar and other night spots... does it give you a picture?": ibid., pp. 177–178; and BV to SV, November 9, 1932, DLAM.

122 "On every street corner... but the strike continues": *KOS*, p. 179.

122 "perhaps it will inspire you": BV to SV, November 9, 1932, DLAM.

122 "he would forget bank notes in hotel rooms": *KOS*, p. 187.

123 "*What* should I say to that?... I am only planning the future in the 'we' form": BV to SV, December 9, 1932, call # 78.860-23, DLAM.

123 He was weighing the offer of a job from Alexander Korda... on the Continent: *KOS*, p. 180.

123 "Alas, I am sure... settle down and finish your books": ibid., p. 180.

123 "In business terms... Are you already so disheartened?": BV to SV, October 7, 1932, DLAM.

124 Garbo remained in Sweden and Salka began to doubt that the picture would ever get made: *KOS*, p. 178.

125 may even have suffered a heart attack: Thalberg's heart attack occurred on December 25, 1932.

125 She was stirred by Franklin Delano Roosevelt's speeches and was sorry she was unable to vote: ibid., p. 179.

126 where with uncontested authority she took dominion everywhere: the observation, with its homage to the line from Wallace Stevens's poem "Anecdote of the Jar," is from Elizabeth Frank.

126 This became clear to her... when... the studio appointed Walter Wanger to serve as producer on *Christina*: Vieira, *Greta Garbo*, p. 177.

126 "assistant and artistic advisor"; "full of snappy dialogue and anachronistic 'Lubitsch touches'": *KOS*, p. 183.

127 while Vajda accused Salka of exploiting her position as Garbo's personal friend: Prager, *"Ich bin,"* p. 155, fn 661.

127 "the prototype of a modern woman, who... shrinks from both marriage and maternity": H. M. Harwood's review of script, March 23, 1933, quoted in Vieira, *Greta Garbo*, p. 178.

127 With the actress's support: Vieira, *Greta Garbo*, pp. 179–180.

127 "Salka has overcome all these difficulties by her own strength... she knows exactly what she owes to Salka and tells her, too": BV to Auguste Steuermann, August 2, 1933, quoted in Prager, *"Ich bin,"* pp. 154–155.

128 seeing no "cultural necessity" for him to be working in Germany: *KOS*, p. 185.

128 "sheer madness to do this film in such times" and "a blond, blue-eyed giant": ibid., p. 185.

129 "Foreigner" was already a dirty word: Isherwood, *Christopher and His Kind*, p. 123.

129 Metro's Berlin representative... then resettled in London, where

the studio hastily moved its European operations base: Thomas Doherty, *Hollywood and Hitler*, pp. 23–33.

129 "One can really say that the world is coming to an end in Europe . . . it will be a question to what degree we saved ourselves from it": Prager, "*Ich bin*," p. 159; BV to SV, February 15, 1933, and March 9, 10, 20, 27, and 30, 1933, DLAM.

130 "expurgated from the culture of the Third Reich": *KOS*, p. 186.

130 In April, the first general boycott . . . and listened without comment: Isherwood, *Christopher and His Kind*, pp. 122 and 124.

131 "Where they burn books, in the end they will also burn human beings": www.ushmm.org, "Book Burnings."

131 "The era of exaggerated Jewish intellectualism is now at an end! . . . From its ruins will arise victorious the lord of a new spirit": www.ushmm.org, "Books Burn as Goebbels Speaks."

131 "See the black souls of the Jews fly away": Palmier, *Weimar in Exile*, p. 46.

131 They would be lucky to be kept alive, and many would be sent to concentration camps: ibid., p. 88.

131 "regardless of how much worse it was going to get . . . in these first months": Klemperer, *The Language of the Third Reich*, p. 48.

132 "Hitler is the triumph of the German *Spiesser*": *KOS*, p. 186.

132 Its writers began to organize into a guild: ibid., pp. 186–187.

132 it might have been caused by deep drilling in nearby oil fields: "So. Cal's deadliest quake may have been caused by oil drilling, study says," *Los Angeles Times*, October 31, 2016.

133 She warned Berthold as well that his visa would expire if he did not return in July: *KOS*, p. 187.

133 "I was sure . . . that after all his wanderings Odysseus would be pleased to have a home": ibid., p. 188.

134 the Viertel boys, dreaming of summer vacation . . . the student's lamp Salka had bought: P. Viertel, *Bicycle on the Beach*, p. 30.

134 Vicki Baum, whose two sons had become friendly with Hans and Peter: *KOS*, p. 174.

134 Salka read the Yiddish writer . . . moved them all to tears: ibid., p. 180.

134 in the mouse-infested writers' building: Eyman, *Lion of Hollywood*, p. 91.

135 gaining a reputation as "Garbo specialists": Marcia Landy and Amy Villarejo, *Queen Christina* (BFI Film Classics), p. 14.

135 "As long as I know that you are well . . . your Jewish girl from Sambor": SV to S. N. Behrman, September 22, 1964, Behrman Archives, NYPL.

135 which contained more historical fidelity than Vajda's or Harwood's versions: Prager, "*Ich bin,*" p. 162, upon reviewing multiple drafts of the script at the Margaret Herrick Library.

135 at least ten writers worked on iterations of the script . . . Ben Hecht: Peter Hay, *MGM: When the Lion Roars*, p. 74. Harvey Gates wrote the famous final scene in which Garbo stares into the distance from the prow of a ship: Prager, "*Ich bin,*" pp. 100–101.

135 Mark A. Vieira's suggestions . . . that more or less became the shooting script: Vieira, *Greta Garbo*, p. 280.

137 the similarity of the sets, camera angles, and action would have been evident to audiences who had seen both pictures: credit for this insight to Horak, *Girls Will Be Boys*; see also the book's film stills on pp. 211–212.

137 "To the unreasonable tyranny of the mob . . . I shall not submit": *Queen Christina* [script]; Rouben Mamoulian; 1933, Dialogue cutting continuity, December 22, 1933, Script Collection, AMPAS (Unpublished), Margaret Herrick Library, Academy of Motion Pictures Arts and Sciences.

138 "Friends and strangers wrote to me praising it": *KOS*, p. 197.

139 One of the reasons Salka feared so for Berthold's safety . . . a weekly magazine serving as the organ for the pacifist left in Germany: ibid., p. 186.

139 “Nothing…you must make your mind and your heart a complete blank”: Vieira, *Greta Garbo*, p. 189, quoting Andrew Sarris, *Interviews with Film Directors*, p. 292.

140 “knights of the inkwell”: quoted in Palmier, *Weimar in Exile*, p. 23.

140 played for a robust forty-four days after its 1943 premiere…who in turn regarded him with absolute authority”: Ben Urwand, *The Collaboration: Hollywood's Pact with Hitler*, pp. 108, 126.

141 “Did I ever tell you…and her pacifism”: SV to S. N. Behrman, September 27, 1968, Behrman Archives, NYPL.

141 “to think of you and me slaving away in the Thalberg building to provide a thrill for the Stalin girl”: S. N. Behrman to SV, October 11, 1967, Behrman Archives, NYPL.

141 “a daily consultant in matters of historical importance”: Swenson, *Greta Garbo*, p. 303.

142 at the hands of the scene designer Alexander Toluboff…and the country inn: Matthew Bernstein, *Walter Wanger: Hollywood Independent*, pp. 110–111.

142 William H. Daniels…with whom he'd worked regularly early in his career: Marcia Landy and Amy Villarejo, *Queen Christina*, p. 12.

142 The final candidate, proposed by Salka, was Rouben Mamoulian: BV to SV, undated 1934, call # 78.864/3, DLAM: “even Mamoulian…was your suggestion…”

142 Mamoulian was born…Drama societies and orchestras thrived”: David Luhrssen, *Mamoulian: Life on Stage and Screen*, p. 9.

142 Garbo was sold on Salka's suggestion…Marlene Dietrich: Swenson, *Greta Garbo*, p. 304.

143 as if eager to trade his foreignness for the demeanor of an East Coast gentleman: Vieira, *Greta Garbo*, p. 178, quoting Maria Riva (Marlene Dietrich's daughter).

143 "to come to my house and go over new problems . . . sure that only he himself could find the solution": *KOS*, p. 192.

143 Thalberg was fond of saying that every great film must have one great scene: Vieira, *Irving Thalberg*, p. 37.

143 "I long to be a human being, a longing I cannot suppress": *Queen Christina*, Script Collection, AMPAS (Unpublished), Margaret Herrick Library, Academy of Motion Pictures Arts and Sciences.

143 "the audience will write in whatever emotion they feel should be there": Paris, *Garbo*, p. 306, quoting Mamoulian interview with Kevin Brownlow, 1970.

144 "This has to be sheer poetry and feeling": Paris, *Garbo*, p. 301.

144 "In the future, in my memory, I shall live a great deal in this room": *Queen Christina*, Script Collection, AMPAS (Unpublished), Margaret Herrick Library, Academy of Motion Picture Arts and Sciences.

144 "This was the suitcase he bought in America . . . I remember when he bought them in Turkey": ibid., pp. 300–301.

145 "Let me remember you with love and loyalty, until memory is no more": *Queen Christina*, Script Collection, AMPAS (Unpublished), Margaret Herrick Library, Academy of Motion Picture Arts and Sciences.

145 "I am so ashamed of *Christina*": Vieira, *Greta Garbo*, p. 190.

145 Audiences there were thrilled to accept Garbo as the remade image of their monarch: Prager, *"Ich bin,"* p. 163; and Vieira, *Greta Garbo*, p. 190.

145 telling Sam Behrman in 1962 that she personally resembled . . . any other character she played . . . grossing $1.843 million: Vieira, *Greta Garbo*, p. 190.

145 a "talking billboard" . . . "Queen Christina is entirely Garbo, and Garbo is entirely Queen Christina": Landy and Villarejo, *Queen Christina*, p. 21; Hay, *MGM: When the Lion Roars*, p. 117.

146 the film brought in a disappointing $632,000 profit in America: Paris, *Garbo*, p. 307.

146 marking the first time that a Garbo film earned less domestically than it did overseas: Vieira, *Greta Garbo*, p. 190.

146 "but the film survives also on its own merits": *KOS*, p. 196.

146 "all in all a decent, coherent work, a clean film": BV to SV, April/May 1934, call # 38.864/8, DLAM.

146 "You didn't want to make anything of your success . . . It was a victory for your character, your personality": BV to SV, undated 1934, call # 78.864/3, DLAM.

146 "If there was ever any argument about a script I always had this woman to fight for me . . . and always found something good that others wouldn't bother about": Swenson, *Greta Garbo*, p. 455, quoting Cecil Beaton, *Memoirs of the 40s*, p. 272.

147 The occasional call back to the *Christina* set: *KOS*, p. 190.

148 He asked Salka's permission to smoke in an endearing way: ibid., p. 191.

148 "I did not jump, but slid into a love affair": ibid., p. 195.

149 "Odysseus resented bitterly that Penelope had not waited patiently for his return": ibid.

149 "He was as dear to me as ever . . . also the sad certainty that never again would we be lovers": ibid., p. 192.

149 "then, exhausted, we all had a nightcap together": ibid.

149 offering Peter money for every French novel he agreed to read: conversation with Ruth Viertel.

150 "remember, never do anything out of your mad generosity . . . only death can cure my addiction to you": *KOS*, p. 193.

5: FATHERLAND

151 "From the very beginning, the studios gave us Papas": A. Scott Berg, *Goldwyn*, first page of Chapter 6.

151 "I once had a beautiful fatherland": quoted in Christa Wolf, *City of Angels, or, The Overcoat of Dr. Freud*, p. 262.

151 The antifascist exodus from Europe was never homogeneous: Palmier, *Weimar in Exile*, pp. 12, 85.

151 "spoke in the meeting of opposites": Alex Ross, *The Rest Is Noise: Listening to the Twentieth Century*, p. 178.

151 In 1933, over 53,000 emigrants left Germany, of whom about 37,000 were Jews: Palmier, *Weimar in Exile*, p. 85.

152 "I consider what is going on here so sickening....But one could be very wrong": Kurt Weill quoted in www.holocaustmusic.ort.org, "Composers In Exile."

152 "For once, no joke. I am taking my own life": Jelavich, *Berlin Cabaret*, p. 231.

152 an estimated 11,000 would reach England: Palmier, *Weimar in Exile*, p. 151.

152 and tried to persuade Brecht and the novelist Leonhard Frank to join him: ibid., p. 150.

152 Conrad Veidt was there: Isherwood, *Christopher and His Kind*, p. 167. The non-Jewish but fiercely antifascist Veidt played a Jew here and, more famously, eight years later, played the Nazi Major Heinrich Strasser in *Casablanca*.

153 Writers had begun to settle in London as well: Palmier, *Weimar in Exile*, pp. 150–151.

153 he had difficulty adjusting to yet another new film culture: *KOS*, p. 196.

153 he hired the boyish and handsome thirty-year-old writer: Isherwood,

Christopher and His Kind, p. 150. Jean Ross was the real-life model for Isherwood's most famous fictional character, Sally Bowles, who first appears in a 1937 novella and in the 1939 novel *Goodbye to Berlin*.

153 "He needed an amateur, an innocent, a disciple, a victim": ibid., p. 152.

153 "I need disciples... if I want to be productive": BV to SV, January 16, 1934, call # 78.864/2, DLAM.

154 "His head was magnificent... the eyes were the dark mocking eyes of his slave": Isherwood, *Prater Violet*, p. 25.

154 "I knew that face": ibid., p. 24.

154 "You have always been safe and protected... I am bitterly ashamed that I am here, in safety": ibid., pp. 120–121.

155 Isherwood spent much of his time seeking permission for Heinz to return to England: ibid., pp. 147–148.

155 These included hours of manic procrastination... when he came to visit them in California he would meet Garbo, would see her every day: ibid., pp. 154–156.

156 an actress named Beatrix Lehmann... an ensemble made mostly of green feathers: ibid., p. 168.

156 and was living with her in her Victorian house on the Thames: *KOS*, p. 203.

156 largely "in seclusion": BV to SV, mid-October 1935, call # 78.865/11, DLAM.

156 "a new and absolutely necessary phase of his education as a writer": Isherwood, *Christopher and His Kind*, p. 171.

156 "He was my father. I was his son. And I loved him very much": Isherwood, *Prater Violet*, p. 159.

157 Rose had been breathing the reek of National Socialism in Dresden since at least 1930: Rose Gielen to SV, November 18, 1930, DLAM.

157 He had fathered a child with the pretty housekeeper at Wychylowka named Hania: *KOS*, p. 166.

157 He accepted financial help from Salka: Rose Gielen to SV, March 9, 1929, call # 80.1.146-7, DLAM.

157 whose weekly Metro paycheck had risen to $550: *KOS*, p. 195.

158 "There was not a day... besieged my American friends for affidavits": ibid. p. 195.

158 denied entrance to anyone who might be "likely to become a public charge"... in case of need: David Wyman, *Paper Walls: Americans and the Refugee Crisis, 1938–1941*, p. 120.

159 through an introduction from the pianist-composer Ferruccio Busoni in Berlin: *KOS*, p. 56.

159 "driven into Paradise": this was the title of a speech Schoenberg gave in 1935.

159 the puckish French playwright Marcel Achard: *KOS*, p. 196.

160 Salka and Gottfried, along with Charlie Chaplin and the film director King Vidor, went backstage to congratulate him: Dorothy Lamb Crawford, *A Windfall of Musicians: Hitler's Émigrés and Exiles in Southern California*, p. 41.

160 known to address their conductor, a stringently formal personage, as "Klempie": Mark Swed, "The Climb of the Century," *Los Angeles Times*, September 23, 2018.

160 "how infinitely grateful I must be to the great America": Crawford, *Windfall of Musicians*, p. 46.

161 In Salka's living room... was the British director James Whale: The story of Franz Waxman's introduction to James Whale comes from a conversation with John Waxman in May 2017 and from David Neumeyer and Nathan Plate, "Franz Waxman's *Rebecca*: A Film Score Guide," pp. 18–19.

162 an entire family in Vienna named Waxman . . . He saved them all: Dorit Beder Whiteman, *The Uprooted: A Hitler Legacy*, p. 79.

163 "the abuse of Greta as a mannequin for the tailor Adrian": BV to SV, December 29, 1934, DLAM, quoted in Prager, "*Ich bin*," p. 166.

163 complaining in letters to Berthold that she didn't want to write only for Garbo: Prager, "*Ich bin*," p. 165; BV to SV, undated; September 16, 1933; February 28, 1934.

163 to explain Garbo's accent and to add some Continental glamour: Prager, "*Ich bin*," p. 165, citing treatments by Vicki Baum, one undated and one from April 25, 1933, Margaret Herrick Library.

164 "I have repressed the memories of *The Painted Veil*": *KOS*, p. 197.

164 she shared Garbo's private opinion of the finished picture as "rubbish": Greta Garbo to Countess Wachtmeister, from Vieira, *Greta Garbo*, p. 200, and Swenson, *Greta Garbo*, p. 325.

164 pinning the blame for its faults squarely on its shoulders: Paris, *Garbo*, p. 311; Vieira, *Greta Garbo*, p. 195.

164 "[Garbo's] reliance on Salka Viertel, who was not qualified to judge literary properties": Vieira, *Greta Garbo*, p. 204.

164 "He is admittedly imaginative": Tagebuch, July 6, 1961.

165 Salka was less enthusiastic about the *Veil* project: Vieira, *Greta Garbo*, p. 174.

165 "a nightmare of a film. . . . The 'mystery-fake' does not work anymore": SV to BV, November 6, 1934, DLAM, quoted in Prager, "*Ich bin*," p. 166.

165 "not all that great a friend . . . my mother was an oarsman in the galley": Eyman, *Lion of Hollywood*, p. 220.

165 "If I had her position . . . what influence I would have in the world": Tagebuch, November 19, 1960, DLAM.

166 "DO NOT BREAK UP YOUR SITUATION OVER THERE": BV to SV, June 21, 1934, DLAM, quoted in Prager, "*Ich bin*," p. 167.

166 "the instinct of the Mother": BV to SV, February 23, 1934, DLAM.

166 "the house is a position, a symbol, it is famous . . . a sort of oasis in the ever-widening desert": BV to SV, June 21, 1940, DLAM.

166 gratefully remembering the help he'd offered in attempting to finance Eisenstein's doomed Mexico picture: *KOS*, p. 158.

167 Thalberg would now head one of four production units . . . and everyone operating under Mayer's prevailing authority: Gabler, *Empire of Their Own*, pp. 231–234; Thomas Schatz, *The Genius of the System: Hollywood Filmmaking in the Studio Era*, p. 165.

167 "Chattering at lunch, Mr. Thalberg and his underlings": "Metro-Goldwyn-Mayer, Playing to a Billion Pairs of Eyes, Has Recently Made the Best and Most Profitable U.S. Pictures. How So?" *Fortune*, December 1932, p. 114.

168 "I'll look after him like my own son": Gavin Lambert, *Norma Shearer*, p. 76.

168 "It was a real father-and-son relationship . . . and you wanted to please father": Vieira, *Irving Thalberg*, p. 270, quoting AFI's "Donald Ogden Stewart Oral History" by Max Wilk, p. 17.

169 "Sure, my nieces and nephews work here . . . help out the others?": Eyman, *Lion of Hollywood*, p. 185.

169 "even the richest Jews were not allowed to join country clubs" . . . "his father who was a god in the theater world of Berlin": Wolf, *City of Angels*, p. 74.

169 "Mr. Mayer's courtesies to U.S. Senators . . . It is his business simply to get the most and give the least": *Fortune*, December 1932, pp. 118–119.

170 "So we shall rely on *your* experience, my dear Salka": *KOS*, p. 198.

171 "And that's what's left of a human being": ibid.

171 "All good luck for a better 1942": Telegram from SV to S. N. Behrman, December 1942, Behrman Archives, NYPL.

171 "We had to eliminate everything that could even be remotely classified as a passionate love scene": David O. Selznick, *Memo from David O. Selznick*, p. 82.

171 to give Salka's son Peter his first job in Hollywood: *KOS*, p. 222.

172 would later put Peter under contract as a writer: ibid., p. 262.

172 "I saw 'Karenina' and found the film nicely told . . . to make a film of your own invention, and where your story is the main and primary thing—whoever acts in it": BV to SV, mid-October 1935, call # 78.865/11, DLAM.

172 Thalberg was back at work: Vieira, *Greta Garbo*, p. 217.

173 the newly built Thalberg bungalow: *KOS*, p. 199.

173 "Since the characters and the events . . . are all historical facts . . . The story looks dangerous to me": December 5, 1935, quoted in Swenson, *Greta Garbo*, p. 362.

173 had the virtue of increasing Thalberg's enthusiasm for the project: *KOS*, p. 200.

174 She arranged to sail for Southampton from New York on June 26: ibid.

174 much more foreign than America had been when she'd first arrived there: ibid., p. 201.

175 she also saw Gottfried's producer brother Wolfgang: ibid., p. 202.

175 All were furiously studying English and hoping for visas: ibid.

176 "I believe in our marriage as I always have . . . know that we will grow old together": ibid., p. 203.

176 *Les absents ont toujours tort*: ibid., p. 202.

177 "must have been hell": ibid., p. 203.

177 asking for old clothes and packages of food for the poor: ibid.

178 "More than ever we are apprehensive about our fate": ibid., p. 205.

178 "Do not think, *mein Herz*, that the wrinkles that are gone now are necessary to your face...I kiss your new old face": BV to SV, undated, DLAM, quoted in Prager, *"Ich bin,"* p. 177.

179 soon to be designated by Goebbels as a prized artist of the National Socialist state: *KOS*, p. 205.

179 "the homecoming was glorious": ibid.

179 "Salka returned from Europe, sick in both body and mind...but entrained directly from the boat": Gene Solow to S. N. Behrman, September 1936, Behrman Archives, Box One, NYPL.

179 "Europe deeply shook me...And then we didn't hold each other tight enough": SV to BV, September 1935; October 28, 1935; November 11, 1935, DLAM, quoted in Prager, *"Ich bin,"* p. 178. Prager mentions that in the letter of November 11 Salka even speaks of a "nervous breakdown."

181 of meeting with the "Zionist Berthold Viertel," though Berthold had not attended the Steuermann family gathering: Prager, *"Ich bin,"* p. 176, fn 777; letters from Rose Gielen to SV and Edward Steuermann, August 18, 1938, and BV to SV, December 3, 1937, DLAM.

181 grateful for the moment to be out from under the boot of Hitlerism: *KOS*, p. 209.

181 so he arranged to move to New York, which remained his home base for the rest of his life: ibid.

182 "I don't write lovely music": ibid., p. 207.

183 Thalberg sent the composer home with a copy of the screenplay and encouraged him to offer more suggestions: More facts about the encounter have recently emerged through the work of the historian Sabine Feisst in the Schoenberg archives, which shows that Schoenberg was more invested in the idea of working on the film than has

been previously suggested; see James Schmidt, "When Arnold Met Irving: A Tale from Hollywood," Boston University.

185 Peter asked to have a room of his own: *KOS*, p. 209; Isherwood, *Lost Years*, p. 74.

186 a serious hearing disability called otosclerosis: *KOS*, p. 222.

186 "the Popular Front extended into my family": ibid., p. 211.

186 made up mostly of affluent right-wing writers including Salka's old nemesis Ernest Vajda: ibid., p. 206.

186 "rescue writer of choice": Patrick McGilligan, *George Cukor: A Double Life*, p. 92.

187 "These were the days of meetings": *KOS*, p. 211.

187 Attending the league's glamorous opening banquet... his fellow Algonquin Round Table mate Dorothy Parker: Thomas Doherty, "The Rise and Fall of the Hollywood Anti-Nazi League," paper presented at annual meeting of the American Studies Association, Washington, DC, 2014.

187 "But Ernst"... And Salka told him she was staying: *KOS*, p. 211. See also Laura B. Rosenzweig, *Hollywood's Spies: The Undercover Surveillance of Nazis in Los Angeles*, p. 130, in which a banner at the Anti-Communist Federation Conference (a Nazi front) in August 1938 accuses the Anti-Defamation League and the Hollywood Anti-Nazi League of persecuting Christian patriots; accuses both groups of being allies of the Communist Party; and urges people to track down the "sponsors" of both groups, including Lubitsch, and to demand a congressional investigation.

188 perhaps three hundred Communist Party members in the film industry from 1936 to 1946: Gabler, *Empire of Their Own*, p. 330.

188 "It is very necessary for me to be able to see clearly and impartially... The ruthlessness was not only stupid, but did not achieve anything": Tagebuch, March 25, 1963, DLAM.

189 the outbreak of the Spanish Civil War: *KOS*, p. 211.

189 Occasionally he emerged to visit with Salka's brother or with Fred Zinnemann: ibid., p. 212.

189 "On these walks Berthold sometimes wore his bathrobe": Isherwood, *Diaries, Volume One*, p. 40.

189 oblivious to the miseries taking place a continent and another ocean away: P. Viertel, *Bicycle on the Beach*, p. 68.

189 "We are Greeks without brains!... That is the song they sing": ibid., p. 5.

190 "Sun, roses, fruit, warmth... We bathe and bask": Sybille Bedford, *Aldous Huxley: A Biography*, p. 240.

190 to worship at the feet of his idol Huxley: Nicholas Murray, *Aldous Huxley*, p. 236.

190 its little head poking out to sniff the wind: Cyril Connolly, *The Unquiet Grave*, p. 111.

191 "into the acerbic scent of the Midi: resin, thyme, hot stone": Sybille Bedford, *Jigsaw: An Unsentimental Education*, p. 147.

191 "potpourri from the local rosemary, geranium, lime, and rose": Bedford, *Aldous Huxley*, p. 234.

191 On Sunday nights the town's ramshackle movie theater... the silent films of Chaplin, Keaton, and Lloyd: Bedford, *Jigsaw*, p. 117.

191 "Thus nothing changed... this will go on; we shall go on": ibid., p. 149.

192 "Rather a dismal crew": Bedford, *Aldous Huxley*, pp. 280–281.

192 after he was jailed for subversive activity in the Weimar Republic: Bedford, *Jigsaw*, p. 94.

192 Julius Meier-Graefe... smoking opium with Jean Cocteau in Toulon: Bedford, *Quicksands: A Memoir*, pp. 280–282.

192 "The communist and Jewish literati who have fled from Germany are now trying to surround Germany with a wall of literary stink-gas":

www.kuenste-im-exil.de/KIE/Content/EN/Objects/mann-klaus-zeitschrift-die-sammlung-en.html?single=1.

193 A short time later he and his wife Marta moved to Sanary... where they remained until 1940: Manfred Flügge, *Fry, Bingham, Sharp: The Americans Who Saved Lion and Marta Feuchtwanger*, p. 50.

193 All his possessions... and his bank accounts were frozen: Lion Feuchtwanger, *The Devil in France: My Encounter with Him in the Summer of 1940*, p. 32.

194 "How do you like my house?... The result of this remark is that you are now living in my house": www.germanhistorydocs.ghi-dc.org; "Thou shalt dwell in houses thou hast not built," Feuchtwanger, *Pariser Tageblatt*, March 20, 1935.

195 stayed only briefly, including Bertolt Brecht... Fritzi Massary: Palmier, *Weimar in Exile*, p. 196.

195 As many as four hundred German and Austrian political refugees found themselves in the district of *le Var* up until the end of the decade: Frank Estelmann, e-paper from ASA Conference, April 2007, London Metropolitan University, quoting Manfred Flügge, 1994.

196 "forerunners of catastrophe": Bedford, *Aldous Huxley*, p. 282.

196 *Dichterfürsten:* princes of poetry: ibid., p. 282. Katharina Prager points out that in one of Berthold Viertel's most influential poems, "Exile," he distanced himself from the company of the *Dichterfürsten*, declaring that he did not leave any kingdoms behind.

196 "We were all victims of intolerance": Marta Feuchtwanger, interviewed by Lawrence Weschler, "An Émigré Life: Munich, Berlin, Sanary, Pacific Palisades," Oral History Program, University of California.

197 the traditional German Sunday roast of veal: Bedford, *Quicksands*, p. 289.

197 "Where I am, is Germany": Mann gave a press conference on February 26, 1938, shortly after arriving in New York, during which he first made this comment. www.dw.com/en/thomas-manns-second-home-in-manhattan/a-16198020.

197 *Weltschmerz* grappling with *luxe, calme, et volupté*: insight by Hilton Kramer, "Oh, that Weltschmerz! German Expressionism About Dark, Not Light," *New York Observer*, September 6, 2004.

198 Ostend for Stefan Zweig and Joseph Roth: Adam Kirsch, review of *Before the Dark: Stefan Zweig and Joseph Roth, Ostend 1936*, *New Statesman*, January 15, 2016.

198 the lush emerald forests of Brazil's Petrópolis: George Prochnik, *The Impossible Exile*, p. 295.

6: MOTHERLAND

199 "One does not wander without punishment under palms": Berthold Viertel, quoted in Isherwood, *Diaries, Volume One*, p. 40.

199 Particularly inspiring to the National Socialists . . . and from Asia: James Q. Whitman, *Hitler's American Model: The United States and the Making of Nazi Race Law*, cited in Rafael Medoff's review of the book in *Ha'aretz*, "Was Hitler Inspired by Racist American Laws?," March 29, 2017.

200 With the Nuremberg Laws in place . . . the persecution of Jews in Germany: www.ushmm.org, Timeline of Events: 1936.

201 About a forty-minute drive northeast . . . there was dancing: The description of the German Day picnic in Hindenburg Park comes from www.archive.org/details/csth_000032, "German Day Festivities in Hindenburg Park, Los Angeles film footage," 1936.

201 two major goals: to Nazify the German-American community . . . Hitler's New Germany: California State University at Northridge

Archives online, https://digital-library.csun.edu/in-our-own-backyard/german-american-bund.

202 "constitution, flag, and a white gentile ruled, truly free America . . . to portray itself as a patriotic American defense organization": Rosenzweig, *Hollywood's Spies*, pp. 103, 111, 112.

202 to mask their German provenance: ibid., p. 94.

202 that also housed the Aryan Bookstore, a restaurant, and a shooting range: ibid., p. 107.

202 into what they hoped would become a headquarters for Hitler: "Heil Hollywood: The Los Angeles Bunker From Which Hitler Planned to Run Nazi Empire After the War," *Daily Mail*, March 18, 2012.

203 The Los Angeles police department was more sympathetic to this homegrown fascism than not: Rosenzweig, *Hollywood's Spies*, p. 38.

203 In the meantime . . . Jack Benny, and Paul Muni: ibid., pp. 137, 250.

205 An Improvisation: biographical details that follow are based on the life of the composer Ernst Toch. Descriptions of Salka are from her step-grand-niece, Elizabeth Frank.

205 his "musical autobiography": Crawford, *Windfall of Musicians*, p. 158, quoting Lawrence Weschler, "My Grandfather's Last Tale," *Atlantic*, December 1996.

205 holed up in a beach hotel writing film scores for Paramount at $750 per week: Crawford, *Windfall of Musicians*, p. 136.

205 and also to resume teaching: Toch's students in Los Angeles included André Previn, Alex North, and Douglas Moore: ibid., p. 137.

205 "a queer step-child": ibid., p. 140.

206 Picasso's *Blue Boy* hanging over the fireplace: Isherwood, *Diaries, Volume One*, p. 40.

206 and a glimpse of some madly blooming rosebushes: ibid.

206 a pair of unruly Irish setters and an old Alsatian: ibid.

206 the huge German shepherd called Prinz . . . if you lean in too closely

over his head: conversation with Sonya O'Sullivan, December 15, 2012.

206 a furious burrow of ashtrays, newspapers . . . and modern American poetry: Isherwood, *Diaries, Volume One*, p. 56.

207 Never an obvious beauty . . . to assume a forceful presence, to make you pay attention: conversation with Elizabeth Frank.

208 as if she were always leaning slightly forward: ibid.

208 Johnny Weissmuller . . . eleven-year-old son Tommy: *KOS*, pp. 196–197.

208 since their neophyte filmmaking days in Berlin: Wilder and Zinnemann worked together on the 1930 landmark film *Menschen am Sonntag (People on Sunday)*, when Wilder was twenty-four and Zinnemann was twenty-three.

208 two screenplays for Pioneer Pictures: these were *Encore* and *Gibraltar*; neither picture was ever made.

209 Salka began to entertain Toch . . . and went to rejoin the others at dinner: The anecdote about Huston and Peter Viertel boxing in the garage is from P. Viertel, *Dangerous Friends*, p. 20.

210 "*The Jew possesses no power or ability to create culture*": this, and the story of Toch's expulsion, are from Lawrence Weschler, "My Grandfather's Last Tale," *Atlantic*, December 1996.

211 "a *zu Hause* . . . and expelled them all": credit for the *zu Hause* insight belongs to Bilski and Braun, *Jewish Women and Their Salons*, p. 145.

211 a position he usually defended but on this occasion considered cowardly: Isherwood, *Diaries, Volume One*, p. 41.

211 Berthold was as temperamental and dramatic as Salka . . . were not only about politics: ibid., p. 92.

212 a view intended to lift your eyes and your spirits: Weschler, "My Grandfather's Last Tale."

213 Irving Thalberg had died . . . Salka did not think they would remember her: *KOS*, p. 212.

213 fans gathered as if for a film premiere: Lambert, *Norma Shearer*, p. 239.

213 "laughed tears": SV to S. N. Behrman, January 9, 1963, Behrman Archives, NYPL.

213 "To be honest... I felt sorry for him": SV to S. N. Behrman, November 3, 1965, Behrman Archives, NYPL.

214 "It is a fascinating theme... He was anti semitic": SV to S. N. Behrman, March 29, 1963, Behrman Archives, NYPL.

214 a big donor, from its earliest days, to the Wilshire Boulevard Temple: Vieira, *Irving Thalberg*, p. 276.

214 to raise funds to expose and combat the active pro-Nazi efforts of the Los Angeles branch of the Bund: Gabler, *Empire of Their Own*, p. 340.

214 "a lot of Jews will lose their lives... The Jews will still be there": David B. Green, "This Day in Jewish History 1936: Hollywood's 'Boy Wonder' Producer... Dies," www.haaretz.com, September 14, 2014, quoting Vieira, *Irving Thalberg*, p. 264.

215 "devoted themselves to assimilation" and "denied their Jewishness": Rabbi Stephen S. Wise, quoted in the Yiddish newspaper *The Day*, January 13, 1935, cited in Richard Breitman and Allan J. Lichtman, *FDR and the Jews*, p. 80.

215 mostly by writing checks to resistance organizations: Rosenzweig, *Hollywood's Spies*, p. 198.

215 "all through my teens I considered myself un- or non-Jewish... with the culture of my forebears": Budd Schulberg, *Moving Pictures*, p. 238.

215 "the ever-recurring—since Egypt—community of expulsion": Crawford, *Windfall of Musicians*, p. 12.

216 Metro, which had the biggest German investment of all the studios, maintained its offices in Berlin as late as 1938, staffed by non-Jews:

Martin Sauter, *Liesl Frank, Charlotte Dieterle and the European Film Fund*, pp. 50–51.

216 while Paramount and Fox remained in business there until at least late 1940: K. Führer and C. Ross, eds., *Mass Media, Culture and Society in Twentieth-Century Germany*, p. 99.

216 Quietly they issued affidavits for Jews seeking to come to America, and wrote checks to the United Jewish Welfare Fund and other organizations: Matthew Bernstein, *Walter Wanger*, p. 175; www.ushmm.org, "American Jewish Joint Distribution Committee and Refugee Aid."

217 Hyman seemed at first to be Salka's ally: *KOS*, p. 212.

217 a "Chassidic soul": ibid., p. 215.

217 "became first a small, then a huge nightmare": ibid.

217 "If you want to feel sorry for Napoleon then let Garbo play him": ibid., p. 214.

217 "I wished to convey my personal feeling . . . since he represented their secret wish-dreams of conquest": S. N. Behrman, *People in a Diary*, p. 162.

218 but fell months behind schedule, piling up costs: *KOS*, p. 26; Swenson, *Greta Garbo*, p. 367.

218 though it did much better in Europe: Paris, *Garbo*, p. 343. The picture lost $1,397,000.

218 "an exhausting experience for everyone . . . from her and Behrman's original script in the final version": *KOS*, p. 216.

218 as the dying Camille: Salka did not get a writing credit for Garbo's *Camille* (1936), as she had been traveling in Europe while the film was being written. But she did coach Garbo's acting for it. Christopher Isherwood noted: "When young, [Garbo] was eager to learn—watched Salka for hours playing out her old roles. Garbo was so inadequate in the last scene of *Camille* that Salka had them give

all the lines to Robert Taylor. Garbo had only to say 'Yes' and 'No,' and it came out great." *Diaries, Volume One*, p. 761 (June 26, 1958).

218 It organized banquets and receptions to save money to buy ambulances, food and medicine for the Republican cause: Palmier, *Weimar in Exile*, p. 594.

219 In early 1937: Palmier (*Weimar in Exile*) says January; others say March.

219 and managed to collect five thousand dollars: *KOS*, p. 215.

219 "ladies in mink rising and clenching their bejeweled hands": ibid. See Peter Viertel's quite different take in *Dangerous Friends* on p. 7, where he says Malraux's "closed-fist salute . . . shocked most of the listeners, the minority of whom belonged to the far left." Where Salka, looking back, attempted to show herself as only one in a large crowd of Communist sympathizers, Peter suggests that few in the audience had those sympathies.

219 Again they stopped first at a private reception on Mabery Road: Larry Ceplair and Steven Englund, *The Inquisition in Hollywood*, p. 115.

219 Their efforts summoned up . . . for ambulances and medicine: *KOS*, p. 215.

219 "stars, producers, writers . . . and practically every German refugee in Los Angeles": ibid.

220 "premature antifascism," meaning antifascist activity that was nefariously controlled by Communists: Kevin Starr, *Embattled Dreams: California in War and Peace*, p. 286.

220 a left-leaning young Metro producer named Frank Davis: *KOS*, p. 220.

221 "Do you think the time has come not to work for Greta any more? . . . it has felt like a burden to you": BV to SV, August 1, 1937, call # 78.867/7, DLAM.

221 her then companion, the conductor Leopold Stokowski: *KOS*, p. 218.

221 amusing stories to recount among the writers' rooms at Metro: ibid., pp. 217–218.

221 while the film star took a dip: Vieira, *Greta Garbo*, p. 240.

221 Salka also wrote at least one draft: Maurice Zolotow, *Billy Wilder in Hollywood*, pp. 80–81.

221 Screenplay credits eventually went to Charles Brackett, Billy Wilder... for the original story: *KOS*, p. 247; and www.tcm.com, "Notes on Ninotchka": "Modern sources indicate that author Melchior Lengyel, S. N. Behrman, and Salka Viertel also wrote drafts of the script, and that Gottfried Reinhardt was originally assigned to direct."

222 Bernie Hyman instructed Salka to go ahead with the treatment: *KOS*, p. 218.

222 and stayed for a time at Frieda Lawrence's ranch in New Mexico: Nicholas Murray, *Aldous Huxley*, pp. 304–306.

223 Huxley turned in a novelistic 145-page treatment: Paris, *Garbo*, p. 359.

223 to discover radium in a squalid one-bedroom laboratory: *KOS*, p. 228.

223 and became the first woman appointed to a lecture chair at the Sorbonne: Paris, *Garbo*, p. 359.

223 Huxley was paid twenty-five thousand dollars for his treatment: *KOS*, p. 220.

223 "it was instantly forgotten"... "it stinks": ibid., p. 223.

223 "were sincerely fond of her but perhaps they tended to take her for granted... Salka's name isn't mentioned": Isherwood, *Lost Years*, p. 71.

223 "above all she is a European... while retaining their charm and personality": Murray, *Aldous Huxley*, p. 320, quoting Maria Huxley to Jeanne Neveaux, July 31, 1939.

224 Thomas Mann, who had also recently landed in Los Angeles: Sauter, *Frank, Dieterle, and the European Film Fund*, p. 62. Mann came over on the same *Normandie* crossing as Aldous Huxley: Murray, *Aldous Huxley*, p. 303.

224 of which Aldous Huxley was one of the founding sponsors: Palmier, *Weimar in Exile*, p. 369.

224 the Franks were living quite handsomely . . . with Metro in 1937: *KOS*, p. 217.

224 Garbo was thoroughly occupied by *Ninotchka*: Prager. "*Ich bin*," p. 127. Shooting began on May 31, 1939.

224 "Like Ariadne's thread . . . the Hitler menace grew": *KOS*, p. 223.

225 "[Hitler] hated Vienna especially . . . It was very, very difficult, and you had to try all kinds of things": Gertrud Zeisl oral history, www.zeisl.com/archive/gertrud-zeisls-oral-history.htm.

225 The Zeisls were among the lucky few . . . settling in Los Angeles in 1941: Crawford, *Windfall of Musicians*, p. 206.

225 She also applied for a quota number for her mother in Poland: *KOS*, p. 223.

225 "with great dignity" . . . to be his assistant and dramaturg: ibid., p. 224.

226 Peter had graduated . . . and continued his studies at UCLA: ibid., p. 222.

226 Berthold remained in London, sending updates to Salka: ibid., p. 224.

226 and he apologized to her for costing so much: BV to SV, August 1, 1937, call # 78.867/7, DLAM.

226 "That you are forced to live and work in Hollywood . . . but even more for me": *KOS*, p. 225.

227 tackling everything from the Viertel boys' untidiness and Salka's chaotic bookkeeping to the tangled coats of the two Irish setters: ibid., p. 217.

228 "the Jewish community of Germany went up in flames": Lucy

Dawidowicz, quoted in Haskel Lookstein, *Were We Our Brothers' Keepers? The Public Response of American Jews to the Holocaust, 1938–1941*, p. 23.

228 German citizens engaged in an orgy of terror and violence . . . and destroyed 267 synagogues: Statistics are from the United States Holocaust Memorial Museum, Holocaust Encyclopedia, "Kristallnacht," www.ushmm.org.

228 All these facts were reported by the American press by early December of 1938 . . . about the Anschluss and mounting refugee crisis: Lookstein, *Were We Our Brothers' Keepers?*, pp. 23 and 26; www.ushmm.org, "Kristallnacht."

229 more vaguely as "political refugees": Lookstein, *Were We Our Brothers' Keepers?*, p. 32.

229 Polls showed that . . . official government position was "sympathy without hospitality": ibid., p. 44.

229 "flight was both necessary and possible in the weeks and months following . . . for the failure of the world to open its doors while there was still time": ibid., pp. 66–67.

229 By 1938 Liesl Frank, along with Charlotte Dieterle . . . had established the European Film Fund in Hollywood: Sauter, *Frank, Dieterle, and the European Film Fund*, p. 149. The EFF was officially incorporated on November 22, 1938.

230 "You paid in . . . for the next guys who were coming along": Paul Andor quoted in *Cinema's Exiles, From Hitler to Hollywood*, PBS, premiere, January 2009.

230 Henry Blanke . . . gotten his start as an assistant to Ernst Lubitsch: Frederick Kohner, *The Magician of Sunset Boulevard: The Improbable Life of Paul Kohner*, pp. 53 and 109.

230 In her memoir she made a point to give proper credit to Liesl Frank and Charlotte Dieterle: *KOS*, p. 217.

230 Salka was both a contributor to the Fund, and, in her later years, a recipient of its largesse: Sauter, *Frank, Dieterle, and the European Film Fund*, p. 153.

230 Donations to the EFF helped refugees in two related ways: ibid., p. 47.

231 a "biographical sketch," preferably written by as distinguished a personage as one could muster . . . and a studio contract or some similar document as proof that one would not become a public charge in America": ibid., p. 185. The requirement for the "biographical sketch" was added later.

231 "generously guaranteed with their bank accounts . . . and I am happy to say that none ever did": *KOS*, pp. 223–224. The precise number of people for whom Salka collected affidavits is unknown. There are thirty-two letters at the DLAM written by people asking her for help, but this is by no means definitive. For one thing, many of Salka's papers and documents were later destroyed in a house fire on Mabery Road; for another, the EFF and other relief organizations avoided paper trails for activity that the government might choose to flag as suspicious.

231 In February 1939, Salka herself became a citizen of the United States": ibid., p. 226.

232 when Gottfried Reinhardt was fired from the picture after arguing with Lubitsch about a plot point: Vieira, *Greta Garbo*, p. 246.

232 "Dear Salka Steuermann . . . so that the ride should be a little easier for me": Alexander Granach to SV, March 1939, DLAM.

232 Some of Alexander Granach's early life . . . by way of Switzerland: Jan-Christopher Horak, UCLA Film & Television blog post, April 4, 2013, www.cinema.ucla.edu/blogs/archival-spaces/2013.

233 In July 1939, Berthold returned again to Mabery Road: Isherwood, *Diaries, Volume One*, p. 39; *KOS*, p. 227.

233 "he always came back and told me that he could not live without me": Tagebuch, January 1, 1963.

234 "Gottfried liked me to get furious at him . . . then cajole and seduce me afterwards . . . either went without him or did something else": Tagebuch, September 16, 1962.

234 "people who considered themselves superior only because they were overpaid": *KOS*, p. 226.

234 which had now reached $650 a week: ibid., p. 242.

234 Gottfried and Sam Hoffenstein had convinced Salka to hire the agent Paul Kohner: Prager, *"Ich bin,"* p. 192. The contract between SV and Kohner in the archives at the Kinemathek Berlin is dated April 21, 1939.

234 could finesse a deal: *KOS*, p. 242.

234 "no pretty girl would ever study chemistry or physics": ibid., p. 227.

235 On the last day of July Salka sailed from New York . . . and Columbia Pictures chief Harry Cohn: ibid., p. 230.

235 Berthold had his own long list of messages for Salka to relay as well: ibid., p. 229.

235 But Salka remembered that nobody aboard this luxury liner was talking about Hitler: ibid., p. 230.

236 All seemed newly fearful because of Hitler's threats against Poland: ibid., p. 232.

236 Both were certain that their parents' story would be cheapened by Hollywood, with or without Garbo: ibid., pp. 234–235.

237 "Not in a position to take full responsibility . . . I remained silent": ibid., p. 234.

237 "Dear Sidney, when [Irène] refuses it is as if the Rock of Gibraltar were to refuse": Michael Troyan, *A Rose for Mrs. Miniver: The Life of Greer Garson*, p. 159; the letter, dated August 21, 1939, is in the USC Archives.

237 planning to fly to Poland on August 23: *KOS*, p. 235.

237 the newspapers were announcing the German-Soviet Non-Aggression Pact: ibid., p. 236. Note that this was probably not announced until August 23.

238 "My American passport made me feel guilty": ibid.

238 when her quota number, which Salka had applied for around the time of the Anschluss, at last arrived: ibid., p. 223.

238 "There were the usual intertwined couples on the boulevard . . . I wrote down addresses and promised help": ibid., p. 237.

239 Nearby was the Viennese novelist Gina Kaus . . . who was emigrating with her husband and sons: ibid.

240 her mother's visa had been forwarded to the American consulate in Bucharest: ibid., p. 239.

240 the eternal sunbathers idled: Tagebuch, September 5, 1962; the fat pelicans . . . the hot Santa Ana winds pummeled the eucalyptus trees: Isherwood, *Diaries, Volume One*, p. 47.

241 "One does not wander without punishment under palms": ibid., p. 40.

241 Isherwood was teaming again with Berthold to work on an idea for a film: ibid., p. 46.

241 "in a coma of nicotine poisoning": ibid., p. 46.

241 "two aliens from doomed Europe . . . Where would these bronzed and muscular boys be, five years from now?": ibid. p. 40.

241 "after much barking and little biting": ibid., p. 42. The producer was Al Rosen and the project was titled *Mad Dog of Europe*.

242 After the outbreak of the war in Europe, the house on Mabery Road was also on edge: *KOS*, p. 241.

242 "snorting like a war-horse": Isherwood, *Diaries, Volume One*, p. 46.

242 a fourteen-year-old compilation of messy red hair and glasses: ibid., p. 56.

242 offering Peter an advance for a novel he had written in secret: *KOS*, p. 241.

242 "The creek bed had gone . . . that was the water's brother": P. Viertel, *The Canyon*, p. 282.

243 "I suppose . . . that people of Salka's temperament . . . as a background to her meetings with Gottfried": Isherwood, *Diaries, Volume One*, p. 73.

244 The party of about thirty people . . . and the Hindu spiritual teacher Krishnamurti: ibid., p. 51.

244 "Berthold—that born city dweller—might just as well have been walking down Fifth Avenue": ibid., pp. 49–51.

244 "Years of the Devil": *KOS*, p. 239.

245 Salka took in Berthold's niece: ibid., p. 241.

245 She also welcomed a thirteen-year-old refugee named Andrew Frank: *KOS*, p. 241. Andrew Frank was not related to Bruno and Liesl Frank.

245 His life would be saved via passage to the U.S. . . . which gathered affidavits for him: Sauter, *Frank, Dieterle, and the European Film Fund*, p. 184. Sauter notes that Lena Frank, Andrew's mother, was also brought to the States via help from the EFF. She was sponsored by the social reformer Dorothy Canfield Fisher, and her "biographical sketch" was written by Thomas Mann, as was that of her ex-husband, Leonhard Frank.

245 her niece Margret, Edward's daughter, who lived at Mabery Road throughout the war years: Margret's nickname was Mausi. She was very talented both musically and theatrically. See also Isherwood, *Diaries, Volume One*, Glossary, p. 997.

245 the Japanese maid . . . the somewhat fearsome German cook: Isherwood, *Diaries, Volume One*, pp. 43, 46, and 57.

246 And now Christmas was coming: *KOS*, p. 242.

246 the studio's general manager Eddie Mannix: Mannix appears as the fear-inspiring studio "fixer" in Joel and Ethan Coen's film about Golden Age Hollywood, *Hail, Caesar!*

246 "She should see if Kohner can get her a better job!": *KOS*, p. 242.

246 grossing $1,187,000 domestically and nearly as well overseas, even without the now-defunct European market: Vieira, *Greta Garbo*, p. 252.

246 at thirty-four, she was preoccupied with the specter of aging . . . a raw-food diet and obsessive skin care: Prager, "*Ich bin*," p. 195; Vieira, *Greta Garbo*, p. 251.

246 "this autumn of tears and anxiety": *KOS*, p. 241.

7: LIFEBOAT

247 "It is a fantastic commentary": quotation from the journalist Dorothy Thompson appears as the epigraph to David Wyman, *Paper Walls: Americans and the Refugee Crisis, 1938–1941*.

247 "Faced by Salka's lost job at MGM": Isherwood, *Diaries, Volume One*, p. 56.

247 Peter gave Salka and Berthold the bound manuscript: ibid., p. 62.

248 "I want to drink blood brotherhood with you" . . . Peter had to take him home and put him to bed: ibid., p. 67.

248 make her think seriously about opening a restaurant in the canyon . . . would be a gold mine: *KOS*, p. 244.

248 The usually generous Ernst Lubitsch . . . feeding all of Hollywood for nothing: ibid.

248 May's second venture . . . failing to attract customers outside the émigré community: Sauter, *Frank, Dieterle, and the European Film Fund*, pp. 168–169.

248 Formerly a contributor to the European Film Fund, in his last years he lived entirely on its donations: Ruth Barton, *Hedy Lamarr: The Most*

Beautiful Woman in Film, pp. 67–68. See Sauter, *Frank, Dieterle, and the European Film Fund*, p. 104, for a sample of May's donations to the EFF.

249 On a random Tuesday in February 1940 . . . "the friendship between Salka and Gottfried has a lot to do with these fights": Isherwood's description of Salka's dinner party in February 1940 appears in *Diaries, Volume One*, p. 92.

250 "the comparative of Kohn": P. Viertel, *Dangerous Friends*, p. 234.

250 an autobiographical novel by Katalin Gero: Prager, "*Ich bin*," 193. The title was *Not a Fairy Tale*.

250 Salka owed money to the bank for back debts on her house: Prager, "*Ich bin*," pp. 193–194.

250 "in the long run the hotdog stand might have given us more permanent security": *KOS*, p. 244.

250 and the picture was shelved: Prager, "*Ich bin*," p. 193.

250 suggestions about putting the house up as collateral to get a new loan: ibid., p. 194.

251 And so . . . "to the perennial search for a Garbo story": *KOS*, p. 247.

251 a comedy—preferably something like an Americanized *Ninotchka*: ibid.

251 "My friend Bruno Frank . . . and, I gather, never recovered until he died": S. N. Behrman, "A Tribute to Fulda," *New York Times*, February 7, 1943.

252 "the imminent conquest of Paris does not aggravate my diabetes so much as the bombings of London and Berlin": *KOS*, p. 245.

252 she "could not write nor work nor think coherently" and "remained glued to the radio in despair": SV to BV, May 20, 1940, DLAM, quoted in Prager, "*Ich bin*," p. 194.

252 "The radio broadcasts claimed large portions of each day . . . tuned it up loud for each new bulletin": Isherwood, *Diaries, Volume One*, p. 45.

252 "I dreaded the thought of his being a pilot . . . the world is rather small when you think of it": *KOS*, p. 243.

253 the first of Peter's "tennis friends" to impress Salka with his love of the theater and literature: P. Viertel, *Dangerous Friends*, pp. 59–60.

253 The Bronx-born Jewish writer . . . to his own large social circle: Michael Shnayerson, *Irwin Shaw*, pp. 104–105.

253 "the azure coast, the mountains, the sea, the pines . . . the gentle call of some bird": Lion Feuchtwanger, *The Devil in France*, p. 27.

254 "All German nationals . . . are to report for internment": ibid., p. 22.

254 Feuchtwanger had already been interned and released: Manfred Flügge, *Fry, Bingham, Sharp: The Americans Who Saved Lion and Marta Feuchtwanger*, p. 51.

255 One of his cats . . . wanting her dinner: Feuchtwanger, *The Devil in France*, p. 23.

255 "a bright room in the sky": Peter Stephan Jungk, *Franz Werfel: A Life in Prague, Vienna and Hollywood*, p. 178.

255 "he smudges so easily": ibid., p. 218. The friend who made that comment was Gustave O. Arlt.

255 "the Hindenburg of the emigration": Anthony Heilbut, *Exiled in Paradise: German Refugee Artists and Intellectuals in America from the 1930s to the Present*, p. 274.

255 the times themselves had become the real novel of the age: Nigel Hamilton, *The Brothers Mann: The Lives of Heinrich and Thomas Mann, 1871–1950 and 1875–1955*, p. 312. Mann's letter was addressed to Eva and Julius Lips, February 12, 1939.

256 one of the few contemporary writers worth his attention: *KOS*, p. 249.

256 "Heinrich Mann, even more stiff and formal than his brother": Bedford, *Aldous Huxley*, p. 282.

256 "the manners of a nineteenth-century *grand seigneur*": *KOS*, p. 249.

256 A collaborationist regime . . . the abandoned hotels of the spa town of Vichy: www.ushmm.org, "World War II in Europe."

256 Many thousands of German and Austrian antifascists and Jews were apprehended and interned as enemy nationals: Memorial to the Shoah in Paris, wall label, "From the Phony War to German Occupation"; see also Hertha Pauli, *Break of Time*.

256 interned again at the Les Milles brickworks . . . made him cough up blood: Feuchtwanger, *The Devil in France*, pp. 38–39.

257 Then he was sent to a military camp . . . outside of Nîmes: Flügge, *Fry, Bingham, Sharp*, p. 52.

257 His wife Marta . . . slept on straw-filled sacks on the floor: ibid.

257 Feuchtwanger was disguised . . . and spirited into a waiting car: ibid., p. 61.

258 Hiram Bingham IV . . . to offer that hospitality: ibid.

258 "I never learned my lesson . . . I must surely be able to keep it": Feuchtwanger, *The Devil in France*, p. 30.

258 Heinrich Mann and his wife Nelly: *KOS*, p. 249. Nelly was twenty-seven years younger than Heinrich, who was sixty-nine at that time.

258 hiding in a small hotel near the city's railway station: Varian Fry, *Surrender on Demand*, p. 58.

259 with the hope of booking passage on any ship they could find leaving the Atlantic coast: Flügge, *Fry, Bingham, Sharp*, p. 62.

259 that Werfel called their "Tour de France": Alma Mahler Werfel, *And the Bridge Is Love*, p. 262.

259 He vowed that if he managed to escape from Europe he would write a book to honor the saint: Jungk, *Franz Werfel*, p. 187.

259 who joined the swelling tide of fugitives to pray at her shrine: Pauli, *Break of Time*, p. 158.

259 Eventually the Werfels managed to obtain a safe-conduct pass . . .

that permitted travel within France: Sheila Isenberg, *A Hero of Our Own: The Story of Varian Fry*, p. 15.

260 and they still needed exit visas to leave the country: Fry, *Surrender on Demand*, pp. 6–7.

260 all bent on their daily hellish missions to petition the consulates: Jungk, *Franz Werfel*, p. 187.

260 risked arrest and deportation to Germany if they remained in Marseille or if they tried to leave: Fry, *Surrender on Demand*, p. 7.

260 The hotels in which they hid were filled with German officers: Mahler Werfel, *And the Bridge Is Love*, p. 262.

260 There was a circulating fear that at any moment the borders might be sealed: Evelyn Juers, *House of Exile: The Lives and Times of Heinrich Mann and Nelly Kroeger-Mann*, p. 280.

261 The husband falls in love with the counterfeit version: Prager, "*Ich bin*," p. 197, which verifies the time as autumn 1940. The writers worked on the script from summer 1940 to summer 1941.

261 She faced comparisons with fresh American actresses like Lana Turner, who was sixteen years younger: Vieira, *Greta Garbo*, p. 256.

261 "As nothing divides people more than difference in their sense of humor": *KOS*, p. 252.

263 sharing the cramped apartment with Salka's brother Dusko, his girlfriend Hania, and their little son: ibid., p. 166.

263 a young woman named Viktoria . . . and had always been treated as a member of the family: ibid., p. 77.

263 "I am thankful that he has become a responsible human being": ibid., p. 246.

263 They were on a Greek steamer on their way to join Josef Gielen in Buenos Aires: ibid.

263 Alexander Granach, Ernst Lubitsch, Henry Blanke, William Wyler,

and Paul Kohner: Sauter, *Frank, Dieterle, and the European Film Fund*, p. 100, from list of "Donations from Non-Members, May 1, 1940–April 30, 1941" and from Paul Kohner Collection; both documents undated.

264 having made a five-thousand-dollar donation to the Finnish Relief Fund . . . under the condition of strict anonymity: Swenson, *Greta Garbo*, p. 402; and Paris, *Garbo*, p. 394.

264 Garbo used her influence to help physicist Niels Bohr escape: Paris, *Garbo*, p. 394.

264 Salka pulled Garbo into her humanitarian network, persuading the actress to donate $500 to the EFF: Sauter, *Frank, Dieterle, and the European Film Fund*, p. 110: "Garbo's donation clearly was a result of her close connection with Salka Viertel . . ."

264 Garbo's donation put her among the top twenty-eight contributors to the EFF: ibid., p. 110.

264 "If anyone has made the suggestion . . . has done the utmost to help me in my work of rescuing antifascist refugees from Europe": Paris, *Garbo*, p. 394, quoting Raymond Daum, *Walking with Garbo*, pp. 173–174.

265 she had a residence of her own on South Amalfi Drive near the Huxleys in the Palisades: Murray, *Aldous Huxley*, p. 319: the Huxleys had moved in April 1939 "to a furnished house at 701 South Amalfi Drive, Pacific Palisades. Garbo lived on the other side of the street."

265 "Salka Viertel, her family and friends remained Garbo's anchor in Hollywood": Swenson, *Greta Garbo*, p. 406.

265 "Everyone was fleeing and everything was temporary . . . or our entire lives": Anna Seghers, *Transit*, p. 32.

265 The ERC was the Amerian extension of an international committee founded by . . . Albert Einstein: Einstein's committee was called the International Relief Association. It still exists today in the form of the International Rescue Committee.

266 while she did not remember the first time she met Thomas Mann, it must have been around this summer of 1940: *KOS*, p. 249.

266 renting a house up the street from the Schoenbergs: Thomas and Katia Mann had not yet committed to moving permanently to Los Angeles from Princeton. They would do so the following year.

266 "the reserved politeness of a diplomat on official duty": *KOS*, p. 249.

266 The committee saw that it needed to focus its initial rescue efforts on high-profile writers . . . to help the many thousands of others to escape: Terence Renaud, "The Genesis of the Emergency Rescue Committee, 1933–1942," Boston University, 2005.

267 Thus the ERC solicited names from the likes of . . . Alfred Barr . . . and . . . Jacques Maritain: ibid.

267 Its initial list of about two hundred refugees: Fry, *Surrender on Demand*, p. xi.

267 Fry arrived in Marseille in mid-August 1940 . . . at that time the only possible exit points out of Europe: Isenberg, *Hero of Our Own*, p. 12.

267 to smuggle more than two thousand people out of France: Fry, *Surrender on Demand*, p. x.

268 "Up to the last moment . . . might in the meantime have run out": Palmier, *Weimar in Exile*, p. 448.

268 Fry added a fourth couple: Isenberg, *Hero of Our Own*, pp. 76–77. Fry left the Adlers out of his account in *Surrender on Demand*, later admitting sheepishly that he did so because Adler was not as famous as the others.

268 Like Lion Feuchtwanger, he was interned at Les Milles and had recently escaped: Isenberg, *Hero of Our Own*, p. 76.

268 These were generally available for anyone who had a valid overseas visa: Fry, *Surrender on Demand*, p. 57. See Isenberg's *Hero of Our Own* for a list of each of the refugees' documents.

268 Their journey would still be illegal . . . the impossible French exit visas: Isenberg, *Hero of Our Own*, p. 15.

269 promising that they could follow as soon as possible: Fry, *Surrender on Demand*, p. 51.

269 They included the musical scores of her former husband . . . novel-in-progress about Saint Bernadette of Lourdes: Juers, *House of Exile*, p. 282.

270 Maybe he was a spy; maybe he would sell them out to the authorities: Fry, *Surrender on Demand*, p. 64.

270 Of this scheme everyone in the group was afraid: Isenberg, *Hero of Our Own*, pp. 77–78; Fry, *Surrender on Demand*, pp. 62–63.

270 "He's too fat . . . and Mann's too old": Fry, *Surrender on Demand*, p. 63.

270 "Half an hour later . . . or resting in its half-shade": ibid., p. 65.

271 a billowing white dress and a pair of old sandals: Isenberg, *Hero of Our Own*, p. 78.

271 "Mountain goats could hardly have kept their footing on the glassy, shimmering slate . . ..nothing but thistles to hold on to": Mahler Werfel, *And the Bridge Is Love*, p. 266.

271 "Not that he wasn't game . . . he couldn't make the grade without help": Fry, *Surrender on Demand*, p. 68.

271 carrying Heinrich most of the way over the mountain: ibid.

271 Some hours later . . . they changed guides: Juers, *House of Exile*, p. 283.

271 "we felt utterly wretched": Mahler Werfel, *And the Bridge Is Love*, p. 266.

272 "We almost fell into one another's arms": Fry, *Surrender on Demand*, p. 68.

272 "Harry can send his friends": Flügge, *Fry, Bingham, Sharp*, p. 63.

272 "Telegram from Golo and Heinrich from Lisbon": Hans Wysling, ed., *Letters of Heinrich and Thomas Mann, 1900–1949*, p. 411, citing Thomas Mann's Tagebuch entry of September 20, 1940, and diary entry of September 22, 1940.

272 "A lost lover is not more beautiful": Hamilton, *The Brothers Mann*, p. 314.

272 "Now America lies before us . . . I hope that it will be favorably disposed toward me": Jungk, *Franz Werfel*, p. 193.

272 with the help of an American Unitarian minister named Waitstill Sharp and his wife Martha: Flügge, *Fry, Bingham, Sharp*, p. 64.

273 and Alfred and Lisl Polgar: Juers, *House of Exile*, p. 288.

273 Some have alleged . . . a cerebral hemorrhage or an overdose of his heart medication: Rebecca Solnit, *Storming the Gates of Paradise: Landscapes for Politics*, p. 73.

273 continued on through Spain and eventually to safety: Isenberg, *Hero of Our Own*, p. 95.

273 From Lisbon, Fry cabled the ERC: Flügge, *Fry, Bingham, Sharp*, p. 63.

273 Other donations . . . went to support the newly arrived refugees in America: ibid., p. 66.

274 "Some may die on the way . . . At least one must try": Pauli, *Break of Time*, p. 215.

274 "Here you feel at home in the landscape . . . it's part of your life": Marta Feuchtwanger, "An Émigré Life," oral history, University of California.

274 "The Riviera is just trash compared to this": Jungk, *Franz Werfel*, p. 196.

275 "Grateful and unhappy": Mahler Werfel, *And the Bridge Is Love*, p. 275.

275 "pedestrians had become extinct . . . I happen to love walking amongst crowds": Juers, *House of Exile*, p. 293.

275 "the people here don't need our stories . . . serve Louis B. Mayer and one's own work": Palmier, *Weimar in Exile*, p. 513.

275 There was even talk that one of his books might once again be made into a film: Wysling, ed., *Letters of Heinrich and Thomas Mann*, p. 238.

Heinrich Mann's novel *Professor Unrat* was published in 1905; the film appeared in 1930.

275 "appeared an odd figure in the Burbank studio": *KOS*, p. 249.

275 had set him up as a screenwriter at six thousand dollars per year: Hamilton, *The Brothers Mann*, p. 317.

275 "to waste the time between 10 and 1 in consultation and chatter": Wysling, ed., *Letters of Heinrich and Thomas Mann*, p. 239.

276 "Care for the house and the car fall to my wife": ibid.

276 "a voluptuous, blond, blue-eyed Teutonic beauty ... to which he heroically consented": *KOS*, p. 249.

276 "the representative, towering literary figure": ibid., p. 259. Mann's house on San Remo Drive was at that time being designed and constructed by the émigré architect J. R. Davidson, but the Manns did not move into it until 1942.

276 "Hollywood could now boast of being the Parnassus of German literature": ibid., p. 248.

277 "Only shortly before Schoenberg's death ... Later Stravinsky paid great homage to Schoenberg and to his music": ibid., p. 259.

277 Garbo was impatient to get things going so as to be finished with it as soon as possible: Vieira, *Greta Garbo*, pp. 257–258.

277 "Nobody's heart was in it": Paris, *Garbo*, p. 374.

277 Gottfried would come home to Mabery Road from the studio: Vieira, *Greta Garbo*, p. 258.

277 "If the war comes here, I won't try to dodge ... Don't be such a sucker!" Isherwood, *Diaries, Volume One*, p. 139.

278 "You can't only help people ... it's probably better to avoid them, and subscribe to charities": Isherwood, *Diaries, Volume One*, p. 158.

279 and would not return until the end of April: *KOS*, p. 250.

279 "I'd rather you didn't speak about my birthday ... the younger natives are waiting": Wysling, ed., *Letters of Heinrich and Thomas Mann*,

p. 243. Italics are Heinrich Mann's and indicate that the original words were in English.

280 The brothers' rivalry had begun long ago . . . had become a senator at age thirty-six: Hamilton, *The Brothers Mann*, p. 19.

280 "I sat in a corner and watched my father and mother . . . on the quiet features of my mother": ibid., p. 23, quoting from Thomas Mann, *The Dilettante* (1897, republished as *Das Bild der Mutter*).

280 As little boys they watched bashfully . . . in the ballroom of the family home: ibid., p. 19.

280 Hans Christian Andersen and Charles Perrault: Anthony Heilbut, *Thomas Mann: Eros and Literature*, p. 10; Hamilton, *The Brothers Mann*, p. 20.

281 She was the daughter of a German-born planter and his Portuguese-Creole-Brazilian wife: Heilbut, *Eros and Literature*, p. 8.

281 and rang with the songs of the slaves on the plantation: Hamilton, *The Brothers Mann*, pp. 14–15, 20.

281 "the primal simplicity of the fairy tale": Wysling, ed., *Letters of Heinrich and Thomas Man*, p. 2.

281 "There is no sharp boundary in my memory between children's games and the practice of art": ibid.

281 "the Starched Collar": Michael Harris, "The Anguish in His Stories Was His Own," review of Anthony Heilbut's *Thomas Mann: Eros and Literature*, *Los Angeles Times*, February 5, 1996.

281 "He looks wonderfully young for his age . . . elderly and staid": Isherwood, *Diaries, Volume One*, p. 100.

281 "the childlike big moments, times of celebration and honors": Thomas Mann, "On the Profession of the German Writer in Our Time: Address in Honor of a Brother," March 27, 1931, Prussian Academy of Arts, Berlin, reprinted in Wysling, ed., *Letters of Heinrich and Thomas Mann*, p. 280.

282 "there behind him, his entire life ... but stole the limelight": Hamilton, *The Brothers Mann*, p. 21.

282 where Heinrich was then serving as president of the poetry department: www.imdb.com, biography of Heinrich Mann.

282 But they published their homages to each other that year: Thomas in March 1936, Heinrich in December.

284 "Decorated with flowers and candles it looked very festive": *KOS*, p. 250; Prager mentions the Ping-Pong table ("*Ich bin*," p. 198), as does Gottfried Reinhardt in his memoir of his father. Descriptions of the event also come from a telegram from BV to SV, May 2, 1941, and from *Aufbau*, the New York–based Jewish émigré newspaper, from May 16, 1941.

284 Walter and Hedy Herlitschek ... Toni Spuhler: *KOS*, pp. 244, 150.

284 "Nelly was opposite us, towering over the very small Feuchtwanger ... All of them represented the true Fatherland to which in spite of Hitler they adhered, as they adhered to the German language": ibid., p. 250.

285 "it gave one some hope and comfort ... crowding each other and wiping their tears": ibid., p. 251.

285 Mann's birthday speech, which was eventually published: Salka says that Thomas Mann's address was published in the periodical *Decision*. It, along with Heinrich's address on the same night, are reprinted in the "Documents" section at the end of Wysling, ed., *Letters of Heinrich and Thomas Mann*, along with the other birthday speeches quoted here.

288 "This glass is for Frau Salka Viertel": Heinrich Mann, "Afterdinner Remarks at Frau Viertel's, Delivered May 2, 1941," ibid., p. 295.

288 her "speciality of the house": *KOS*, p. 251.

289 "Perhaps one had to live her life to make it ... the rich, moist, slightly undercooked core": email from Adam Shaw.

289 because he heard that Salka was bringing the cake: conversation with Elizabeth Frank.

290 "I've started work on a film... when war is on our doorstep": Swenson, *Greta Garbo*, p. 411.

290 It was Garbo's twenty-sixth picture for Metro: ibid., p. 414; but Mark A Vieira writes that Garbo appeared in only twenty-four American films: *Greta Garbo*, p. 271.

290 on location at the Sugar Bowl Lodge near Donner Summit: McGilligan, *George Cukor*, p. 165.

290 "I'm only very sorry that the story has changed so much... it will have turned out like it has": Vieira, *Greta Garbo*, p. 261.

290 Often the blame went to Salka: ibid.: "Cukor, Viertel, or Behrman was often named as a fatal element."

291 with another picture remaining under her current contract": Paris, *Garbo*, p. 379.

291 "immoral and un-Christian attitude toward marriage... suggestive costumes": Swenson, *Greta Garbo*, pp. 417–418.

291 asked him to make an assessment of its wickedness: *KOS*, p. 253.

292 "More incensed than his minions... against my sinful *Two-Faced Woman*": Gottfried Reinhardt, *The Genius: A Memoir of Max Reinhardt*, p. 104.

292 "when each day brought news more horrible than one could bear": *KOS*, p. 248.

292 "Oh, these! I just slipped into these": *Two-Faced Woman* [script]; George Cukor; 1941; Dialogue cutting continuity, revised version, December 19, 1941; Script Collection, AMPAS (Unpublished), Margaret Herrick Library, Academy of Motion Pictures Arts and Sciences.

293 based on a novel called *The Paradine Case*... as a possible Garbo vehicle: Prager, *"Ich bin,"* p. 202.

293 But the actress was not keen to play another femme fatale: *KOS*, p. 253. Metro eventually gave up on the screenplay and resold it to David O. Selznick, who had bought it in 1933 when he was at Metro, and who eventually completed the picture with Alfred Hitchcock in 1947. Salka's drafts were unused and she received no credit.

294 an emblem of the hardships she had endured: ibid., p. 256.

294 with Garbo's help had secured promises of intervention from the U.S. ambassador: ibid., p. 253. Garbo had become acquainted with the ambassador, Lawrence Steinhardt, during his earlier assignment in Stockholm.

294 could only pray that he had fled from Sambor with the retreating Soviets: ibid., p. 254.

294 as the Nazis advanced on the capital: ibid., p. 255.

294 after which they put her on the train which would take her to Los Angeles: ibid., p. 256.

295 "Everyone brought friends . . . Old age even gallantly borne frightened them": ibid., p. 257.

295 their Swedish ship forced to dawdle through the Panama Canal: ibid., p. 256.

295 quietly supported the evacuation of Brecht and a number of other refugees through its bureaucratic channels: Sauter, *Frank, Dieterle, and the European Film Fund*, p. 36.

295 until the release of the Molotov Report in 1942: *KOS*, p. 269.

296 by shooting them or poisoning them in gas vans: www.ushmm.org, "Final Solution" and "*Einsatzgruppen*."

296 As of late October, it was unlawful for Jews to emigrate from Germany or any of its territories: David Wyman, *Paper Walls*, p. 205.

296 In July all the American consulates in German territory were closed: ibid.

296 "a complete solution of the Jewish question": Hermann Goering to

Reinhard Heydrich, July 31, 1941, cited in www.ushmm.org, "Final Solution."

296 up to 1,700,000 Jews were murdered in Eastern Europe: ibid.

297 Viktoria was not Jewish, so unlike Dusko she had some measure of protection against German persecution: *KOS*, p. 257 and 280.

297 a few weeks before the release of *Two-Faced Woman*: the premiere took place on November 30; a censored version was released on December 31.

297 Gottfried Reinhardt was sitting in a dubbing room at Metro: Paris, *Garbo*, p. 379.

297 "Arthur Rubinstein was just finishing the first movement... and sunk the American fleet in Pearl Harbor": *KOS*, p. 260.

8: ILIUM

299 "In Hollywood there are only two categories of writers": Alfred Döblin quoted in Sauter, *Frank, Dieterle, and the European Film Fund*, p. 193.

299 "All the Japanese living in California were sent to concentration camps": *KOS*, p. 261.

299 Policemen warned that it was forbidden to speak German on the street: Juers, *House of Exile*, p. 342.

300 The FBI rounded up many of the prominent Reich sympathizers: Steven J. Ross, *Hitler in Los Angeles: How Jews Foiled Nazi Plots Against Hollywood and America*, pp. 316–317.

300 "there was no curfew in the East... convinced that a 'fifth column' existed and caution was necessary": *KOS*, p. 261.

300 Gottfried... was in uniform immediately... to make training films for the Signal Corps: ibid., p 262.

300 "to build my place in life so that I do not have to reproach myself": ibid., p. 263.

300 on a loan-out from David Selznick: P. Viertel, *Dangerous Friends*, p. 21.

300 The news filled Salka with dread: *KOS*, p. 262.

301 "is compelled to face the monster, man to man": ibid., p. 263.

301 "it tortured me to think that Peter had become a tiny, passive particle": ibid.

302 In the Benedict Canyon house of Budd's unsuspecting father: Nancy Lynn Schwartz, *The Hollywood Writers' Wars*, p. 94.

302 among them Dalton Trumbo, Ring Lardner Jr., Albert Maltz, Robert Rossen, and Maurice Rapf: ibid., p. 298.

303 Her political convictions grew from her sympathy: conversation with Vicky Schulberg.

303 But she found Marxist texts tedious: Schwartz, *Hollywood Writers' Wars*, p. 184.

303 drank and flirted and jousted: Jigee at this point never drank alcohol, and Peter rarely did.

303 for a time she was an active Marxist: ibid.

303 "strong reservations" . . . "destructive character": *KOS*, p. 267.

303 "would need a lot of courage to face the future . . . we would need each other": ibid., p. 266.

304 "We spent Sundays on the beach . . . she also took hold of my heart": ibid., p. 267.

305 chugged off to war in a sea teeming with enemy submarines: P. Viertel, *Dangerous Friends*, p. 79.

305 the new woman in Berthold's life . . . "Berthold was much more at peace with himself, and also with me and Gottfried": *KOS*, p. 267.

305 "A surprisingly large number of elevator boys . . . at the ends of the corridors": Isherwood, *Diaries, Volume One*, p. 256.

305 and was helping the Swami write a translation of the *Bhagavad Gita*: ibid., p. 240. Isherwood's and the Swami's translation was published

in 1944 as *Bhagavad Gita: The Song of God*, with an introduction by Aldous Huxley.

306 "What am I doing with this old, unfashionable Indian stuff? What relation can it possibly have to America?": Isherwood, *Diaries, Volume One*, p. 265.

306 "For Garbo and her contemporaries, 1942 was the Twilight of the Goddesses": Vieira, *Greta Garbo*, p. 268.

306 With England the only remaining European market for Metro's pictures: Thomas Doherty, *Projections of War: Hollywood, American Culture, and World War II*, p. 40.

306 prompting Goebbels to shut down Metro's Berlin office and to forbid the screening of its films in all German territories: www.tcm.com, "The Mortal Storm."

306 On this autumn afternoon the excitable Saville . . . hoped for the shooting of French collaborators: Isherwood, *Diaries, Volume One*, p. 257.

307 It was the story of a wounded soldier and a nurse . . . updated to the Soviet-German conflict: *KOS*, p. 268.

307 Hyman suddenly died of heart failure: Vieira, *Greta Garbo*, p. 268.

307 His death provoked much anxiety: *KOS*, p. 269.

307 He offered to buy her out . . . saying she had not earned it: Vieira, *Greta Garbo*, p. 269.

308 A gaggle of Metro employees . . . Lana Turner: ibid., p. 270.

308 published in the United States to blockbuster sales and was chosen in July as a main selection for the Book-of-the-Month Club . . . for the huge sum of $125,000: Kevin Starr, *The Dream Endures: California Enters the 1940s*, pp. 370–372.

308 The screenwriting contract . . . and the studio did not renew it: Sauter, *Frank, Dieterle, and the European Film Fund*, p. 131.

309 "that prevented us from destitution": ibid., p. 193.

309 Heinrich Mann's contract at Metro . . . fell behind on the rent: Juers, *House of Exile*, p. 317.

309 his only lifeline: ibid., p. 320.

309 Nelly wrote out her will: ibid., p. 318. This occurred on April 27, 1942.

310 "Mama is no expert in the treatment of technical implements": SV to BV, 1945, call # 78.916/10, DLAM.

310 still trying to believe that Dusko had escaped from Sambor: *KOS*, p. 269.

310 arrested by the FBI and were currently in jail, awaiting trial: Ross, *Hitler in Los Angeles*, pp. 322, 323.

310 There were no more pro-Nazi rallies . . . occupied by U.S. troops on the day after Pearl Harbor: ibid., p. 316.

310 Much of it was inspired by nationwide campaigns . . . for America First: ibid., pp. 312, 325.

310 G. Allison Phelps . . . immorality in the film community: ibid. p. 332. See also Louis Pizzitola, *Hearst Over Hollywood: Power, Passion, and Propaganda in the Movies*, p. 388.

311 Germany might institute a pro-Soviet government . . . heads of state": Juers, *House of Exile*, p. 313.

311 Heinrich Mann sometimes went outside . . . in a neighbor's yard: ibid., p. 317.

311 "We learned to speak freely only at home . . . an ever more controlled life": Fritz Stern, *Five Germanys I Have Known*, p. 95.

311 Beginning in January 1942 . . . "165 Mabery Road": Alexander Stephan, *"Communazis": FBI Surveillance of German Émigré Writers*, pp. 194–197.

311 "anti-capitalistic and communistically-inclined": Swenson, *Greta Garbo*, p. 448.

311 "no indication that either [Berthold or Salka] has important Communist Party connections": ibid.

312 "strong, handsome young men . . . harassing the refugees": *KOS*, p. 261.

312 Von Bucovich . . . a low-paying job at Warner Bros.: ibid., p. 217.

312 "Oh, you people, you are anti-fascist but": ibid., pp. 261–262.

313 "Since the human capacity for empathy . . .": Heinrich Mann's words paraphrased in Juers, *House of Exile*, p. 361.

313 The British actor Charles Laughton . . . at Birmingham General Hospital in the San Fernando Valley: Simon Callow, *Charles Laughton: A Difficult Actor*, p. 153; Charles Higham, *Charles Laughton: An Intimate Biography*, pp. 112, 116.

314 "The death of this love is horrible": SV to BV, undated 1943, DLAM.

314 "it was difficult to extricate myself" . . . "it is senseless to compare one's own grief": *KOS*, p. 269.

315 "Just as he had resented my happiness": ibid., p. 270.

315 His girlfriend Liesel Neumann followed from New York: Isherwood, *Diaries, Volume One*, p. 311.

315 "the air full of spray and falling light" . . . and her intention to visit Isherwood's Swami Prabhavananda: ibid., p. 290.

315 "played up outrageously, sighing about how wonderful it must be to be a nun": ibid., p. 308.

316 "Everything in the household was just as usual . . . the other about refugee domestic servants": ibid., p. 307.

316 "I am convinced he meant it": *KOS*, p. 272.

316 That same July she sold a treatment for a domestic comedy to Paramount: Prager, "*Ich bin*," p. 143. The treatment was called *Keeping House*.

316 a love story for Garbo set in Iceland: ibid.

316 Neither was produced . . . relieving her mortgage worries: *KOS*, p. 274.

317 The fund declared itself in dire financial straits by 1943: Sauter, *Frank, Dieterle, and the European Film Fund*, p. 236.

317 The movement was hoping to install Thomas Mann as the leader of a German government-in-exile: Stephan, *"Communazis,"* p. 58.

317 earned him a place on the U.S. National Censorship Watch List: ibid., pp. 112–113.

317 At the Mabery Road meeting were Salka . . . and Hanns Eisler: Juers, *House of Exile*, p. 331.

317 Bruno Frank and Ludwig Marcuse likewise withdrew their signatures: Stephan, *"Communazis,"* p. 114.

318 Mann believed that the entire German nation was at fault for Nazism: Juers, *House of Exile*, p. 331.

318 Liesel Neumann also returned to New York, having been cast in a play: the play was called *Tomorrow the World*.

318 Isherwood moved into her room across the street . . . "Only Tommy is nearly always available": Isherwood, *Diaries, Volume One*, p. 311. Hans was a night owl throughout his life, reading or working into the early morning hours and sleeping until the early afternoon.

318 "about politics, Buddhism, literature, everything . . . listening very carefully and earnestly to my replies": ibid., p. 312.

319 "the Red composer . . . with whirring wittiness": ibid.

319 "They were all very apologetic about this . . . I felt like a fake": ibid., p. 313.

320 Observing the curfew . . . throwing darts at a board painted with Hitler's image: I have seen the dartboard, which according to the current administrators of the Villa Aurora is original and was found in the house after Marta Feuchtwanger's death. The artist is unknown.

320 "a specialist in musicals": *KOS*, p. 270.

320 "To be 'discovered' by Reinhardt had meant more to me": ibid.

320 had even influenced . . . the Third Reich: see Gerwin Strobl, *The Swastika and the Stage: German Theatre and Society, 1933–1945*, p. 53. Reinhardt's techniques that were appropriated by the National

Socialists included his use of theater in the round, Expressionistic light and sound, emotionalism, and ritual.

321 "He once called himself a 'negotiator between dream and reality'... but he defined the essence of *all* art": Thomas Mann, from a 1944 memorial service for Max Reinhardt, published in *Max Reinhardt 1873–1973, A Centennial Festschrift*, p. 93.

321 "We jumped when the telephone rang... his father was dead": *KOS*, p. 271.

322 "Jigee had gotten her divorce... to marry her right away": ibid. See also ibid. for the following description of Peter and Jigee's wedding.

323 Salka could barely drive through her tears on the way home: ibid., p. 274.

324 "For many years you have given me the possibility... one day will justify me before my children": ibid., p. 275.

324 "At that time, and this is now twenty years ago... Because he needed me?": Tagebuch, January 1, 1963.

324 "Why didn't I let the house go dirty... made me loathe disintegration": *KOS*, p. 282.

325 "At the stalls previously owned by Japanese... If only one could send some of it to Europe": ibid.

326 "the social glue that made the exiles into a community": E. Randol Schoenberg, ed., *The Doctor Faustus Dossier: Arnold Schoenberg, Thomas Mann, and Their Contemporaries 1930–1951*, p. xii.

326 "benevolent connoisseurs": Adrian Daub, introduction to E. R. Schoenberg, ed., *Doctor Faustus Dossier*, p. 20.

326 including Schoenberg, Stravinsky, Ernst Toch, and Hanns Eisler: Crawford, *Windfall of Musicians*, p. 109, fn 31.

327 even writing some descriptions of Leverkühn's fictional music: Daub, introduction to E. R. Schoenberg, ed., *Doctor Faustus Dossier*, p. 1.

327 Those essays of Adorno's became important source material for the

book: Christoph Gödde and Thomas Sprecher, eds., *Adorno-Mann Correspondence 1943–1955*, pp. 3–5.

327 Mann made use of Adorno's writing . . . that featured Schoenberg: ibid., p. 4.

327 Adorno accepted no payment for his efforts: Stefan Müller-Doohm, *Adorno: A Biography*, footnotes on pp. 216–218.

328 He startled Marta Feuchtwanger . . . did not in fact have syphilis: Crawford, *Windfall of Musicians*, p. 109; M. Feuchtwanger, *An Émigré Life*, p. 1068.

328 "Wiesengrund should be excluded altogether": Crawford, *Windfall of Musicians*, p. 110.

328 There were impassioned arguments . . . he had never intended to use him as a model for his hero: *KOS*, p. 314.

329 "Every intellectual in emigration is mutilated without exception": quoted in Gerd Gemünden, *Continental Strangers*, p. 8.

330 "To the Germans I am a Jew . . . for Hindemith and Stravinsky": Arnold Schoenberg to Thomas Mann, February 24, 1948, quoted in E. R. Schoenberg, ed., *Doctor Faustus Dossier*, p. 235.

331 "it was impossible to conceal from Mama . . . After a while we would cease talking and plunge into our separate gloom": *KOS*, pp. 280–281.

332 the visitors who came to discuss the war with Brecht: ibid., p. 258.

332 a rival of Isherwood's guru: Juers, *House of Exile*, p. 343.

332 Alfred Döblin's wife Erna also stayed there: ibid., p. 348.

332 glad to see Heinrich looking improved: ibid.

333 His son Tim was a little boy at the time and remembered . . . always the center of the show: anecdote from a conversation with Tim Zinnemann, June 12, 2017.

334 "When the warning sounds after dark . . . report the fact to the nearest policeman": *A Handbook for Air Raid Wardens*, issued by the U.S. Office of Civilian Defense (U.S. Government Printing Office, April 1942).

334 "completely hypnotized": *KOS*, p. 282.

334 "The very fact that their meeting took place . . . the community of artists, could flourish": Callow, *Charles Laughton*, p. 165.

335 during a 1936 stint at the Comédie-Française: ibid.

336 "I have done enough for you . . . I cannot do more": SV to BV, July 28, 1944, DLAM.

336 "I haven't read the script . . . to know how much damage you have done to Salka": SV to BV, July 28, 1944, call # 78.916/5, DLAM.

336 they did not speak for a number of months: Prager, *"Ich bin,"* p. 209.

337 his slow coordination made him unfit for combat: *KOS*, p. 278.

337 "as far as both of us are concerned . . . as long as we live": ibid.

337 Now she was scheduled to appear in court . . . filled her with panic: Juers, *House of Exile*, pp. 336, 350; *KOS*, p. 279.

338 this was the fifth time Nelly had set out to end her life: Juers, *House of Exile*, p. 353.

338 "such as they use on movie sets": *KOS*, p. 279.

339 "Heinrich's unhappy wife, who had brought him a lot of trouble": Juers, *House of Exile*, p. 353.

339 insisting that Nelly appeal to her own relatives in America to act as her sponsors: ibid., p. 297.

339 Klaus Mann, then serving in Italy: ibid., p. 350.

339 "She should have stayed in Germany with people of her own kind": ibid.

339 "We were together, she and I, and now I'm alone": ibid., p. 356.

339 "But even those she shocked had no doubts about her devotion to her husband": *KOS*, p. 249.

340 "Nelly's death was the last, sad event of this depressing year": ibid., p. 280.

340 Ruth Berlau . . . also as a paying guest: ibid., p. 282.

342 "it was fun": Sonya Schulberg O'Sullivan to Ad Schulberg, April 6, 1945, courtesy of Christine O'Sullivan.

342 "I'm particularly impressed with her handling of her terribly bad luck...and scrubs the kitchen floor as if she enjoyed it": Sonya Schulberg O'Sullivan to Ad Schulberg, March 20, 1945, courtesy of Christine O'Sullivan.

342 Peter had finished his officer training...a second lieutenant: P. Viertel, *Dangerous Friends*, p. 12.

342 where his language skills enhanced his service in tactical intelligence operations: ibid., p. 105.

342 Peter's letters home described the wholesale destruction as the Allies bombed Dresden, American troops crossed the Rhine, and the Russians marched into Berlin: *KOS*, p. 282.

342 "The well-known streets were now a bloody, senseless battlefield...bloody dogs were still on the loose": ibid., p. 283.

343 "I had never seen him so happy": ibid.

343 Jigee and Vicky came to join the household when Peter left: ibid., p. 288.

343 "combat fatigue": ibid., p. 282.

343 "I know we are winning the war...but it is as if one had suffered a great personal loss": ibid.

343 Brecht tried to cheer up Salka...to justify their high salaries": ibid., p. 283.

344 "At the end I had to speak...Garbo came and was much noticed but not bothered": ibid., p. 286.

344 At some point before June 1945, Salka accepted a donation of two hundred dollars: Sauter, *Frank, Dieterle, and the European Film Fund*, pp. 150, 202.

344 "He'd been among the most stalwart of the exiles...and had

remained a faithful champion of refugee causes": Bedford, *Aldous Huxley*, pp. 281–282.

344 "was comforted by the thought that he had lived long enough to see the crumbling of the Nazi power": *KOS*, p. 288.

345 "a well-made bad book": quoted by John Simon in review of Jungk, *Franz Werfel*, *New York Times*, April 29, 1990.

345 Salka was glad to see that Werfel . . . had survived to see the Germans surrender: *KOS*, p. 288.

345 "had not been evident in the fates of his fellow writers who, almost without exception, lived at subsistence level": Jungk, *Franz Werfel*, p. 201.

345 "I find it disgusting . . . What a monstrous self-adoration Alma has!": Tagebuch, July 22, 1960, DLAM.

346 "among them my own friends . . . we try to cope with the sins of the past and their reverberations upon the present": *KOS*, p. 289.

9: UN-AMERICANS

347 "The ultimate logic of racism is genocide": Martin Luther King Jr., "The Other America," speech given at Grosse Pointe High School, Grosse Pointe Farms, Michigan, on March 14, 1968. Transcript available at www.gphistorical.org

347 "The Nuremberg Trials were coming to an end . . . haunted me in sleepless nights": *KOS*, p. 294.

348 "but as we are living in a rented place I could not do it . . . I have not heard from him again": ibid.

348 "The German word '*Aktion*' . . . that Dusko was alive": *KOS*, p. 295.

348 An *Aktion* was the National Socialists' name . . . to slave-labor or death camps: Jewish Virtual Library, Holocaust Memorial Center, Zekelman Family Campus, "Aktion."

348 In Sambor all those efforts had occurred at regular intervals . . . and

many suffered from hunger and typhus: Yizkor Books, New York Public Library, "Sambir," p. xxxix. See also www.wikipedia.com, "Sambor Ghetto."

349 In the early morning hours the Gestapo hounded thousands of screaming Jews to the sports square near the railway station: Numbers here vary depending on sources and the definitive numbers may never be known. According to www.deathcamps.org/belzec/galiciatransportlist.html, 6,000 Jews from the county of Sambor, Stary Sambor, Felsztyn, Chyrow, and Strzylki were sent from the sports square on railway trains to Bełżyce. The NYPL Yizkor Books on Sambir say variously "some four thousand" and "some thousand people," while Yitzhak Arad's 1987 work, *Belzec, Sobibor, Treblinka: The Operation Reinhard Death Camps* (Indiana University Press), says 4,000.

349 The second *Aktion*, . . . with another several thousand Jews forcibly removed to Bełżyce: Again, the numbers differ. According to Yitzhak Arad's *Belzec, Sobibor, Treblinka: The Operation Reinhard Death Camps*, the second *Aktion* involved 2,000 Jews on October 17 and 18, with another 2,000 on October 22; the Yizkor Books for Sambir say "thousands" and "about two thousand."

350 On April 14, they brought somewhere around twelve hundred Jews: Numbers are variable according to sources. The Yizkor Books say variously 1,000; 1,200 in April and "over a thousand Jews" in May; other sources say 1,200 or 1,500.

350 The trucks arrived at a wood . . . where all the Jews were shot and killed: NYPL Yizkor Books, Sambir.

350 In a 1931 census, Jews had comprised nearly 29 percent of the population of Sambor: Of the 21,923 total population, the census counted 6,274 Jews, 1,338 ethnic Ukrainians, 1,564 ethnic Ruthenians, and 13,575 ethnic Poles.

350 In the early years of the twentieth century . . . the Jewish orphans of the town continued to be accepted into the city orphanage: Details of Sambor's history and of Josef Steuermann's efforts as mayor are from Yizkor Books, NYPL, "Sambir," p. xvii.

351 Before the war, Salka's brother Dusko had been a star player . . . on the Polish team: ibid., p. xxvi.

352 "I wrote her . . . that she had allied herself with murderers and torturers": *KOS*, p. 295.

353 In 1938, Fred Zinnemann's parents . . . killed in Auschwitz: conversation with Tim Zinnemann.

353 Alfred Döblin learned . . . including his mother: Sauter, *Frank, Dieterle, and the European Film Fund*, p. 193. Information about Franz Waxman's brother and Billy Wilder's family is from Daniel Bernardi, ed., *Hollywood's Chosen People: The Jewish Experience in American Cinema*, Detroit: Wayne State University Press, p. 49.

353 "How can one possibly stand what has been stood by millions and millions of suffering people?" . . . left California to seek psychiatric treatment in Illinois: Crawford, *Windfall of Musicians*, p. 147.

353 On the evening in 1942 after Salka had first learned from the Molotov Report: *KOS*, p. 269.

353 Called "I, the Survivor," . . . his loved ones were dead: ibid., p. 240. Salka quotes the poem in the original German.

354 "I don't want to cook or wash for strangers again . . . Oh, how I would like to have two hours without worrying about anybody": SV to BV, December 20, 1945, call # 78.916/9 and 1945 undated, call # 78.916/10, DLAM.

354 she could no longer write to Rose in Buenos Aires or Edward in New York: *KOS*, p. 295.

354 Salka had to shout to make sure she understood: SV to BV, January 23, 1947, call # 78.917/4, DLAM.

354 Peter had been demobilized: P. Viertel, *Dangerous Friends*, p. 14; *KOS*, p. 288.

354 accompanied by a good friend of Irwin's, the Hungarian photographer Robert Capa: *KOS*, p. 288.

355 "were united in a common front against the European regular guests . . . a flippant remark that provoked only polite laughter at the tea table": P. Viertel, *Dangerous Friends*, p. 60.

355 "my great joy": SV to BV, December 20, 1945, call # 78.916/9, DLAM.

355 Vicky entertained herself . . . in different languages: Vicky Schulberg's recollections of her life on Mabery Road are from a conversation dated July 20, 2014.

355 They found a parcel of nine acres . . . with Vicky by her side holding handfuls of nails: P. Viertel, *Dangerous Friends*, p. 18; *KOS*, p. 291.

356 Vicky ended up again in Salka's care: *KOS*, p. 292.

356 In Switzerland Peter and Jigee learned to ski: P. Viertel, *Dangerous Friends*, pp. 3–4.

356 Tommy had gone off to college . . . and eager to spend his holidays with him: *KOS*, p. 290.

356 Dorothy Thompson's Twin Farms in South Pomfret, Vermont: BV to Virginia Viertel, July 8, 1944, courtesy of Christine O'Sullivan.

356 Isherwood moved into Salka's garage apartment . . . as he loved having sex outside: Isherwood, *Lost Years: A Memoir, 1945–1951*, p. 70.

357 "Salka was always glad to see you," and the following anecdote about Garbo: ibid., pp. 71–72.

357 "thus reviving . . . the old Wychylowka breakfast tradition": *KOS*, p. 291.

357 In 1946–1947 alone . . . "Work is a habit and she lost it": McGilligan, *George Cukor*, p. 182.

358 she immediately hired a Viennese woman . . . she also hired a gardener: *KOS*, p. 293.

358 “a strong and simple story”: ibid.

358 So it wedged *Deep Valley* into its already bustling schedule: www.tcm.com/this-month/article/159662%7C0/Deep-Valley.html.

359 Blanke was keen on *Deep Valley*: “Production Notes for *Deep Valley*,” Warner Bros. Archives.

359 “very nice but deadly boring”: SV to BV, 1945, call # 78.916/10, DLAM.

359 “This is practically a first draft . . . on improving it all the way through”: Henry Blanke to Jack Warner, Interoffice Memo, May 31, 1946, Warner Bros. Archives.

359 “Blanke is nice and not hurrying me”: SV to BV, March 14, 1946, call # 78.917/1, DLAM.

359 Again it’s impossible to determine . . . “Would reward notices for Folsom escapees be posted in a small-town post office?”: *Deep Valley* #669, folder 8056, Warner Bros. Archives.

360 “only goes from week to week” . . . a lien of six thousand dollars on her salary for tax debts: SV to BV, August 16, 1946, call # 78.917/4, DLAM.

360 “will not do anything that requires any courage . . . is also no pleasure but a big star here in the studio”: ibid.

360 “work in the studio was pleasant”: *KOS*, p. 293.

360 *Deep Valley* was his sixty-eighth production for the studio . . . until 1961: “Production Notes for *Deep Valley*,” Warner Bros. Archives.

361 William Dieterle, a friend from his Berlin theater days: Gemünden, *Continental Strangers*, p. 203, fn 9.

361 Through affidavits, Dieterle was instrumental . . . the coordinating force behind the European Film Fund: ibid., p. 203, fn 11.

361 And Blanke was a significant benefactor to the fund . . . and June 1945: Sauter, *Frank, Dieterle, and the European Film Fund*, p. 110.

361 When the EFF reinvented itself after the war . . . and raised money to help insolvent refugees in the U.S. to return to Europe: ibid., p. 252.

361 "They were the descendants of pioneers... long since discarded by the world outside": Dan Totheroh, *Deep Valley*, p. 2.

363 "I've worked 14-16 hours a day in the last 3 years... I am simply dead tired": SV to BV, January 23, 1947, DLAM.

363 "rocked to sleep by the waves"... "That room in which I have been so miserable and so happy... This and Wychylowka": Tagebuch, August 27, 1962, DLAM.

364 "the entrancing, velvety quality of a dream world brought to life": David Thomson, "Jean Negulesco," *New Biographical Dictionary of Film*, p. 699.

365 It was he who so memorably incorporated the "Marseillaise"... along with "As Time Goes By": Noah Isenberg, *We'll Always Have Casablanca*, p. 194.

365 Max Steiner was so busy in the 1940s... finishing both projects in six weeks: Peter Wegele, *Max Steiner: Composing, Casablanca, and the Golden Age of Film Music*, p. 76.

366 "European and American cultures have always been a two-way interchange": Clive James, review of Joseph Horowitz, *Artists in Exile: How Refugees From Twentieth-Century War and Revolution Transformed the American Performing Arts*, *Times Literary Supplement*, July 9, 2008.

366 Irwin Shaw to Salka Viertel, December 9, 1946: courtesy of Adam Shaw.

366 hoping to do what he could to help with Salka's financial problems: P. Viertel, *Dangerous Friends*, pp. 18–19; *KOS*, p. 294.

367 "like a medium size haystack": *KOS*, p. 293.

368 Salka had nearly completed the *Deep Valley* screenplay... went on strike, preventing the use of the studio backlot: Thomas Doherty, *Show Trial: Hollywood, HUAC, and the Birth of the Blacklist*, p. 49.

368 scrambled to move locations from the Warner Ranch to Palos Verdes: "Daily Production and Progress Report," *Deep Valley*, September 27, 1946, to October 12, 1946, Warner Bros. Archives.

368 "swayed them by insisting that the strikers were just a bunch of communists . . . to be against them": *KOS*, p. 296.

368 well after Salka's work at the studio was done: at least through March 1947. The Taft-Hartley Act was passed on June 23, 1947 (Doherty, *Show Trial*, p. 51).

369 the Taft-Hartley Act . . . loyalty oaths disavowing any Communist sympathies: ibid.

369 "the *Gemütlichkeit* when Stalin's staff was dining with their boss": *KOS*, p. 297.

369 Salka may have believed this, but . . . long lines for inadequate supplies of food: "Liquidation of the Jewish Community of Sambor," Yizkor Books, NYPL, p. xxxviii.

369 "Salka is a Communist, Mr. Warner" . . . As no one could deny that anti-Semitism existed in America, the discussion ended: *KOS*, p. 297.

370 The picture did a modest box-office business of $1.4 million: www.wikipedia.com, "*Deep Valley*."

370 "The two of us need very little . . . perhaps I will even dare to try a book": SV to BV, May 23, 1947, call # 78.917/9, DLAM.

371 "the last time I was to work at a major studio, but it took me several years to realize why": *KOS*, p. 297.

371 to the radio broadcasts . . . in Washington: SV to BV, October 3, 1947, call # 78.917/12, DLAM.

371 "The Un-American Committee is giving a great performance . . . could not have done it better and more successfully": ibid.

371 he had rather desultorily joined the party in Germany back in 1926: Doherty, *Show Trial*, p. 90.

372 The former first lady's recommendation on Eisler's behalf . . . who took advantage of American hospitality during the war: ibid., p. 89.

372 "it was too late for Hitler to gas him": ibid., p. 91.

372 "I could well understand it when in 1933 . . . in this ridiculous way": www.eislermusic.com, "Hanns Eisler: A Composer's Life."

373 "I am a guest in this country and do not want to enter into any legal arguments": Doherty, *Show Trial*, p. 283.

373 "The Committee was utterly unprepared for this . . . and even some of Brecht's friends were surprised": *KOS*, p. 302.

373 Three months earlier . . . premiered at the Coronet Theatre on La Cienaga Boulevard: The premiere of *Galileo* took place on July 30, 1947. The Coronet Theatre still exists today.

373 "so that the audience can think": Callow, *Charles Laughton*, p. 188.

374 "I saw Galileo . . . a mixture of megalomania and rank dilettantism": SV to BV, September 1947, call # 78.917/10, DLAM.

375 "As an American citizen of German birth": Mann had become a U.S. citizen in 1944.

375 "What followed was fascism and what followed fascism was war": Thomas Mann, "All-American Opinion on the Un-American Committee," *The Screen Writer*, December 1947, p. 8.

375 "the ritual enactment of a great Constitutional conflict": Doherty, *Show Trial*, p. 103.

376 "the first ones to be denounced and verboten . . . and no sorcerer has been able to banish them": Salka Viertel, "Sorcerer's Apprentice," *The Screen Writer*, December 1947, p. 14.

377 "Democracy is a precious thing . . . I dare to express the hope that the screen shall remain free of the censorship of moronic haters": ibid., p. 15.

378 "It is the beginning of my journalistic career . . . I will probably work in a restaurant if our film project does not come to fruition": SV to BV, December 12, 1947, call # 78.717/11, DLAM.

378 and Laurence Olivier's production company in London: Swenson, *Greta Garbo*, pp. 457–458.

379 "We will not knowingly employ a Communist ... by force or by illegal or unconstitutional methods": Doherty, *Show Trial*, p. 306.

379 failed to establish through its surveillance of her house and activities that she was or had ever been a Communist: Swenson, *Greta Garbo*, p. 457.

379 "Technically she avoided the blacklist ... as long as Salka remained in Hollywood": ibid.

380 She explained in her memoir ... "even ... if it represented 25 percent of the screenplay": *KOS*, p. 312.

380 "I don't have any credit in the Jean Renoir movie, political reasons": Prager, "*Ich bin*," p. 252, quoting SV to BV, July 22, 1951, DLAM.

380 "Financially it is bleak ... I'm going to starve to death": Prager, "*Ich bin*," p. 252, quoting SV to BV, March 23, 1953 and August 1, 1953, DLAM.

381 "like a second emigration, ... and scarred by a horrible disease": *KOS*, p. 306.

381 "Thirty years ago, when I married you ... Nothing will ever change that": ibid., pp. 306–307.

381 "You must know that I consider this formality ... If only you were happier" ... "I never had the temperament nor the leisure to become aware of it": ibid., p. 308.

383 "There are no words to describe what this place looks like ... The people here pick up exactly where they left off in 1928": ibid., p. 310.

384 "the major disagreement between Berthold and me ... the anti-Semitic, false, corny city of Gemütlichkeit": SV to S. N. Behrman, March 2, 1965, Behrman Archives, NYPL.

384 a diligent father figure to twenty-four-year-old Tommy who was sorely missing Berthold: *KOS*, p. 309.

384 "Fascism is here": SV to BV, June 24, 1950, call # 78.918/7, DLAM.

384 "I couldn't give a damn about freedom of the press . . . But any government is preferable to the one we have here": SV to BV, July 22, 1950, call # 78.918/8, DLAM.

385 "seek my fortune or my living there but Mama is weak . . . Sometimes I think, Thank God!": SV to BV, January 27, 1948, call # 78.918/1, DLAM.

385 bailed out at the last minute by loans from Donald Ogden Stewart and Charlie Chaplin: *KOS*, p. 313.

385 James Agee, who sat at the piano and played Schubert: ibid., p. 316.

385 for a trio of Peruvian performers . . . John Huston, and John Houseman: Isherwood, *Diaries, Volume One*, p. 425.

386 For the actor Montgomery Clift, off-putting to many who met him socially: Isherwood, *Lost Years*, p. 174.

386 "He always presses his sex towards me when he embraces me like Francesco": Tagebuch, August 22, 1957, DLAM.

386 was not above kissing them impetuously on the lips: conversation with Chester Aaron.

386 "necking in a rather sexual manner": Shelley Winters quoted in Michelangelo Capua, *Montgomery Clift: A Biography*, p. 53.

386 Once a week Salka picked up fifteen-year-old Arianne . . . the girl's hopeless American diction: conversation with Arianne Ulmer Cipes, February 4, 2014.

386 "Now say *faaaaaaahzer* . . .": conversation with Elizabeth Frank.

387 At sixty-three she still drove recklessly around the canyon: *KOS*, p. 314.

387 who was full of resentment at being taken for a Nazi when anyone could see that he was very nearly a martyr: Palmier, *Weimar in Exile*, p. 637, citing Klaus Mann, *The Turning Point*.

388 "I do not wish to survive this year": Frederic Spotts, *Cursed Legacy:*

The Tragic Life of Klaus Mann; and www.spartacus-educational.com, "Klaus Mann," citing diary entry by Klaus Mann, January 1, 1949.

388 that he might become a propaganda tool of the German Democratic Republic: Anthony Heilbut, ed., *Letters of Thomas and Heinrich Mann*, p. xvii.

388 "the most merciful outcome": Palmier, *Weimar in Exile*, p. 633; and Thomas Mann, "Letter on the Death of My Brother Heinrich," *Germanic Review*, December 1950.

388 and asked Salka to take her to his funeral: *KOS*, p. 316.

388 "He would have approved": Thomas Mann, "Letter on the Death of My Brother Heinrich."

388 "Hollywood did not recognize his genius and only very few attended his funeral": *KOS*, p. 316.

389 Ilse managed to sell two of her scripts: ibid., p. 313.

389 refusing to acknowledge that Salka was on any kind of blacklist: ibid., p. 315.

389 Vicky enrolled in a Swiss school: ibid., p. 317.

389 on the day of Salka and Berthold's wedding anniversary: ibid., p. 318.

389 "I am terribly sorry for Peter and Jigee . . . that she has inherited your lioness's strength": ibid.

390 Irwin Shaw to Salka Viertel, January 8, 1953: courtesy of Adam Shaw.

391 "At the horrible moment when one had to leave her in this foreign earth . . . many Negroes and German refugees and young Americans": *KOS*, p. 321.

392 Berthold at age sixty-eight had recently been hospitalized: ibid., p. 318.

392 "because it supported the fight against fascism": ibid., p. 326.

392 "He had been my constant companion . . . The shackles of love were falling off": ibid., p. 327.

393 "Berthold died last night": ibid., p. 330.

393 Hans arrived in Vienna . . . but in time to carry him to his grave: P. Viertel, *Dangerous Friends*, p. 195.

394 "He was the mainspring of my life . . . I am catching myself writing *to* him and *for* him": SV to S. N. Behrman, January 30, 1964, Behrman Archives, NYPL.

394 where he had declared with absolute certainty that he was going to marry her: *KOS*, p. 323.

395 in a hospital in White Plains, with no visitors allowed: ibid., p. 331.

395 "The name Mendelssohn obliges": ibid., p. 299.

395 "compassionate, unchanged, and very dear": ibid., p. 331.

395 "Gruscha" or "Miss G": from an unpublished reminiscence by Jack Larson, courtesy of Vicky Schulberg.

395 "Ernest C.": *KOS*, pp. 331–332.

395 "the list of my sins . . . as thick as the New York telephone book": ibid., p. 333.

395 Had she said that she'd prefer *any form of government* to the one in the United States?: ibid.

395 FBI agents had been opening her mail since the early 1940s: Stephan, *"Communazis,"* pp. 194–197, see especially p. 195.

396 he had regained his Austrian citizenship . . . or a threat to the nation: ibid., p. 197.

396 would give up her home by the Pacific for good, selling it to John Houseman: John Houseman, *Front and Center*, p. 447.

396 "It would be wonderful to know . . . is a happy home for you and your family": SV to John Houseman, December 1, 1953, John Houseman Papers, Box 6, Folder V, UCLA, quoted in Saverio Giovacchini, *Hollywood Modernism: Film and Politics in the Age of the New Deal*, p. 189.

397 The two women lit the candles on a tiny Christmas tree: *KOS*, p. 334.

10: HOME

400 She rented an apartment on Veteran Avenue in Westwood: Isherwood, *Diaries, Volume One*, p. 467.

400 After she left London, Salka traveled with Hans and Violette . . . *Prisoner of the Volga*: ibid., p. 590.

400 Violette reluctantly agreed to accompany her: the descriptions of Salka's and Violette's trip to Dachau are courtesy of Violette Viertel in a letter to me dated March 9, 2013.

401 "The world is certainly not big enough for the Jews . . . only the gas chambers were big enough": Tagebuch, July 16, 1957, DLAM.

402 "a small female family" . . . "held together by our love for Christine": ibid.

402 "the last grand passion of my life": SV to S. N. Behrman, 1957 undated, Behrman Archives, NYPL.

402 "I am an old woman . . . it is all my present life": Tagebuch, June 14, 1959, DLAM.

403 "my heart bled. Nothing is so terrible to watch than the human degradation of an addict": Tagebuch, August 1, 1959, DLAM.

403 "from falling down while drunk": Isherwood, *Diaries, Volume One*, p. 819.

403 "I went to see her at the hospital Sunday the 24th of January . . . which I noticed in Mama's eyes before she died": Tagebuch, February 24, 1960, DLAM.

404 Before dawn on February 1, 1960, age forty-four, Jigee died: Nancy Lynn Schwartz, *The Hollywood Writers' Wars*, p. 299; Tagebuch, February 23, 1960, DLAM: "Virginia died . . . on January 31st. No—Feb. 1 4:30 a.m."

404 "She was such an audience for me . . . And now there is nothing left of her": Tagebuch, March 5, 1960, DLAM.

404 "she would have suffered beyond words . . . The whole population turning out to wish Peter happiness with another woman": Tagebuch, July 22, 1960, DLAM.

405 the "utter honesty" of Jigee's decline: Tagebuch, September 5, 1962, DLAM.

407 and told Sam Behrman in confidence that her purpose for moving to Klosters . . . had been crushed when the girl was sent away to school: SV to S. N. Behrman, January 18, 1968, Behrman Archives, NYPL.

407 "I never ceased regretting that I sold 165 Mabery Road": SV to Vicky Schulberg, February 27, 1969.

407 "I remember how she sat in my kitchen . . . BUT she has courage and this I admire": Tagebuch, March 31, 1963, DLAM.

408 "The first sentences I put on paper are always horrible": Tagebuch, February 3, 1963, DLAM.

408 "I don't want you to think, Darling, that I was kissed by the Muse ten to twelve hours a day": SV to S. N. Behrman, August 16, 1966, Behrman Archives, NYPL.

408 "This is a *secret*, don't mention it yet to anybody": ibid.

408 "The only thing I can leave to my granddaughters": SV to S. N. Behrman, July 22, 1965, Behrman Archives, NYPL.

408 "The content is not gossipy enough . . . To hell with them": Tagebuch, April 6, 1962, DLAM.

409 "politically irreproachable": SV to S. N. Behrman, March 29, 1963, Behrman Archives, NYPL.

409 "American, martini-addicted Madison Avenue editor" . . . met instead a sympathetic Viennese-born Jewish intellectual: SV to S. N. Behrman, October 23, 1967, Behrman Archives, NYPL.

409 "although he himself is not a pleasant man": SV to S. N. Behrman, October 14, 1967, Behrman Archives, NYPL.

410 “Couldn’t you have had those three in one day?”: S. N Behrman to SV, August 25, 1967, Behrman Archives, NYPL.

410 “he is such a Puritan”: SV to S. N. Behrman, December 14, 1966, Behrman Archives, NYPL.

410 “One governess and the menstruation are already out”: SV to S. N. Behrman, October 23, 1967, Behrman Archives, NYPL.

410 “Wallace’s Follies”: conversation with Tom Wallace, September 30, 2018.

410 “although I don’t think I will get rich . . . and make it a best seller”: SV to S. N. Behrman, January 18, 1968, Behrman Archives, NYPL.

410 Isherwood, who praised the book for maintaining a clear narrative line . . . tended to dissolve into crowds of people: SV to S. N. Behrman, December 3, 1968, Behrman Archives, NYPL.

410 “in spite of the filthy young people . . . I love and cherish in my ‘adopted country’”: SV to S. N. Behrman, July 3, 1969, Behrman Archives, NYPL.

410 “the middle-aged ones go around in such fantastic costumes that they reminded me of Purim in Sambor . . . unbelievable how dirty people are”: SV to S. N. Behrman, November 19, 1968, Behrman Archives, NYPL.

411 “She was not a person of pretense . . . and make you feel important”: memories of Salka are from an email to me from Valérie Viertel.

411 “Everyone, even only fleeting acquaintances” . . . “spontaneity and especially generosity”: Carl Zuckmayer, foreword to Salka Viertel, *Das unbelehrbare Herz: Ein Leben in der Welt des Theaters, der Literatur und des Films* (Claassen Verlag, 1970).

411 The publication of *Kindness* brought all kinds of correspondence to Salka . . . to complete strangers: SV to S. N. Behrman, July 3, 1969, Behrman Archives, NYPL.

412 “all the Poles and Ruthenians had been deported (or killed) during

the Stalin era . . . a party functionary of course": SV to S. N. Behrman, December 22, 1971, Behrman Archives, NYPL.

412 "the tenacity is there": Tom Viertel to Vicky Schulberg, September 7, 1975, courtesy of Vicky Schulberg.

412 "this gift of love, this passion for life . . . all the rest would be vanity": Harold Clurman, "Salka's Incorrigible Heart," *The Nation*, May 5, 1969.

412 "is what you did *not* say": Marta Feuchtwanger to SV, August 1, 1969, DLAM.

413 "One knows the working world of Hollywood only from the perspective of glorification or satire, of worship or disgust": Zuckmayer, foreword to *Das unbelehrbare Herz.*

413 "Without Salka's mind and bravery . . . would never have been made": ibid.

414 "was two years old when he left Europe . . . means to him and his wife": SV to S. N. Behrman, April 19, 1971, Behrman Archives, NYPL.

415 They threw a little party for Salka . . . she was taken aback to see that a swimming pool had replaced her rose garden: conversation with Judi Davidson, August 29, 2011.

415 "so shaky and deaf and it is sadly dreary and exhausting being with her . . . understanding what you're saying": Isherwood, *Liberation: Diaries, 1970–1983*, p. 410.

415 "The intricate tortures of old age make me indignant": SV to S. N. Behrman, February 17, 1973, Behrman Archives, NYPL.

415 Salka had reacted badly to the drugs . . . "She asked for her comb and slowly and painfully she combed and brushed her hair to receive the gentlemen": James Bridges to Katharine Hepburn, February 8, 1975, "Bridges, James 1974–1994," 59.f-740, Katharine Hepburn papers, Margaret Herrick Library, Academy of Motion Picture Arts and Sciences.

416 "The new medication seems to work and I am less shaking and stronger . . . for Americans living in foreign countries": SV to Vicky Schulberg, January 22, 1976.

416 "The mere fact that I need a nurse is depressing beyond words": SV to Vicky Schulberg, February 18, 1977.

416 "What a dreary way to wait for death": James Bridges to Katharine Hepburn, February 8, 1975, Margaret Herrick Library.

416 "made me homesick for my youth . . . my father liked apples very much and had all kinds of them": SV to Vicky Schulberg, October 31, 1977.

417 *The sunsets at Wychylowka were blue and golden in summer, and purple-red in winter*: *KOS*, p. 2.

417 *There were hundreds of fruit trees in the orchard*: ibid., p. 3.

417 *Papa is feeding Viktoria corn kernels out of his palm as if she were a little bird*: ibid., p. 295: "it was the same little Viktoria, who in her nightshirt had followed me to Papa's room and climbed on his bed and like a bird ate the corn kernels from his hand."

417 *Darling Vick, when I think of my youth in Sambor . . . under the supervision of my Niania*: SV to Vicky Schulberg, May 8, 1976.

417 *I also remember the peacocks promenading in the garden*: SV to Vicky Schulberg, March 17, 1971.

417 *When I remember the beach in Santa Monica . . . and melting into the foam of the waves*: Tagebuch, September 5, 1962, DLAM.

417 *In 1921 I was bringing the children to Dresden from Wychylowka . . . so much jam that my boys were covered in raspberries*: *KOS*, p. 97.

418 Telegram to Fred Zinnemann in London from Klosters, October 27, 1978: Peter Viertel to Fred Zinnemann, Fred Zinnemann papers, Margaret Herrick Library, Academy of Motion Picture Arts and Sciences.

BIBLIOGRAPHY

Adorno, Theodor W. *Letters to His Parents, 1939–1951*. Cambridge, UK: Polity Press, 2006.

Anderson, Mark M., ed. *Hitler's Exiles: Personal Stories of the Flight from Nazi Germany to America*. New York: New Press, 1998.

Anger, Kenneth. *Hollywood Babylon*. New York: Dell, 1975.

Bach, Steven. *Marlene Dietrich: Life and Legend*. New York: William Morrow, 1992.

Bachardy, Don. *Stars in My Eyes*. Madison: University of Wisconsin Press, 2000.

Bahr, Ehrhard. *Weimar on the Pacific: German Exile Culture in Los Angeles and the Culture of Modernism*. Oakland: University of California Press, 2007.

Banham, Reyner. *Los Angeles: The Architecture of Four Ecologies*. London: Allen Lane, 1971.

Bankhead, Tallulah. *My Autobiography*. New York: Harper, 1952.

Barron, Stephanie, Sabine Eckmann, and Matthew Affron. *Exiles and Émigrés*. Catalogue for LACMA's 1997 exhibition. New York: Harry N. Abrams, 1997.

Barton, Ruth. *Hedy Lamarr: The Most Beautiful Woman in Film*. Lexington: University Press of Kentucky, 2010.

Basinger, Jeanine. *The Star Machine*. New York: Knopf, 2007.

Basten, Fred E. *Santa Monica Bay: The First 100 Years: A Pictorial History of Santa Monica, Venice, Ocean Park, Marina del Rey, Pacific Palisades, Topanga & Malibu*. Los Angeles: Douglas-West, 1974.

Baum, Vicki. *It Was All Quite Different*. New York: Funk & Wagnalls, 1964.

Beaton, Cecil. *Memoirs of the 40s*. New York: McGraw-Hill, 1972.

Beauchamp, Cari. *Without Lying Down: Frances Marion and the Women of Early Hollywood*. Oakland: University of California Press, 1997.

———, ed. *My First Time in Hollywood*. Los Angeles: Asahina & Wallace, 2015.

Bedford, Sybille. *Aldous Huxley: A Biography*. New York: Knopf, 1974.

———. *Jigsaw: An Unsentimental Education*. New York: Knopf, 1989.

———. *Quicksands: A Memoir*. Berkeley, CA: Counterpoint, 2005.

Behrman, S. N. *People in a Diary*. Boston: Little, Brown, 1972.

Belletti, Valeria. *Adventures of a Hollywood Secretary: Her Private Letters from Inside the Studios of the 1920s*. Edited by Cari Beauchamp. Oakland: University of California Press, 2006.

Berg, A. Scott. *Goldwyn: A Biography*. New York: Knopf, 1989.

Bergan, Ronald. *Sergei Eisenstein: A Life in Conflict*. New York: Overlook, 1999.

Berger, Doris. *Light & Noir: Exiles and Émigrés in Hollywood, 1933–1950*. Catalogue for the Skirball Cultural Center's 2015 exhibition in Los Angeles.

Bergstrom, Janet. "Murnau in America: Chronicle of Lost Films." *Film History* 14 (2002): 430–460. www.jstor.org/stable/3815442.

Bernstein, Matthew. *Walter Wanger: Hollywood Independent*. Berkeley: University of California Press, 1994.

Bilski, Emily D., and Emily Braun. *Jewish Women and Their Salons: The*

Power of Conversation. Catalogue from the Jewish Museum's 2005 exhibition in New York. New Haven, CT: Yale University Press with the Jewish Museum, 2005.

Bingen, Stephen, Michael Troyan, and Stephen X. Sylvester. *MGM: Hollywood's Greatest Backlot.* Solana Beach, CA: Santa Monica Press, 2011.

Braudy, Leo. *The Hollywood Sign: Fantasy and Reality of a Hollywood Icon.* New Haven, CT: Yale University Press, 2011.

Brecht, Bertolt. *Poems 1913–1956.* New York: Methuen, 1976.

Breitman, Richard, and Allan J. Lichtman. *FDR and the Jews.* Cambridge, MA: Belknap/Harvard University Press, 2013.

Brook, Vincent. *Driven to Darkness: Jewish Émigré Directors and the Rise of Film Noir.* New Brunswick, NJ: Rutgers University Press, 2009.

Buckley, Veronica. *Christina, Queen of Sweden: The Restless Life of a European Eccentric.* New York: Fourth Estate/HarperCollins, 2004.

Callow, Simon. *Charles Laughton: A Difficult Actor.* New York: Grove/Atlantic, 1988.

Capua, Michelangelo. *Montgomery Clift: A Biography.* Jefferson, NC: McFarland, 2002.

Carr, Steven Alan. *Hollywood and Anti-Semitism: A Cultural History up to World War II.* Cambridge, UK: Cambridge University Press, 2001.

Ceplair, Larry, and Steven Englund. *The Inquisition in Hollywood: Politics in the Film Community, 1930–1960.* New York: Anchor/Doubleday, 1980.

Chandler, Charlotte. *Nobody's Perfect: Billy Wilder, A Personal Biography.* New York: Simon & Schuster, 2002.

Chaplin, Charles. *My Autobiography.* New York: Simon & Schuster, 1964.

Collier, John. *Fancies and Goodnights.* New York: Doubleday, 1951.

Connolly, Cyril. *The Unquiet Grave.* New York: Harper, 1945.

Crawford, Dorothy Lamb. *A Windfall of Musicians: Hitler's Émigrés and Exiles in Southern California.* New Haven, CT: Yale University Press, 2009.

Crowe, Cameron. *Conversations with Wilder.* New York: Knopf, 1999.

Dawidowicz, Lucy S. *The War Against the Jews 1933–1945.* New York: Holt, Rinehart & Winston, 1975.

De Acosta, Mercedes. *Here Lies the Heart.* New York: Viking-Reynal, 1960.

De Waal, Edmund. *The Hare with Amber Eyes.* New York: Farrar, Straus & Giroux, 2010.

Doherty, Thomas. *Projections of War: Hollywood, American Culture, and World War II.* New York: Columbia University Press, 1993.

______. *Hollywood's Censor: Joseph I. Breen and the Production Code Administration.* New York: Columbia University Press, 2007.

______. *Hollywood and Hitler 1933–1950.* New York: Columbia University Press, 2013.

______. *Show Trial: Hollywood, HUAC, and the Birth of the Blacklist.* New York: Columbia University Press, 2018.

Edwards, Anne. *Leaving Home: A Hollywood Blacklisted Writer's Years Abroad.* Lanham, MD: Scarecrow Press, 2012.

Eisner, Lotte. *The Haunted Screen: Expressionism in the German Cinema and the Influence of Max Reinhardt.* Berkeley: University of California Press, 1969.

______. *Murnau.* Berkeley: University of California Press, 1973.

Epstein, Leslie. *Pandaemonium.* New York: St. Martin's, 1998.

______. *San Remo Drive.* New York: Handsel/Other Press, 2003.

Ewen, Frederic. *Bertolt Brecht: His Life, His Art, His Times.* New York: Citadel Press, 1967.

Eyman, Scott. *Ernst Lubitsch: Laughter in Paradise.* New York: Simon & Schuster, 1993.

______. *The Speed of Sound: Hollywood and the Talkie Revolution.* New York: Simon & Schuster, 1997.

______. *Print the Legend: The Life and Times of John Ford.* New York: Simon & Schuster, 1999.

———. *Lion of Hollywood: The Life and Legend of Louis B. Mayer.* New York: Simon & Schuster, 2005.

Feisst, Sabine. *Schoenberg's New World: The American Years.* New York: Oxford University Press, 2011.

Fest, Joachim C. *Hitler.* New York: Harcourt Brace Jovanovich, 1974.

———. *Not I.* New York: Other Press, 2012.

Feuchtwanger, Lion. *The Oppermanns.* London: M. Secker, 1933.

———. *Moscow 1937.* New York: Viking, 1937.

———. *Paris Gazette (Exil).* New York: Viking, 1940.

———. *The Devil in France: My Encounter with Him in the Summer of 1940.* New York: Viking, 1941.

Feuchtwanger, Marta. *An Émigré Life: Munich, Berlin, Sanary, Pacific Palisades.* Los Angeles: Oral History Project, University of California, 1976.

Fittko, Lisa. *Escape through the Pyrenees.* Evanston, IL: Northwestern University Press, 1991.

Fitzgerald, F. Scott. "Crazy Sunday." *American Mercury,* October 1932.

———. *The Pat Hobby Stories.* New York: Scribner, 1962.

———. *The Last Tycoon.* New York: Cambridge University Press, 1993 reprint.

Flügge, Manfred. *Fry, Bingham, Sharp: The Americans Who Saved Lion and Marta Feuchtwanger.* Los Angeles: Villa Aurora, 2016.

Ford, Elizabeth A., and Deborah C. Mitchell. *Royal Portraits in Hollywood: Filming the Lives of Queens.* Lexington: University Press of Kentucky, 2009.

Frank, Elizabeth. *Cheat and Charmer.* New York: Random House, 2004.

Frankel, Glenn. *High Noon: The Hollywood Blacklist and the Making of an American Classic.* New York: Bloomsbury, 2017.

Freeman, Judith. *The Long Embrace: Raymond Chandler and the Woman He Loved.* New York: Pantheon, 2007.

Friedländer, Saul. *When Memory Comes.* New York: Farrar, Straus & Giroux, 1979.

______. *Where Memory Leads: My Life.* New York: Other Press, 2016.

Friedrich, Otto. *Before the Deluge: A Portrait of Berlin in the 1920s.* New York: Harper & Row, 1972.

______. *City of Nets: A Portrait of Hollywood in the 1940s.* New York: HarperCollins, 1986.

Fry, Varian. *Surrender on Demand.* New York: Random House, 1945.

Fuchs, Daniel. *The Golden West: Hollywood Stories.* Boston: Black Sparrow/David R. Godine, 2005.

Führer, Karl Christian, and Corey Ross, eds. *Mass Media, Culture and Society in Twentieth-Century Germany.* Hampshire, UK: Palgrave Macmillan, 2006.

Gabler, Neal. *An Empire of Their Own: How the Jews Invented Hollywood.* New York: Crown, 1988.

Gay, Peter. *Weimar Culture: The Outsider as Insider.* New York: Norton, 1968.

Gemünden, Gerd. *Continental Strangers: German Exile Cinema 1933–1951.* New York: Columbia University Press, 2014.

Giovacchini, Saverio. *Hollywood Modernism: Film and Politics in the Age of the New Deal.* Philadelphia: Temple University Press, 2001.

Gödde, Christoph, and Thomas Sprecher. *Adorno-Mann Correspondence 1943–1955.* Cambridge, UK: Polity Books, 2006.

Granach, Alexander. *There Goes an Actor.* New York: Doubleday, Doran, 1945.

Grobel, Lawrence. *The Hustons.* New York: Scribner, 1989.

Grosz, George. *A Little Yes and A Big No.* Illustrated by the author. New York: Dial, 1946.

Haidt, Jonathan. *The Righteous Mind: Why Good People Are Divided by Politics and Religion.* New York: Pantheon, 2012.

Hamilton, Nigel. *The Brothers Mann: The Lives of Heinrich and Thomas Mann, 1871–1950 and 1875–1955.* New Haven, CT: Yale University Press, 1979.

Hampton, Christopher. *Tales from Hollywood.* London: Faber & Faber, 1984.

Harmetz, Aljean. *Round Up the Usual Suspects: The Making of* Casablanca—*Bogart, Bergman, and World War II.* New York: Hyperion, 1992.

Harris, Mark. *Five Came Back: A Story of Hollywood and the Second World War.* New York: Penguin, 2014.

Hart, Moss. *Act One.* New York: Random House, 1959.

Haskell, Molly. *From Reverence to Rape: The Treatment of Women in the Movies.* New York: Holt, Rinehart & Winston, 1974.

Hay, Peter. *MGM: When the Lion Roars.* Kansas City, MO: Turner Publishing, 1991.

Hecht, Ben. *A Child of the Century.* New York: Simon & Schuster, 1954.

Heilbut, Anthony. *Exiled in Paradise: German Refugee Artists and Intellectuals in America from the 1930s to the Present.* Berkeley: University of California Press, 1983.

______. *Thomas Mann: Eros and Literature.* New York: Knopf, 1996.

Heller, Erich. *The Ironic German: A Study of Thomas Mann.* Boston: Little, Brown, 1958.

Henreid, Paul. *Ladies Man: An Autobiography.* New York: St. Martin's, 1984.

Higham, Charles. *Charles Laughton: An Intimate Biography.* New York: Doubleday, 1976.

Hill, Erin. *Never Done: A History of Women's Work in Media Production.* New Brunswick, NJ: Rutgers University Press, 2016.

Hirschhorn, Clive. *The Warner Brothers Story.* New York: Crown, 1979.

Hoberman, J., and Jeffrey Shandler. *Entertaining America: Jews, Movies, and Broadcasting.* Princeton, NJ: Princeton University Press, 2003.

Horak, Jan-Christopher. "The Palm Trees Were Gently Swaying: German Refugees from Hitler in Hollywood." *Image* 23, no. 1 (1980).

Horak, Laura. *Girls Will Be Boys: Cross-Dressed Women, Lesbians, and American Cinema, 1908–1934.* New Brunswick, NJ: Rutgers University Press, 2016.

Houseman, John. *Front and Center.* New York: Simon & Schuster, 1979.

———. *Unfinished Business.* London: Columbus Books, 1986.

Huston, Anjelica. *A Story Lately Told: Coming of Age in Ireland, London, and New York.* New York: Simon & Schuster, 2013.

Huston, John. *An Open Book.* New York: Knopf, 1980.

Huxley, Aldous. *After Many a Summer Dies the Swan.* New York: Harper, 1939.

———. *Selected Letters.* New York: Ivan R. Dee, 2007.

Huxley, Laura. *This Timeless Moment: A Personal View of Aldous Huxley.* Berkeley, CA: Ten Speed Press, 1975.

Isenberg, Noah. *Edgar G. Ulmer: A Filmmaker at the Margins.* Berkeley: University of California Press, 2014.

———. *We'll Always Have Casablanca: The Life, Legend, and Afterlife of Hollywood's Most Beloved Movie.* New York: Norton, 2017.

Isenberg, Sheila. *A Hero of Our Own: The Story of Varian Fry.* New York: Random House, 2001.

Isherwood, Christopher. *The Berlin Stories.* New York: New Directions, 1945.

———. *Prater Violet.* New York: Random House, 1945.

———. *A Single Man.* New York: Simon & Schuster, 1964.

———. *Christopher and His Kind: 1929–1939.* New York: Farrar, Straus & Giroux, 1976.

———. *Diaries, Volume One, 1939–1960.* London: Vintage, 1997.

———. *Lost Years: A Memoir, 1945–1951.* London: Chatto & Windus, 2000.

———. *The Sixties: Diaries, 1960–1969.* London: Chatto & Windus, 2010.

———. *Liberation: Diaries, 1970–1983.* London: Chatto & Windus, 2012.

Jelavich, Peter. *Berlin Cabaret.* Cambridge, MA: Harvard University Press, 1993.

Juers, Evelyn. *House of Exile.* New York: Farrar, Straus & Giroux, 2011.

Jungk, Peter Stephan. *Franz Werfel: A Life in Prague, Vienna, and Hollywood.* New York: Grove/Weidenfeld, 1990.

Kahn, Lothar. *Insight and Action: The Life and Work of Lion Feuchtwanger.* Madison, NJ: Fairleigh Dickinson University Press, 1975.

Kanin, Garson. *Hollywood: Stars and Starlets, Tycoons and Flesh-Peddlers, Moviemakers and Moneymakers, Frauds and Geniuses, Hopefuls and Has-Beens, Great Lovers and Sex Symbols.* New York: Viking, 1974.

Kanon, Joseph. *Stardust.* New York: Atria Books, 2009.

Kazan, Elia. *A Life.* New York: Knopf, 1988.

Kemper, Tom. *Hidden Talent: The Emergence of Hollywood Agents.* Berkeley: University of California Press, 2009.

Klemperer, Victor. *I Will Bear Witness: A Diary of the Nazi Years, 1933–1941.* New York: Random House, 1998.

———. *The Language of the Third Reich: LTI: Lingua Tertii Imperii: A Philologist's Notebook.* London: Athlone Press, 2000.

Kohner, Frederick. *The Magician of Sunset Boulevard: The Improbable Life of Paul Kohner, Hollywood Agent.* Palos Verdes, CA: Morgan Press, 1977.

Korda, Michael. *Charmed Lives: A Family Romance.* New York: Random House, 1979.

Kracauer, Siegfried. *From Caligari to Hitler: A Psychological History of the German Film.* Princeton, NJ: Princeton University Press, 1947.

Kreimeier, Klaus. *The Ufa Story.* New York: Hill & Wang, 1996.

Lally, Kevin. *Wilder Times: The Life of Billy Wilder.* New York: Henry Holt, 1996.

Lambert, Gavin. *The Slide Area: Scenes of Hollywood Life.* New York: Viking, 1959.

———. *Inside Daisy Clover.* New York: Viking, 1963.

———. *On Cukor.* New York: Putnam, 1972.

———. *Norma Shearer, A Biography.* New York: Knopf, 1990.

———, ed. *The Ivan Moffat File: Life Among the Beautiful and Damned in London, Paris, New York, and Hollywood.* New York: Pantheon, 2004.

Landy, Marcia, and Amy Villarejo. *Queen Christina.* London: BFI Film Classics, 1995.

Lardner Jr., Ring. *I'd Hate Myself in the Morning.* New York: Nation Books, 2000.

Larson, Erik. *In the Garden of Beasts: Love, Terror, and an American Family in Hitler's Berlin.* New York: Crown, 2011.

Laurents, Arthur. *Original Story By: A Memoir of Broadway and Hollywood.* New York: Applause Books, 2000.

Levant, Oscar. *Memoirs of an Amnesiac.* New York: Putnam, 1965.

Lloyd, Norman. *Stages.* Lanham, MD: Scarecrow Press, 1990.

Lookstein, Haskel. *Were We Our Brothers' Keepers? The Public Response of American Jews to the Holocaust, 1938–1941.* Bridgeport, CT: Hartmore House, 1985.

Lord, Rosemary. *Hollywood Then and Now.* San Diego: Thunder Bay Press, 2003.

Luhrssen, David. *Mamoulian: Life on Stage and Screen.* Lexington: University Press of Kentucky, 2013.

Mahler Werfel, Anna. *And the Bridge Is Love.* New York: Harcourt Brace, 1958.

Mann, Erika. *The Last Year of Thomas Mann.* Translated by Richard Graves. New York: Farrar, Straus & Cudahy, 1958.

Mann, Katia. *Unwritten Memories.* New York: Knopf, 1958.

Mann, Klaus, and Hermann Kesten, eds. *Best of Modern European Literature 1920–1940.* Philadelphia: Blakiston Company, 1945.

Mann, Thomas. *The Story of a Novel: The Genesis of Doctor Faustus.* New York: Knopf, 1961.

———. *Diaries.* New York: Harry N. Abrams, 1982.

———. *Letters of Heinrich and Thomas Mann, 1900–1949.* Edited by Hans Wysling. Berkeley: University of California Press, 1998.

Mann, William J. *Behind the Screen: How Gays and Lesbians Shaped Hollywood 1910–1969.* New York: Viking, 2001.

Marino, Andy. *A Quiet American: The Secret War of Varian Fry.* New York: St. Martin's, 1999.

Marquez, Ernest. *Santa Monica Beach: A Collector's Pictorial History.* Santa Monica, CA: Angel City Press, 2004.

McGilligan, Patrick. *George Cukor: A Double Life.* New York: St. Martin's, 1991.

McLellan, Diana. *The Girls: Sappho Goes to Hollywood.* New York: St. Martin's, 2000.

Mérigeau, Pascal. *Jean Renoir: A Biography.* Philadelphia: Running Press, 2017.

Müller-Doohm, Stefan. *Adorno: A Biography.* Cambridge, UK: Polity Press, 2005.

Murray, Nicholas. *Aldous Huxley: A Biography.* New York: St. Martin's, 2003.

Navasky, Victor. *Naming Names.* New York: Viking, 1980.

Negulesco, Jean. *Things I Did and Things I Think I Did.* New York: Simon & Schuster, 1984.

Norman, Marc. *What Happens Next: A History of American Screenwriting.* New York: Crown Archetype, 2007.

O'Brien, Darcy. *A Way of Life, Like Any Other.* New York: Norton, 1978.

Orlean, Susan. *Rin Tin Tin.* New York: Simon & Schuster, 2011.

Palmier, Jean-Michel. *Weimar in Exile: The Antifascist Emigration in Europe and America.* London: Verso, 2006.

Paris, Barry. *Garbo.* New York: Knopf, 1994.

Parker, Peter. *Isherwood: A Life Revealed.* New York: Random House, 2004.

Parrish, Robert. *Growing Up in Hollywood.* New York: Harcourt Brace Jovanovich, 1976.

———. *Hollywood Doesn't Live Here Anymore.* Boston: Little, Brown, 1987.

Pauli, Hertha. *Break of Time.* New York: Hawthorn Books, 1971.

Pizzitola, Louis. *Hearst Over Hollywood: Power, Passion, and Propaganda in the Movies.* New York: Columbia University Press, 2002.

Prager, Katharina. *"Ich bin nicht gone Hollywood!": Salka Viertel—Ein Leben in Theater und Film.* Vienna: Braumüller, 2007.

Prochnik, George. *The Impossible Exile.* New York: Other Press, 2014.

Reinhardt, Gottfried. *The Genius: A Memoir of Max Reinhardt.* New York: Knopf, 1979.

Remarque, Erich Maria. *The Night in Lisbon.* New York: Harcourt Brace & World, 1964.

———. *Shadows in Paradise.* New York: Harcourt Brace Jovanovich, 1972.

Robinson, Edward G. *All My Yesterdays.* New York: Hawthorn Books, 1973.

Rosenzweig, Laura B. *Hollywood's Spies: The Undercover Surveillance of Nazis in Los Angeles.* New York: New York University Press, 2017.

Ross, Alex. *The Rest Is Noise: Listening to the Twentieth Century.* New York: Farrar, Straus & Giroux, 2007.

Ross, Lillian. *Picture.* New York: Rinehart, 1952.

———. *Moments with Chaplin.* New York: Dodd, Mead, 1980.

Ross, Steven J. *Hollywood Left and Right.* New York: Oxford University Press, 2011.

———. *Hitler in Los Angeles: How Jews Foiled Nazi Plots Against Hollywood and America.* New York: Bloomsbury, 2017.

Roth, Joseph. *What I Saw: Reports from Berlin 1920–1933.* New York: Norton, 2002.

Sakall, S. Z. *The Story of Cuddles: My Life under The Emperor Francis Joseph, Adolf Hitler, and the Warner Brothers.* London: Cassell, 1954.

Sauter, Martin. *Liesl Frank, Charlotte Dieterle and the European Film Fund.* Ph.D. dissertation. Coventry, UK: University of Warwick, 2010.

Schary, Dore. *Heyday: An Autobiography.* Boston: Little, Brown, 1979.

Schatz, Thomas. *The Genius of the System: Hollywood Filmmaking in the Studio Era.* New York: Pantheon, 1988.

Schnauber, Cornelius. *Hollywood Haven: Homes and Haunts of the European Émigrés and Exiles in Los Angeles.* Riverside, CA: Ariadne Press, 1997.

Schoenberg, E. Randol, ed. *The Doctor Faustus Dossier: Arnold Schoenberg, Thomas Mann, and Their Contemporaries 1930–1951.* Berkeley: University of California Press, 2018.

Schulberg, Budd. *What Makes Sammy Run?* New York: Random House, 1941.

———. *The Disenchanted.* New York: Random House, 1950.

———. *Moving Pictures: Memories of a Hollywood Prince.* Briarcliff Manor, NY: Stein & Day, 1981.

Schulz, Bruno. *The Street of Crocodiles.* New York: Walker, 1963.

Schwartz, Nancy Lynn. *The Hollywood Writers' Wars.* New York: Knopf, 1981.

Seghers, Anna. *Transit.* Boston: Little, Brown, 1944.

Selznick, David O. *Memo from David O. Selznick.* Edited by Rudy Behlmer. New York: Viking, 1972.

Semenov, Lillian Wurtzel, and Carla Winter, eds. *William Fox, Sol M. Wurtzel and the Early Fox Film Corporation.* Jefferson, NC: McFarland, 2001.

Seton, Marie. *Sergei M. Eisenstein: A Biography.* New York: A.A. Wyn, 1958.

Shaw, Irwin. *The Young Lions.* New York: Random House, 1948.

———. *The Troubled Air.* New York: Random House, 1951.

———. "Instrument of Salvation." *New Yorker,* April 24, 1954.

———. *Two Weeks in Another Town.* New York: Random House, 1959.

———. *Short Stories, Five Decades.* New York: Delacorte, 1978.

Shnayerson, Michael. *Irwin Shaw: A Biography.* New York: Putnam, 1989.

Smyth, J. E. *Fred Zinnemann and the Cinema of Resistance.* Jackson: University Press of Mississippi, 2014.

Solnit, Rebecca. *Storming the Gates of Paradise: Landscapes for Politics.* Berkeley: University of California Press, 2007.

Solomon, Aubrey. *Twentieth Century-Fox: A Corporate and Financial History.* Lanham, MD: Scarecrow Press, 2002.

Spalek, John M., ed. *Lion Feuchtwanger: The Man, His Ideas, His Work.* Los Angeles: Hennessey & Ingalls, 1972.

Spotts, Frederic. *Cursed Legacy: The Tragic Life of Klaus Mann.* New Haven, CT: Yale University Press, 2016.

Starr, Kevin. *Inventing the Dream: California Through the Progressive Era.* New York: Oxford University Press, 1985.

———. *The Dream Endures: California Enters the 1940s.* New York: Oxford University Press, 1997.

———. *Embattled Dreams: California in War and Peace, 1940–1950.* New York: Oxford University Press, 2002.

Stephan, Alexander. *"Communazis": FBI Surveillance of German Émigré Writers.* New Haven, CT: Yale University Press, 2000.

Stern, Fritz. *Five Germanys I Have Known: A History and Memoir.* New York: Farrar, Straus & Giroux, 2006.

Stewart, Donald Ogden. *By a Stroke of Luck! An Autobiography.* New York: Paddington Press, 1975.

Strobl, Gerwin. *The Swastika and the Stage: German Theatre and Society, 1933–1945.* Cambridge, UK: Cambridge University Press, 2007.

Styan, J. L. *Directors in Perspective: Max Reinhardt.* Cambridge, UK: Cambridge University Press Archive, 1982.

Swenson, Karen. *Garbo.* New York: Scribner, 1997.

Symonette, Lys, and Kim H. Kowalke, eds. and trans. *Speak Low (When You Speak Love): The Letters of Kurt Weill and Lotte Lenya.* Berkeley: University of California Press, 1996.

Taylor, John Russell. *Strangers in Paradise: The Hollywood Émigrés, 1933–1950*. New York: Henry Holt, 1983.

Thomas, Bob. *Thalberg: Life and Legend*. New York: Doubleday, 1969.

Thomson, David. *The New Biographical Dictionary of Film*. New York: Knopf, 1975.

———. *Beneath Mulholland: Thoughts on Hollywood and Its Ghosts*. New York: Knopf, 1997.

Totheroh, Dan. *Deep Valley*. New York: L.B. Fischer, 1942.

Troyan, Michael. *A Rose for Mrs. Miniver: The Life of Greer Garson*. Lexington: University Press of Kentucky, 1999.

Urwand, Ben. *The Collaboration: Hollywood's Pact with Hitler*. Cambridge, MA: Harvard University Press, 2013.

Vasey, Ruth. *The World According to Hollywood, 1918–1939*. Madison: University of Wisconsin Press, 1997.

Vieira, Mark A. *Greta Garbo: A Cinematic Legacy*. New York: Harry N. Abrams, 2005.

———. *Irving Thalberg: Boy Wonder to Producer Prince*. Berkeley: University of California Press, 2009.

Viertel, Peter. *The Canyon*. New York: Harcourt, Brace, 1940.

———. *Line of Departure*. New York: Harcourt, Brace, 1947.

———. *White Hunter, Black Heart*. New York: Doubleday, 1953.

———. *Love Lies Bleeding*. New York: Doubleday, 1964.

———. *Bicycle on the Beach*. New York: Delacorte, 1972.

———. *American Skin*. Boston: Houghton Mifflin, 1984.

———. *Dangerous Friends: At Large with Hemingway and Huston in the Fifties*. New York: Doubleday, 1992.

Viertel, Salka. "The Sorcerer's Apprentice." *The Screen Writer*, December 1947.

———. *The Kindness of Strangers*. New York: Holt, Rinehart & Winston, 1969.

———. *Das unbelehrbare Herz*. Hamburg, Germany: Claassen, 1970.

Wallace, David. *Lost Hollywood*. New York: Macmillan, 2002.

———. *Exiles in Hollywood*. New York: Limelight Editions, 2006.

Wegele, Peter. *Max Steiner: Composing, Casablanca, and the Golden Age of Film Music*. Lanham, MD: Rowman & Littlefield, 2014.

Weinberg, Herman G., ed. *The Lubitsch Touch: A Critical Study*. New York: Dutton, 1968.

Welles, Orson, and Peter Bogdanovich. *This Is Orson Welles*. New York: HarperCollins, 1992.

Wellwarth, George E., and Alfred G. Brooks, eds. *Max Reinhardt 1873–1973: A Centennial Festschrift*. New York: New York Cultural Center, 1974.

Weschler, Lawrence. "My Grandfather's Last Tale." *Atlantic*, December 1996.

Whiteman, Dorit Beder. *The Uprooted: A Hitler Legacy*. New York: Da Capo, 1993.

Whitman, James Q. *Hitler's American Model: The United States and the Making of Nazi Race Law*. Princeton, NJ: Princeton University Press, 2017.

Wieland, Karin. *Dietrich and Riefenstahl: Hollywood, Berlin, and a Century in Two Lives*. New York: Liveright, 2015.

Winters, Shelley. *Shelley: Also Known as Shirley*. New York: Morrow, 1980.

Wolf, Christa. *City of Angels, or, The Overcoat of Dr. Freud*. New York: Farrar, Straus & Giroux, 2013.

Wyman, David. *Paper Walls: Americans and the Refugee Crisis, 1938–1941*. New York: Pantheon, 1968.

———. *The Abandonment of the Jews: America and the Holocaust 1941–1945*. New York: Pantheon, 1984.

Zeisl, Gertrud. "Gertrud Zeisl's Oral History," www.zeisl.com.

Zinnemann, Fred. *My Life in the Movies: An Autobiography*. New York: Scribner, 1992.

Zolotow, Maurice. *Billy Wilder in Hollywood*. New York: Limelight Editions, 1987.

ACADEMIC PAPERS

Prager, Katharina. "Berthold Viertel: A Migration Career and No Comeback in Exile." Quiet Invaders Conference, 2015.

Renaud, Terence. "The Genesis of the Emergency Rescue Committee, 1933–1942." Boston University, 2005.

Schmidt, James. "When Arnold Met Irving: A Tale from Hollywood." Contested Legacies Conference, Bard College, Annandale-on-Hudson, New York, August 14, 2002.

Schreckenberger, Helga. "'They Say Hollywood Is a Paradise!': Salka Viertel's Perseverance During Hollywood's 'Inquisition.'" *To Stay or Not to Stay*, Fifth Conference of the International Feuchtwanger Society, University of Southern California, Los Angeles, September 14–16, 2011.

———. "Salka Viertel's Transnational Network." *Networks of Exile*, International Conference on Exile Studies, University of Vermont, Burlington, September 26–29, 2013.

ARCHIVES

AMPAS at Margaret Herrick Library, Academy of Motion Pictures Arts and Sciences, Beverly Hills, CA: Fred Zinnemann Papers, Katharine Hepburn Papers, John Huston Papers

Deutsches Literaturarchiv, Marbach, Germany (DLAM): Salka Viertel Papers

New York Public Library: S. N. Behrman Archives

UCLA Special Collections: Henry Blanke Papers, Ernst Toch Papers

USC Feuchtwanger Memorial Library, Exile Collections

Warner Brothers Archive at USC

CREDITS

EPIGRAPH CREDITS

Opening epigraphs: Max Beerbohm, "Hosts and Guests," from his essay collection *And Even Now* (Dutton, 1921); Jane Gardam, quoted in "Retrospective" by Lauren Collins, *New Yorker*, June 30, 2014.

Epigraph on page 103 from *Thalberg: Life and Legend* by Bob Thomas, copyright © 1969 by Robert Joseph Thomas. Used by permission of Doubleday, an imprint of the Knopf Doubleday Publishing Group, a division of Penguin Random House LLC. All rights reserved.

Epigraph on page 151 by Lucille Ball printed by permission of Desilu, too, LLC. Copyright © Desilu, too, LLC.

Epigraph on page 265 from *Transit* by Anna Seghers. Copyright © 1951 by Aufbau-Verlag GmbH, Berlin. Translation copyright © 2013 by Margot Bettauer Dembo. Published in English by *New York Review Books*. All rights reserved.

Epigraph on page 299 from *The Righteous Mind: Why Good People Are Divided by Politics and Religion* by Jonathan Haidt, copyright © 2012 by Jonathan Haidt. Used by permission of Pantheon Books, an imprint of the Knopf Doubleday Publishing Group, a division of Penguin Random House LLC. All rights reserved.

Epigraph on page 313 from *The Letters of Heinrich and Thomas Mann*, 1900–1945. Edited by Hans Wysling, translated by Don Reneau. Copyright © 1998 by The Regents of the University of California. Used by permission of the University of California Press.

Epigraph on page 333 from a public service announcement fox-trot written by Les Burness and John Morris.

Epigraph on page 347 copyright © 1968 Dr. Martin Luther King, Jr., copyright © renewed 1996 Coretta Scott King.

IMAGE CREDITS

Pages 13, 304, 325, 367: Collection of Vicky Schulberg. The image on page 304 was taken by William Caskey, who in 1945 had met and begun a relationship with Christopher Isherwood.

Pages 21, 33 (left), 82, 87, 382: Wienbibliothek im Rathaus

Page 33 (right): Source unknown. The author has made every effort to identify the owner of this image, and asks that such person contact the publisher.

Pages 55, 64, 322: Estate of Peter Viertel

Page 99: U.S. Department of Labor, Southern District of California, County of Los Angeles

Pages 195, 254, 257, 319: USC Digital Library, Lion Feuchtwanger Papers Collection

Pages 227, 258, 262, 331, 406: Deutsches Literaturarchiv Marbach

Page 259: United States Holocaust Memorial Museum, courtesy of Hiram Bingham

Page 376: Courtesy of Writers Guild Foundation Archive

Page 405: Collection of Adam Shaw

Page 419: Author photo, 2014

INDEX